Contents

INTERNATIONAL POLITICAL ECONOMY SERIES

General Editor: Timothy M. Shaw, Professor of Political Science and International Development Studies, and Director of the Centre for Foreign Policy Studies, Dalhousie University, Nova Scotia, Canada

Recent titles include:

Pradeep Agrawal, Subir V. Gokarn, Veena Mishra, Kirit S. Parikh and Kunal Sen
ECONOMIC RESTRUCTURING IN EAST ASIA AND INDIA: Perspectives on Policy Reform

Solon L. Barraclough and Krishna B. Ghimire
FORESTS AND LIVELIHOODS: The Social Dynamics of Deforestation in Developing Countries

Kathleen Barry (*editor*)
VIETNAM'S WOMEN IN TRANSITION

Jorge Rodríguez Beruff and Humberto García Muñíz (*editors*)
SECURITY PROBLEMS AND POLICIES IN THE POST-COLD WAR CARIBBEAN

Ruud Buitelaar and Pitou van Dijck (*editors*)
LATIN AMERICA'S NEW INSERTION IN THE WORLD ECONOMY: Towards Systemic Competitiveness in Small Economies

William D. Coleman
FINANCIAL SERVICES, GLOBALIZATION AND DOMESTIC POLICY CHANGE: A Comparison of North America and the European Union

Paul Cook and Frederick Nixson (*editors*)
THE MOVE TO THE MARKET? Trade and Industry Policy Reform in Transitional Economies

Mark E. Denham and Mark Owen Lombardi (*editors*)
PERSPECTIVES ON THIRD-WORLD SOVEREIGNTY: The Postmodern Paradox

John Healey and William Tordoff (*editors*)
VOTES AND BUDGETS: Comparative Studies in Accountable Governance in the South

Noeleen Heyzer, James V. Riker and Antonio B. Quizon (*editors*)
GOVERNMENT–NGO RELATIONS IN ASIA: Prospects and Challenges for People-Centred Development

George Kent
CHILDREN IN THE INTERNATIONAL POLITICAL ECONOMY

NAPIER UNIVERSITY LIBRARY

David Kowalewski
GLOBAL ESTABLISHMENT: The Political Economy of North/Asian Networks

Laura Macdonald
SUPPORTING CIVIL SOCIETY: The Political Role of Non-Governmental
Organizations in Central America

Gary McMahon (*editor*)
LESSONS IN ECONOMIC POLICY FOR EASTERN EUROPE FROM
LATIN AMERICA

David B. Moore and Gerald M. Schmitz (*editors*)
DEBATING DEVELOPMENT DISCOURSE: Institutional and Popular
Perspectives

Juan Antonio Morales and Gary McMahon (*editors*)
ECONOMIC POLICY AND THE TRANSITION TO DEMOCRACY: The Latin
American Experience

Paul J. Nelson
THE WORLD BANK AND NON-GOVERNMENTAL ORGANIZATIONS:
The Limits of Apolitical Development

Archibald R. M. Ritter and John M. Kirk (*editors*)
CUBA IN THE INTERNATIONAL SYSTEM: Normalization and Integration

Ann Seidman and Robert B. Seidman
STATE AND LAW IN THE DEVELOPMENT PROCESS: Problem-Solving and
Institutional Change in the Third World

Tor Skålnes
THE POLITICS OF ECONOMIC REFORM IN ZIMBABWE: Continuity and
Change in Development

John Sorenson (*editor*)
DISASTER AND DEVELOPMENT IN THE HORN OF AFRICA

Howard Stein (*editor*)
ASIAN INDUSTRIALIZATION AND AFRICA: Studies in Policy Alternatives
to Structural Adjustment

Deborah Stienstra
WOMEN'S MOVEMENTS AND INTERNATIONAL ORGANIZATIONS

Sandra Whitworth
FEMINISM AND INTERNATIONAL RELATIONS

David Wurfel and Bruce Burton (*editors*)
SOUTHEAST ASIA IN THE NEW WORLD ORDER: The Political Economy
of a Dynamic Region

Social Reconstructions of the World Automobile Industry

Competition, Power and Industrial Flexibility

Edited by

Frederic C. Deyo
Professor of Sociology
State University of New York at Brockport

WITHDRAWN

in
association
with

International Institute
SUNY BROCKPORT

Selection, editorial matter and Chapters 1, 5 and 10 © Frederic C. Deyo 1996
Chapters 2–4, 6–9 © Macmillan Press Ltd 1996

All rights reserved. No reproduction, copy or transmission of
this publication may be made without written permission.

No paragraph of this publication may be reproduced, copied or
transmitted save with written permission or in accordance with
the provisions of the Copyright, Designs and Patents Act 1988,
or under the terms of any licence permitting limited copying
issued by the Copyright Licensing Agency, 90 Tottenham Court
Road, London W1P 9HE.

Any person who does any unauthorised act in relation to this
publication may be liable to criminal prosecution and civil
claims for damages.

First published 1996 by
MACMILLAN PRESS LTD
Houndmills, Basingstoke, Hampshire RG21 6XS
and London
Companies and representatives
throughout the world

ISBN 0–333–61067–9 hardcover
ISBN 0–333–66034–X paperback

A catalogue record for this book is available
from the British Library.

10   9   8   7   6   5   4   3   2   1
05   04   03   02   01   00   99   98   97   96

Printed and bound in Great Britain by
Antony Rowe Ltd, Chippenham, Wiltshire

Published in the United States of America 1996 by
ST. MARTIN'S PRESS, INC.,
Scholarly and Reference Division
175 Fifth Avenue, New York, N.Y. 10010

ISBN 0–312–12736–7 cloth
ISBN 0–312–12737–5 paperback

NAPIER UNIVERSITY LIBRARY

AC

ON
14170

LOC   SHMK

M   338. 476292 DEY

CON

SUP
Mi

PR
16.99

List of Tables

Preface

This volume is based on the proceedings of a conference entitled 'Global Competition in the Automobile Industry', held at the State University of New York, Brockport, 7–8 May 1991. The conference was attended by representatives of both management and labor in automobile plants of upstate New York. Given the resulting diversity of views among conference participants, and against a backdrop of many years of dialogue and bargaining which has substantially influenced the extent and nature of industrial restructuring in the American auto industry, it is not surprising that the discussion strongly suggested a view of industry change centering on a contested social process occurring within the constraints of competition, markets and technology, rather than an alternate and more prevalent view of such change as flowing primarily from the imperatives of competition alone. Indeed, it quickly became clear from the presentations on industry change outside the United States that competitive requirements do not force a global convergence of industrial organization, but rather only create broad constraints on the strategies contending groups may successfully pursue in their efforts to realize their own goals in industrial restructuring. This volume seeks to contribute to a growing corpus of work on industrial change which has sought to deepen our understanding of the social implications of the current restructuring of world industry, and the way in which workers have sought, with greater or lesser success, to shape this process.

The conference and this volume were sponsored by the International Institute of SUNY, Brockport, with funding from SUNY, Brockport, Cornell University's Institute of Industry Studies, and a title VIB grant from the United States Education Department. The City University of New York kindly granted permission for the reprinting of Kevin Middlebrook's chapter on Mexico, previously published in *Comparative Politics*. The German journal *Industrielle Beziehung* similarly provided permission for the reprinting of Lowell Turner and Peter Auer's chapter 'A Diversity of New Work Organization'.

FREDERIC C. DEYO

Notes on the Contributors

Peter Auer is a senior research fellow and project head at the Social Science Research Center in Berlin (WZB) and has done major comparative studies on work organization, workforce adjustment and labour market policy. He is also programme manager for the European employment policy network, MISEP (Mutual Information System on Employment Policies).

Frederic C. Deyo is Professor of Sociology at the State University of New York, Brockport. His publications on industrial development include *The Political Economy of the New Asian Industrialism* (ed.) and *Beneath the Miracle: Labor Subordination in the New Asian Industrialism*. He has served as chair of the Political Economy of the World System section of the American Sociological Association and is conducting research on industrial restructuring in Latin America and East Asia.

Richard Florida is co-author of *Beyond Mass Production: The Japanese System and Its Transfer to the United States* and *The Breakthrough Illusion: Corporate America's Failure to Move from Mass Production to Innovation*. He is currently writing a book entitled *For Knowledge and Profit*, with Wesley Cohen, which examines the evolution of university–industry–government research relationships in the American system of innovation.

Stephen Herzenberg has written on work organization and labor relations in the auto industry, labor aspects of North–South economic integration, and, most recently, the US service sector. He served on the US negotiating team for the labor side agreement to the North American Free Trade Agreement. His recent publications on the auto industry include essays in *The Challenge of Restructuring* and *Driving Continentally*.

John Holmes is Professor of Geography at Queen's University in Kingston, Ontario, where he teaches courses on the political economy of contemporary industrial change. His recent writings include *Front-yard/Backyard: The Americas in the Global Crisis* (co-edited) and auto industry chapters in Drache and Gertler (eds), *The New Era of Global Competition*, and J. Britton (ed.), *Canada and the Global Economy*.

Martin Kenney is Professor in the Department of Applied Behavioral Sciences at the University of California, Davis. He has been a visiting scholar at Hitotsubashi University, University of Tokyo and Osaka City University. He is the co-author (with Richard Florida) of *Beyond Mass Production: The Japanese System and Its Transfer to the US*, and *The Breakthrough Illusion*.

Pradeep Kumar is Professor of Industrial Relations and Associate Director of the School of Industrial Relations at Queen's University, Kingston, Ontario. He and John Holmes are currently engaged in a study of restructuring in the Canadian automobile industry, with particular attention to changes in labor relations polices and practices. His recent publications include *From Uniformity to Diversity: Industrial Relations in Canada and the United States*, and an article on union responses to work reorganization in a recent issue of *Economic and Industrial Democracy*.

Solomon B. Levine is Professor Emeritus at the University of Wisconsin-Madison, where he served for many years as chair of the East Asian Studies Program and was a member of the School of Business, Department of Economics, and Industrial Relations Research Institute. He is the author of numerous books and articles on labor and management in Japan, and continues to be active as a scholar and arbitrator in the field of labor relations.

Kevin J. Middlebrook is Director of Research at the Center for US–Mexican Studies, University of California–San Diego. He is the author of *The Paradox of Revolution: Labor, the State, and Authoritarianism in Mexico*. His edited books include *The Politics of Economic Restructuring: State-Society Relations and Regime Change in Mexico, Unions, Workers, and the State in Mexico*, and *The United States and Latin America in the 1980s: Contending Perspectives on a Decade of Crisis*.

Ronald A. Rodgers studied law (J.D., 1985) and industrial relations (Ph.D., 1993) at the University of Wisconsin-Madison. He is currently a lecturer in Organizational Behavior at the National University of Singapore. His earlier professional work and research centered around industrial relations and international business in the Republic of Korea.

Lowell Turner is Associate Professor in the School of Industrial and Labor Relations at Cornell University. His main teaching and research interests are in international and comparative labor, with a focus on Western Europe, especially Germany, and the US. His 1991 book, *Democracy at Work: Changing World Markets and the Future of Labor Unions*, is a comparative study of unions and new work organization in Germany and the United States.

List of Abbreviations

AFTA	Asean Free Trade Agreement
AIF	Annual Improvement Factor
ASEAN	Association of Southeast Asian Nations
CAW	Canadian Auto Workers Union
CBA	Collective Bargaining Agreement
CKD	Completely Knocked-down Unit (Automobile)
COLA	Cost of Living Allowance
CROC	Revolutionary Confederation of Workers and Peasants
CTM	Confederation of Mexican Workers
DQP	Diversified Quality Production
EC	European Community
GATT	General Agreement on Tariffs and Trade
GHO	General Headquarters (Japan)
GM	General Motors Co.
GNP	Gross National Product
HRM	Human Resource Management
ICFTU	International Confederation of Free Trade Unions
IFF	Internal Functional Flexibility
IG METALL	German Metalworkers' Union
ILO	International Labor Organization
IMF	International Monetary Fund
IMF-JC	International Metalworkers Federation – Japan Council
IR	Industrial Relations
JIT	Just-in-time Production and Delivery
JNAAP	Japan–North American Auto Pact
JPC	Japan Productivity Center
LDP	Liberal Democratic Party (Japan)
LMC	Labor–Management Council
LO	Labor Organisation (Swedish Confederation of Trade Unions)
NAFTA	North American Free Trade Agreement
NIC	Newly Industrialized Country
OECD	Organization for Economic Cooperation and Development

OPEC	Organization of Petroleum Exporting Countries
RENGO	Japanese Trade Union Confederation
R&D	Research and Development
ROK	Republic of Korea
SAF	Swedish Employers Confederation
SCAP	Supreme Commander of Allied Powers (Japan)
SME	Small and Medium-Sized Enterprise
TCO	Central Organization of Salaried Employees
TGMA	Thai Garment Manufacturers' Association
UAW	United Automobile Workers
UOI	Independent Workers Union

1 Introduction: Social Reconstructions of the World Automobile Industry

Frederic C. Deyo

The world automobile industry, like many other industries, is undergoing a fundamental restructuring in response to new competitive pressures and requirements. To a degree, these pressures stem from more versatile micro-electronics-based production technologies along with an increased pace of technological advance and a corresponding need to accelerate research and development activities, including quick follow-through to marketable products. In part, too, such pressures emanate from a changing market environment, one increasingly characterized by fragmentation and volatility. The liberalization of world trade under the General Agreement on Tariffs and Trade, alongside the creation of regional free-trade zones in Asia, Europe and North America have forced auto companies both to share domestic markets with new foreign entrants and to compete with many other firms in virtually all major markets. Such fragmentation occurred earliest in Britain and West Germany where relatively liberal trade and/or foreign investment policies eventuated, by the late 1970s, in the division of domestic auto markets among a large number of foreign and local firms (Reich, 1989). While more protectionist countries like France and Italy have fostered greater market consolidation favoring a few domestic firms, the instituting of a single European market beginning from 1993 is expected to subject national firms to intensified competition over future years. While Japanese automakers had captured only an 11–12 per cent market share during 1993–94 (*Ward's Automotive Yearbook*, 1994), a 1991 EC–Japan agreement will open European markets to increasing Japanese participation during the late 1990s.

Market fragmentation in the United States began with the influx of small, fuel-efficient European imports in the wake of escalating gasoline prices during the 1970s, and continued through the 1980s and early 1990s with dramatic increases in US market share by Japanese companies. During the 1980s, the 'Big Three' automobile companies (General

1

Motors, Ford and Chrysler) lost substantial market share to Toyota, Honda and Nissan. Even in Japan itself, where foreign companies together shared only about 8 per cent of the domestic auto market in 1993 (*Wall Street Journal*, 2 February 1995: A14), imports have increased sharply during the mid-1990s.

Market fragmentation was fostered as well by a progressive segmentation of consumer markets as increasingly differentiated categories of buyers sought vehicles to meet their special interests and requirements. By the early 1990s, the best-selling cars in the US were achieving market volumes half or less than those of best-selling cars in the 1960s and early 1970s. In addition, consumers have demanded ever higher standards of safety, quality and reliability.

Processes of market fragmentation have both contributed to and paralleled a more general increase in market volatility. Internationally, increased reliance on diverse global markets has reduced predictability and stability in the face of uncertainties relating to government policies, currency exchange rates and differential national economic performance. Domestically, a progressive tightening of safety, emission and fuel efficiency requirements has created a constantly changing economic environment.

To the extent that standardized mass production, most fully developed in the large, relatively insulated, North American market, relies on economies of scale for its competitive advantage, increasing technological and market volatility and market fragmentation have undercut the competitive position of firms which have failed to adapt to the new economic environment. Conversely, these changes have favored companies which have been able to meet the new competitive challenges. By the mid-1980s, it was clear that a new, and competitively superior, model of industrial organization pioneered by Toyota and other Japanese firms was to prove the successor to more traditional Fordist mass-production. This new model has been variously termed lean production (Womack *et al.*, 1990); flexible mass-production; flexible-specialization (Sabel, 1986); internal functional flexibility (Standing, 1989); systemofacture (Hoffman and Kaplinski, 1988); and innovation-mediated production (Kenney and Florida, 1993). The defining characteristics of this post-Fordist model of industrial organization, here more generally termed flexible production, include a close integration of all parts of the production process, rapid product and process innovation, efficient small-lot production, continuous efforts to enhance quality and productivity at all organizational levels, including on the shopfloor, and close interaction with suppliers and customers.

These characteristics have permitted Japanese and other automobile companies to manufacture a larger number of differentiated products for diverse export markets and market niches, to develop new products rapidly, to respond quickly to market shifts and instability, and to continually improve productivity and quality through constant changes in work process and organization. Womack statistically documents many of these advantages in his comparison of US and Japanese firms.

By the late 1980s, Japanese companies produced twice as many car models as did American or European companies; replaced models every four years (compared to nine years for the Big-Three); were able to achieve normal quality standards after the introduction of new models in less than two months (compared to 11–12 months for US and European producers); and maintained a significant lead in avoidance of defects (Womack, 1990; Hill and Lee, forthcoming). More recent *Consumer Reports* car ratings suggest a continuing quality and reliability lead on the part of Japanese producers over Big-Three and European companies in US markets. Setting aside the 'large car' class in which Japanese producers have not competed in the US, Japanese cars comprised 23 of the 28 'recommended 1994 models' for small, compact, mid-sized and luxury cars rated by *Consumer Reports*. For these same classes of cars, of the 18 models rated 'much better than average in predicted reliability' (based on 1991–93 data), only two were non-Japanese (the Volvo 850 and Saturn) (*Consumer Reports*, April 1994).

By consequence of these advantages, 'Toyotaism', the Japanese variant of flexible production, has redefined the conditions of global competition while at the same time establishing a new model of industrial organization which is rapidly displacing older variants of Fordist, standardized mass-production (see Table 1.1). In 1979, Japan became the world's largest national producer of automobiles, and had already mounted a vigorous export program in US markets, thus prompting the US government in 1981 to negotiate an agreement with Japan which imposed 'voluntary' quotas on Japanese auto exports to the US. In response to these quotas, alongside subsequent growing pressure from an increasingly strong yen, Japanese auto makers began to establish 'transplant' facilities to produce cars in the US. In 1993, Japanese sales of cars produced in Japan and in Japanese 'transplant' factories in the US accounted for 34 per cent of total US sales (*Automotive News*, 2 July 1994).

By consequence of the shift on the part of Japanese auto companies from exporting to direct-foreign-investment strategies for penetrating

4 *Introduction*

export markets, Japan's share of total world motor vehicle production
stabilized during the 1980s (see Table 1.1).

Table 1.1 Percentage of world motor vehicle production by major automobile
manufacturing centers

	US	United States and Canada	Japan	Europe*	W. Europe
1960	47.9%	50.4%	2.9%	41.5%	
1965	45.9	49.4	7.7	39.4	
1970	28.2**	32.1	18.0	44.3	
1971	31.9				
1975	27.2	31.4	21.0	40.8	
1980	20.8	24.2	28.7	40.1	
1985	26.0	30.3	27.4	35.7	
1990	20.5	24.6	28.3	34.9	32.7
1991	19.8	24.0	28.2	31.8	30.7
1992	19.5	24.6	25.0	34.0	33.0
1993	23.0	27.7	23.6	33.8	29.4
1994	24.5	29.2	21.1	34.2	31.2

*Includes Eastern European countries.
**A major General Motors strike substantially reduced US production in 1970.
Sources:
(1960–85) calculated from Motor Vehicle Manufacturers' Association
(1990–94) from *Ward's Automotive Yearbook* 1994, 1995.

By the late 1980s, it was felt by some that adoption of key elements of
Japanese flexible production systems had become a condition for survival on the part of automobile companies everywhere (Womack, Jones
and Roos, 1990; Kenney and Florida, 1993). And, indeed, major companies in the US and Europe have sought to emulate their Japanese
competitors, whose successes have come to define world best-practice
benchmarks.

FLEXIBILITIES: DYNAMIC AND STATIC

Colclough and Tolbert (1990) draw an important distinction between
'static' forms of organizational and production flexibility which, while
responsive to market volatility and segmentation and increased cost
pressure, fail to provide a basis for long-term growth and development,
and other more 'dynamic' forms which do. Static flexibility may seek
to reduce production costs, increase cost flexibility and reduce excess

capacity and overheads during market downturns through 'external' or 'numerical' flexibility (Standing, 1989). This form of flexibility fosters quick adjustments in employment levels, skill mixes and production through hiring and firing workers, employment of temporary and contract workers, and reliance on short-term subcontracting. These measures replace fixed with variable labor and other costs, even as they foster product flexibility. On the other hand, they may undercut longer-term investments in employee skills, technological innovation, work reorganization, and supplier capabilities. Noting the long existence of static flexibilities everywhere, including under Fordist mass-production, Sayer (1989) argues that current organizational changes reflect not so much an increase in flexibility *per se*, as a shift in flexibility 'profiles'.

Intensified competitive pressures, it is clear, may reduce rather than enhance the likelihood of substantial investments in long-term organizational, human resource and technological change. Such investments, it may be felt, give competitors a short-run cost advantage, or directly benefit competitors through externalities such as improved worker skills which may subsequently be expropriated by competing firms. Under such circumstances, other more cost-focused measures may be preferred. In this sense, urgent cost pressures during periods of intensified competition may reduce the incentive to make the investments needed for dynamic flexibility. It will be argued later that some of the important organizational innovations now associated with Toyotaism were in fact introduced largely in response to political rather than economic pressures, and that these elements, especially relating to labor policy, have been harder to introduce under the more difficult competitive circumstances facing auto firms in the US and Europe today.

STATE, LABOR AND DYNAMIC FLEXIBILITY

Dynamic flexibility is often seen as fostering an especially close linkage between labor policy and enterprise competitiveness (Streeck, 1987; Kochan and Katz, 1988, pp. 46, 469). In particular, dynamic flexibility is strengthened by such human resource practices as extensive, broad-based training (Schrage, 1990), some degree of shopfloor participation in quality improvements, in-process inspection and correction of problems, performance-based pay, and a fluid deployment of workers to a variety of different tasks as dictated by changing needs and circumstances (Hirschhorn, 1984; Cole, 1989).

Much of the literature suggests that such flexibility-enhancing human resource practices are most easily implemented where other employment conditions (including job security and stability, adequate wages and work conditions, information sharing and an equitable distribution of productivity or profit gains) foster trust, commitment and workforce stability (Katz and MacDuffie, 1994). Further, this literature suggests that the possibilities for implementing both human resource and employment-relations requisites for dynamic flexibility are in turn influenced by broader sectoral and national 'governance' systems, loosely defined here as the institutional environments of economic activity comprising states, associations, social and communal networks, labor-management bargaining structures, and organizations which influence and constrain the decisions and strategies of firms (see Hollingsworth, Schmitter, and Streeck, 1994). Of particular importance for the introduction of flexible work structures within industrial plants are unions and states.

The role of unions in instituting flexibility is problematic. On the one hand, strong unions may force management to institute progressive labor policies which favor dynamic flexibility. But then again, those same unions may oppose managerial efforts to institute flexibility itself for fear of granting management too much discretionary control over work assignment and allocation, or of compromising other labor goals such as humanization of work, reduced stress and enhanced union/worker control over scheduling and work organization.

Severe competitive pressures may be expected to both motivate and weaken union opposition to reforms. On the one hand, fear of layoffs and threats to union strength may trigger confrontation and opposition. But on the other hand, competitive pressures and reforms may themselves undercut union membership and bargaining power. The net outcome may well be a situation in which reforms become easy to formally introduce but, in a climate of distrust and fear, difficult to render effective. Under such circumstances, union strategies may become somewhat less coherent and unified as union leaders thrash about for an appropriate response (Katz and MacDuffie, 1994). In addition, flexibility reforms may well take a relatively autocratic form as managers force organizational change on ambivalent workers and internally divided unions, as seen in the United States during the 1980s and early 1990s.

For these reasons, too, one might expect flexibility-enhancing work reforms to be easiest under conditions of low to moderate, rather than severe economic pressure. Paradoxically, of course, moderate to low competitive threat may also encourage greater attention to non-

competitive issues in work restructuring, which in part explains why
existing flexible production systems in Europe and Japan are as often
historically rooted in political and social circumstances under moderate competitive pressures as in strictly economic considerations. At a
minimum, it can be assumed that union strength and strategy, along
with the broader governance environment which influences both of
these, play an important, if problematic, role in the instituting of
dynamic flexibility.

Similarly complex is the role of states in current industrial transformation. The state and its various agencies have historically comprised a critical component of the institutional complex of governance,
thus suggesting a correspondingly important role in flexibility reforms
within and among firms (Piore and Sabel, 1994; Scott, 1992; Hirst and
Zeitlin, 1991). Most obvious is the role of the state in providing or col-
laborating in the provision of basic and vocational education, an essential element in Germany's industrial achievements (Streeck, 1987). As
important is state encouragement of enterprise strategies favoring intra
and inter-organizational dissemination of information, collaborative
research and development, flexibility-enhancing work reforms, and
close working relationships with suppliers. Third, state agencies may
(often in response to political pressures from organized labor) promote
effective trade unions and labor representation in enterprise and sectoral decision-making; employment policies and practices which enhance labor-management cooperation; and flexibility-enhancing
human resource policies, including multi-skill training, quality circles
and so forth.

Since unions and state agencies comprise but two elements of larger
governance systems, their relative importance in fostering dynamic
flexibility varies depending on the institutional salience of other elements of governance. In some instances, business associations or even
community and kinship networks may be the more central actors in encouraging industrial flexibility. While we do not explore the influence
of these alternative governance actors in this volume, their importance
is clear.

FLEXIBLE PRODUCTION AND AUTO INDUSTRIES IN
DEVELOPING COUNTRIES

Because of its extensive backward and forward linkages to a large number of industries and sectors, the automobile industry is often seen as

critical to the industrialization efforts of developing countries. Global industrial restructuring, however, raises important questions regarding the continued advance of the industry in all but a small handful of these countries. Given the technological, marketing and financial dominance of major global auto companies in developed countries, the international production, sourcing and marketing strategies of these companies largely determines the parameters within which developing-country producers must operate.

During the 1950s and 1960s, import-substitution efforts on the part of developing-country governments forced major world automobile companies to relocate production facilities to those countries in order to serve domestic auto markets (Doleschal, 1992). Depending on domestic content and other political regulation, such production ranged from simple assembly of premanufactured vehicle 'kits' to localization of more complex operations such as chassis and even engine production. Growing cost pressures in the 1970s added further impetus to world automobile industry dispersal to developing countries as companies increased the sourcing of simple parts from low-cost export platforms on the one hand, and globalized more capital-intensive components under 'worldcar' schemes on the other (Froebel, Heinrichs and Kreye, 1980; also see Ross and Trachte, 1990, pp. 103–14; and Doleshchal, 1992).

These various forms of production dispersal to developing countries shared an important foundation: that of standardized production utilizing relatively stable technologies to serve mass markets. For this reason, the global ascendancy of flexible production may pose a threat to the continued growth of developing-country auto industries. In particular, efforts by international companies to de-standardize production processes, and to enhance dynamic organizational flexibility through greater emphasis on product and process innovation, quality improvements and more tightly integrated supplier production chains which permit just-in-time delivery and closer assembler–supplier collaboration in product design and development may place these countries at a special disadvantage (Katz and MacDuffie, 1994, p. 198). Additionally, such countries may often lack the social and physical infrastructure, educational levels and labor-relations climates to support flexible production.

By the late 1980s, several auto analysts were suggesting that further relocation of higher-value-added auto production to developing countries for global production was becoming less and less likely, thus locking developing countries into stagnant, standardized production niches in the global division of labor. Such a scenario, supported by findings for other industries (for example Appelbaum, Smith and Christerson, 1994) was further strengthened by the continued decline in the percentage of total vehicle production costs accounted for by labor and a corresponding diminution in the attractiveness to investors of cheap labor in developing countries (Karmokolias, 1990). At best, more advanced developing countries such as South Korea and Mexico would be confined to inexpensive, entry-level cars and complex components, while less advanced countries would produce only stable-technology parts and components (Hoffman and Kaplinski, 1988; Womack *et al.*, 1990; Karmokolias, 1990).

Whether such a pessimistic account is accurate is not yet clear. On the one hand, available evidence suggests continued moderate growth in the percentage of world automobile production accounted for by developing countries in the 1970s (Jenkins, 1985) and 1980s (Karmokolias, 1990). And even in the early 1990s, the percentage of world car production occurring in the six largest developing-country auto producers (Mexico, South Korea, Taiwan, India, Brazil and Argentina) increased from 7.2 per cent in 1990 to 12.3 per cent in 1993 (calculated from Ward's Automotive Yearbook, 1993, 1994).

On the other hand, significant recent growth has been increasingly confined to a few developing countries like South Korea, Mexico (Table 1.2) and, more recently, Thailand; while other previously dynamic auto production centers (for example Argentina and Taiwan) have faltered. Thus, we may be seeing a pattern of continuing dispersal of auto production to developing countries alongside a growing concentration of such production among those countries themselves. Such concentrated dispersal (dubbed 'global localization' by Hill, forthcoming) provides a parallel to 'greenfielding' strategies of auto companies in developed countries, in affording a compromise between pressures for dispersal to new markets and production sites on the one hand and contrary pressures for integrated production systems on the other.

The success of the auto industries in several developing countries seems to challenge the assumption, discussed earlier, that dynamic flexibility presupposes governance structures which encourage cooperation within and among firms, progressive employment practices and participative decision-making. A number of recent case studies of firms in Mexico (Shaiken, 1991), Malaysia (Rasiah, forthcoming) and elsewhere (see case studies in this volume) suggest that dynamic flexibility may in fact be successfully instituted under authoritarian politics and repressive labor regimes. This observation suggests that dynamic flexibility may not pose such rigid requirements for labor policy and labor relations as previously thought, or, alternately, that flexibility may take a number of different forms (Hirst and Zeitlin, 1991, p. 10) each with a different set of labor regime requirements. It is this latter alternative, that of multiple forms of dynamic flexibility, that we pursue here.

Table 1.2   Vehicle production in the three largest developing-country auto producers (000 units)

	South Korea		Mexico		Brazil	
	Autos	Total vehicles	Autos	Total vehicles	Autos	Total vehicles
1970			193		416	
1971	12					
1975	18		361		930	
1980	57	123	303	490	600	1165
1981	69	133	355	597	406	780
1982	94	163	301	473	718	861
1983	122	221	207	285	576	896
1984	159	265	232	344	538	847
1985	238	378	247	398	714	967
1986	455	602	208	341	829	1066
1987	790	980	266	395	788	920
1988	872	1084	354	513	783	1069
1989	856	1129	439	641	731	1012
1990	987	1322	346	542	653	915
1991	1158	1498	720	939	705	960
1992	1307	1730	776	1081	816	1075
1993	1593	2050	835	1080	1100	1391
1994	1806	2312	840	1106	1249	1583

Source: Ward's Automotive Yearbook, various issues.

SUPPLIER RELATIONS

While this volume focuses mainly on the introduction of flexible production systems within firms, it must be noted that intra-organizational transformation is closely linked with corresponding changes in a firm's supplier relations. It is commonly assumed that external subcontract relations bear similarities to intra-firm work organization (Altshuler et al., 1984; Florida and Kenny, this volume). Such isomorphism follows in part from the requirements of dynamic flexibility itself. For example, organizational flexibility encourages closer collaborative interaction with suppliers and customers to improve quality and market responsiveness, and to accelerate product innovation and development (Olea, 1991; Smitka, 1991, pp. 195–6). Creating appropriate incentives and support for production improvements on the part of suppliers is thus the external counterpart of internal investments for improved flexibility and quality. Conversely, a cost-driven organizational strategy may spill over to an obsession with supplier costs, thus encouraging displacement of quality efforts by short-term cost-cutting measures among supplier firms as well. A second basis for isomorphorism stems from the frequent association between governance institutional encouragement of trust-based, participative employment relations within firms on the one hand, and of interorganizational cooperation and mutual support on the other.

A somewhat more complex set of possibilities is suggested by the observation that most firms in fact pursue 'mixed' strategies which seek simultaneously to achieve static and dynamic flexibilities. For example, firms may adopt policies among permanent employees and first-tier suppliers which encourage stability, trust and long-term development in critical production processes. At the same time, they may pursue short-term, cost-focused strategies among temporary or contract workers and among lower-tier suppliers for routine, standardized production. External, static flexibility among temporary workers and some suppliers functions here to compensate for internal rigidities such as relatively fixed labor costs in the core sector (see, for example, Portes and Schauffler, 1993). The possibility for mixed strategies is enhanced where firms seek selectively to adopt elements of dynamic flexibility in the absence of strong governance pressure to generalize such policies to a broader range of production processes and suppliers.

* * *

The foregoing discussion suggests that the global diffusion of dynamic flexibility in auto and other industries is uneven, and contingent on a number of factors including management strategic choice along with sectoral technological and market characteristics, sectoral governance institutions, and resource availabilities which influence such choice. It further suggests the possibility of divergent organizational forms, including multiple types of flexibility, as firms seek to enhance their competitive strength in varying circumstances.

This volume explores these issues through an examination of industrial reorganization in the automobile industries of a number of industrialized and developing countries. Presentation of the varied experience of industrial change in these countries is guided by the following more specific questions:

1. Where and under what conditions have such flexible production systems been most effectively introduced? Is organizational flexibility confined primarily to established industrial centers in developed and semi-industrialized countries, or is it being diffused globally?
2. Do these systems display variation in form and function, and can this variation be explained by differences in sociopolitical or economic contexts? What roles, for example, do government and organized labor play in discouraging, shaping or supporting the introduction of dynamic flexibility?
3. What is the relationship between intra-organizational and inter-firm flexibility?
4. How do firms balance the often conflicting requirements for short-term cost-cutting and for longer-term improvements in quality and flexibility?
5. What sorts of labor and industrial relations policies are compatible with dynamic flexibility?
6. Under what circumstances is flexibility supportive of improved worker welfare and real decision-making participation?

*   *   *

The chapters in Part I describe the origins and spread of flexible production associated with the growing international competitive challenge of Japanese industry. Chapter 2, by Levine, traces the development of Japanese industrial organization, rooting it in part in early labor struggles during the immediate post-World War II period. Levine shows that Japanese industrial relations and production systems may be understood less as a reflection of long-standing Japanese cultural traits than as the outcome of labor struggles, state policy and managerial strategies. Levine refutes the frequent assertion that unions have played a largely passive role in the construction of Japanese industrial relations institutions.

Florida and Kenney, in Chapter 3, document the successful diffusion to North America of several elements of Japanese organization through the rapid growth of transplant auto assembly and supplier firms. In the course of their discussion they pose several important

questions. First, how successfully have Japanese companies transferred organizational practices which have often been assumed to be incompatible with the American cultural emphasis on individualism and
market competition? How have these companies selected or altered
their organizational environments in the US in order to achieve a better
organization–environment compatibility? And to what extent have
these organizations created a beachhead for the diffusion of Japanese
flexible production to US industry?

The chapters in Part II address the issue of further global industrial
dispersion of flexible production through an examination of the success
with which organizational flexibility is being introduced in South
Korea and Thailand, two major developing-country auto producers.
In Chapter 4, Rodgers argues that Korean firms have largely retained
low-wage, autocratic management practices, achieving continued productivity improvements instead through tight unilateral controls over
the work process, capital intensification and technology upgrading. Indeed, government support for autocratic management, coupled with
repression of independent unions, has encouraged retention of traditional management practices. While Rodgers suggests that long-term
success may require adoption of elements of dynamic flexibility, he argues that such factors as labor–management conflict and lack of employment stability will make such a transition difficult at best. On the
other hand, his account suggests that some elements of flexibility have
in fact been implemented in South Korean companies despite labor–
management conflict.

Deyo, in Chapter 5, describes responses by companies and government to intensified international competition in the Thai automobile
industry. He argues that in the absence of government leadership, labor
casualization and cost-cutting efforts have dominated managerial responses to intensified competition. Where dynamic flexibility has been
introduced, it has taken an autocratic form which minimizes and discourages substantial shop-floor participation in decision-making.
And, insofar as auto assemblers and first-tier suppliers have sought to
meet the often contradictory demands of both cost-cutting and quality
enhancement, they have adopted a strategy of tiered subcontracting
under which subcontract suppliers in simple-technology production
processes are strongly pushed to cut costs, while assistance and encouragement are given to higher-tier suppliers to enhance quality and
flexibility.

Whereas Parts I and II emphasize managerial strategies as keys to
the implementation and diffusion of new flexible production systems,

14 *Introduction*

Part III shifts to a consideration of the response of organized labor to such managerial initiatives, and to the ways in which labor may seek to negotiate, defer or block new patterns of work organization which are seen as challenging union strength or compromising employee wages and working conditions.

In Chapter 6, Holmes and Kumar discuss the greater intransigence of Canadian auto union leadership (especially since the 1984 UAW-CAW split) to management demands for union wage concessions, union-management cooperation and shop-floor teamwork, and other elements of Japanese production systems, rooting this more aggressive union stance in corresponding Canadian–US differences in industry performance and political ideology. They also point to long-term consequences for both industry and workers of this difference in union response to common managerial initiatives in the context of increasing North American auto market integration.

Middlebrook's chapter on the implementation of flexible production in Mexico (Chapter 7) similarly stresses the importance of labor politics for an understanding of the success of flexibility strategies. Middlebrook shows that early management efforts to implement flexibile production was hindered by the presence of strong, independent unions in industrial districts in the Mexico City region. Here, unions have been able to maintain control over the production process and worker deployment on the shop floor through contractual provisions relating to seniority, hiring and promotions, work rhythm and pace, and restrictions on the use of temporary workers. By contrast, weaker unions in the 'greenfield' auto industry sites of northern Mexico have been less successful in maintaining control over production and employment, with the result that managers there have exercised greater discretion in introducing work reforms. Based on his study of Mexico, Middlebrook suggests that international auto firms will continue to seek out investment sites in developing countries.

In Chapter 8, Turner and Auer provide a comparative account of cross-national differences in the implementation of dynamic flexible production schemes in the US, Germany and Sweden. Their findings suggest that characteristics of industrial relations systems substantially shape emergent systems of flexible production; and that continuing divergence, rather than convergence on Japanese production systems, will prevail in the industry.

In Part IV, Herzenberg addresses the issue of public policy in shaping the future course of work reorganization and social welfare in North America. Herzenberg poses two alternative future scenarios for the

American auto industry. Under the first scenario, a small percentage of the workforce will find high-skill, high-wage employment in major assembly plants and first-tier suppliers, while most other workers in the industry (especially in lower-tier supplier firms) will be employed at low wages, with minimal job security, in low-skill jobs without union protection.

The second, more optimistic, scenario is one of larger numbers of workers employed at higher wages in higher-skilled, more secure, unionized, high-productivity jobs in both assembly and supplier firms. Herzenberg argues that current efforts by American companies to reduce union power, force concessionary bargaining on workers, outsource to cheaper suppliers, and relocate work to cheap-labor countries represent cost-cutting responses to intensified competition which will eventuate in a two-tiered employment structure and declining living standards throughout North America. The more optimistic scenario, he says, requires greater US corporate commitment to increased productivity and quality, and greater investment in human resource development. In support of the latter alternative, he proposes a number of national and local policy initiatives relating to trade, labor standards and training.

Finally, the concluding chapter returns to the questions guiding this volume, seeking their further clarification through the country cases described in these chapters.

References

Altshuler, Alan, Martin Anderson, Daniel Jones, Daniel Roos and James Womack (1984) *The Future of the Automobile: The Report of MIT's International Automobile Program* (Cambridge, MA: MIT Press).
Appelbaum, Richard P., David Smith and Brad Christerson (1994) 'Commodity Chains and Industrial Restructuring in the Pacific Rim: Garment Trade and Manufacturing', in Gary Gereffi and Miguel Korzeniewicz (eds), *Commodity Chains and Global Capitalism* (Westport, CT: Praeger).
Automotive News (various issues).
Chu, Yun-Han (1989) 'The State and the Development of Automobile Industry in South Korea and Taiwan'. Paper presented at the Conference on State Policy and Economic Development in Taiwan, Republic of China. Taipei, ROC, 4–5 December.
Colclough, Glenna and Charles M. Tolbert (1990) *Work in the Fast Lane: Flexibility, Divisions of Labor and Inequality in High-Tech Industries* (Albany, NY: SUNY Press).
Cole, Robert E. (1989) *Strategies for Learning: Small-Group Activities in American, Japanese and Swedish Industry* (Berkeley: University of California Press).

16   *Introduction*

Consumer Reports (various issues).

Dankbaaar, Ben (1994) 'Sectoral Governance in the Automobile Industries of Germany, Great Britain and France', in J. Rogers Hollingsworth, Philippe C. Schmitter and Wolfgang Streeck (eds), *Governing Capitalist Economies* (New York: Oxford University Press).

Doleschal, Reinhard (1992) 'Internationalization and the Reorganization of Production and Marketing in the Volkswagen Corporation', in William D. Graf (ed.), *The Internationalization of the German Political Economy* (London & New York: Macmillan & St Martin's).

Froebel, Folker, Jurgen Heinrichs and Otto Kreye (1980) *The New International Division of Labor: Structural Unemployment in Industrialized Countries and Industrialization in Developing Countries* (Cambridge: Cambridge University Press).

Hill, Richard Child and Yong Joo Lee (forthcoming) 'Japanese Multinationals and East Asian Development: The Case of the Automobile Industry', in Leslie Sklair (ed.), *Capitalism and Development* (London: Routledge).

Hirschhorn, Larry (1984) *Beyond Mechanization* (Cambridge, MA: MIT Press).

Hirst, Paul and Jonathan Zeitlin (1991) 'Flexible Specialization vs. Post-Fordism: Theory, Evidence and Policy Implications', *Economy and Society*, 20(1) (February) pp. 1–56.

Hoffman, Kurt and Raphael Kaplinsky (1988) *Driving Force: The Global Restructuring of Technology, Labour and Investment in the Automobile and Components Industries* (Boulder, Co: Westview Press).

Hollingsworth, J.R. and W. Streeck, (1994) 'Countries and Sectors: Concluding Remarks on Performance, Convergence and Competitiveness', in J. Rogers Hollingsworth, Philippe C. Schmitter and Wolfgang Streeck (eds), *Governing Capitalist Economies* (New York: Oxford University Press).

Jenkins, Rhys (1985) 'Internationalization of Capital and the Semi-Industrialized Countries: The Case of the Motor Industry', *Review of Radical Political Economics*, 17(1/2) pp. 59–81.

Karmokolias, Yannis (1990) 'Automotive Industry Trends and Prospects for Investment in Developing Countries'. Discussion Paper No. 7, International Finance Corporation (Washington, DC: The World Bank).

Katz, Harry and John Paul MacDuffie (1994) 'Collective Bargaining in the U.S. Auto Assembly Sector', in Paula B. Voos (ed.), *Contemporary Collective Bargaining in the Private Sector* (Madison, WI: Industrial Relations Research Association).

Kenney, Martin and Richard Florida (1993) *Beyond Mass Production: The Japanese System and its Transfer to the U.S.* (New York: Oxford University Press).

Kochan, Thomas A. and Harry C. Katz (1988) *Collective Bargaining and Industrial Relations: From Theory to Practice* (Homewood Ill: Irwin).

Lee, Naeyoung and Jeffrey Cason (1994) 'Automobile Commodity Chains in the NICs: A Comparison of South Korea, Mexico and Brazil', in Gary Gereffi and Miguel Korzeniewicz (eds), *Commodity Chains and Global Capitalism* (Westport, CT: Praeger).

Motor Vehicle Manufacturers' Association, various issues. *Motor Vehicle Facts and Figures* (Detroit, MI).

Olea, Miguel Angel (1991) 'The Mexican Automotive Industry in the NAFTA Negotiations'. Paper presented at the Auto Industry Workshop Program, Centre for Trade Policy and Law, Ottawa, Canada, 3–4 October.

Piore, Michael and Charles Sabel (1984) *The Second Industrial Divide: Possibilities for Prosperity* (New York: Basic Books).

Portes, Alejandro and Richard Schauffler (1993) 'Competing Perspectives on the Latin American Informal Sector', *Population and Development Review*, 19(1) (March) pp. 33–60.

Rasiah, Rajah (forthcoming) 'Flexible Production Systems and Local Machine Tool Subcontracting: the Case of Electronics Components Transnationals in Malaysia', *Cambridge Journal of Economics*.

Rehder, Robert R. (1992) 'Building Cars as if People Mattered: The Japanese Lean System vs. Volvo's Uddevalla System', *The Columbia Journal of World Business* (Summer).

Reich, Simon (1989) 'Roads to Follow: Regulating Direct Foreign Investment', *International Organization* 43(4) pp. 543–84.

Ross, Robert J.S. and Kent C. Trachte (1990) *Global Capitalism: The New Leviathan* (Albany: State University of New York Press).

Sabel, Chamles F. (1986) 'Changing Models of Economic Efficiency, and Their Implications for Industrialization in the Third World', in A. Foxley, M. McPherson, and G. O'Donnell (eds), *Development, Democracy, and the Art of Trespassing: Essays in Honor of Albert O. Hirschman* (Notre Dame, Indiana: University of Notre Dame Press) pp. 27–55.

Sayer, Andrew (1989) 'Postfordism in Question', *International Journal of Urban and Regional Research*, 13(4) (December) pp. 666–95.

Schrage, Michael (1990) *Shared Minds: New Technology of Collaboration* (New York: Random House).

Scott, Allen (1992) 'The Roepke Lecture in Economic Geography: The Collective Order of Flexible Production Agglomerations: Lessons for Local Economic Development Policy and Strategic Choice', *Economic Geography*, 68(3) (July) pp. 219–33.

Shaiken, Harley (1991) 'The Universal Motors Assembly and Stamping Plant: Transferring High-Tech Production to Mexico', *The Columbia Journal of World Business*, 26(2) (Summer) pp. 124–37.

Smitka, Michael J. (1991) *Competitive Ties: Subcontracting in the Japanese Automotive Industry* (New York: Columbia University Press).

Standing, Guy (1989) 'The Growth of External Labour Flexibility in a Nascent NIC: Malaysian Labour Flexibility Survey (MLFS)'. World Employment Programme Research Working Paper No. 35 (November).

Streeck, Wolfgang (1987) 'Industrial Change and Industrial Relations in the Motor Industry: An International View', in *Economic and Industrial Democracy*, 8(4) pp. 437–62.

Turner, Lowell (1991) *Democracy at Work: Changing World Markets and the Future of Labor Unions* (Ithaca: Cornell University Press).

Wards Automotive Yearbook, various issues (Detroit: Ward's Communications).

Womack, James P., Daniel T. Jones and Daniel Roos (1990) *The Machine that Changed the World* (New York: Rawson Associates).

Part I
Origins and Diffusion of Flexible Production

2 The Transformation of Industrial Relations in Postwar Japan

Solomon B. Levine

Industrial relations and human resource management in Japan have experienced steady change since the sweeping labor reforms instituted by the Allied occupation immediately following the end of World War II. The argument of this paper is that the postwar reforms laid the basis for the subsequent transformation although that was not necessarily the intended outcome. On the other hand, the changes which evolved in the decades after 1945 were hardly a reversion to the kind of industrial relations and human resource management of prewar Japan. Little of what exists today are such throwbacks. Rather, the present-day system is largely a product of the leading actors and environmental conditions which sprang up in the aftermath of the war and occupation and then continued to adapt in the years since. Even the major rules of the postwar industrial relations system were essentially new and then underwent modifications in subsequent decades.

The basic assumption here is that the postwar Japanese industrial relations system has not been static. In this view, it is incorrect to assign unchanging characteristics to the Japanese system. Unfortunately, however, a commonly held perception is that industrial relations in Japan has three major fixed features (often referred to as 'treasures' or 'pillars'), namely, 'lifetime employment', 'seniority wages', and 'enterprise unionism'. Constant dwelling in the scholarly literature and popular media upon these three concepts, often poorly defined, has not only distorted understanding of the Japanese system, especially in making comparisons with other industrialized societies, but has also long stood in the way of pursuing methodologically-sound research into many of the more important facets of the system. Following the Dunlopian notion of industrial relations systems,[1] moreover, those three notions are an oversimplified characterization of a highly complex set of evolving relationships in industry. At best, they allude to but an especially limited segment of the entire system. There are many other key elements,

involving government as well as employers and workers and their
organizations, which need to be taken into account for accurate com-
prehension of industrial relations in contemporary Japan.
Further, the focus on the three features has given rise to incorrect
stereotyping of Japanese industrial society as a whole. It has generated
such persistent notions as worker submissiveness and loyalty to employer, company paternalism, hierarchical control and authority, exclusive groupism and 'welfare corporatism' as predominant practices
in the Japanese nation. In other words, the widely-held image of Japan
remains one of neo-feudalism carried forward from the Tokugawa Era,
before that country began to industrialize. This is frequently epitomized
as 'Japan Inc'. While postwar Japan has perhaps not produced the kind
of independent individualism, social democracy and political pluralism
envisioned in the revolutionary reforms of the occupation, after almost
50 years since Japan's surrender political, economic and social relations
are so different and so much more varied than in earlier periods that
one should reasonably conclude that those goals have been approached
if not somewhat approximated. The system of industrial relations and
human resource management is not an exception to this conclusion.
    In the materials presented below, first are outlined in brief major
shifts of special importance to industrial relations and human resource
management which have taken place since 1945 in Japan's economic
environment; for example, industrial structure, labor force composition, demographic change, income distribution and living standards.
Then follows an analysis of the principal changes in Japan's system of
industrial relations and human resource management which accompanied the transformation of the Japanese economy. This approach to
the postwar Japanese system readily, although arbitrarily, divides itself
into five successive periods of about ten years each beginning in 1945.
In this depiction, appropriate reference is made to developments in the
automotive industry as that case is often utilized as a prime example of
Japanese industrial relations as a whole. A concluding section summarizes the trends over the 50 years and speculates on changes likely to
emerge in the next decade or two.

CHANGES IN JAPAN'S ECONOMIC ENVIRONMENT,
1945–1990[2]

It may be argued that the sweeping economic, political and social reforms imposed upon Japan by the Allied occupation laid the basis not

only for achieving democracy in that nation but also for generating an almost unheard of high rate of industrial growth for any nation in modern times. In sweeping aside the military for the first time in Japan's history, the reforms concentrated instead upon developing human resources which could be productively employed in a civilian economy. This outcome emerged from a drastic revision in Japan's educational system, a wholesale redistribution of agricultural land, a far-reaching breakup of financial and industrial oligopolies, and fundamental changes in the legal relationships between workers, employers and government bodies charged with supervising industrial relations – to mention only the most important of the sociodemocratic reforms affecting human resources in economic development.

Japan's shift to high-speed economic growth did not evidence itself immediately upon the end of the war. Initially, occupation policy aimed at reducing Japanese living standards to a bare level of subsistence incapable of recovering enough industrial strength ever again to mount a military challenge (as dramatized in Article 9 of the new war-renouncing constitution of 1947). For the first few years, near starvation, widespread unemployment and rampant inflation plagued most of the Japanese population. In 1945, with a GNP at merely 60 per cent of the 1934–36 peak, Japan stood shorn of any overseas possessions and at least one-third of its prewar productive capacity. Several million military personnel had been killed or maimed, not to mention the hundreds of thousands of civilians bombed out of their homes, and cities such as Hiroshima and Nagasaki almost totally destroyed. To keep alive, Japan had to import vital foodstuff, fuel and other materials far exceeding in value the meager exports it was allowed to ship. At that time, economic recovery seemed all but impossible. Efforts to achieve reconstruction and stability encountered one failure after another. While the occupying powers adopted the basic policy of relying on a system of private enterprise rather than a socialist strategy, the central Japanese government, constantly under the watchful eye of GHQ, moved to launch initiatives for economic recovery. Its approach was gradual and stop-and-go, utilizing a series of monetary and fiscal measures as stimuli; but most important was the government's establishment of production priorities to assure a rise in output of the most essential commodities while at the same time allowing the banks to issue new credit which swelled the money supply and fed inflation. Assistance from the United States, continuing at an average of $500 million per year for close to ten years, was also needed to help stabilize the Japanese economy.

These steps by themselves might have proved successful in due time, but they became academic matters after 1947 once it became clear that the Cold War between East and West had begun, and it was advantageous for the United States and its allies to rebuild Japan quickly as a strong industrial state arrayed on their side. The Allied Occupation then began to reverse course by curbing social protest and intervening more directly to bring about economic reconstruction. The most visible step in this wholesale shift was the institution of the so-called Dodge Plan (named after the man who authored the new policy), which imposed in one fell swoop austerity measures to end inflation, eliminate overstaffing in businesses, reduce and balance the government's budget, raise household taxes, encourage savings, fix exchange rates (at ¥360 to $1.00) to promote exports, strengthen price controls (and stabilize wages), enforce rationing of essential commodities and raise domestic production of food, to develop mining (especially coal) and manufacturing. Remarkably, these measures seemed to work very quickly as inflation rapidly declined and unemployment mounted. Again, it is not known whether they would have continued to be effective; for with the outbreak of the Korean War in June 1950 the Japanese economy suddenly began to enjoy a tremendous boom as Japan soon became a major supply base for the Allied forces.

While there was a short let-down in the economy after the Korean conflict ended in 1952, this sizeable stimulus, heaped upon the brief period of sharp austerity under the Dodge Plan and the production priorities scheme of the Japanese government, proved lasting. By the time of the 1951 San Francisco Peace Treaty, which ended the occupation in April 1952, booms in both consumption and investment had set in. The Japanese economy recovered to its prewar peak by the mid-1950s and began galloping ahead in real terms at a rate which would hardly slow down for the subsequent two decades. Government policy stabilized with the beginning in 1955 of the rule by the Liberal Democratic Party (LDP), which continued without interruption to 1993. An efficient government bureaucracy, essentially left intact by the occupation, assisted in carrying out consistent policies.

At the same time, Japan began to re-enter the world community of nations, having gained admission in 1951 to the International Labor Organization (ILO), in 1952 to the International Monetary Fund (IMF), in 1955 to the General Agreement of Tariffs and Trade (GATT), and in 1956 to the United Nations. Japan came firmly and permanently under the nuclear umbrella of the United States, reaffirmed amid considerable social and political tension by the renewal in

1960 of the 1952 US–Japan Mutual Security Treaty. Japanese defense expenditures, however, were minimal, thus avoiding any large drain of resources for a military establishment. By 1960, real GNP was more than double its level ten years earlier. It was to double again by 1965.

The 'miracle' growth era from 1955 to 1975 actually was a series of successive booms, interrupted either by short periods of balance of payments deficits or threats of inflation which called for credit restraints and economic slowdowns. In retrospect, none was a serious dip until the outbreak of the first oil crisis of 1973–74. The indicative 'double the income plan' set forth by the government under Prime Minister Ikeda in 1960 with hopes of fulfillment in ten years was actually accomplished in five. High rates of household, corporate and even government savings matched by equally high rates of capital investment underlay rapid advances in productivity. Ample supplies of well-educated labor accompanied continuous technological improvement with importation or licensing of increasingly sophisticated technologies from abroad, mainly from the United States. Unemployment disappeared toward the end of the 1950s, and within the next ten years severe labor shortages began to emerge. (Population expansion, greatly feared in the 1950s, began to disappear as a threat to economic growth with birth rates falling rapidly in the 1960s.) Major gains in productivity were registered, with widespread substitution of fairly inexpensive petroleum imported especially from the Middle East and Indonesia for high-cost domestic coal. Increasing success in exporting Japanese manufactures, first with light goods such as textiles and then moving upscale to more advanced products such as electronics, financed the growing importation of fuel and raw materials, technology, machinery and food. With an increasingly favorable fixed exchange rate, deficits in the balance of trade were now being left behind. Throughout the entire period, Japan did not resort to foreign borrowing. Indeed, unlike Western Europe at that time there was little 'invasion' by American multinationals. The automobile industry, for example, began to come into its own in the 1960s, almost entirely financed by domestic capital. Mounting of the 1964 Olympic games in Tokyo celebrated Japan's total recovery from the wartime devastation and the era of unprecedented economic growth. In the same year, Japan joined the Organization for Economic Cooperation and Development (OECD).

All this occurred as Japan's population grew from less than 80 million at the end of the war to well above 100 million by 1970, going up steadily to close to 124 million by 1990. At the same time, during those years there was a spectacular shift of Japan from a semi-agrarian society with almost half the population living in rural areas at the end of the war, to a highly urbanized nation with 90 per cent of the population living in cities and towns of at least 10 000 persons each by the 1970s. Also, the Japanese labor force, growing from about 25 million in 1945 to more than 62 million in 1990, moved heavily percentage-wise into wage and salaried employment in industry and commerce, and away from unpaid family work and self-employment. A mere 12 million were wage and salary earners following the surrender. By 1990, more than 58 million were in that category.

After growing on the average by 10 per cent a year in real terms for almost two decades, the postwar Japanese economy finally suffered a serious setback only when it encountered the first oil crisis and registered negative growth in 1973. By that time the yen had been revalued following the Nixon shocks of 1971, and in 1973 with the Smithsonian agreement allowed to float freely. Monetary policy faltered, and not only was Japan beset, along with the other industrial democracies, by a sudden rise in costs as the OPEC countries doubled petroleum prices, but also for the first time in almost 25 years faced the spectre of rampant inflation. The consumer price index rose above 30 per cent by early 1974 amid widespread fear, if not panic, that the immediate postwar runaway inflation would repeat itself. It took two years to bring the abnormal rise of prices under control but only after concerted joint efforts by the government, big business and big labor (discussed more fully later).

It was now clear that the high growth era had come to end. The Japanese economy prepared for structural shifts that would require new technologies and labor force adjustments as many industries and enterprises shifted to new products and services and reorganized themselves to cut costs in order to remain competitive in world markets. These changes, nevertheless, were launched successfully in time for the second oil crisis of 1979 so that needed adjustments were made smoothly, setting the stage for great increases in exports and in overseas investments by Japan. It was within that context of fairly uneventful readjustments that the Japanese automobile companies, for example, slimmed down operations with their newly learned lean and flexible production methods and made even greater inroads into foreign markets. Japan's balance of trade, especially with the United States, began to skyrocket as a result.

After 1975 the Japanese economy grew relatively moderately, averaging only about four or five per cent a year in real terms, with some years as low as 2.5 per cent. Nonetheless, Japan's real economic growth rate in most years exceeded those of the other industrially advanced nations; per capita real income rose steadily and in the 1980s surpassed the levels of the United Kingdom and Italy among others. However, Japan's large trade surpluses have invited growing pressures from abroad to reduce exports and expand imports. Throughout the period, until recently, Japanese households and corporations maintained high rates of saving, so that, despite the rising value of the yen, there was a continuing strong force to increase exports without a commensurate increase in imports. Further, especially as a result of huge deficits accumulated especially in the operation of the publicly owned railways, the central government resolved by the early 1980s to reduce the national debt with austere budgeting, economic deregulation, and divesting itself of ownership of the large debt-ridden national enterprises and public corporations. These steps were well underway by the end of the decade.

Responding to foreign pressure, it also became the resolve of the central government to induce Japan's population, now well above 120 million, to reduce savings and increase consumption. Spurred on by the G5 Agreement in 1985 to devalue the US dollar especially relative to the yen, the government appealed to management and labor to step up purchases of foreign goods. In 1986 a highly publicized report from a well-respected government-appointed commission headed by Haruo Maekawa urged the Japanese to enjoy the fruits of their prosperity more fully by expanding consumption. The turnaround has proceeded slowly, although some of the most visible results were seen in a highly speculative land boom at the end of the 1980s and early 1990s which ended in a stock market crash and the bursting of the economic 'bubble'. By 1991 and 1992, the Japanese economy was in the doldrums along with much of the rest of the world. Even so, unemployment has risen slowly in Japan; indeed, labor shortages have continued and, for the first time, Japan has been confronted with a problem of relatively large numbers of illegal foreign workers in the labor markets.

Most important in light of these recent developments is that Japan has emerged as a potential international leader, perhaps an inevitable outcome as the world's second largest economy with a strong likelihood of becoming the largest within the next decade or two. This presumes, of course, that The United States would continue to lose its relative economic position and would be willing to share hegemonic leadership with Japan now that the Soviet super state is gone.[3] Such questions have come to the forefront in public discussion in Japan for the first time in more than 50 years. They affect the outlook of the leaders of many Japanese institutions, perhaps none more so than in the relationships among employers, workers and government in this most industrialized of the world's societies. The remainder of this paper focuses on those relationships.

INVENTING THE POSTWAR JAPANESE INDUSTRIAL RELATIONS SYSTEM, 1945–1955

Few areas of Japanese life were more affected by the reforms of the Allied occupation than labor–management relations. Immediately upon the cessation of hostilities in 1945, SCAP (Supreme Commander of the Allied Powers, also referred to as GHQ) called for wide-scale unionization of wage and salaried workers. The aim was to establish democracy in industry and to prevent re-emergence of powerful employers suspected of having supported the militaristic government. Within a few months new laws were adopted, formally put into effect, along with the new Constitution, in 1946 and 1947. Not only did the postwar Constitution guarantee the right of workers to self-organize, engage in collective bargaining, and to conduct strikes and other dispute actions; but also the 1945 Trade Union Law strongly encouraged formation of unions, while the 1946 Labor Relations Adjustment Law laid down procedures for dispute settlement and for prosecution of employers for committing unfair labor practices. It was notable that while basically patterned after the American Wagner Act, these laws went beyond in applying to all workers in both the private and public sectors (except police, firefighters, and security personnel) and in setting no limits to union recognition, such as the requirement of exclusive representation elections. Any two workers, in effect, could form a legitimate union which the employer had to recognize. Still another departure was the creation of tripartite commissions, paralleling both the US National Labor Relations Board and the Federal Mediation and Conciliation Service combined, with functions to determine the legitimacy of unions, decide on unfair labor practice cases, and offer services for settling labor–management disputes. In April 1947, moreover, the government passed the Labor Standards Law, the Workmen's Compensation Law, the Employment Security Law and the Unemployment Insurance Law.

Thus, for the first time in Japanese history Japan adopted a set of comprehensive protections for labor, most taken from the conventions of the ILO and experience of the industrially advanced Western democracies. These new legal pillars represented a complete about-face for labor policy in Japan, which had seen unions disappear to be replaced by a fascist-type 'labor front' during the wartime years. To supervise administration of the new laws the Ministry of Labor was created, also beginning in April 1947 and modelled closely after the US Department of Labor in its organization.

With such strong encouragement, if not decided favoritism, workers rushed to form unions of their own choosing. The long proclaimed-as-dead labor organizations of the prewar era suddenly sprang back to life, especially with the release from jail of numerous leftist leaders upon the war's end. Re-establishment of *Sōdōmei* on the right, and *San-betsu* on the left, both in August 1946, spearheaded the organizing drives, which over the next three years saw union membership soar to six million or more than 50 per cent of all the eligible wage and salary earners –nowhere had unionism ever spread so fast. The *Sōdōmei–San-betsu* rivalry, pitting social democrats and business unionists against left-wing socialists and communists, assured that many Japanese unions would be involved in politics to gain control of the new government. This sharp ideological rift continued to characterize the Japanese labor movement almost to the present. Only in the late 1980s, as discussed later, was the left–right split substantially closed.

The period from 1945 to 1955 was one of instability in union–management relations in Japan. Of course, in those years, the new industrial relations institutions were only becoming established. There were many disputes both economic and political in nature. At first, in pursuing its policy of achieving pacification and democratization, SCAP did not allow employers to put up much resistance to the new unions. Top management leadership was purged because of its role in assisting the war effort. Younger personnel rose suddenly to many of the highest company positions; but, themselves often imbued with the fervor for a new democratic Japan, were not at all certain about their prerogatives to manage. Many managements, it appeared, either became paralyzed in their passivity or actually welcomed union predominance. One of the most startling developments in the immediate postwar years was the workers movement for 'production control', whereby the union by itself would operate a company or plant.[4] Eventually, however, this type of activity was declared illegal by the courts as an invasion of private property rights.

The most telling disputes came in the fall and winter of 1946, which culminated in a threat of a general strike scheduled by the union leadership for 1 February 1947. Seen as a challenge to the supreme authority of GHQ itself, the strike was banned by General Macarthur at the final hour and never took place. However, the threat set in motion a reversal in occupation policy for union encouragement over the ensuing five years. By that time, of course, the East–West conflict was clearly apparent. The Allied powers were now more interested in seeing to it that Japan become a reliable and industrially strong ally rather than continuing to exact retribution for its role in World War II and to convert itself to a political democracy.

In the field of industrial relations, the main objective of the 'reverse course' was to de-emphasize political action among the unions while continuing to support union–management collective bargaining over wages, hours and working conditions. At the urging of the occupation authorities, the government, now controlled by the conservatives after brief socialist and coalition reigns, made several important revisions in labor relations law in the following several years. By December 1948, the government completely forbade public sector workers at the national level from going out on strike, a prohibition that has continued to the present. At the same time, revision of the National Public Service Law also deprived central government civil servants from engaging in collective bargaining, although it permitted them to form 'personnel associations' within their respective administrative units for purposes of presenting petitions and consulting with management. In 1948, also, a new labor relations law solely for public corporations and national enterprises (which included some of the most important operations in the Japanese economy, such as the government-owned railroads, postal service, and the telephone and telegraph network) allowed unions to continue within them and to engage in collective bargaining, but with impasses to be settled by a special tripartite labor relations commission (LRC) for that sector. These restrictions were later extended to local government employees, notably the public school teachers in 1950, and to local government-owned enterprise workers in 1952. Since the public sector was highly unionized from the outset and often led nation-wide walkouts and protests, the changes in law crimped the political force of the national labor organizations. Another major blow to the politically oriented unions was a 'purge' in 1950, ordered by the occupation, of as many as 10 000 leftist workers, many of them union officials in both government and private employment, in the name of both cutting excess staff and eliminating 'subversives'.

Of key importance to industrial relations were the 1949 changes in the Trade Union Law and the Labor Relations Adjustment Law. New requirements were set down through a 'qualifications examination' for a labor union to gain management recognition and to utilize the services of the labor relations commissions. Unions not only had to show that they were completely free of employer control, but also that they provided internal democratic practices and were fully accountable to the membership. A union was prohibited from striking unless it secured approval from a majority of its members in a secret ballot. Also, a union would be found 'qualified' only if its main objective was to engage in collective bargaining with an employer or employers over wages, hours and working conditions. Worker organizations primarily established to carry on political activity or only to provide mutual welfare benefits would not meet the new tests to be qualified as bona fide unions. While these changes in requirements were more exacting than in the original Trade Union Law, the close government supervision of unions that that act had imposed was lifted for the sake of promoting union autonomy.

For a while, it appeared that the labor movement itself would embrace the 'collective bargaining' model. After the 1947 general strike threat, both *Sanbetsu* and *Sōdōmei* began to crumble, mainly as the result of democratization movements within, and debilitating left–right struggles for control of major constituent unions. By 1950, the internal conflicts had become so divisive that these federations were dissolved, and in July was proclaimed the establishment of *Sohyo* as a new peak center which aimed to bring together left, right and neutral unions while de-emphasizing political movement in favor of industry-wide collective bargaining.

This dramatic shift, however, did not last long. The outbreak of the Korean War just a few days before *Sohyo's* founding almost immediately led *Sohyo* back to the political sphere. *Sohyo* not only denounced the war, but also declared its neutrality between East and West and its opposition to signing a peace treaty which did not include the Soviet Union, to a proposed US–Japan mutual security pact and rearmament of Japan. *Sohyo*'s unity, never complete, immediately began to crumble. Its right-wing union constituents, most of which originally had been affiliated with *Sōdōmei*, soon withdrew from *Sohyo* and in April 1954 founded *Zenrō Kaigi*, ten years later renamed *Domei*, as the rival to *Sohyo*. By that time, labor union membership had gone into decline, and both centers engaged in severe competition to enlist constituents, especially from among the unions which had not affiliated with any national federation.

One interesting example was the then small automobile workers union, originally organized within the several companies struggling in the years immediately after the end of the war to keep alive and get back to making vehicles. But unity among the several enterprise-level auto unions was very fragile. While the national organization joined *Sohyo* upon the latter's formation, the auto unions quit along with the other right-wing unions when *Sohyo* became politicized after the Korean War broke out. But, in turn, they broke into two competing although overlapping federations as one wing joined *Zenrō Kaigi* and another remained 'neutral'. Later, in 1956, many neutral or independent private-sector unions like those in the auto industry formed a loosely organized national confederation known as *Chūritsu Rōren*.

Despite the new legal requirements and restrictions placed on the unions, there was little let up in dispute activity. Employers themselves became more aggressive and confrontational once SCAP restored them to a more authoritative role in the reconstruction of Japan. At first prohibited from forming employer associations, by the Spring of 1947 national, regional and industrial employer groups (including the auto industry) were allowed to form associations for the primary purpose of dealing with unions and defending management prerogatives. *Nikkeiren*, which has remained the employers' peak industrial relations organization to the present, was launched in May 1947.

Some of Japan's severest strikes occurred between 1950 and 1954, arising not only over wages and salaries, but also especially over employment security as many companies reduced their work forces in response to the Dodge Plan austerity measures and the SCAP-ordered 'red purge' of left-wing unionists. Especially bitter were prolonged walkouts in electric power and coal mining, which in 1952 prompted special legislation limiting strikes in those industries. Two years later a more general Taft–Harley type restriction of 'national emergency' strikes was enacted. The labor–management conflicts of the late 1940s and early 1950s fundamentally arose over national economic policy for streamlining industry, particularly given the new opportunities at that time for exporting and earning foreign exchange. The strife in the auto industry was especially bitter in 1949 and 1950 as companies resorted to large lay-offs and wage cuts under presure from the Dodge Plan.

Yet, despite this turmoil, considerable headway was made in this period to establish collective bargaining as a lasting institution in Japanese industrial relations. Labor agreements became commonplace, providing for union security such as the union shop and dues check-off at the enterprise level. It should be noted that union recognition as derived from the union qualifications examination procedure at the labor relations commissions was largely at the enterprise or plant level where the workers formed their unions. This meant that collective bargaining tended to be highly decentralized, even though in the early, postwar years industry-wide negotiations were prevalent in major industries such as coal mining and iron and steel due to the need for national-level planning for reconstruction. Because of skyrocketing inflation quickly followed by deflation, layoffs and wage cutting, collective bargaining became widely practiced at the enterprise level where these problems were directly felt by the workers and managements. In many cases settlements were not easily reached, so that the parties had to turn to the labor relations commissions for assistance or intervention in the form of conciliation or mediation.

The role of the LRCs, especially of the Central Labor Relations Commission (CLRC), was undoubtably critical for restoring industrial peace in many cases and of devising compromise solutions to disputes which were to become established industrial relations practice throughout Japan. One notable example was the adoption of 'periodic wage increases', whereby the individual employee normally could expect a regular pay rise with each additional year of work in a company. Still another was the spread of large lump-sum payment of 'seasonal' bonuses (usually at the time of the Buddhist holidays in July and at year's end) in lieu of regular wage and salary increases. These payments were adopted, after serious collective bargaining, not simply because of traditional gift giving on seasonal holidays but because of great economic uncertainty as Japan strove to recover and attain stability. By the mid-1950s, also, many collective bargaining relationships had become so firmly established at the enterprise level that they had begun to include joint consultation on a regular basis and to experiment with union–management cooperation. By that time, too, as in the auto unions, radical left-wing union leaders had been replaced by moderates in numerous cases.

INSTITUTIONAL STABILIZATION, 1955–1965

1955 is perhaps the most memorable year in Japan's postwar industrial relations. The first *Shuntō*, or 'Spring Wage Struggle', was mounted, continuing annually ever since without interruption.[5] The same year also saw establishment of the Japan Productivity Center (JPC), which today still remains a vital organization. One should note as well that by 1958 Japan adopted its first Minimum Wages Law, thus implementing a fundamental provision in the Labor Standards Law of 1947 and removing wage minima as a contentious issue in collective bargaining.

It was during this decade that *shuntō*, originated by the leaders of *Sohyo* and almost from the beginning supported by *Chūritsu Rōren*, became the mainstay of collective bargaining in Japan. The principal aim of *shuntō* was to achieve a degree of uniformity in annual wage settlements at a time that industry-wide collective bargaining was in decline, and enterprise-level negotiations were producing diverse outcomes even in the same industry. Another purpose was to mobilize the political strength of labor to support the then newly merged socialist party in opposition to the newly unified conservatives.

After an uncertain start, by about 1960 *shuntō* was embraced by most of organized labor and by the major enterprises and government agencies as the principal means for determining annual wage level adjustments for virtually the entire economy. Also, although many employers and the *Zenrō Kaigi* unions at first resisted the spread of *shuntō* in its early years in favor of decentralized bargaining, actually by the mid-1960s they too came to rely upon the process to 'take wages out of competition' at the time of very rapid industrial expansion. *Shuntō* became an institution in both the private and public sectors for establishing national and industrial wage policy in Japan.

It should be emphasized that from the beginning *shuntō* combined both centralized and decentralized collective bargaining. While formal collective bargaining in Japan takes place mainly at the enterprise level, because legal authority to conclude labor agreements resides there, *shuntō* actually has consisted of successive waves of simultaneous negotiations coordinated, if not directed, by national industrial union federations and employer's associations. Bargaining, thus, goes forward together at both industrial and enterprise levels, once *Sohyo* and the national union constituents each year give the signal to begin by announcing the goals for wage and salary increases, usually issued months in advance of the eventual settlements in the Spring. In the interim, as the beginning of the fiscal or budget year approaches (1 April), bargaining mounts in intensity at the different levels within most industries. Settlements at major firms are typically reached within a few days or weeks following that 'deadline', usually after short walkouts or demonstrations by the workers, lasting a few hours or a day or two, on a mass basis industry by industry. In the first two decades of *shuntō*, virtually the entire union membership would participate in *shuntō* stoppages. After the process became so ritualized and the outcome so predictable, such mass activity was no longer necessary to demonstrate labor solidarity.

In the earlier years of *shuntō*, the leading pattern setters were in most cases the iron and steel industry and the private railways; later, particularly following the first oil crisis in 1973–74, the metalworking industries, including automobiles and electric products, became the leaders. Especially by the 1960s, not uninfluential in the process were the prospective settlements in the government-owned enterprises, especially the national railways. Bargaining in the private sector would often attempt to anticipate the outcome in the public sector even though the formal decision for the latter awaited the mediation awards (and subsequent negotiations) of the tripartite Public Corporation and National Enterprise Labor Relations Commission (PCNELRC) issued retroactively later in the summer. That settlement, of course, was of great importance for both central and local governments in the making of budgets by 1 April.

In essence, then, most of the wage and salary settlements in *shuntō*, whether at the industrial or enterprise level, have long been tied together. A major outcome of the process was assurance of a role for the union movement in determining how the fruits of economic growth would be distributed. *Shuntō* thus helped to gain popular acceptance for unionization. Eventually, the *shuntō* approach has embraced other major issues in Japanese collective bargaining. For example, while determined at other times of the year, seasonal bonuses, in some cases accounting for a third of the average worker's annual wage income, came to be settled mainly in relation to the *shuntō* outcome on the basis of industry-level patterns although variations were allowed at the firm level depending on profitability. By the 1970s, *shuntō* broadened into such issues as starting wages, hour reductions, pension benefits, housing and even income tax rates for workers.

On the other hand, *shuntō* bargaining has not dealt directly with fringe benefits such as health and hospitalization insurance and unemployment compensation, because they have been negotiated on a comprehensive basis through social security legislation since the late 1950s. Moreover, as discussed later, following the first oil crisis most social security programs saw significant improvements as the result of government action. Similarly, particularly under conditions of full employment, raising of minimum labor standards has depended on legislation rather than collective bargaining. Despite its conservatism, the ruling Liberal Democratic Party (LDP) almost from its founding in 1955 declared itself in favor of developing a welfare state and often has seemed more effective in achieving advances for working people than the two disunited socialist parties in the opposition.

Japan's productivity improvement movement also contributed to widespread acceptance of unions and collective bargaining, but it went beyond the negotiation of labor agreements by strongly advocating union–management consultation, information sharing and worker participation programs. Much of the movement was initiated by the Japan Productivity Center (JPC), which at the outset was assisted in its establishment by the United States. By the 1960s, the JPC, advised by many of the neutral members of the labor relations commissions, often themselves leading scholars, provided an effective forum for information and education. One of its important activities, along with the study of production systems and technologies, was the dispatching of management and labor teams aboad to learn first-hand about industrial relations practices in other countries, especially the US. While not a public agency, the JPC received government support as well as financing from employers and right-wing unions. Along with still other new organizations such as the Japan Institute of Labor founded in 1959, the JPC promoted concepts of professional human resource management and advocated systematic personnel administration. For years, *Sohyo*, dominated by public-sector and left-socialist unions, refused to cooperate with the JPC, which it believed was merely another means for exploiting workers. However, as more and more of the collective bargaining at the enterprise level formally embraced union–management consultation in the 1960s and 1970s, *Sohyo*'s opposition gradually faded.

With the emergence of collective bargaining and union–management consultation and cooperation as well-established institutions in Japan, large-scale labor disputes of long duration virtually disappeared in the private sector. The last of these clashes was the near year-long strike at the Miike coal mines in 1960, essentially over the question of mass worker dismissals as Japanese industry began to substitute petroleum for coal as a principal source of fuel. While the outcome of this at times violent dispute favored the employers, it also convinced many managers of the need to consult closely with the unions before resorting to workforce reductions. They came to fear repetitions of the Miike experience especially at a time when Japan was scoring its first postwar successes in exporting to foreign markets and beginning to liberalize its own economy. Throughout the period, in the meantime, unions resumed their growth, while labor shortages were becoming increasingly apparent. There was a notable spread of collective bargaining agreements, including provisions for regular union–management joint consultation at the enterprise level. With stronger enforcement of the labor standards law, employment security of regular workers became firmly established. The government of Japan itself, which had been accused by the ILO of denying full rights of association to public sector employees in contravention of one of its conventions (No. 87), was subjected to an intensive public investigation in 1965. As a result, the government soon thereafter revised the law to remove the objectionable restrictions and ratified the ILO convention in question.

MAKING OF A SOCIAL COMPACT, 1965–1975[6]

Japanese industrial relations became relatively stable by the second half of the 1960s and early 1970s. As already noted, collective bargaining and joint consultation had become fully institutionalized. The parties no longer challenged each other's legitimacy. *Shuntō*, increasing in its rate of union participation, grew in importance as the chief instrument for determining national wages and incomes policy. More and more joint deliberations were taking place at the national and industrial levels in addition to the enterprise, often initiated by government ministries or the labor relations commissions. There was a spread in the use of tripartite advisory committees for public policy concerning labor, notably minimum wages, employment measures, education and training and social security. A quiet but highly significant development was the initiation at the end of the 1960s of the so-called Industry and Labor Round Table Conference (*Sanrōkon*), which was formally organized by the Ministry of Labor and brought together leading members of the government, private industry, labor movement and academia for regular discussion of labor matters. While in no sense a negotiating body, this Conference no doubt served to enhance communications and narrow differences among the participants. It has not failed to hold its scheduled monthly meetings in all the years since its founding.

With developments like these, the Japanese industrial relations system was well prepared to ride out the economic disruptions brought on by the first oil crisis of 1973–74. While the initial reaction of the labor unions was to seek protection for workers against the sudden rise in living costs, the union leadership soon realized that a collaborative approach was needed to stem the consequences of the 'oil shock'. The *shuntō* of 1974 saw a pattern of almost 33 per cent in wage increases, the highest experienced, as Japanese employers and the government, fearful of disruptive walkouts, put up little resistance to union demands. Yet, it was also clear that mass layoffs could be in the offing as Japanese industry adjusted to new cost structures.

By the *shuntōs* of 1975 and 1976, however, the deliberations among all the parties at the national level had led to a mutual understanding, or 'social compact', that each had to share in the sacrifices as well as in any rewards involved in the economic readjustments. On the government side, there was a pledge to utilize fiscal, monetary and industrial policies to maintain full employment, stabilize prices and bring about structural change; but at the same time to improve social security, industrial safey and health measures, employment and training programs and labor market services. Employers, too, essentially promised to avoid dismissals and !ayoffs and support joint consultation and worker participation even though they adopted technological and organizational change. The unions, even including many from *Sohyo*, vowed that as long as worker employment security was maintained and inflation subdued, they would restrain their wage increase demands and, provided there was genuine joint consultation and information sharing, would not obstruct management efforts to cut costs and improve productivity. These understandings essentially were carried out in the ensuing years, thereby solidifying the new era of mutual cooperation in Japanese industrial relations. It is notable that following achievement of this consensus, the labor share of national income rose significantly and, even with the recovery of profits since that time, permanently.

Particularly notable after 1975 was the decline of the use of the strike.[7] As labor union membership steadily rose throughout the 1960s and early 1970s, so did workdays lost as the result of stoppages, although prolonged strikes appeared to be a thing of the past. Much of the loss of workdays had resulted from the expansion of *shuntō* to larger and larger proportions of the workforce. The new social compact of the mid-1970s meant a sharp reduction in such overt conflict as union attention shifted to protecting employment security and cooperating with management in improving efficiency and cutting costs. The most dramatic strikes now occurred in the public sector, notably in the national railways, where the right to strike, denied since 1948, had become a major demand.

SLOW ECONOMIC GROWTH AND INDUSTRIAL RESTRUCTURING, 1975–1985[8]

The test of the new social compact came quickly with the second oil crisis of 1979. Clearly, the cooperative industrial relations which had been established helped the Japanese economy to adjust rapidly to the new cost and market conditions. Already well underway was a shift from conventional manufacturing to high-tech production processes and to services. The steep rise in educational levels of the labor force that had been emerging ever since the school reforms of the occupation eased the transition. The new government programs for subsidizing employment adjustment and retraining at the firm level avoided sharp increases in unemployment. Workforces within enterprises quickly adapted to new technologies and organizations through established training methods, usually right on the job. Changes in production were made only after thorough airing of plans and problems with unions and workers directly affected. In the *shuntō* negotiations, settlements were kept within the limits of productivity growth and cost-of-living increases.

It was at that time that Japan began to make its greatest inroads into foreign markets, especially the United States; now with automobile, machinery and electronics exports leading the way rather than textiles and steel. As foreign exchange surpluses piled up, Japanese enterprises also contemplated making sizeable production investments abroad, and soon afterward built or acquired plants in North America led by such companies as Honda, Nissan and Toyota.

This period also saw the first serious moves toward unifying the long-divided Japanese labor movement. The old generation of rival leaders had now passed into history. New leadership, experienced with the success of collective bargaining and joint consultation in achieving economic gains and employment security for union members within a market-type economy, were far less interested than their predecessors in achieving ideological goals. Despite the intense rivalry between *Domei* and *Sohyo*, there had long been potential for labor unification. Philosophically, the two major federations agreed on the need for a centralized labor movement based on industrial unionism. Even the small *Shinsanbetsu* federation had remained over the years as the symbol of pure industrial unionism for *Domei* and *Sohyo* to emulate.

As early as 1964, the metalworking industry unions, including the automobile workers as a prominent participant, had formed the International Metalworkers Federation-Japan Council (IMF-JC), not only to achieve coordination with other affiliates of the international trade union secretariat but also to centralize collective bargaining strategy, particularly for *shuntō* and bonus negotiations within Japan. IMF-JC straddled the national federations. Like the IMF-JC, the neutral *Chūritsu Rōren* also continuously urged unity by downplaying political and ideological differences between *Domei* and *Sohyo*.

After numerous attempts to prepare the ground for unification, it was not until 1982 that the process appeared to be on its way for certain. By that time, it should be noted, the public sector unions, which had almost completely dominated *Sohyo*, had begun to lose strength.

Not only had private sector unions such as the auto and electrical products unions grown larger, but even among them leadership had shifted from industrial federations such as the steelworkers and private railways to the electrical workers and auto workers, especially within the IMF-JC. Further, the Liberal Democratic government now proposed to 'privatize' major government enterprises – notably telecommunications, the national railroads and the tobacco and salt monopoly – which through breakup, reorganization and competition, meant the weakening if not destruction of their enterprise-level unions even though they would be accorded full rights under the Trade Union Law, including the right to strike. Privatization was well underway by the mid-1980s.

Because of the turmoil among the public sector unions which resulted from those proposals, plans for unification of the labor movement were confined to the private sector for the time being. The *Zenminrōkyō*, or Private Sector Trade Union Council, formed at the end of 1982, brought together almost all *Domei*, *Chūritsu Rōren* and *Shinsanbetsu* affiliates and the leading private sector constituents of *Sohyo*. However, five more years were to pass before that preparatory council was converted into a new national peak center, called *Rengo*, the Japanese Private Sector Trade Union Confederation, replacing all the other centers except *Sohyo*.

The shift in industrial structure from manufacturing to services and from blue to white-collar work resulted in stagnation of organized labor membership after the mid-1970s. Union membership had steadily grown from the late 1950s to the early 1970s reaching a peak of about 12.5 million members, or 35 per cent of the eligible wage and salary earners. With a relatively large shift to white collar employment and increased numbers of women as temporary workers, unions found it difficult to organize new members of the labor force. Accordingly, while the total number of unionists has declined only slightly to about 12.3 million, the percentage organized has steadily fallen over the years to less than 25 per cent at present.

ERA OF GLOBALIZATION, 1985–?

With the ascendancy of the Japanese economy in the 1980s to become the world's second largest, the relative decline of the American economy in the same period, and by the end of that decade the demise of the

Soviet Union as a viable economic entity, clearly Japan had been thrust into a new role as a potential hegemonic power in the world. However, the era of ideological struggle within Japan to shape the nature of Japanese society now appeared long dead. The 40 years since the end of World War II had seen the transformation of Japan from centralized state capitalism to a democratic market-oriented 'mixed' economy. In that transformation, industrial relations also underwent a parallel change. Employers and unions had learned to work together with little animosity. The conservative governments, continuously in power from the late 1940s, had come to embrace the goals sought in the occupation reforms: industrial democracy, worker participation, collective bargaining, unionization and welfare programs to protect workers. Notably throughout the 1980s to the present, the government enacted steady improvements in labor standards, especially for maximum work hours, minimum wages, equal treatment (notably between men and women), skill training and retraining, child care leave, labor market operations and the like.

By the mid-1980s, especially as the result of pressures from foreign countries like the US which suffered from large trade deficits with Japan, public policy began to shift consciously to an emphasis upon increasing consumption and decreasing savings among the Japanese population. The time had come, in the minds of many Japanese, for the citizens of Japan to partake more fully in that nation's economic success. The turn toward increased consumption was already in the works, it was assumed, as the result of very rapid ageing of the population. A sharp revaluation of the yen against the dollar and other currencies in September 1985, agreed upon by the five leading Western powers, was supposed to facilitate the shift toward consumption especially of foreign imports. A series of influential reports in 1986 and 1987, commissioned by the government of Japan, set forth the steps to be taken for Japan to become a nation of consumers. New tax measures, instituted in 1989, were intended to bring greater equity in income distribution, although hotly opposed as regressive by housewives and labor unions because they included taxes on consumption.

Under these circumstances, *shuntō* and bonus bargaining became increasingly important institutions for assuring an equitable distribution of income. Even though the rate of union membership continued to decline slowly throughout the late 1980s into the early 1990s, labor–management negotiations hardly lost relevance for income and wages policy. Private sector bargaining still clearly set the pattern for settlements in both organized and unorganized industry, even as the public sector declined in influence. In recognition of this development, the government merged the special labor relations commission for the public sector enterprises with the Central Labor Relations Commission in 1988. This was a part of the general deregulation of the economy followed by the government as Japan became increasingly prominent in foreign markets, an overseas investor, and provider of assistance abroad.

Hardly had the private-sector *Rengo* been established when it began serious negotiations for bringing in the public-sector unions. Not only had collective bargaining leadership for the entire economy shifted to the private-sector unions, but also the time appeared ripe to launch unified labor efforts in the political arena. Among *Sohyo*'s public sector constituents, there still remained sharp ideological divisions and disagreement over whether to have a separate peak federation for the government workers or unify with the private-sector unions. Now led by privatized former public employee unions, notably the telecommunications workers, *Rengo* determined it would attempt to achieve a consolidated federation and at the same time bring about the long sought-after merger of the socialist and social democratic parties. The first objective was reached in November 1989 with the founding of the merged organization, continuing with the same name of *Rengo* (Japanese Trade Union Confederation). Thus, for the first time since the establishment of *Sohyo* in 1950 was so much unity achieved in the Japanese labor movement. Most of *Sohyo* had joined, and the new *Rengo* boasted of at least 80 industrial union affiliates with a total membership of 7.6 million, making it the third or fourth largest national peak center in the non-communist world. Like its predecessor, the merged *Rengo* affiliated with the ICFTU as the sole spokesperson for Japanese labor. While *Rengo* opposed the conservative Liberal Democrat government, actually it was welcomed by the conservatives because of its declared moderation and acceptance of the on-going economic and political system.

The new *Rengo* not only vowed to concentrate upon economic gains for workers rather than achieving political control, but also to expand its membership to 10 million within two years by bringing about mergers of rival unions in the same industry, enlisting still neutral or unaffiliated unions, and stepping up efforts to organize the unorganized. The new confederation was very accommodating. Its dues levy was much smaller than had been the case for *Sohyo* or *Domei*, and it brought under its umbrella without any alteration the political organizations which had been parts of the predecessor centers. Thus, it wished to avoid any divisiveness from the very beginning. *Rengo*'s long-term goals, in addition to reversing the relative decline in union density, included establishing a single opposition political party as well as an internal organizational structure of fewer than two dozen IMF-JC-like industrial union federations modelled after the DGB of West Germany.

Unification, however, remained far from complete, and even to the present has not made much progress since November 1989.[9] The sought-for increase in union membership has yet to be achieved. At least one-fourth of Japan's 70 000 basic unions and 12.5 million union members remain unaffiliated with any national-level union body. Two small federations continue to compete with *Rengo*: *Zenrōren* (National Confederation of Trade Unions) with about 800 000 members mainly from the radical unions formerly within *Sohyō* and opposed to joining *Rengo*; and *Zenrōkyō* (National Trade Union Council) with about 200 000 members, composed primarily of erstwhile government enterprise employees, for the most part from the former national railways, who lost their jobs under privatization or who favor a separate public sector federation.

Rengo's goal of forming a single opposition party in the hope of establishing a true two-party system in Japan appears as if it could be within its grasp. With the fall of the Takeshita government on the heels of scandals, and widespread public dissatisfaction over the introduction of a consumption tax, the upper house (councillors) election in the summer of 1989 resulted in the Liberal Democrat government losing its majority in that chamber for the first time in almost 35 years. While the opposition parties increased their seats in the upper house, what was most surprising was that a group of 12 newly elected councillors had run under the new banner of *Rengo*, unattached to either the socialists or democratic socialists because there had not been time in the few weeks allowed between the initial announcement and the election itself to reach agreement among the rival opposition parties for candidates they would mutually support. The *Rengo* councillors, it should be noted, gained a sufficient number of seats to hold the balance of power within the upper house. Thus, it appeared that by the time the merged *Rengo* was established in November there was great promise for achieving its vow to launch a single opposition party to challenge the Liberal Democrats.

By the end of 1992, once again the Liberal Democrat government encountered serious financial scandals which caused divisions in the ruling party. At the same time, in part reflecting worldwide conditions, the Japanese economy had slid into a prolonged recession, experiencing negative growth for the first time since the 1973–74 oil crisis. With the rapidly moving political events of the summer of 1993, *Rengo*'s hope for a two-party system was on the brink of realization. A coalition of most opposition parties and of scores of defectors from the Liberal Democrats who formed three new parties achieved victory in the lower house elections of 18 July 1993. For the first time since 1955, the LDP was no longer in power. The new eight-party coalition government was led by former Liberal Democrat Morihiro Hosokawa as Prime Minister. Included in the coalition was the *Rengo*-supported Social Democrat Party, the largest party in the group although actually a heavy loser of seats in the election. A major reason for the new coalition was mutual opposition to continued LDP rule. Not included, however, were the communists.

While it is unclear exactly what role *Rengo* played in bringing about this dramatic change, there is little question that Akira Yamagishi, the president of the labor federation, was a significant actor in brokering the formation of the new coalition. This ruling coalition proved highly fragile and in 1994, following the resignation of Hosokawa in April, another coalition lasted only 10 weeks in office, followed by a third coalition, made up, surprisingly, of the social Democrats and LDP headed by socialist Tomiichi Murayama. The era of the '1$\frac{1}{2}$ party' system in Japan now seems to have ended. In the wake of these events President Yamagishi retired, giving poor health as the reason. However, these developments in the longer run could strengthen *Rengo*'s unity and the tendency to centralize the locus of decision-making in the Japanese labor movement.

INDUSTRIAL RELATIONS IN JAPAN'S AUTO INDUSTRY

The evolution of industrial relations and human resources in the Japanese automobile industry in the postwar decades closely parallels the history of the system in general.[10] Some detailed characteristics of the system may be portrayed better at the industrial and enterprise level than for the nation as a whole. It is important to point out that, unlike the American case in which the auto industry was among the most prominent in the newly developing US system as early as the 1930s, the Japanese industry did not rise to the forefront until the 1970s. In the course of that development, close ties had been forged among the various metalworking industries, as exemplified by the IMF-JC from 1964 on, led in the earlier years especially by the iron and steel, electrical machinery and shipbuilding industries, all prominent in Japan's re-entry into world markets well before the rise of Japanese-made automobiles. Even after autos became Japan's leading exports by the 1980s, the ties among the metalworking industries remained extremely close, culminating in the emergence of *Rengo* toward the end of the decade. Undoubtedly, this helps to explain the continuing cohesiveness in the Japanese industrial relations system in contrast to the industry-by-industry separateness and disappearance of pattern bargaining that occurred in the United States after the 1950s.

The prewar Japanese auto industry was tiny compared to that in America, and left little legacy for industrial relations after the war. The American industry, of course, was characterized by mass production and 'Fordism', the breakdown of work into numerous small and repetitive tasks and, as a result, a proliferation of job wage rates, seniority hierarchies and rigid work rules. No such industrial relations legacy was willed to the Japanese. In prewar Japan, both Ford and General Motors had assembly plants which they were forced to leave upon order of the militaristic government. The other major vehicle makers, notably Toyota and Nissan, manufactured vehicles primarily for the military and with the wartime period followed the techniques advocated by the Industrial Patriotic Association or *Sampō*, Japan's labor front, such as rewarding length of service and forbidding labor mobility, none of which proved especially successful in increasing production.

After Japan's surrender, the future of a Japanese automobile industry was quite dubious. While the plants had been bombed, they were quickly rehabilitated to make products more essential than autos and only with the boom of the Korean War could serious contemplation be given to expanding vehicle production. In the meantime, as in so many other Japanese industries and major firms, the workers almost immediately formed unions at the enterprise and plant level primarily in order to protect their employment against reductions in the workforces. The first auto unions tended to be radical, mainly responding to the left-wing *Sanbetsu*. Serious walkouts beset the industry until the mid-1950s, especially as management attempted to streamline employment following adoption of the Dodge Plan and the 'red purge' of radical workers. Prolonged strikes in 1954 at Toyota and Nissan resulted in the split of their enterprise-level unions into 'first' and 'second' unions, with the latter in favor of labor–management cooperation to increase productivity and leaning toward the right-wing *Zenrō Kaigi*, the break-away from *Sohyo* eventually to become the *Domei* federation. After considerable internal conflict, 'second' unions, led by well-educated white collar and highly skilled employees, became predominant. On the employer side, the industry association, founded soon after the end of the war, soon become an effective instrument for management to formulate a common labor policy among the companies and to coordinate negotiations with unions.

With Japan's economic growth well underway by the mid-1950s, more than a dozen auto companies were in competition for the small but growing domestic market. Because of the limited availability of capital, and high market risk, these enterprises found it impossible to adopt the kind of vertical and horizontal integration in their operations for which the Big Three of the US had become famous. Rather, the Japanese approach was to keep the 'parent' firm to a minimum and rely heavily upon dependable subcontractors and other associates who would share the problems of production planning, management and risk-taking. This strategy alone would make it impossible to follow American-style labor relations based on a minute division of work and employment of semi-skilled workers in large-scale comprehensive organizations. Instead, it meant that management had to rely upon knowledgeable, well-trained, multi-skilled workers within the firm for carrying out rapidly changing production operations efficiently and with the most advanced technology.

One reason for this approach was the evolving system of industrial relations itself. As the result of collective bargaining, strikes and mediation efforts, the management of large firms had become more committed to the employment security of the unionized regular workers, blue and white collar workers alike, within plants and enterprises. Also, there was growing acceptance of the practice of granting annual wage increases and bonuses to those workers. With the shift of union leadership toward moderation in their demands and ideology, the employers no longer fought the existence of unions within their enterprises. Instead, the unions at that level were seen as supportive of management efforts to improve productivity and cut costs.

Against this background, companies began to experiment with new techniques such as 'flexible' and 'just-in-time' production, worker participation and self-management schemes like zero-defect programs and quality control circles, and regularly scheduled consultation and sharing of information on long-run production planning and human resource needs with their respective enterprise-level unions. In the light of these industrial relations and human resource management approaches, management became increasingly willing to accept worker unionization and collective bargaining as legally required.

Thus, after the late 1950s work stoppages essentially ceased among the major auto producers. Following the advice of the new JPC, moreover, union–management cooperation for enhancing productivity and product quality rested on assuring employment security for those regularly employed, steadily improving working conditions for safety and health of employees, sharing the gains in productivity on an equitable basis through collective bargaining, and communicating systematically with the unions on a wide range of subject matter vital to the future of the industry and enterprises.

For example, Toyota and its enterprise-level union embodied these principles in a joint declaration issued as early as 1962, thereby fortifying the process of achieving mutual consensus among all members of the firm.[12] Over the ensuing years, an elaborate network of councils, conferences and other means for employer–employee communications as well as machinery for settling worker grievances was put into place through negotiations. Usually covered in the joint discussions have been such matters as production plans; expected technological change; assignment, transfer and training of personnel; human resource needs; and overtime requirements. As necessary, work rules were revised regularly through collective bargaining to reflect changes mutually agreed to. The great success of companies such as Toyota in turn inspired the widespread use of these institutions as basic elements in the industrial relations system of postwar Japan.

Of particular importance in the Japanese auto industry have been the special relationships which grew up over the years between the parent companies, subcontractors and distributors.[13] These took the form of tight-knit chains of alliances, known as *keiretsu*, through contracts, stockownership, shared management know-how and technology, and close tutelage and communications. Even though with *keiretsu* structures industrial relations in automobiles became decentralized by leaving each of the affiliated firms to determine many details with their respective workforces, at the same time the alliances provided a high degree of centralized coordination for producing uniform and consistent rules and practices. This was the case for both the employer and worker sides.

Taking Toyota again as an example,[14] in 1990 about 85 firms provided the *keiretsu* network for manufacturing operations alone, while another 158 firms were devoted to marketing. Predominant among these were five major enterprises, both assemblers and principle suppliers. The more than 240 companies involved ranged from small to large-scale organizations and in total employed close to 300 000. The companies were affiliated with the Japan Automobile Manufacturers Association, while the unions, one in each enterprise, formed the Federation of All Toyota Workers' Union. The latter has been a constituent of the Confederation of Japan Automobile Workers Union (*Jidōsha Sōren*), a *Rengo* affiliate, along with similar enterprise-wide federations for the 11 other major auto and auto parts makers. Collective bargaining over major issues affecting the entire automobile industry is centered in on-going discussions and informal negotiations between the employers' association and *Jidōsha Sōren* and between top company management and company-wide union federations, although the signing of the collective bargaining agreements takes place formally at the individual enterprise level. As mentioned earlier, the IMF-JC, of which *Jidōsha Sōren* is a member, strongly influences both the auto labor confederation and the enterprise-level affiliates in their bargaining positions, especially on issues of national import. With close to 750 000 union members in a dozen of Japan's most important enterprises, the settlements made for the auto industry become key patterns or benchmarks for the remainder of the metalworking sector and for the national economy as a whole, unionized or not. On the union side, moreover, both *Jidōsha Sōren* and the enterprise-wide union federations carry out political and lobbying functions nationally and at prefectual and local government levels. The same may be said of the employers association.

CONCLUSIONS

The system of industrial relations which evolved in Japan after World War II has proved to be both highly dynamic yet well-institutionalized. It has coped with enormous and rapid economic, political, social and technological change during the past 48 years, and today still promises to sustain its ability to adapt to the changes expected in the decades ahead. The most notable feature of the system are the prominent roles played, and mutually accepted, by the three major actors – government, employers and organized labor – in the making of both procedural and substantive rules for human resource management and industrial relations. Despite assertions to the contrary, it is difficult to assign continuing predominance to any single actor. The transformation of the Japanese system in the postwar era has been precisely that: from totalitarian control to the emergence of pluralistic tripartitism for industrial relations rule-making.

Three important institutional features especially have characterized the postwar system. The first is vigorous collective bargaining activity, with each of the parties accepting one another as equals and key settlements having economy-wide influence. The second is the widespread practice of joint labor–management consultation at all levels – national, industrial, regional and enterprise – often involving government as well as management and labor, with as a major result the decline of overt conflict as seen in strike rates. Third is reliance upon government to establish and enforce basic labor standards throughout the economy and to underpin the industrial relations system with capable mediation facilities and substantial investments in human skill development.[15]

The history of the Japanese system deserves close study for the important lessons it provides for other nations, developing as well as economically advanced. In order to understand its essential features, the close to 50-year evolution of the system commands special attention. Tripartitism in Japanese industrial relations took several decades to emerge full-blown, and then only after receiving an initial strong impetus. While various elements in the system are surely the products of historical and cultural circumstances particular to Japan, at the same time the Japanese system evinces characteristics long advocated as desiderata for any national system of industrial relations in which democratic values are to predominate.

Notes

1. See John T. Dunlop (1958) *Industrial Relations Systems* (New York: Henry Holt).
2. For comprehensive treatments of Japan's postwar economic growth, see, for example, Hugh Patrick and Henry Rosovsky (1976) (eds), *Asia's New Giant: How The Japanese Economy Works* (Washington DC: The Brookings Institution); and Takafusa Nakamura (1981) *The Postwar Japanese Economy* (Tokyo: University of Tokyo Press); and Kozo Yamamura and Yasukichi Yasuba (1987) (eds), *The Political Economy of Japan: the Domestic Transformation*, vol. I (Stanford: Stanford University Press).
3. For a thoughtful statement regarding this development, see Koji Taira (1991), 'Japan, An Imminent Hegemon?', in Solomon B. Levine and Koji Taira (eds), *Japan's External Economic Relations: Japanese Perspectives*, *Annals of the American Academy of Political and Social Science*, vol. 513 (January) pp. 151–63.
4. For a full analysis of 'production control' in postwar Japan, see Joe Moore (1983) *Japanese Workers and the Struggle for Power* (Madison, WI: University of Wisconsin Press).

5. A detailed treatment is found in Akira Takanashi, *et al.* (1989) *Shunto Wage Offensive: Historical Overview and Prospects*, Japanese Industrial Relations Series No. 15 (Tokyo: The Japan Institute of Labour).
6. See Koji Taira and Solomon B. Levine (1985) 'Japan's Industrial Relations: A Social Compact Emerges', in Hervey Juris, *et al.* (eds), *Industrial Relations in a Decade of Economic Change* (Madison, WI: Industrial Relations Research Association), pp. 247–300.
7. See Solomon B. Levine and Koji Taira (1980) 'Interpreting Industrial Conflict: The Case of Japan', in Benjamin Martin and Everett M. Kassalow (eds), *Labor Relations in Advanced Industrial Societies: Issues and Problems* (Washington, DC: Carnegie Endowment for International Peace).
8. For a comprehensive analysis in English, see Taishiro Shirai (1983) (ed.), *Contemporary Industrial Relations in Japan* (Madison, WI: University of Wisconsin Press).
9. For basic information, see The Japan Institute of Labour (1992) *Labour–Management Relations in Japan* (Tokyo).
10. An extensive literature on the Japanese auto industry has appeared in recent years. For a comprehensive history, see M.A. Cusumano (1989) *The Japanese Automobile Industry: Technology and Management at Nissan and Totota* (Cambridge, Mass: Harvard University Press).
11. For a detailed treatment of skill formation in Japanese industry, see Kazuo Koike (1988) *Understanding Industrial Relations in Modern Japan* (New York: St Martin's Press).
12. Based on the Federation of All Toyota Workers' Union (1990) *Union Activities: Basic Concepts, Organization, Activities* (April) Toyota, Aichi, Japan.
13. For an analysis of these relationships, see Michael J. Smitka (1991) *Competitive Ties: Subcontracting in the Japanese Automotive Industry* (New York: Columbia University Press).
14. All Toyota Workers' Union, *Union Activities, op. cit.*
15. An English-language history of Japanese human resources is available in Solomon B. Levine and Hisashi Kawada (1980) *Human Resources in Japanese Industrial Development* (Princeton, NJ: Princeton University Press).

3 Japanese Automotive Transplants and the Transfer of the Japanese Production System[†]

Richard Florida and Martin Kenney

> The key to success of Toyota Motor Manufacturing USA, Inc, will depend upon the support and contribution of our human resources in implementing the Toyota Production System . . . The very basis of the Production System is respect and dignity of team members through effective utilization of their time – allowing team members to use their ingenuity and to participate in the design of their jobs.
> (Toyota, Motor Manufacturing USA, Inc., *Team Member Handbook*)[1]

> The idea is to work smarter, not harder.
> (Joel Smith, original UAW representative to NUMMI)[2]

INTRODUCTION

Since 1980, Japan's major automobile companies have set up 12 major automobile assembly plants or *transplants* in North America – nine of these are in the US another three are in Canada. These transplants

[†] This chapter is an expanded and updated version of our article, 'Transplanted Organizations: The Transfer of Japanese Industrial Organization to the United States' (1991) originally published in the *American Sociological Review*, 56, pp. 381–98. The research was funded in part by the National Science Foundation, the Economic Research Service of the US Department of Agriculture and the Ohio Board of Regents and more recently by the Alfred P. Sloan Foundation. The authors would like to thank Nicole Biggart, Robert Cole, Norman Glickman, Akio Kida, Donald Smith, Shoko Tanaka and Fred Deyo for their comments. We gratefully acknowledge the collaboration of the Ritsumeikan University Automobile Industry Research Group, particularly Akio Kida, on site visits and interviews, and the research assistance provided by Donald Smith, Davis Jenkins, Mitsumasa Motoya, James Curry, W. Richard Goe, James Gordon and Marshall Feldman at various phases of the research. The authors are equally responsible for this article.

NAPIER UNIVERSITY LIBRARY

produce more than 2.5 million cars per year, roughly 20 per cent of total US production. These transplants are supported by more than 350 transplant component suppliers, some 75 steel facilities, and more than 20 Japanese affiliated rubber and tire producers (Florida and Kenney, 1992a). In addition, the automotive assembly transplants operate 22 research, development and design centers in the United States (Kenney and Florida, 1993; Florida and Kenney, 1994). By 1993, transplant investment in the automotive related industries in the US was more than $25 billion dollars, and it continues to increase. Taken as a whole, these automotive-related transplants employ more than 100 000 American workers.

The transplants have generated a great deal of attention both among scholars and other experts and in the popular media. Although a number of research studies have been published, myths and misconceptions about the transplants continue to abound. Perhaps the most widely studied transplant is NUMMI, the GM–Toyota joint venture located in Fremont, California. In an important early study which was to inform many of the key ideas in the best-selling book, *The Machine that Changed the World*, John Krafcik, then a graduate student at MIT and a former engineer at NUMMI (Krafcik, 1986), found that NUMMI was able to recreate many of the key elements of the fabled Toyota production system, including reduced numbers of job classifications, use of work teams, rotation of workers, and a focus on *kaizen* or continuous improvement. Krafcik's findings have been reinforced by more recently published studies by Brown and Reich (1989) and, more recently, by Gronning (1992) and Adler (1993). In a series of papers and a forthcoming book, Welford Wilms (Wilms *et al.*, 1994a; Wilms, 1996) and a group of industrial anthropologists at UCLA who have spent five years working on NUMMI's factory floor have documented the emergence of 'third culture', a core of Japanese production techniques and the Toyota production system, wrapped with elements of American management and organizational style.

In *The Machine that Changed the World*, which summarized the key findings of MIT's International Motor Vehicle Program, James Womack, Daniel Roos and Daniel Jones (Womack, Jones and Roos, 1990) suggested that the automobile industry – and to some extent manufacturing industry more generally – was in the midst of a paradigm shift from the traditional mass production model to a new model built largely around the Japanese production system which they referred to as 'lean production'. This book, which reached a large audience and had a significant impact not only within the academy but also within the industry, suggested that the core characteristics of lean production were the products of organizational design rather than culture, and that, as such, amenable to transfer and diffusion across national boundaries. A more recently published study by Tetsuo Abo and his collaborators at the University of Tokyo (Abo, 1994), explored the experience of Japanese transplants in the automotive assembly, automobile component parts and electronics sectors. Their work suggests that the automotive industry has seen a significantly higher rate of transfer of core elements of the Japanese production system than the electronics sector. They also found a relatively lower rate of transfer to North America, and suggested that the ability to effectively transfer core elements of the Japanese production system to the North American environment tends to require a relatively higher level of commitment of managerial and other resources by the firm. An intriguing case study of the Subaru–Izusu plant in Indiana by Graham (1993) found that there was considerable resistance to the transfer of Japanese production methods; however, evidence provided in the study indicated that those production methods; were still being transferred. In a more journalistic exposition based upon off-site interviews with employees and union officials, Fucini and Fucini (1990) argued that the Mazda plant in Flat Rock Michigan has experienced numerous problems in the transfer of Japanese production methods including high rates of injury, worker discontent and labour–management conflict.

This chapter provides a summary and update of our own research on the Japanese automotive-related transplants (see especially Florida and Kenney, 1991; Kenney and Florida, 1988, 1993). That work has consisted of nearly a decade of data collecting and analysis based upon field research at dozens of plants in the US and Japan, survey research of hundreds of others, and the development of both conceptual and analytical models of the transfer of elements of the Japanese production system and the location decisions and geographic organization of Japanese automotive-related manufactures in the United States. The bottom line contribution of our work is two-fold. First, we argue that the Japanese production system represents a major advance over the previous model of Fordist mass production. The key to this new model of production organization – or production system – lies in the fact that it has more effective organizational forms and divisions of labor for harnessing the intellectual as well as physical capabilities of the entire workforce from the R&D laboratory to the factory floor. We thus find ourselves more or less in agreement with management theorists such as Peter Drucker (1993) and Ikujiro Nonaka (1991) who suggest that the new age of capitalism is one of 'knowledge creating capitalism'. We have elsewhere (Kenney and Florida, 1993) advanced the concept of 'innovation-mediated production' to capture the synthesis of intellectual and physical labor, or innovation and production, under this new system of capitalism (for a debate and discussion of our work see Kato and Steven, 1993). Second, and related to this, we suggest that this new model of capitalism is premised upon new organizational forms. As the leading edge of this new model, the Japanese production system represents a set of organizational practices which are not reducible to culture. Indeed, our research indicates that these organizational techniques and practices can be lifted out of the Japanese context and transferred abroad. Furthermore, we find that Japanese transplants have not adapted to their environment as existing organizational and management theory would have predicted; rather, they have effectively transformed their environments to meet their needs and functional requirements.

We believe that the Japanese automotive transplants provide an ideal lens from which to view these issues. We note that the US industrial environment is typically said to be individualistic, diverse and market-oriented, while Japan is said to be group-oriented, homogeneous, paternalistic and corporatist (see Dore, 1973). And, of course, traditional US firms are distinguished by high levels of functional specialization, large numbers of job classifications, extensive internal labor markets (Edwards, 1979), adversarial labor–management relations (Kochan, Katz and McKersie, 1986; Katz, 1985) and arm's-length relations between corporations and their suppliers (Womack, Jones and Roos, 1990), while Japanese corporations have pioneered new organizational forms such as small numbers of job classifications (Aoki, 1988), team-based work organization (Koike, 1988), consensual relations between labor and management (Shirai, 1983), and long-term supplier relations (Dore, 1983).[3]

RESEARCH DESIGN

For the purposes of this study, we defined *transplants* as firms that are either wholly Japanese-owned or have a significant level of Japanese participation in cross-national joint ventures in the automobile assembly and automotive component parts industries. We developed a database of Japanese transplant assemblers and suppliers from data provided by the Japan Economic Institute, US government sources, industry trade journals and newspaper reports. Eight assembly centers

Richard Florida and Martin Kenney 55

were identified in the United States, of which one operated two plants at one site and the rest operated single plants. In addition, 229 transplant suppliers were identified; this number has since grown to more than 350. These transplants are heavily concentrated in a transplant corridor of the lower Midwest and upper South – an area with a legacy of traditional US (Fordist) organizational practices (see Florida and Kenney, 1992a). Four of the assembly transplants, Mazda, NUMMI, Diamond-Star and the Ford–Nissan joint venture are unionized; four others, Honda, Nissan, Toyota and Subaru–Isuzu (SIA), are not.

Field research was conducted at six of the seven operating transplant assembly plants in the US (Honda, Nissan, Toyota, Mazda, NUMMI and Subaru–Isuzu) and at various supplier firms including Nippondenso which has the largest investment in the US of any transplant supplier.[4] More than 100 personal interviews were conducted with Japanese and American executives, managers and engineers; shopfloor workers and trade union officials; and state and local government officials.

A mail survey was administered to the universe of Japanese-owned or Japanese–US joint-venture suppliers in the United States. The survey questionnaire collected data on start-up date, employment, sales, industry, end-users, information on work organization, number of job classifications, use of teams, rotation, quality control circles, wages and wage determination, employment security and work-force characteristics, and information on interfirm relationships such as delivery times, frequency of communication, shared personnel, and cooperation in R&D and product design. Addresses were located for 196 of the 229 suppliers in the original database. (Some of the firms for whom addresses were unavailable had probably not yet begun operations.) Each establishment was then contacted by telephone to identify the appropriate person to complete the survey. The survey was mailed in 1988, and a series of follow-up post cards and letters resulted in 73 completed surveys for a response rate of 37.2 per cent, which is comparable to the rates in other research of this type (see Lincoln and Kalleberg, 1985, for example).

TRANSFER OF THE JAPANESE PRODUCTION SYSTEM

Work and Production Organization

Table 3.1 summarizes the main characteristics of work and production organization for transplant assemblers and for representative Big Three

Table 3.1 Comparison of organizational practices in the automotive transplants and the Big Three

	Work teams	Rotation	Job classifications	Worker QC	Annual wage $ US	Hourly wages $ US*	Union
Auto Alliance	+	+	2	0	–	16.22	Yes
Diamond-Star	+	+	2	0	38 406	17.00	Yes
Honda	+	+	3	0	36 982	16.20	No
NUMMI	+	+	4	0	41 545	17.85	Yes
Nissan	+	+	4	0	36 294	15.62	No
Subaru–Isuzu	+	+	3	0	–	–	No
Toyota	+	+	3	0	39 582	16.43	No
Big Three	–	–	90	–	–	17.59	Yes

Notes: + = similar to Japan
  0 = modified
  – = different from Japan

However, in the last five years, many Big Three plants are adopting Japanese-style work practices.
*This does not count the cost of living wages received in unionized transplants which are calculated separately, but increase worker's pay quarterly.
Source: Author's compilation from various sources.

automobile company at the time our original study was conducted (1988). Table 3.2 presents similar information for transplant suppliers.[5]

Table 3.2 Percentage of transplant parts suppliers with selected Japanese intraorganizational practices, US, 1988

Characteristic	Per cent	Number of cases
Work organization		
Work teams	76.7	73
Rotation within teams	87.0	69
Rotation between teams	66.2	68
Just-in-time inventory control	68.5	73
Worker involvement		
Production workers maintain their own machines	79.5	73
Production workers do routine quality control	98.6	73
Production workers help design their own jobs	60.9	69
Division of labor		
Number of job classifications		
1	34.3	67
2	14.9	67
3	16.4	67
4	14.9	67
5	6.0	67

Source: Survey of Japanese Automotive Transplant Suppliers, 1988.

Work teams

In Japan, work is organized on the basis of teams that are responsible for planning and carrying out production tasks (Aoki, 1988; Koike, 1988). Teams socialize production tasks and assign immediate managerial tasks to shopfloor workers. Table 3.1 indicates that work teams are used at all of the transplant assemblers. At Honda, Toyota and NUMMI teams meet daily to discuss production improvements and redesign of tasks; meetings at the other transplants take place at least once a week. More than three-fourths of transplant suppliers organize production on the basis of work teams (Table 3.2).

Rotation

Rotation of workers among tasks within a team is a key feature of Japanese production organization. Rotation functions to train workers in multiple tasks and to reduce the incidence of repetitive motion injuries. While rotation is used by all transplant assemblers, its frequency varies, as it does in Japan. Toyota, Honda and NUMMI rotate workers in the same team quite frequently. Toyota workers in high stress jobs, for example those that require the use of a high impact torque gun or involve constant bending or lifting, rotate as frequently as once an hour, others rotate at break times, at lunch or every other day. According to a NUMMI worker:

> We would be rotating every time we had a break or change. If we had a break in the morning, we rotated. And then lunchtime, we rotated. And if we had a break in the afternoon, we rotated. Every time the line stopped, a break or whatever, we rotated.

Rotation is less frequent at Mazda, Nissan and SIA. While these companies consider rotation a long-term goal, each has slowed or even stopped the use of rotation during production scale-ups. Our interviews with Mazda workers confirm that infrequent rotation has been a major cause of repetitive motion injury at the Mazda plant. Rotation from team to team is less common both in Japan and in the transplants. In Japan, this type of rotation is typically mandated by management; in the US, it is more common for workers to apply for job transfers.

According to the supplier survey, roughly 87 per cent of suppliers rotate workers within teams, while approximately 66 per cent rotate among teams. Nippondenso rotates workers in high-stress jobs every hour or two, and encourages workers to apply for rotation from team to team. Both US and Japanese managers at all the transplants we visited, as well as many workers, felt that it was too early for implementation of a full Japanese-style rotation system and that it may be a few years before workers have enough basic skills and knowledge to be moved regularly from team to team.

Inventory control

In Japan, production takes place according to the just-in-time system of inventory control in which materials are forwarded as needed and inventory is kept to a minimum. All the assemblers and over two-thirds of suppliers (68.5 per cent) use a just-in-time system of production control.

The supplier survey asked: 'How similar is your manufacturing process to one that might be found in Japan?' Eighty-six per cent of the respondents said that their US manufacturing practice was either 'exactly the same' or 'very similar' to one that might be found in Japan; only one supplier said that it was not at all similar.

The Division of Labor

Job classifications

Few job classifications are a key characteristic of the Japanese model. This contrasts sharply with traditional US production organization in which virtually every job has its own job classification and these are seen by workers and unions as a 'job ladder' that provides the basis for wage increases and employment security. Kochan *et al.* (1986) report that the unionized plants in a multidivisional US manufacturing firm had an average of 96 job classifications. Table 3.1 indicates that transplant assemblers use no more than four job classifications, whereas a representative traditional US Big Three auto maker had 90. Although the implementation of few job classifications might seem especially difficult at transplants which employ large numbers of managers and workers that were originally socialized to traditional Big Three practices, for example NUMMI which has a large percentage of former GM workers, interviews with NUMMI officials and workers indicated few adaptation problems.

More than 85 per cent of transplant suppliers use five or fewer job classifications for production workers; and one-third use only one job classification. Several indicate that they have instituted more job classifications than would be ideal (as many as ten) to keep American workers happy by providing the appearance of an internal career ladder.

Team leaders

Japanese production organization includes a class of workers, referred to as team leaders, who are members of shopfloor work groups but also have managerial responsibility for immediate production activities. There are no foremen or low-level managers whose job is to supervise shopfloor workers. Team leaders are used at all the transplant assemblers we visited, and 84 per cent of suppliers use them as well. At Honda, Toyota, NUMMI, Nissan and SIA, team leaders are the first line of supervision and play a crucial role in the organization, design and allocation of work on a daily basis. At some transplants, team leaders are selected by management, while at others, especially the unionized transplants, team leaders are selected by joint labor–management committees. All the transplants consider the input of workers to be an important criterion for the selection of team leaders.

Status

Overt status distinctions between management and blue-collar workers are less evident in Japan than in the US. For example, in Japan workers and managers eat in the same cafeteria; middle-level managers wear the same uniforms as shopfloor workers. Managers typically do not have enclosed offices but sit at desks on a large open floor adjacent to the production facility. All transplants we visited had single cafeterias. At Nippondenso, all executives including the President work at desks on the floor. Nissan is the only transplant in which status distinctions are more visible, for example, a separate parking lot for top managers' cars and plush American-style offices. This may be because Nissan has a much higher percentage of former American automobile executives than other transplants. All the transplants provide uniforms, although some give workers the option of wearing street clothes. Transplant officials we interviewed suggested that uniforms create an identification between workers and the company. Most top executives wear company uniforms, although Nissan is again the exception. In fact, the transplants tend to have greater visible status equality than in Japan where top executives have chauffeured company automobiles and wear suits and ties rather than work uniforms.

Hierarchy

Lincoln, Hanada and McBride (1986) indicated that management hierarchies are taller in Japan than in the US. Our findings suggest that management hierarchies in the automotive transplants are relatively flat. At Honda, there are nine levels in the internal hierarchy: associate, team leader, coordinator, department manager, plant manager, assistant vice president, senior vice president, executive vice president and president. This structure is typical of the other transplants as well. At Honda, the various vice presidents do not form separate levels in the reporting structure, but are part of Honda's senior management team, which includes the plant manager and the president of Honda America Manufacturing. This senior management team makes decisions as a group and thus functions to some extent as a single reporting level. The president of Honda America is a member of and reports to the Board of Directors for Honda Japan. A number of shopfloor workers have risen to management ranks at Honda and the company actively encourages such mobility. Toyota officials indicate that shopfloor workers are recruited for middle-level management positions in the factory and the front office.

Worker Participation and Quality Control

It is important to distinguish between the form of Japanese organization and its substance; that is, its effects on worker behavior. A main objective of the Japanese system of work and production organization is to harness the collective intelligence of workers for continuous product and process improvement (Kenney and Florida, 1988, 1993). This stands in sharp contrast to traditional American automobile industry practices in which there are formal and informal organizational barriers and norms that inhibit the use of worker intelligence (Braverman, 1974). In Japan, workers actively participate in company suggestion programs and quality control circles as well as informal, everyday *kaizen*, or continuous improvement activities. In Japan, different automobile corporations emphasize different aspects of *kaizen* activity. Toyota places greater emphasis on team activities, like quality circles, whereas Honda emphasizes individual initiative and innovation. Japanese scholars use the term *voluntarism* to explain the extraordinary initiative of workers in Japan. However, Japanese automobile companies vary significantly in their ability to generate voluntaristic behavior – with Toyota being the most effective.

Worker initiative

Transplants encourage worker initiative through the delegation of managerial authority and responsibility to shopfloor workers. Workers at the transplants, especially Honda and Toyota, have significant input into the design of their jobs. More than 60 per cent of respondents to the supplier survey indicate that workers are involved in the design of their tasks. At Toyota and Nippondenso, work teams actually design standardized task descriptions for their work units and post them in the form of drawings and photographs with captions at their work stations. Roughly 80 per cent of suppliers indicate that workers are responsible for routine maintenance on their own machines.

Japanese corporations use suggestion systems to harness workers' knowledge and ideas. Honda and Toyota have fairly well-developed suggestion systems. Although Mazda has a suggestion system, Mazda workers have occasionally, at times, boycotted it to express their dissatisfaction with management policy. SIA does not yet have a suggestion system, although management indicates that the company will institute one in the future. Thirty per cent of transplant suppliers provide cash awards for worker suggestions, and two-thirds report that 'willingness to suggest new ideas' is a key criterion for evaluating production workers.

Quality circles

Quality circles are an important element of the Japanese system (Cole, 1989; Lillrank and Kano, 1989). In Japan, quality circles are groups of workers who devote effort outside regular working hours to improving an element of the production process. According to Lincoln *et al.* (1986, p. 354), 76 per cent of employees in a sample of Japanese plants participated in quality circles compared to 27 per cent of workers in US plants. The transplants vary in the extent and intensiveness with which they employ quality circles. Toyota and Honda use quality circles extensively, Mazda and NUMMI 'moderately,' and SIA not at all. Slightly less than half of suppliers use quality circles, and 68 per cent of those who do not use quality control circles plan to do so in the future.

Transplant assemblers pay workers for quality circle activity. Of suppliers that use quality circles, 83 per cent pay workers for hours spent working on quality circles. In both transplant assemblers and suppliers, participation in quality circles usually occurs immediately before or after shift work. Several transplants set up competitions between quality control circles and use prizes, plaques and cash awards as additional incentives for quality circle participation. Some transplants have sent American quality circles to Japan to participate in anual company competitions. All the transplant assemblers and suppliers that we visited indicated that they will devote significant effort to establishing quality control circles on a par with Japan. We thus agree with Cole's assessment (1989, pp. 111–12) that it is still too early in the transfer process to expect full use of quality control circles. Such activity will likely increase as the transplants complete the process of implanting organizational forms and move on to more subtle techniques of shaping and motivating worker initiative.

We also asked Japanese managers to tell us how much, in percentage terms, Japanese *kaizen* or continuous improvement activity they have been able to replicate in their American work force. Honda executives feel they have completely replicated Japanese practice in their Marysville, Ohio plant. A Toyota manager who has worked in numerous

Toyota plants in Japan as well as at NUMMI and Georgetown, Kentucky, indicated that the Georgetown plant is at 60 per cent of Japanese practice and NUMMI at 40 to 50 per cent. Management is actively trying to implement greater *kaizen* activities. Nippondenso, a Toyota group member, has also closely replicated Japanese practice. Mazda and Nissan have had more difficulty implementing *kaizen* activity, and stand at roughly 50 per cent of Japanese practice. Executives of SIA, which is the most recent transplant, estimate that the plant is currently at about 30 per cent of Japanese practice. Still, the progress of the transplants on this dimension is remarkable, given the time they have had to socialize American workers to the requirements of Japanese production. The central role played by worker initiative and the use of workers' knowledge contradicts the view that the Japanese model is simply an extension of Fordist mass production. It lends support to the alternative conceptualization that it is a new and potential successor model based upon harnessing workers' intellectual *and* physical capabilities.

Transplants recognize this deficit and are working hard to replicate the worker initiative and voluntaristic behavior of Japanese firms. Numerous Japanese executives see the lack of independent initiative of American workers as a product of previous attitudes and socialization, and suggest that it can be changed by education and socialization to Japanese practices. According to the Japanese president of a transplant supplier, education and effort is required to 'remove American barriers to worker initiative'. Japanese transplants indicate that they will concentrate on this issue in the next few years. Going even further, Toyota is working with the local school system to redesign curriculum and other socialization mechanisms to impart group-oriented behavior, problem solving and initiative to students. SIA has also sent local school officials to Japan so that they can learn more about Japanese group-oriented educational practice.

Workforce Selection and Socialization

Japanese corporations do not simply impose Japanese production organization and manufacturing practices on their American workforces. Instead, they use a number of selection and socialization mechanisms to ensure effective transfer.

Selection

Recruitment and selection processes identify workers who possess initiative, are dedicated to the corporation, work well in teams and do not miss work. The process differs from the recruitment policies of Japanese corporations in Japan (Rosenbaum and Kariya, 1989) but serves a similar function. Moreover, the process differs markedly from the typical US practice of hiring off the street. The transplants subject potential workers to cognitive and psychological tests and other screening procedures to identify workers who fit the Japanese model. Previous job records or high school records are scrutinized for absenteeism. Potential employees go through extensive interviews with personnel officials, managers, and even members of their potential work teams to rate their initiative and group-oriented characteristics. While theorists have generally treated the so-called loyalty of the Japanese workforce as a product of Japanese culture, the screening and selection process constitutes an organizational mechanism that selects potentially loyal workers from a large, diverse population. Simply put, this long held cultural effect is also a product of organizational practice.

Socialization

Prior to start-up, all the assembly transplants sent key employees (for example, managers and team leaders) to Japanese sister plants for three to six months. There they received both formal training and informal socialization to Japanese practice (for example, team work and *kaizen*). They worked closely with veteran Japanese trainers, who transfer formal and tacit knowledge of production and who function as role models to some extent. Workers and trainers also spend time together outside work to continue the socialization process. These trainers then came to the US for periods from three months to two years to work alongside the same US employees and their teams. The supplier survey indicates that 33 per cent of American managers were sent to Japan for training. According to workers at different transplants, trainers provided the most substantial and significant exposure to Japanese practices.

    The transplants use ongoing training and socialization programs to acclimate workers to Japanese production. Most employees begin with a six to eight-week introductory session that includes an overview of automotive assembly and fairly rigorous socialization in the Japanese model. After this, workers are assigned to teams where they continue to learn from senior employees. According to the survey, suppliers provide an average of eight days of training for factory workers before they assume shopfloor activities (range = 0–180 days); assemblers have longer training periods. This is supplemented by an average of 61 days additional training on the shopfloor (range = 1–302 days).

Adaptation

Shopfloor workers in the US have experienced few problems adapting to the Japanese system. NUMMI workers who previously worked for GM indicate that they prefer the Japanese model to US Fordist practice. According to one:

> I was at GM and the part I didn't like ... is that we had a lot of drug and alcohol problems. It was getting to the point, even with me, when it got around lunchtime I had to go out ... and take down two or three beers.

Mazda has had the most adaptation problems including significant worker discontent and the recent election of a new local union that is less conciliatory. However, Mazda workers indicate that such adaptation problems are largely due to management's failure to fully implement Japanese production organization; for example, not rotating workers to prevent repetitive motion injury.

Management has been the site of recurring adaptation problems at the transplants. During site visits and interviews, we were told repeatedly that American middle managers, especially those recruited from US automobile corporations, have experienced great difficulty adapting to Japanese production organization and management. Honda officials indicate that the previously formed attitudes and prejudices of US middle managers toward factory workers are a serious problem. NUMMI workers complain that American managers are still operating in the GM style and are a major obstacle to implementation of a full-blown Japanese system that they see as more favorable to workers than the old Fordist system. According to a NUMMI worker:

> A lot of things have changed. But see, you hear people talk. You hear them saying once in a while: 'Oh, we're going back to the GM ways.' I hope not. That was rough ... I think to completely bring back the Japanese way, Japan would have to take over the plant completely and have nothing to do with General Motors at all.

Japanese transplant managers indicate that problems with American middle managers have encouraged them to promote shopfloor workers to supervisory positions.

Wages and Industrial Relations

In any industrial system, the immediate organization of production is reflected in rules, regulations and norms that create the context in which production takes place. This broader production environment includes wage rates, wage determination, the organization and function of the internal labor market, degree of tenure security, type of unionization and pattern of labor relations. These factors create incentives for work effort, establish the context for labor–management relations, and form the framework for mobilizing employee demands and mediating disputes. In Burawoy's (1979) terminology, they provide a sociological context for *manufacturing consent*.

Wages and bonuses

The Japanese *nenko* system of wage determination is based on a combination of seniority, job-related performance and the ability to work in a group context (Suzuki, 1976; Gordon, 1985; Kagono, Nonaka, Sakikabara and Okumura, 1985). Semiannual bonuses constituting roughly 30 per cent of total remuneration are used to supplement regular pay (Aoki, 1988).

Both the transplant assemblers and suppliers are relatively high-wage employers. At the time of our original study (1988), the transplant assemblers had average annual compensation between $28 598–$36 013, compared to an average of $36 089 for Big Three auto makers. Hourly wages for production workers ranged from $13.94–$16.81 per hour, compared to an average of $16.41 for Big Three firms. As Table 3.1 shows, by 1993 average annual compensation had increased to $36 294–$41 545; and average hourly wages had increased to $15.62–$17.85. Note that average annual compensation refers to regular pay plus bonuses, but does not include overtime pay or the value of benefits. When overtime is taken into account, a significant number of workers at the transplants achieved average annual compensation in excess of $50 000.

Transplant suppliers also paid relatively high wages as of 1988 when our original survey was conducted: $7.21 per hour to start and $8.00 after a year on the job for low-skill workers, to more than $11.00 for high-skill workers – a rate which is slightly below the wage levels at US parts suppliers (US International Trade Commission, 1987). Total annual compensation at the transplant suppliers averaged $21 200 per year. This wage differential between assemblers and suppliers is thus roughly similar to that in Japan.

The wage determination policies of the transplants are more standardized and uniform than in Japan. This is somewhat striking because academic studies and conventional wisdom contrast American individualism to Japanese groupism. Transplant assemblers pay uniform wages for each class of workers, with raises at regular intervals. Transplant suppliers report that work effort, absenteeism, 'willingness to work in teams', and 'willingness to suggest new ideas' are the major criteria used to evaluate workers for wage increases and promotions.

Bonuses are not as common in the transplants as they are in Japan, and they are not an important component of employee wages. Bonuses at the transplants tend to be across-the-board, equal-percentage wage supplements to all workers. Honda provides a monthly bonus of $100 for perfect attendance. Bonuses represent only 1 per cent of total compensation for transplant suppliers. However, 49 per cent of transplant suppliers provide small cash awards for attendance, 30 per cent provide small cash awards for suggestions, and 18 per cent provide small cash awards for participation in quality circles.

Job security

Long-term employment tenure is a much discussed feature of the Japanese system (Abegglen, 1958; Dore, 1973; Cole, 1979; Lincoln and Kalleberg, 1985). The pattern of employment security differs between unionized and non-unionized assembly transplants, and between assemblers and suppliers. Our review of the labor–management agreements for the unionized assembly transplants indicates that all of them have formal contractual agreements that stipulate tenure security, guaranteeing jobs except under conditions that jeopardize the financial viability of the company. Both NUMMI and Mazda have fulfilled their commitment to no layoffs. NUMMI has kept full employment during periods of up to 30 per cent reduction in output by eliminating overtime, slowing the work pace, offering workers voluntary vacation time, placing workers in special training programs or transferring them to other jobs. Mazda workers have been loaned to local governments during slowdowns. The non-unionized transplants provide informal assurance of tenure security, although this is not reflected in contractual agreements with workers. Nissan and Toyota have redeployed workers to other jobs to avoid layoffs. However, it is impossible to know at this stage whether the non-unionized transplants will remain committed to tenure security in the event of a severe economic downturn.

Transplant suppliers do not offer formal guarantees of tenure security. However, more than two-thirds of the supplier respondents indicate that the Japanese long-term employment system *should* be transferred to the US. Nevertheless, they offered a wide range of opinions on this issue – some saw long-term employment as a source of long-run productivity increases, others saw the threat of termination as a way to motivate American workers.

Unionization

The Japanese system of unionization is one of enterprise or company unions (Taira, 1961; Shirai, 1983), which differs markedly from the prevailing US practice of industrial unionism. Levine (1958), Taira (1962), and Koike (1988) observed that the US has always had a system of decentralized plant-specific locals that operate in a way that is similar to enterprise unions by aggregating worker demands and establishing the context of labor–management relations at the plant level.[6]

The transplants have developed two basic strategies to cope with US labor relations, and to recreate some elements of Japanese industrial relations. Most automobile transplants have simply chosen to avoid unionization. Only four of the 71 supplier respondents were unionized. The four non-unionized assemblers – Honda, Toyota, Nissan and SIA – have chosen rural *greenfield* locations at least in part to avoid unionization. Nissan went to great lengths to defeat a unionization drive. SIA has implemented an in-plant video system to communicate messages to workers in anticipation of a unionization campaign. Non-unionized transplants, notably Nissan and Toyota, use employee handbooks that provide plant rules and regulations and have formed employee associations that collect employee input and create a stable structure through which work-related grievances can be addressed. The unionized transplants, Mazda, NUMMI and Diamond-Star, have established independent agreements with their respective union locals that enlist the union in the implementation of Japanese work organization. These agreements make possible fewer job classifications and more flexible work rules and the utilization of pay systems that differ markedly from the typical US assembly plant. However, recent research by Smith and Florida (1994) which explored the location choices of a large sample of Japanese automotive-related transplants found no statistical evidence that transplant manufacturers were avoiding relatively unionized locations. In fact, transplant manufacturers tended to cluster in manufacturing-intensive areas with relatively higher concentrations of union locals.

Dualism

The transplants are recreating aspects of Japan's highly segmented or dual labor markets (see Koike, 1988; Kalleberg and Lincoln, 1988). In Japan, for example, a large manufacturing facility will typically have non-unionized temporary workers or lower-paid workers from subcontractors working side-by-side with regular employees. The transplants use part-time or temporary employees to provide flexibility. At both Mazda and Diamond-Star, temporary employees were laid off during a downturn in the automobile market in early 1990 (Guiles and Miller, 1990). The use of temporary workers has been a source of ongoing labor–management conflict at Mazda where (in contrast to Japan) union leaders see temporary workers as a threat to labor solidarity.

Gender is the most common basis of workforce segmentation in Japan. Japanese women are prohibited from working in assembly plants by Japanese laws that make it illegal for women to work the night shift. The transplants do not show the extreme pattern of gender-based segmentation that is common in Japan. The supplier survey indicates that women comprise 34 per cent of production workers. However, women are only 10 per cent of the management workforce.

Race is a typical line of workforce segmentation in the US. Earlier research (Cole and Deskins, 1988) inferred racial bias from the site selection and workforce composition of Japanese transplants. We did not see large or even representative numbers of minorities in site visits. According to the supplier survey, minorities fill 11 per cent of production positions and 9 per cent of management slots. Recent data indicate that the transplant assemblers are hiring relatively more minority workers in production jobs. For example, Honda has increased minority employment from 2.8 per cent in 1989 to 10.6 per cent in 1990. Similarly, Toyota in Kentucky reports that 15 per cent of its employees are non-white (Cole, 1989b). In all likelihood, this is a response to the political pressure that resulted from publicizing earlier hiring practices. Furthermore, recent research by Smith and Florida (1994) explored the locational choices of automotive-related transplants, and found no statistical evidence that transplants manufacturers were avoiding areas with relatively higher concentrations of minority populations.

TRANSFER OF JAPANESE SUPPLIER RELATIONS

The Japanese supplier system differs markedly from that of the US. The Japanese just-in-time system of supplier relations is characterized by close geographic proximity of producers, long-term relationships, and tight interfirm linkages characterized by personnel sharing, joint participation in product development, and regular communication and interaction (Asanuma, 1985; Odaka, *et al.*, 1988). In Japan, suppliers provide as much as 70 per cent of a car's components, while US automobile assemblers rely on suppliers for 30 to 50 per cent of inputs (Mitsubishi Research Institute, 1987; US. International Trade Commission, 1987). The Japanese supplier system is organized in a pyramidal structure with 500 first-tier suppliers, a few thousand second-tier suppliers and more than 20 000 tertiary automotive parts suppliers (Sayer, Andrew, 1986). The parent or *hub* company plays a key role by structuring linkages and coordinating flows within the network (Florida and Kenney, 1992a). The Japanese supplier system is embedded in a set of organizational relationships that structure economic behavior. Dore (1983) advanced the concept of relational contracting to capture elements of the Japanese system and to contrast it with the arm's-length system of the US (see also Nisiguchi, 1994).

Japanese assembly transplants initially located facilities in the lower-Midwestern region of the United States to take advantage of the indigenous infrastructure of domestic automobile parts suppliers. However, indigenous supplier firms were unable to adapt to the delivery and quality requirements of the Japanese just-in-time system. Dismayed by the performance of US suppliers, assembly transplants encouraged their first-tier Japanese suppliers to locate in the US. The Japanese suppliers, in turn, found it in their interest to expand overseas. In effect, the creation of a Japanese-like supplier system in the US can be understood as a *creative response* (Schumpeter, 1947) to the deficiencies of the US environment.

Transplant assemblers have played an active role in the creation of this new production environment by financing and helping to set up US branches for key suppliers. For example, Honda encouraged two of its Japanese suppliers to form Bellemar Parts to supply it with seat subassemblies. In another instance, Honda provided technical and financial assistance to a group of Japanese suppliers to form KTH Parts Industries, a company that took over US production of chassis parts that were once produced in-house by Honda at Marysville. Nearly half of Honda's main suppliers in Japan now operate US plants. The suppli-

er survey indicates that 12 of 73 suppliers are partially owned by the assemblers they supply.

Furthermore, assemblers played a key role in influencing both
the original decision of transplant suppliers to relocate production in
the US and their choice of locations in the US. According to the supplier survey, more than 75 per cent set up US operations to maintain
close ties to a major Japanese customer, and 90 per cent chose their specific locations to be close to a major customer. Traditional environmental factors like the local labor market or local labor costs have
relatively little impact on locational choices. Recently, other Japanese
parts suppliers have opened US plants on their own initiative to access
the growing market for their products. Most of the supplier plants are
located in states with transplant assembly plants. The strong role
played by large assemblers in orienting and structuring the transplant
supplier complexes contradicts the claim (Sabel, 1989; Friedman,
1988) that the Japanese model is converging toward flexible specialization.

Supplier Relations

Table 3.3 summarizes data from the supplier survey on the main
characteristics of relations among transplant assemblers and suppliers.
This table reports the responses of 73 transplant suppliers on their
supply relationships with transplant assemblers and with their own
second-tier suppliers. Geographic proximity is a basic characteristic
of the Japanese supplier relations (Sayer, 1986). Among transplant
suppliers, 40 per cent are located within a two-hour shipping radius
of end-users, and almost 90 per cent are located within an eight-
hour radius. Eighty per cent make just-in-time deliveries. Still, the
distances separating end-users from suppliers are somewhat greater
in the United States than in Japan. Transplant complexes are essentially stretched out versions of Japan's dense just-in-time supplier
system, probably due to the greater availability of land, well-
developed highway systems, larger trucks and greater storage capacity
in the US.

Interaction and information exchange

Table 3.3 reveals a continuous exchange of information between transplant assemblers and suppliers. Approximately 97 per cent of transplant suppliers are contacted immediately by phone when they deliver

a defective product. Eighty-two per cent indicate that engineers from their major customer came on-site while they were setting up US operations, three-quarters report that engineers from their major customer make ongoing site visits to deal with production problems, and 97 per cent indicate that engineers from their major customer make ongoing site visits to deal with quality control problems.

Table 3.3   Percentage of transplant first-tier suppliers with selected Japanese interorganizational linkages, US, 1988

Characteristic	Linkages to assemblers	Number of cases	Linkage to second-tier suppliers	Number of cases
Transit time				
1/2 hour	6.9	72	–	–
1/2 hour–2 hours	33.9	72	–	–
2–8 hours	38.9	72	–	–
8–24 hours	9.7	72	–	–
Deliver according to just-in-time schedule	80.0	70	43	72
Immediate feedback on defective parts	90.2	72	97.2	72
Customers' engineers visit plant site				
For quality control problems	96.8	62	96.9	65
For production problems	74.2	62	83.1	65
Interaction in design				
Close interaction between supplier and customer	50.0	72	33.8	71
Supplier bids on customer design	31.9	72	62.0	71
Supplier can alter customer design	22.2	72	11.3	71
Supplier designs subject to customer approval	15.3	72	11.3	71
Supplier designs but customer can alter	6.9	72	8.5	71

Source: Survey of Japanese Automotive Transplant suppliers, 1988.

Joint product development

Joint participation in design and development is another key characteristic of Japanese supplier relations. Fifty per cent of suppliers said they participate closely with assemblers in the development of new products. This includes interaction with US-owned firms as well. Honda engineers, for example, developed new production techniques for a small Ohio plastics firm that became a Honda supplier. Honda, Toyota and SIA send teams of engineers and shopfloor workers to consult with suppliers on new product designs and production machinery. Honda intends to use its Marysville R&D center to integrate both transplant and US suppliers into the future design of cars. We thus conclude that Japanese-style supplier relations, like high levels of interaction, joint development and long-term contracts, which typically have been viewed as a function of Japan's sociocultural environment, are actually a product of the organizational relation itself.

Supplier tiers

In Japan, first-tier suppliers play a critical role in organizing and coordinating supply flows between lower-level suppliers and main assembly plants. They are located close to assemblers, interact frequently with them, and often are at least partially owned by them (Asanuma, 1985). First-tier suppliers are probably more important in transplant complexes. For example, the windshields for Honda's American-made vehicles originate at PPG, an American producer. PPG supplies windshields to a Japanese supplier, AP Technoglass, twice a week. AP Technoglass screens them for defects, cuts and grinds them, and delivers them to a Honda subsidiary, Bellemar Parts, twice a day. Bellemar, which is located one mile from the Honda plant, applies rubber seals to the windshields and makes just-in-time deliveries to Honda every two hours. Bellemar also screens for defects, so that Honda receives much higher-quality windshields than it would without its suppliers. In this way, first-tier suppliers serve as a buffer between assemblers and the environment.

Table 3.3 reveals the pyramidal nature of transplant supplier relations. Second-tier suppliers, who supply to the first-tier suppliers, have less interaction in design or development of new products. One-third of first-tier suppliers integrate second-tier suppliers in new product development. Just 43 per cent of the first-tier suppliers receive just-in-time deliveries from their second-tier suppliers, whereas in Japan, tight supplier relations extend to second and third-tier suppliers. However, this may be due to the fact that the transplant complex is still in the process of formation, so that linkages are at an early stage of development. Other evidence indicates that linkages are being extended down through the hierarchy to producers of basic inputs like steel and automotive plastics (Florida and Kenney, 1992a, 1992b).

Integration of and diffusion to US suppliers

Transplant assemblers are forging linkages to US producers, leading to the rapid diffusion of Japanese practices among US producers. Over half of Mazda's US suppliers are US-owned firms: 43 of Mazda's 96 suppliers are independent US-owned firms, 10 are owned by Ford, and 43 are Japanese-owned or Japanese–US joint ventures (*Automotive News*, 1989). Helper, (1990) indicated that 41 per cent of 437 US automotive suppliers surveyed, supplied at least one component to the transplants.

Transplant assemblers work with US suppliers to accelerate the diffusion of Japanese practices. As in Japan, Toyota has set up an organization of its Kentucky suppliers, the Bluegrass Automotive Manufacturers Association (BAMA), and has held meetings with US suppliers in Las Vegas and Japan to encourage diffusion of Japanese practices. NUMMI has organized a supplier council of 70 mostly US-owned suppliers to share information and facilitate product improvement (Krafcik, 1986). SIA has organized teams of engineers, purchasing representatives and manufacturing people who work with suppliers to improve quality. Johnson Controls, an American-owned automotive supplier in Georgetown, Kentucky, is now the sole source supplier of seats for the Toyota Camry. Toyota has worked with the company to implement a full-blown Japanese production system. Johnson Controls delivers completed subassemblies to Toyota according to just-in-time requirements every four hours. We visited a ten-person small machine shop in rural Ohio that formerly rebuilt tractor engines, but now rebuilds robot heads for Honda and Honda suppliers.

The emergence of a new system of Japanese supplier relations in the US is exerting a sizable demonstration effect on US practice. Helper (1989) provided empirical evidence of US convergence toward the Japanese model. A recent study by the McKinsey Global Institute (1993) provides cross-national evidence that transplant firms increase the productivity of domestic industries by accelerating the adoption and diffusion of best-practice production organization and management. Osterman (1994) indicates that roughly one-third of US manufacturers are making the transition to best-practice or high-performance production organization and management, suggesting that there may be increasing convergence of production and management practices among Japanese-affiliated manufacturers and traditional US-owned firms. Rather than taking on characteristics of US suppliers or the broader environment of US supplier relations, the Japanese transplants are transforming existing patterns of supplier relations in the US.

CONCLUSIONS

Our findings indicate that both transplant assemblers and suppliers have been remarkably successful in implanting the Japanese system of work organization in the US environment. The basic form of Japanese work organization has been transferred with little if any modification. There are differences in the extent to which the transplants have been able to replicate Japanese behavior in *kaizen*, quality circles and other such activity, but they are working hard to increase the participation of US workers in these activities. Japanese wage determination and labor relations practices have been somewhat modified to fit the US context. However, these practices still resemble Japanese more than US traditions. Our findings also indicate that the transplants have effectively recreated key elements of the Japanese supplier system in the US. Our findings are thus in line with the hypothesis that the Japanese model is a set of organizational practices that can be removed from the Japanese environment and successfully implanted elsewhere. However, we do not imply that the transfer process has occurred automatically. Japanese firms have taken great care to select and even to alter the environment to make it conducive to new organizational forms.

Our findings may come as a surprise, given the legacy, conceptual orientation and predictions of industrial sociology and organization theory. These theories imply that the environment has a strong effect on organizations, that it is difficult to transfer organizations between dissimilar environments, and that once transferred, organizations tend to take on characteristics of the new environment. The transplants have effectively recreated the basic Japanese system of production organization and are working hard to implant it fully. They have also recreated Japan's relational contracting system, establishing a new production environment for automobile manufacture. Thus, our findings suggest that too much explanatory power has been given to cultural factors in organizational development. Outside the plant as well as inside, the Japanese model forms a set of organizational practices that has been effectively transferred to the US.

On a more general level, our research suggests a general symmetry between intra- and interorganizational characteristics. The Japanese transplants have replicated long-term, interactive, participative and/ or mutually dependent relations at both the intra- and interorganizational levels. These findings are not specific to the transplants but are reflected in comparative institutional research – the US pattern of short-term adversarial labor–management relations is reflected in the short-term arm's-length pattern of US supplier relations. We believe that there may be an underlying rationale for such symmetry. Organizational pressures and incentives may lead to increasing continuity in the governance structures inside and outside the firm. Firms that effectively organize intraorganizational activity are likely to replicate it in dealings with external firms as well. More research and theory-building are needed on this crucial issue, using other sectors, industries and types of organizations.

Our research indicates that organizations can and do shape their environments. Thus, the concept of environmental embeddedness should be revised to incorporate measures of the power, intentions, and purposeful activities of organizations. Transferring organizational practices and forms from one society to another means that they must be uncoupled from the environment in which they are embedded and recreated in the new environment. The transplants provide clear evidence that organizational forms can be effectively lifted from an originally supportive context and transferred to a foreign environment. Furthermore, they show that organizations can mold the new environment to their needs and to some degree create the conditions of their own embeddedness. In general terms then, organizations have the resources to alter the environment. Large powerful firms, for example, can control the machines, the organization of production, the hiring of employees and the establishment of interorganizational connections. These organizational resources can be used to offset and transform the social matrix of the environment.

We do not wish to imply that any type of organization can be made to fit any environment. The German automobile manufacturer, Volkswagen, failed to implement its production organization in the US context – its US plant experienced high levels of worker discontent, serious strikes, and was closed after less then ten years of operation. Successful organizational transfer is neither natural nor automatic; it hinges on the strategic action organizations take to shape the environment to meet their requirements. Based on our findings, we conclude that the organizational–environmental tie works in both directions.

Finally, our research provides useful insights for the debate over new forms of production and industrial organization. The findings resonate with the general notion of a movement toward new models of production organization; the transplants reflect the more general restructuring of production organization, supplier relations and industrial networks. We find little evidence to support the claim made by Sabel (1989) that the Japanese model, as manifested by the transplants, is coverging toward flexible specialization. In fact, the evidence clearly suggests that US firms are converging toward the Japanese model. By focusing on what is or can be transferred, our research reveals three defining features of the Japanese model:

1.　High levels of task integration;
2.　Integration of workers' intelligence as well as physical capabilities;
3.　Tightly networked production complexes.

In organizational terms, the transplants, and the Japanese model in general, display a high degree of *functional integration* that differs markedly from previous forms of functional (and/or flexible) specialization. Based on our findings here and related research on US high-technology industrial organization (Florida and Kenney, 1990; Kenney and Florida, 1993), we believe that these features may be the underlying and defining elements that will determine the success, survival and diffusion of the competing models of industrial organization that are emerging around the world. It remains for future research to further assess the broad generality of these trends.

Notes

1.　First Edition, February 1988, p. 17.
2.　Joel Smith and William Childs (1987) 'Imported from America: Cooperative Labor Relations at New United Motor Manufacturing, Inc.', *Industrial Relations Law Journal*, 9(1) p. 78.

3. These are ideal-typical characterizations of large manufacturing firms, particularly automobile firms, in these countires, designed to focus attention on salient differences highlighted in the literature. In reality, there are significant differences among firms in each country, and there are likely to be hybrid or mixed forms.
4. We were unable to arrange a visit to Diamond-Star, and the Ford–Nissan venture was not yet operational.
5. Here, we note that not all Japanese automobile firms are organized the same way; each has its individual "company way."
6. The US industrial relations system is experiencing a general decentralization of such functions to the local level. For example, the new GM Saturn plant in Tennessee has instituted an agreement with unique provisions.

References

Abegglen, James (1958) *The Japanese Factory* (Cambridge, MA: MIT University Press).

Abo, Tetsuo (ed.) (1994) *Hybrid Factory: The Japanese Production System in the United States* (New York: Oxford University Press).

Adler, Paul (1993) 'Time-and-Motion Regained', *Harvard Business Review*, 71(1) pp. 97–109.

Aiken, Michael and Gerald Hage (1968). 'Organizational Interdependence and Intra-organizational Structure', *American Sociological Review*, 33 (December) pp. 912–30.

Altshuler, Alan *et al.* (1987) *The Future of the Automobile* (Cambridge, MA: MIT Press).

Altshuler, Alan, Martin Anderson, Daniel Jones, Daniel Roos, and James Womack (1984) *The Future of the Automobile* (Cambridge, MA: MIT Press).

Aoki, Masahiko (1988) *Information, Incentives and Bargaining in the Japanese Economy* (Cambridge: Cambridge University Press).

Arensen, Paul, Robert Cole and A.R. Krishna (1987) 'Japanese Auto Parts Companies in the US and Japan: Implications for US Competitors' (Ann Arbor: University of Michigan, East Asia Program, manuscript).

Asanuma, Banri (1985) 'The Organization of Parts Purchases in the Japanese Automotive Industry', *Japanese Economic Studies* (Summer) pp. 32–53.

Automotive News (1989) 'Mazda: $1 Billion to Suppliers' (23 October): E29.

Baron, James and William Bielby (1986) 'The Proliferation of Titles in Organizations', *Administrative Science Quarterly*, 31, p. 561–86.

Benedict, Ruth (1946) *The Chrysanthemum and the Sword* (Boston: Houghton Mifflin Publishers).

Bradley, Keith and Stephen Hill (1987) 'Quality Circles and Managerial Interests', *Industrial Relations*, 26(1) pp. 68–82.

Brown, Clair and Michael Reich (1989) 'When Does Union–Management Cooperation Work: A Look at NUMMI and GM-Van Nuys', *California Management Review*, 31(4) pp. 26–44.

Burawoy, Michael (1983) 'Between the Labor Process and the State: The Changing Face of Factory Regimes Under Advanced Capitalism', *American Sociological Review*, 48, pp. 587–605.

Burawoy, Michael (1979) *Manufacturing Consent* (Chicago: University of Chicago Press).

Chappell, Lindsay (1989a) 'Increased Capacity and Flexible Production Schedules are Built Into the Design of the Plant', *Automotive News* (7 August) p. 53.

Chappell, Lindsay (1989b) 'UAW Battered in Nissan Vote, Finds Old Pitches Don't Work', *Automotive News* (31 July) p. 2.

Clark, Rodney (1979) *The Japanese Company* (New Haven, CT: Yale University Press).

Cole, Robert (1971) *Japanese Blue Collar* (Berkeley: University of California Press).

Cole, Robert (1979) *Work, Mobility and Participation* (Berkeley: University of California Press).

Cole, Robert (1989a) *Strategies for Learning* (Berkeley: University of California Press).

Cole, Robert (1989b) 'Reflections on Japanese Corporate Citizenship: Company Reactions for a study of Hiring Practices in the United States', *Chuo Korean*, 10, pp. 122–35.

Cole, Robert and Donald Deskins (1988) 'Racial Factors in Site Location and Employment Patterns of Japanese Automobile Firms in America', *California Business Review*, 31, pp. 9–22.

Cool, Karel and Cynthia Legnick-Hall (1985) 'Second Thoughts on the Transferability of the Japanese Management Style', *Organization Studies*, 6 pp. 1–22.

Dillman, Donald (1978) *Mail and Telephone Surveys: The Total Design Method* (New York: John Wiley).

DiMaggio, Paul and Walter Powell (1983) 'The Iron Cage Revisited: Institutional Isomorphism and Collective Rationality in Organizational Fields', *American Sociological Review*, 48 (April) pp. 147–60.

Dohse, Knuth, Ulrich Jurgens and Thomas Malsch (1986) 'From Fordism to Toyotism? The Social Organization of the Labor Process in the Japanese Automobile Industry', *Politics and Society*, 14(2) pp. 45–66.

Dore, Ronald (1983) 'Goodwill and the Spirit of Market Capitalism', *British Journal of Sociology*, 34, pp. 459–82.

Dore, Ronald (1973) *Japanese Factory, British Factory* (Berkeley: University of California Press).

Drucker, Peter (1993) *Post-Capitalist Society* (New York: Random House).

Dunphy, Dexter (1987) 'Convergence/Divergence: A Temporal Review of the Japanese Enterprise and Its Management', *Academy of Management Review*, 12(3) pp. 445–59.

Edwards, Richard (1979) *Contested Terrain* (New York: Basic Books).

Ennis, Peter (1987) 'NUMMI Struggles to Close the Culture Gap', *Tokyo Business Today* (September) pp. 32–6.

Florida, Richard and Martin Kenney (1991) 'Transplanted Organizations: The Transfer of Japanese Industrial Organization to the United States', *American Sociological Review*, 56, pp. 381–98.

Florida, Richard and Martin Kenney, 'The Globalization of Innovation: The Economic Geography of Japanese R&D in the U.S.,' *Economic Geography* (October 1994), 70, 4, pp. 344–69.

Florida, Richard and Martin Kenney (1992a) 'The Japanese Transplants, Production Organization and Regional Development', *Journal of the American Planning Association* (Winter 1992) pp. 21–38.

Florida, Richard and Martin Kenney (1992b) 'Restructuring in Place: Japanese Investment, Production Organization, and the Geography of Steel', *Economic Geography*, 68(2) (April) pp. 146–73.

Florida, Richard and Martin Kenney (1990) *The Breakthrough Illusion* (New York: Basic Books).

Friedman, David (1988) *The Misunderstood Miracle: Industrial Development and Political Change in Japan* (Ithaca, NY: Cornell University Press).

Fucini, J. and S. Fucini (1990) *Working for the Japanese* (New York: Free Press).

Gordon, Andrew (1985) *The Evolution of Labor Relations in Japan: Heavy Industry, 1853–1955* (Cambridge, MA: Harvard University Press).

Graham, Laurie (1993) 'Inside a Japanese Transplant', *Work and Occupations*, 20(2) pp. 147–73.

Granovetter, Mark (1986) 'Labor Mobility, Internal Markets, and Job Matching: A Comparison of the Sociological and Economic Approaches', *Research in Social Stratification and Mobility*, 5, pp. 3–39.

Granovetter, Mark (1985) 'Economic Action and Social Structure: The Problem of Embeddedness', *American Journal of Sociology*, 91(3) (November) pp. 481–510.

Gronning, Terje (1992) 'Human Value and Competitiveness: On the Social Organization of Production at Toyota Motor Corporation and New United Motor Manufacturing, Inc.', Ph.D. dissertation, Ritsumeikan University.

Guiles, Melinda and Krystal Miller (1990) 'Mazda and Mitsubishi–Chrysler Venture Cut Output, Following Big Three's Lead', *Wall Street Journal* (12 January): A2, A12.

Hannan, Michael and John Freeman (1988) 'The Ecology of Organizational Mortality: American Labor Unions, 1836–1985', *American Journal of Sociology*, 94(1) (July) pp. 25–52.

Helper, Susan (1989) 'Changing Supplier Relationships in the US: Results of Survey Research' (Cambridge, MA: MIT International Motor Vehicle Project).

Hill, Richard Child, Michael Indergaard and Kuniko Fujita (1988) 'Flat Rock, Home of Mazda: The Social Impact of a Japanese Company on an American Community'. Paper presented at the Eighth Annual Automotive Conference, University of Michigan, March.

HAM (Honda America Manufacturing) (1988) 'The New Wage Plan', *The Stamping Press* (7 March) p. 2.

Helper, Susan (1990) 'Selling to Japanese Automonile Assembly Plants: Results of a Survey', Case Western Reserve University, Cleveland, unpublished MS.

Jacoby, Stanford (1993) 'Pacific Ties: Industrial Relations and Employment Systems in Japan and the US since 1900', in Howell Harris and Nelson Lichtenstein (eds), *Industrial Democracy in the Twentieth Century* (New York: Cambridge University Press).

Jacoby, Sanford (1979) 'The Origins of Internal Labor Markets in Japan', *Industrial Relations*, 18 (Spring) pp. 184–96.

Judge, Paul (1990) 'U.A.W. Faces Test at Mazda Plant', *New York Times* (27 March): D1, D8.

Kagono, Tadao, Ikujiro Nonaka, Kiyonori Sakakibara and Akihiro Okumura (1985) *Strategic vs. Evolutionary Management* (Amsterdam: North Holland).

Kalleberg, Arne and James Lincoln (1988) 'The Structure of Earnings Inequality in the United States and Japan'. *American Journal of Sociology*, 94, pp. 121-53.

Kamata, Satoshi (1982) *Japan in the Passing Lane* (New York: Pantheon).

Kato, Tetsuro and Rob Steven (eds) (1993) *Is Japanese Management PostFordist? An International Debate* (Tokyo: Madosha Publishers), in Japanese and English.

Katz, Harry (1985) *Shifting Gears* (Cambridge, MA: MIT Press).

Kenney, Martin and Richard Florida (1993) *Beyond Mass Production: The Japanese System and Its Transfer to the US* (New York: Oxford University Press).

Kenney, Martin and Richard Florida (1988) 'Beyond Mass Production: Production and the Labor Process in Japan', Politics and Society, 16(1) pp. 121-58.

Kertesz, Louise (1989) 'Injury, Training Woes Hit New Mazda Plant', *Automotive News* (13 February) pp. 1, 52-3.

Kochan, Thomas and Joel Cutcher-Gershenfeld (1988) 'Institutionalizing and Diffusing Innovation in Industrial Relations' (Washington, DC: US Department of Labor, Bureau of Labor–Management Relations and Cooperative Programs).

Kochan, Thomas, Harry Katz and Robert McKersie (1986) *The Transformation of American Industrial Relations* (New York: Basic Books).

Koike, Kazuo (1988) *Understanding Industrial Relations in Japan* (New York: St Martin's Press).

Krafcik, John (1986) 'Learning From NUMMI', MIT International Motor Vehicle Program, unpublished manuscript.

Levine, Solomon (1958) *Industrial Relations in Postwar Japan* (Urbana: University of Illinois Press).

Lillrank, Paul and Noriaki Kano (1989) *Continuous Improvement: Quality Control Circles in Japanese Industry* (Ann Arbor, MI: Center for Japanese Studies, The University of Michigan).

Lincoln, James and Arne Kalleberg (1985) 'Work Organization and Workforce Commitment: A Study of Plants and Employees in the US and Japan', *American Sociological Review*, 50 (December) pp. 738-60.

Lincoln, James Mitsuyo Hanada and Kerry McBride (1986) 'Organizational Structures in Japanese and US Manufacturing', *Administrative Science Quarterly*, 31 pp. 338-64.

Mair, Andrew, Richard Florida and Martin Kenney (1988) 'The New Geography of Automobile Production: Japanese Transplants in North America', *Economic Geography*, 64 pp. 352-73.

Marsh, Robert and Mannari, Hiroshi (1976) *Modernization and the Japanese Factory* (Princeton, NJ: Princeton University Press).

Meyer, John and Brian Rowen (1977) 'Institutionalized Organizations: Formal Structure as Myth and Ceremony', *American Journal of Sociology*, 83(2) (September) pp. 340-63.

Mitsubishi Research Institute (1987) *The Relationship Between Japanese Auto and Auto Parts Makers* (Tokyo: Japanese Automobile Manufacturers Association, Inc).

Nakane, Chie (1970) *Japanese Society* (Berkeley: University of California Press).

Nishiguchi, Toshihiro (1994) *Strategic Industrial Sourcing: The Japanese Advantage* (New York: Oxford University Press).

Nonaka, Ikujiro and Hirotaka Takeuchi, (1995). *The Knowledge Creating Company*, (New York: Oxford University Press).

NUMMI (1986) 'New United Motor Manufacturing, Inc. and the United Automobile Workers: Partners in Training'. A Case Study for the ILO/ Turin Center Seminar on Labor–Management Cooperation in Training and Retraining, 21 May.

Odake, Konuska *et al.* (1988) *The Automobile Industry in Japan: A study of Ancillary Firm Development* (Tokyo: Kinokuniya).

Ouchi, William (1980) 'Markets, Bureaucracies and Clans', *Administrative Science Quarterly*, 25 (March) pp. 129–41.

Parker, Michael and Jane Slaughter (1988) 'Management by Stress', *Technology Review* (October) pp. 36–46.

Patterson, Gregory (1990) 'GM Has a New Worry: Tough UAW Official Could Lead Fall Strike', *Wall Street Journal* (10 January): A1, A8.

Patterson, Gregory (1989) 'The UAW's Chances at Japanese Plants Hinge on Nissan Vote', *Wall Street Journal* (25 July): A1, A12.

Perrow, Charles (1981) 'Markets, Hierarchies and Hegemony: A Critique of Chandler and Williamson', in Andrew Van de Ven and William Joyce (eds), *Perspectives on Organization Design and Behavior* (New York: Wiley Interscience) pp. 371–86.

Robins, James (1987). 'Organizational Networks: Notes on the Use of Transaction Cost Theory in the Study of Organizations,' *Administrative Science Quarterly* 32: 68–86.

Robins, James (1987) 'Organizational Economics: Notes on the Use of Transaction-Cost Theory in the Study of Organizations', *Administrative Science Quarterly*, 32 (March) pp. 68–86.

Rosenbaum, James and Takehiko Kariya (1989) 'From High School to Work: Market and Institutional Mechanisms in Japan', *American Journal of Sociology*, 94, pp. 1334–65.

Sabel, Charles (1989) 'Flexible Specialization and the Re-emergence of Regional Economics', in *Reversing Industrial Decline? Industrial Structure and Policies in Britain and her Competitors* ed. Paul Hirst and Jonathan Zeitlin (New York: St. Martin's.

Sayer, Andrew (1986) 'New Developments in Manufacturing: The Just-in-Time System', *Capital and Class*, 30, pp. 43–72.

Schlesinger, Jacob (1987) 'NUMMI Keeps Promise of No Layoffs by Setting 'Nonproduction Workdays'', *Wall Street Journal* (29 October): A26.

Schumpeter, Joseph (1947) 'The Creative Response in Economic History,' *Journal of Economic History*, 7, pp. 149–59.

Sheard, Paul (1983) 'Auto Production Systems in Japan: Organizational and Locational Features', *Australian Geographical Studies*, 21 (April) pp. 49–68.

Shimada, Haruo (1986) 'Japanese Industrial Relations in Transition', MIT Sloan School of Management Work Paper No.1854–88, December.

Shirai, Taishiro (ed.) (1983) *Contemporary Industrial Relations in Japan* (Madison, WI: University of Wisconsin Press) pp. 29–62.

Smitka, Michael (1992) *Competitive Ties: Subcontracting in the Japanese Automotive Industry* (New York: Columbia University Press).

Smith, Donald and Richard Florida (1994) 'Agglomeration and Industrial Location: An Econometric Analysis of Japanese-affiliated Manufacturers in Automotive-related Industries', *Journal of Urban Economics* (1994) 35: 1–19.

Suzuki, H. (1976) 'Age, Seniority and Wages', *International Labour Review*, 113 (January–February) pp. 67–83.

Taira, Koji (1962) 'The Characteristics of Japanese Labor Markets', *Economic Development and Cultural Change* (January) pp. 150–68.

UAW (1989) *UAW–DSM Special Report: Highlights of a Tentative UAW–Diamond-Star Agreement* (Normal, IL: UAW Local 2488).

US General Accounting Office (GAO) (1988) *Foreign Investment: Growing Japanese Presence in the US Auto Industry*, Report to Congressional Requesters, GAO/NSIAD-88-111 March.

US International Trade Commission (1987) *US Global Competitiveness: The US Automotive Parts Industry* (Washington, DC: US International Trade Commission).

Ward's Auto World (1990) 'The Transplants: The State of the Industry' (January) pp. 23–43.

White, Joseph (1989) 'Joint Venture UAW Members Accept Contract', *Wall Street Journal* (29 August): A2.

Wilms, Welford (1995) *Restoring Property* (New York: Times Books).

Wilms, Welford, Alan Hradcastle and Deone Zell (1994) 'A Cultural Transformation: New United Motor Manufacturing Inc.' Paper presented at a conference on 'The Challenge of Multinational Competition', Stuttgart, Germany, May 1993.

Williamson, Oliver (1975) *Markets and Hierarchies* (New York: Free Press).

Womack, John, Daniel Jones, and Daniel Roos (1990) *The Machine that Changed the World* (New York: Rawson Associates).

Young, Ruth (1988) 'Is Population Ecology a Useful Paradigm for the Study of Organizations', *American Journal of Sociology*, 94 (1) pp. 1–24.

Zucker, Lynne (1986) 'Production of Trust: Institutional Sources of Economic Structure', in Barry Staw and L.L. Cummings (eds), *Research in Organization Behavior*, vol. 6 (Greenwich, CT: JAI Press) pp. 53–111.

Part II
Dispersion to Developing Countries

4 Industrial Relations in the Korean Auto Industry: The Implications of Industrial Sector Requirements and Societal Effects for International Competitiveness

Ronald A. Rodgers

INTRODUCTION: INDUSTRIAL RELATIONS/HUMAN RESOURCE MANAGEMENT AND THE INTERNATIONAL COMPETITIVENESS OF THE KOREAN AUTO INDUSTRY

The automobile industry is widely recognized as the world's largest manufacturing industry and as the trend-setter for other industries (Womack, Jones and Roos, 1990). Besides providing many high-wage, high-value-added jobs, an integrated automobile industry also offers very extensive linkages to a wide array of supplier industries. The automobile industry may, thus, have the potential of contributing more than any other industrial sector to an advanced high-productivity national economy. But, though developing an automobile industry is a desirable goal, the barriers of entry are so formidable that no newly industrialized country other than the Republic of Korea has been able to foster the emergence of indigenous automobile manufacturers that have been able to become significant players in the international markets.

The history of Korean industrialization reveals a pattern of repeated advances into increasingly capital and technology-intensive industries that have posed ever more formidable barriers to entry. Economic advisors had considered many projects overly ambitious at the time they were initiated, but in retrospect it is evident that Korean firms that began operations in advanced industries (typically at the urging of national economic planners and with strong government support) have often been able to devote sufficient resources to their new ventures to become internationally viable. While in many cases the resources could have undoubtedly been utilized more efficiently in the short run in industries that corresponded more closely to Korea's comparative advantage in low labor costs, the early forays into more sophisticated industries and capital-intensive production processes correctly anticipated Korea's rising labor costs and the increased vulnerability of Korean firms in labor-intensive industries to competitors in lower-cost locations.

Sustained productivity growth and prosperity at the national level depend on firms that are able to compete in 'structurally attractive' industries; that is, high value-added industries with sustainable entry barriers (Porter, 1990, pp. 8, 36). That may be the reason why Korean public policy makers supported the emergence of large conglomerates (*chaebol*) that were willing and able to channel a substantial portion of the nation's resources into capital and technology-intensive industries (Clifford, 1994), even though such industries offered lower earnings in the short run than traditional labor-intensive industries (Amsden, 1989, pp. 85–9). The formal and *de facto* policies of restricting foreign multinationals to only those industrial sectors and activities in which indigenous firms were not yet able to perform independently facilitated the development of strong indigenous firms at the vanguard of the Korean economy. Arguably (but the point is intensely debated), this policy contributed more to the upgrading of the Korean economy than what would have been possible if Korea had consistently maintained policies to attract foreign investments and had been content to play host to the affiliates of foreign multinational corporations (Kim and Leipziger, 1993). As explained by Porter (1990, p. 19):

... the home base is the nation in which the essential competitive advantages of the enterprise are created and sustained ... [It is] the location of many of the most productive jobs, the core technologies, and the most advanced skills.

On the other hand, new entrants that attempt to survive independently in advanced industrial sectors face the risk that if they ultimately prove unable to overcome the high barriers to entry, they are unlikely to be able to recoup more than a small fraction of the resources they have expended in the unsuccessful attempt.

The dramatically rising standards that a firm must meet in order to achieve international competitiveness in the auto industry are more than the Korean government officials who decided to target the industry, and the Korean firms that made the first major investments, had initially bargained for. In the 1970s it was widely assumed that the maturing auto industry was a likely candidate for progressive migration from the advanced industrialized countries toward newly industrialized countries (NICs) that offered substantially lower wage rates and expanding domestic markets (Jones and Womack, 1985). As a result of the vastly improved production systems and new technologies, however, the standards for competitive performance in the auto industry have risen far beyond the reach of most new entrants.[1] The new consensus is that the automobile industry has entered into a period of 'de-maturation'. Some industry analysts contend that even many established companies and national industries will fall behind unless they are able to merge or enter into strategic alliances with one of the few remaining major international companies (Green, 1992). In contrast to the earlier view, the prevailing view today is that no independent integrated automobile manufacturers in any of the NICs will have any realistic chance of becoming internationally competitive for many years to come (Jones and Womack, 1985; Womack and Jones, 1989; Gwynne, 1991; Green, 1992).

The literature on the automobile industry enumerates many elements (ranging from organizational structure, to capital and technological resources, supply and distribution networks, and so on) that must be brought together by any world-class automobile company. There is not room in this chapter to systematically address all of those issues. Instead, the focus will be on one other set of issues that has recently received extensive attention in the academic, business and popular press: the industrial relations and human resource management (IR/HRM) institutions and practices that are associated with 'best practice' production systems.[2] In the traditional Fordist/Taylorist type of mass production system that has traditionally characterized most Korean manufacturing industries, the predominant national institutions and enterprise-level practices are primarily oriented toward maintaining managerial control and minimizing labor costs. This system naturally gives rise to rigidity, antagonistic labor–management relations, minimal skill formation, an alienated work force and a lack of employee involvement in raising productivity or improving quality. Due to the elevated performance standards that have become a prerequisite for competitiveness in the auto industry, many authors contend that firms that continue to adhere to this traditional form of mass production will never be able to make the grade. That proposition sets the stage for the key question to be considered here: *Given the existing national institutions and enterprise-level IR/ HRM practices, is it possible for Korean automobile manufacturers to advance beyond the old mass production model to some alternative system that contributes to greater flexibility and improved quality?*[3]

The following section will briefly describe the historical development of the automobile industry in the ROK, and the current accomplishments and ambitions of the major companies. Data on the economic performance of the major firms, and the national industry as a whole, show that the Korean auto industry must be taken seriously. It also helps to relate the outcomes achieved thus far to the objectives of the top managers and public officials who are primarily responsible for selecting and implementing the general strategies and specific practices in the Korean automobile industry.[4] Having described the prospects in the Korean auto industry in terms of economic performance, the essential features of traditional mass production and several alternative 'models' will then be examined. (As used herein, a model may be considered a package of overall corporate strategies with the corresponding set of IR/HRM institutions and practices.) By hypothesis, each model carries different implications for international competitiveness, but the opportunities and constraints posed by external conditions at the national, regional or industry-sector level may limit the choices that are realistically available to individual firms in different economic, social and political environments.

In the penultimate section of this chapter, the dominant national institutions, and the most prevalent enterprise-level practices involving industrial relations and human resource management, are first analyzed in terms of the relative weight given to the two alternative priorities facing employers and public policy makers: minimizing labor costs to improve firms' cost competitiveness through mass production or raising the quality of firms' (or the nation's) human resources to support flexible quality-oriented production strategies. The information that is available on the practices of the leading auto companies will then be examined in the context of the norms and expectations engendered by the practices that prevail throughout the Korean economy. In the final section, the prospects for a transition in the Korean auto industry away from the mass production model toward a more flexible quality-oriented model of 'international best practice' will be examined.

HISTORICAL DEVELOPMENT, CURRENT PERFORMANCE
AND FUTURE PROSPECTS FOR THE KOREAN AUTO
INDUSTRY

The automobile industry was selected by the government and business
elites of the ROK as one of the target industries in conjunction with
the 'Big Push' into capital intensive industries beginning in the early
1970s, and far greater investments were made in the 1980s to enable
the Korean automobile industry to become internationally competitive.[5] The center-piece of the early 1970s initiative was the highly natio-
nalistic 'Long-term Plan for the Promotion of the Auto Industry',
promulgated in 1974. That plan required Korean auto producers to develop original models as well as to achieve a high local content ratio.
The plan was not fully realized in practice, but it prompted Hyundai
Motors to develop an original model, the Pony, with the extensive help
of an Italian consulting firm and with many key parts designed or supplied by Mitsubishi. This model quickly came to dominate the local
market and it may have helped to provide a base for the export drive
that began in the mid-1980s. Nonetheless, the entire Korean auto industry (and many other industries as well) faced a serious crisis beginning in the late 1970s, and it had to be fundamentally reorganized.[6] It
was only after this reorganization that the two surviving Korean automobile producers seriously targeted the export markets as a means of
achieving the minimum economies of scale necessary for viability.

Prior to the 'take off' dating from the early 1980s, the Korean auto
industry completely lacked international competitiveness. Jones and
Womack (1985) cite a Korean Ministry of Commerce (subsequently renamed the Ministry of Trade and Industry) report showing that the
production cost for a Hyundai Pony in 1979 amounted to US $3972,
while a Toyota Carolla could be produced in Japan for US $2300.
Worse still, the Hyundai vehicle was plagued by so many defects and
technological deficiencies that it could only be exported to countries
that did not have rigorous environmental or safety standards at a
dumping price that was less than half of the domestic price (N.Y. Lee,
1994). The volume of auto exports from the ROK declined from 31 000
in 1979 to 20 000 in 1982.

To the amazement of the many sceptics, the Korean auto industry
staged a remarkable turn-around in the 1980s. Whereas production
of commercial vehicles and passenger cars stood at a mere 123 000
vehicles in 1980, the total figure came to 1.084 million vehicles in
1988, and it has continued to expand in subsequent years. As shown in

Table 4.1, total production and exports have expanded steadily in recent years, and the expansion is expected to continue at a rapid pace. In fact, the Korean auto producers have revised their projection target for 1994 upward to 2.63 million vehicles. If those targets are realized, Korea will soon become the world's fifth largest motor vehicle producing country (*Business Korea*, January, 1994).

Table 4.1   Production and exports of the Korean auto industry

Year	Total production (000 units)	Annual change %	Passenger cars (000 units)	Domestic sales (000 units)	Exports (000 units)	Annual change %
1990	1320	17.1	986	954	347	(−2.3)
1991	1498	13.3	1158	1104	390	12.4
1992	1730	15.5	1306	1268	456	16.9
1993*	2020	16.7	1580	1440	580	27.1
1994*	2290	13.4	1810	1630	660	15.7

*projected.
Source: *Business Korea*, November, 1993, p. 17.

The export performance of the Korean auto industry is worthy of special attention. Prior to 1985 there were almost no exports, but by 1988 exports, aimed primarily at the North American markets, had surged to a peak of 564 000 vehicles. In that year, Hyundai Motors was the fourth leading car exporting company to the United States, and Korea was the third leading nation, behind only Japan and Canada. But the well-known fact is that exports from Korean auto companies fell precipitously, by almost 40 per cent, in the next two years.[7] When the exports from the Korean auto companies to the United States and Canada declined significantly after an early peak, many analysts were very quick to write-off the entire industry as nothing more than a flash in the pan. A consensus quickly emerged that a sustainable competitive advantage was (permanently?) beyond the reach of the Korean auto makers (Womack, Jones and Roos, 1990; N.Y. Lee, 1994; Green, 1992).

Despite the poor prognosis offered by auto industry analysts, the rapid growth of the Korean auto industry has continued unabated. That is primarily because the explosive growth in the much more profitable domestic markets more than offset the decline in exports.[8] Success in the protected domestic market does not prove that the firms are internationally competitive, but the revenues that Hyundai Motors and Kia Motors earned in recent years from their domestic sales have

helped them to build up their resources and their confidence for a renewed advance into the international (not merely North American)
markets. The fierce competition that has emerged in the domestic markets among Korean auto makers is also forcing Korean firms to make
the improvements that are essential for successful exports.[9]

News reports on individual firms and the Korean auto industry as a
whole present a picture of enormous investments and reckless expansion of production facilities.[10] The total annual investments made by
all Korean auto companies (final assemblers) in the years 1986–89
averaged more than one trillion won (US$ 1.4 billion) – almost an
eight-fold expansion over the total average investments for the years
1982–84 (N.Y. Lee, 1994). Total investments in 1991 and 1992 were estimated at 1.5 trillion won and 1.7 billion won, respectively (*Korea Economic Report*, September, 1993) and for the years 1993–97 total annual
investments are expected to amount to about US$ 3.0 billion (2.4 tril-
lion won) (*Business Korea*, November, 1993). Hyundai has immediate
plans to construct three new plants in Korea that will add 870 000 to its
current capacity of 1.15 million vehicles, and, in its ambitions to become the world's tenth largest auto manufacturer, it plans to double its
current capacity by the year 2000 (*Business Korea*, December, 1993).
Kia is following Hyundai's lead in constructing new facilities and introducing new models (*Business Korea*, February, 1994). Daewoo and
General Motors broke-up in 1992 primarily because GM was unwilling
to go along with Daewoo's ambitious expansion plans, and since the
break-up Daewoo Motors, under the sole control of the Daewoo
Group, has proceeded full speed ahead to make up for lost time (*Korea
Economic Report*, October, 1993). In addition to the Korean 'big three',
Hyundai, Kia and Daewoo are all producing cars in affiliated companies.[11] A member of another *chaebol*, Ssangyong, manufactures a variety of specialty vehicles (including recreational vehicles) and expects to
expand production to include passenger cars in cooperation with Mercedes Benz. Finally, it is generally believed that the huge Samsung
Group will soon realize its dream to begin manufacturing passenger
cars.

The continuing expansion of the existing Korean auto companies
and the entry of new players shows that the companies, as well as public
policy makers and financial institutions, do not accept the view that
Korean firms cannot succeed in the auto industry. The record production and exports in 1993, and the large increase in domestic and export
sales that is expected in coming years, provide some confirmation for
their optimistic view. But the fact that companies have been pouring

money into the industry and expanding the volume of output still does not prove that the industry has been able to reach internationally competitive levels of productivity or quality. Korean auto exports continue to compete primarily at the low end of the markets, and are increasingly aimed at price-sensitive consumers in Asia and Eastern Europe. As in 1988, the primary stimulus for the current expansion of exports is favorable foreign exchange rates (a high Japanese yen and a low US dollar, with the Korean won pegged loosely to the dollar) that make Korean exports relatively less expensive (*Korea Economic Report*, Nov. 1993).

The Korean auto companies fully understand that their long-term success will depend on their ability to develop their own technology, reduce their dependence on foreign components suppliers and distributors, and improve productivity, quality and flexibility. On the basis of their extensive investments in research and development, Hyundai Motors and Kia Motors have both designed their own new models and engines,[12] and Kia is also following Hyundai's lead in developing its own overseas distributors. Daewoo is also investing in its own design and engineering capabilities and is busily developing independent distribution networks. All the major Korean companies are working hard to cultivate local components suppliers, and the proportion of imported components for the entire Korean auto industry is steadily declining.

Korean firms, including the major automobile producers, have invested heavily in advanced capital equipment designed to boost labor productivity, raise quality standards and increase managerial control. Porter (1990, p. 470) notes that the combination of highly-productive workers, relatively new and large-scale facilities and near state-of-the-art capital equipment allow Korean firms in various industries to approach the world frontier in productivity. In the automobile industry, Krafcik (1989) found that the productivity and quality levels achieved by Hyundai Motors in the late 1980s was superior to the industry averages in North America and Europe. He attributed this positive outcome to their having successfully learned many aspects of 'lean production' from their Japanese neighbors. Kia Motors, which was not included in Krafcik's study, has certainly progressed much further than Hyundai Motors in quality and in its adoption of lean production (Jo, 1992). Hyundai Motors has also progressed since Krafcik's study, partially as a result of the company's continuing investments in sophisticated capital equipment and its efforts to automate as many functions as possible.[13] Indeed, aggregate data on labor productivity show a

60 per cent increase in direct labor productivity in the Korean motor vehicle industry between 1990 and 1993.

Hyundai Motors and Daewoo Motors have both found it more difficult to reduce the number of reported defects per 100 vehicles than to raise labor productivity. Jo (1992) cites J.D. Powers data indicating that the number of defects per 100 vehicles dropped from 315 in 1987 to 178 in 1989, but Kim and Lee (1992) report an increase in Hyundai's defect rate to 249 in 1991, and an article in *Business Korea* (November, 1993) reported a defect rate in 1992 of 194 per 100 vehicles. Jo's data show that Daewoo Motors had a reported defect rate in both 1988 and 1989 of 246 per 100 vehicles, but in Kia Motors the defect rate dropped from 162 in 1988 to 122 in 1989. In subsequent years, cars produced by Kia have continued to enjoy an excellent reputation for quality.[14]

Assessing whether the Korean auto industry has sustainable international competitive power is more complex than compiling data on total sales, exports, productivity levels and quality ratings. In the analytical framework proposed by Porter (1990), only dynamic and evolving competitiveness is sustainable. The long-term strength of the Korean auto industry depends on the ability of the leading companies to advance from their current strength in producing cars of acceptable quality at low cost to higher bases of advantage. This can only be done through the sustained investments of effort and resources that are necessary for continuous improvements and innovations in product technology and production processes.

The preceding pages note the enormous investments that the Korean auto companies have made in expanding their production capacity, upgrading production processes, launching new models, developing indigenous research and design capabilities, cultivating local suppliers and building their own distribution networks. The proliferation of new models being introduced by the major Korean automobile companies, and the establishment of new companies, may also enhance the international competitiveness of the national automobile industry (though the impact of the fierce competition on the existing companies' profit margins is undoubtedly negative in the short run). There is competition and cross fertilization among firms; an increasingly rich network of components suppliers is emerging, and vocational research institutes and research centers are focusing on the industry's needs. All of this contrasts with the situation in other NICs where subsidiaries of the foreign multinationals that dominate the auto industry are managed in accordance with the parent companies' global rationalization strategies. The Korean auto companies' reckless expansion of production capacity, and their costly investments in developing independent capabilities, are probably irrational from an intermediate-term profit maximizing perspective, but it may be what will enable them to achieve the economies of scale and to move rapidly along the learning curve to the point where they can upgrade their technology and advance to higher bases of competitive advantage.

Despite these positive developments, to achieve sustainable international competitiveness the Korean auto industry faces a formidable task. Porter (1990, pp. 53–4) characterizes automobiles as a global industry in which 'firms are compelled to compete internationally in order to achieve or sustain competitive advantage in the most important industry segments'. Even more ominously, Womack and Jones (1989, p. 5) contend that:

... firms which cannot establish multiregional presence in the 1990s have little prospect of surviving as even single region players after the turn of the century. Thus countries seeking an internationally competitive but domestically owned industry may have no choice but to go global.

In their view, this requires more than massive surpluses in exports. 'Global status' can only be attained by firms that have mastered the current best practice in their home country operations *and* are able to introduce manufacturing practices that are superior to the host countries' norms (and comparable to the best Japanese transplants) in affiliates they have established in diverse regions. Even if all elements of that prescription are not absolutely essential for survival, the prospects for the Korean auto industry are dim unless they can at least approach international best practice in their own domestic operations.

INDUSTRIAL RELATIONS/HUMAN RESOURCE MANAGEMENT IN ALTERNATIVE PRODUCTION SYSTEMS

An Interactive Societal Effects Perspective

Due to the rising standards that are emerging in the auto industry, a firm that hopes to be internationally competitive cannot afford to fall substantially below world-class performance levels in any crucial aspect of its operations. IR/HRM matters, in particular, may be more important in the auto industry than in almost any other industry (Abo, 1990; Itagaki, 1989). Labor costs continue to be a substantial component of the overall cost of production, so auto companies cannot afford to implement practices that raise labor costs or undermine efficiency in excess of their long-term benefits. At the same time, however, many authors contend that the type of flexible high-quality production system that has become the *sine qua non* of international competitiveness in the auto industry depends on loyal, highly motivated employees with broad technical and interpersonal skills (MacDuffie and Krafcik, 1992).

As noted in the introduction, a recurring theme in scholarly literature on the auto industry is the debate as to whether successful companies in every country have no choice but to conform to a single emerging model that represents international best practice. Womack, *et al.* (1990) seem to think so. They claim that the model they have labelled 'lean production' will eventually overtake all companies in every country and in every industry. In their words:

> Manufacturers around the world are now trying to embrace lean production ... the adoption of lean production, as it inevitably spreads beyond the auto industry, will change everything in almost every industry – choices for consumers, the nature of work, the fortune of companies and, ultimately, the fate of nations.
>
> (p. 12)

There are many sceptics who question whether 'lean production' is qualitatively different than,[15] and superior to,[16] all alternative systems, and whether it can be successfully transferred from auto companies in Japan (especially the Toyota Motor Company) to firms in different industries and/or countries.

From a contingency perspective, the desirability and feasibility of adopting practices that conform to the lean production model (or any other model) would depend on conditions in the external environment ('societal effects'), the distinctive requirements for success in the relevant industrial sector, and the organization's own strategic objectives and capabilities. The relationship between the factors is interactive. Conditions that are present at the starting point in the external environment (including various social institutions and business norms, the climate of government/business relations, substantive and procedural aspects of the regulatory framework, the nature of academic and vocational training programs, the availability of workers having various types of qualifications and ambitions, the strength and character of labor unions and employers' associations, and the overall economic, geographic and demographic conditions) limit the ability of firms to successfully implement one type of production system while providing the necessary preconditions for some other type of production system. Success in a particular industrial sector (for example, automobiles), or for firms pursuing a particular market strategy (for example, differentiation as opposed to cost-leadership), might depend on the ability of a firm to implement IR/HRM practices that contribute to the successful implementation of a particular type of production system (for example, lean production). If that is true, then the external conditions that limit which type of production system can be successfully implemented would indirectly influence which industrial sector or which market strategy could prevail (Porter, 1990; Sorge, 1991; Kitschelt, 1991). At the same time, however, the type of external conditions that enable firms to successfully implement policies that contribute to international competitiveness in the industrial sector that is dominant in a particular nation or region, and the strategic choices of the most powerful actors, may influence various aspects of the external environment. As the outcome of this interaction, conditions that are most conductive for mass production industries emerge in certain nations or regions (and in such circumstances individual firms may have little choice but to adopt practices that conform to the mass production model), while in regions where the external conditions are more conducive for specialized small batch or craft production, different industries prosper and different production strategies prevail (Piore and Sabel, 1984). The conditions in still other regions may facilitate the type of operating systems that are most appropriate in sophisticated technical, professional and financial services.

Three Alternative Models

The introduction stated that an important theme in this chapter is the extent to which Korean auto makers have found it possible or necessary to advance beyond traditional mass production to a more advanced production system oriented towards flexibility and quality. Before presenting a detailed examination of the IR/HRM practices adopted by the leading auto companies, and the relationship between the situation in the auto industry and the institutions, norms and practices that prevail throughout the Korean economy, it will be useful to briefly digress by providing a conceptual explanation of traditional cost-oriented mass production and the two most widely advocated alternatives: 'diversified quality production' and 'lean production'.

Cost leadership through mass production

The logic of the IR / HRM policies adopted by market-oriented firms in pursuit of a cost leadership strategy is straightforward. The primary objective of these firms is to reduce overall production costs by minimizing labor costs while maximizing output. Firms pursuing this strategy typically recruit employees with the requisite skills from external labor markets when they are needed, and then lay off or dismiss employees whose specific skills no longer fit the firm's needs. They rely primarily on extrinsic rewards rather than attempting to cultivate their employees' long-term commitment and loyalty. They provide little training beyond the narrow on-the-job training that is needed to perform specific tasks; they tend to adopt Taylorist or machine-paced production processes that can be performed by unskilled workers subject to strict controls; and they maintain narrow managerial hierarchies that leave little space for employee participation or integration vertically or across functions.

Employers whose only objective is to maximize output at the lowest possible cost still need to be able to effectively control their typically unskilled and alienated workers; but if workers can easily find equally attractive opportunities elsewhere they may resign or risk dismissal rather than submitting to harsh discipline (Cho, 1987). In low-wage countries, employers can overcome this limitation by paying wages that exceed the local norms but that are still below the prevailing wages in advanced countries. Studies show that many workers will work very diligently for long hours under harsh conditions, and will not willingly resign until they are dismissed or become utterly unable to continue working, as long as there are no alternatives by which they could obtain similar rates of pay (see, for example, Humphrey, 1982).

The inherent rigidities of the mass production strategy pose a more serious problem. According to the traditional logic of mass production, specialized machines that are dedicated to the production of one specific type of product can be operated by poorly motivated unskilled or semi-skilled workers pursuant to standardized operating procedures formulated by white-collar managers and industrial engineers. Even if this is true (a debatable point!) such specialized equipment, and the formulation of standardized operating procedures, are only economical for very long production runs. With workers relegated to the mindless performance of routine tasks, there is no space for them, on the basis of their intelligence or pride in workmanship, to enhance product quality or improve the production processes; instead, management assumes (and via the self-fulfilling prophecy effect, ensures) that workers will exert no more effort or intelligence than what they are forced to exert in order to retain their jobs. As argued by Dertouzos, Lester and Solow (1989, pp. 79–93) in relation to manufacturing in the United States, the fragmentation of tasks and the rigid antagonistic relations between labor and management that are engendered by this system lead to a devaluation of skills, and may result in a workforce that is unable to keep up with the heightened requirements of an internationally competitive production system.

Diversified quality production

Since Piore and Sabel's (1984) polemical attack against the mass production model, many authors have noted the growing need, and the growing possibilities, for more flexible, specialized high quality production systems. Piore and Sabel's own preferred model is a high technology version of craft production which they call 'flexible specialization'. They envision networks of artisinal firms in which highly-skilled workers utilize sophisticated general purpose tools incorporating advanced micro-electronic circuitry to cooperatively produce a wide array of specialized, or even customized, products. Piore and Sabel do not provide concrete examples of auto manufacturers attaining international competitiveness by implementing practices consistent with their idealized model. Other authors who recommend an alternative model, which may be called 'Diversified Quality Production' (DQP), are able to point to specific examples. Indeed, the idea of DQP is based on experience of German and Swedish auto companies that have been able retain their competitiveness through a production system that is simultaneously highly efficient and socially desirable (Berggren, 1992a, 1992b; Streeck, 1991a, 1987).

Achieving premier product quality and operating a flexible production system with general purpose equipment requires firms to place greater emphasis on attracting excellent employees, cultivating broad skills, and drawing out the employees' intelligence and responsibility than on lowering labor costs and/or maintaining strict labor control. Streeck (1991a, p. 41) contends that 'a "professional" work motivation and a quality consciousness among workers that do not need to be supported by specific monetary incentives or the possibility of negative sanctions are indispensable resources for . . . diversified quality production' and that these traits, in turn, require the type of 'mutual trust and loyalty between employer and worker . . . that can only grow on the basis of stable social peace'.

It is clear from the German and Swedish examples that firms following the DQP strategy can achieve high levels of efficiency and quality, but few individual firms would be willing or able to pursue this strategy outside of the context of a national or industry-wide structure of opportunities and constraints based on social and political institutions.[17] Thus, as conceptualized in this chapter, a distinctive feature of this type of production system is its embeddedness in the context of:

1. National or regional institutions which effectively limit the types of strategies employers may realistically pursue;
2. Labor markets that reduce the dependence of employees on their employers by recognizing non-firm-specific skills and enabling employees to transfer to other firms without an undue loss in long-term earnings;
3. Independent, legally protected, channels of employee representation.

Lean production and 'Japanese-style' IR/HRM

The discussion of lean production in the following pages is based primarily on Womack *et al.* (1990). That text acknowledges the close relationship between lean production and the type of production system (supported by appropriate IR/HRM institutions and practices) implemented by large Japanese firms (especially the Toyota Motor Company)[18] but the authors are more interested in the contribution that a rational set of practices make toward an efficient high quality production system than on the practices that happen to characterize Japanese firms and their foreign affiliates. Korea shares with Japan a rather similar cultural tradition, as well as many continuing similarities in laws, institutions, and industrial governance structures. Furthermore, many Korean firms apply certain characteristically 'Japanese-style' IR/HRM policies to certain segments of their workforce. In evaluating the applicability of the lean production model to firms in the ROK, it will therefore be helpful to incorporate 'Japanese-style' IR/HRM practices into an explicitly 'Japanese-style lean production model'.[19]

In contrast to the DQP model described above, firms that adhere to the Japanese-style lean production model typically do so at the employer's initiative in the context of weak labor movements and minimal regulations (Dore, 1990). On the other hand, firms adhering to the latter model share with firms following the DQP model a form of work organization that maximizes employee initiative, responsible autonomy and flexibility rather than strict labor control.[20] As for production and market strategies, the focus may be low-cost production for mass markets or small-scale premium-quality production for specialized markets, or a combination of both. The distinctive feature of this alternative is the close identification of core employees with the firm, and their active involvement in promoting its objectives.

The HRM policies of this type of firm feature careful selection (emphasizing general aptitude, a cooperative attitude and a compatible social background over prior work experience or advanced technical skills), extensive internal training (in interpersonal skills and problem-solving techniques as well as general technical matters), extensive job rotation, socialization into the corporate family, benevolent paternalism, promotions from within and credible assurances of long-term employment. The result is a workforce with the ability and the motivation for teamwork, vertical and horizontal integration, and the involvement of employees at all levels in a continuous endeavor to improve quality and efficiency and to eliminate any wasted efforts or materials.

Several widely publicized management practices that are consistent with this type of organization include just-in-time processes, total quality control at the point of production, team-oriented production (based on broad job classifications, flexible assignments, cross-training among team members, and an extensive delegation of authority to teams for self-management), and non-adversarial channels for employee involvement. The finely-tuned production system that emerges has no buffers and would be extremely vulnerable to disruption from individual opportunism or collective action, but this risk is minimized by the high dependence of the employees and their representatives on the firms.

An enormous literature exists on the benefits of the whole package, and of specific practices; and on the feasibility of transplanting the model, in whole or in part, to different environments.[21] There is now no disputing the impressive accomplishments of firms that correspond to this model in terms of efficiency and quality, but there is considerable debate as to the conditions that must be present if the desired outcomes are to occur. It would seem that only employers who provide a solid assurance of long-term employment (at least to the core employees) could come within the limits of this model, but at least one study argues that the positive outcomes associated with the model can be obtained in firms that do not provide such assurances and that have high rates of labor turnover (Shaiken, 1990). Many earlier studies suggested that the cooperative team-oriented production system associated with

large Japanese firms depended on a favorable cultural environment
and/or on encompassing enterprise-level socialization,[22] but other studies indicate that the desired aspects of this management system can be
effectively transferred to other countries in disaggregated form.[23]
Enterprise unions are frequently cited as one of the pillars of Japanese-
style industrial relations, and the Japanese management literature
also stresses other forms of employee involvement, including labor–
management councils, quality circles and consensus-based decisions,
but in practice employee involvement (in Japan, in Japanese transplants overseas, and in other firms that attempt to follow the Japanese
model) is almost entirely on management's terms, and the independent
power of unions to struggle against management to uphold the employees' interests is severely circumscribed (Oliver and Wilkinson, 1988;
Fucini and Fucini, 1990).

Societal Effects in a Rapidly Advancing Economy

The Korean experience illustrates the interaction between the three sets
of factors discussed at the beginning of this section: external environmental conditions, the distinctive requirements for competitiveness
that apply to specific industrial sectors, and enterprise-level strategies
and practices. In earlier years, the Korean environment was considered
appropriate for labor-intensive industries in which the key to competitiveness was low labor costs. Almost all entrepreneurs who sought to
engage in manufacturing in the ROK selected such industries and
adopted mass production strategies and IR/HRM policies designed to
minimize labor costs. In turn, the overwhelming predominance of such
firms shaped the emerging business norms and social institutions in the
ROK. In recent years, Korea's declining comparative advantage in
low labor costs has upset the congruence between environmental conditions, industrial sectors and corporate strategies. Some entrepreneurs are now attempting to enter industries where cost-competitive
mass production strategies are less viable, and where effective operations require more flexible forms of work organization and more sophisticated human resources.

The automobile industry is the prime example of an industry where
international competitiveness is now said to depend on the successful
implementation of a production system that overcomes the limitations
of traditional mass production. Evidence presented in the next section
shows that traditional mass production is still the dominant strategy
in most Korean industries, however, and that most Korean auto

companies have retained IR/HRM practices that are most appropriate for the low-cost mass production strategy. The national institutions, norms and expectations that emerged in response to the needs of the mass production model may, therefore, be an obstacle for firms that are now attempting to pursue a different strategy.

As noted above, the primary objectives that firms adhering to the traditional mass production model seek to achieve through their IR/HRM policies and practices are the minimization of labor costs and the maintenance of managerial control. Firms that attempt to implement the other models described above (diversified quality production or lean production) place relatively greater emphasis on raising the quality and commitment of their employees. Evaluating the IR/HRM institutions and practices that prevail among Korean firms in terms of that dichotomy will provide a basis for accessing the size of the gap that an auto company would have to bridge to implement one of the alternatives to traditional mass production.

THE PREVAILING IR/HRM INSTITUTIONS AND PRACTICES IN KOREA, AND IN THE KOREAN AUTO INDUSTRY

The Prevailing IR/HRM Institutions and Norms throughout the Korean Economy

The way that institutions that have emerged at the national level in response to general economic, social and political developments determine the range of choices available to firms in specific industrial sectors may be seen most clearly in the area of labor relations. Especially since the mid-1980s, labor relations for firms in all industries have been swept along by the surge of labor conflict and union organizing, and then by the nation-wide offensive to restore order, reassert managerial prerogatives, and halt the escalating wage spiral. The differences that have emerged over time in each of the major auto companies in accordance with the changing national institutions and business norms have arguably been greater than the differences among the companies at any given time.

In their selection of HRM practices, on the other hand, the existing web of regulations, institutions and social conventions imposes relatively few effectively binding obligations or constraints.[24] Employers are quite free to choose the policies they will apply to various categories of employees in accordance with their business strategies or personal preferences. As will be explained below, this has led to widely divergent HRM policies among firms in different industrial sectors, and in relation to different categories of employees. But paradoxically the absence of effectively enforced legal obligations or consistently observed social norms may also limit the types of HRM practices and forms of work organization that individual firms can realistically expect to implement. For example, credible assurances of employment security and fair treatment may be essential preconditions for forms of work organization that depend on the long-term commitment and loyalty of highly-skilled employees (Streeck, 1991a; Kochan and Dyer, 1993). Individual firms acting on their own initiative are likely to find it prohibitively difficult to implement practices that satisfy those preconditions in geographical areas and industrial sectors where pre-employment education and training is inadequate, and where authoritarian management and high labor turnover rates are the norm.

In the pages that follow, Korea's changing industrial relations institutions and norms will be described first, and then the norms and expectations in relation to a few selected HRM issues will be more briefly explained. That will provide the context for an examination of the IR / HRM practices of the leading Korean auto companies.

Labor relations in Korea

Throughout modern history, Korean government and business elites have generally considered labor unions and collective bargaining to be luxuries that their country could not afford. Insofar as the competitiveness of the predominantly labor-intensive mass production industries was based on well disciplined low-cost labor, the primary considerations have always been to prevent disruptive labor conflict, maintain managerial control, and hold down labor costs. Arrangements to alleviate the causes of employee dissatisfaction in order to reduce absenteeism and turnover, and to elicit a higher degree of commitment and conscientious cooperation are, at best, granted only secondary importance. Lofty notions of industrial democracy through effective employee representation and broadly-based employee participation schemes are always deferred into the indefinite future.

Early experiments in worker control of production were crushed together with the radical labor movement in the late 1940s, and when liberals again began to insist that there was a legitimate role for labor unions, what they had in mind was limited 'job control' unions that conformed to the American model. Today, despite frequent exhortation from scholars and government officials for labor–management cooperation, neither labor nor management see much scope for labor involvement in efforts to improve the production processes for the benefit of both parties.[25]

The Korean government's heavy-handed intervention to suppress union organizing and collective action prior to 1987 led one Korean scholar to comment, 'One may wonder if what we observed . . . was "labor-government relations" rather than "labor-management relations" ' (S.K. Kim, 1989, p. 10).[26] In the few cases where collective labor disputes did break out, heavy-handed government intervention to restore order on terms favorable to the employer was swift and sure (Asia Watch, 1986; S.K. Kim, 1988; Rodgers, 1990; Ogle, 1990). Strike statistics provide particularly clear evidence of the government's dominant role. Sharp peaks in the number of labor disputes, towering above the very low numbers in normal years, occurred in 1960–61, 1979–80, and 1987–89, beginning in the months immediately after the successive regimes of Presidents Rhee, Park and Chun had broken down.[27] It does not appear that economic factors relating to the business cycle had any significant impact on the number of strikes (Y.K Park, 1991; D.O. Kim, 1992). There was a strike wave whenever, but only whenever, there was a gap in the willingness or ability of the government to suppress labor militancy. When the succeeding authoritarian regimes consolidated their power, the anti-labor policies were resumed and the number of strikes fell back to the normal low levels.

The ready availability of government intervention on employers' behalf to prevent labor from successfully challenging even harsh and arbitrary management practices resulted in a fundamental change in the cost-benefit analysis for all kinds of management policies relating to labor. It may take a credible threat of disruptive collective action to make some employers willing to accept any effective form of employee representation scheme that could limit management's unilateral authority. A basic tenant of IR theory is that effective channels for employee representation bring a host of benefits in terms of improved morale, loyalty and commitment (Freeman and Medoff, 1984; Hirschman, 1970). Recent literature also suggests that unions may contribute to more effective programs for training (Streeck, 1989), and they may facilitate employee involvement in innovative arrangements to boost productivity (Mishel and Voos, 1991). When the threat of disruptive collective action is effectively removed, however, employers are likely not to consider these auxiliary benefits to be worth the cost.

There have undoubtedly been some significant changes since 1987. The strike wave beginning in that year was much bigger than anything that had gone before, and it did not subside until late 1989. There were more strikes, involving many more workers and resulting in the loss of far more working days.[28] For the first time, large firms in capital and technology intensive industries, including the major auto assemblers and their first-tier components suppliers, were particularly vulnerable to strikes. Revisions were made in the exclusionary labor law framework that now make it easier for moderate unions to be established and for disputes to be handled pursuant to legal procedures (Rodgers, 1990). A surge in union organizing that accompanied the political liberalization and labor law reform resulted in almost 900 000 new union members between the end of 1986 and the end of 1989, raising the density rate among eligible employees from 15.5 per cent to 23.7 per cent (Y.K. Park, 1991, Table 5, citing MOL statistics). Militant workers embraced dissident unions, and pressured the normally tame established unions to adopt a more independent, aggressive stance.

In contrast to previous years when unions had generally been unable to significantly influence management policies (Bognanno and Kim, 1981; Bognanno, 1988; Y.K. Park, 1991), many unions have, since 1987, succeeded in winning large wage increases and favorable collective agreements. Studies on the union-wage premiums (the differential between wages for union members and non-union members after controlling for individual human capital and industry-related variables) in various years between 1976 and 1987 showed a very small union-wage premium (ranging from −2.27 per cent to 6.7 per cent), but on the basis of wage data for 1989, Song (1991) found a significant union-wage premium which he estimated to be 10.2 per cent.[29]

On the other hand, it is evident from an analysis of the grievance procedures in unionized work places that Korean labor unions do not have the power to ensure that collective agreements are fairly interpreted and enforced, or that the rights of individual employees are protected.[30] Whereas in most industrial democracies neutral arbitrators or labor courts are used to adjudicate disputes regarding individual rights or the interpretation of CBAs, the ultimate decision-making power in almost all companies in Korea is retained by management.[31] Korean companies do usually include provisions for the handling of grievances in their internal Rules of Employment and/or in their CBAs, and they have Grievance Committees as a subordinate function of the inherently non-adversarial Labor–Management Councils (see below). These grievance procedures give employees a chance to pursue their complaints, individually or through representatives, up through several levels of review. It is extremely rare for the employees' representatives to be given an equal voice,[32] however, and it does not appear that any company has committed itself to follow the decision of an external labor arbitrator for the final resolution of grievances. The absence of effective protections for the rights of employees and their representatives follows from the fact that, in contrast to the situation in countries where labor would require a solid assurance of neutral grievance procedures as an inducement to foreswear its use of the strike weapon during the term of a contract, management in Korea is often able to get a peace obligation clause inserted into a CBA without accepting grievance arbitration procedures. Even without such a clause, a peace obligation during the term of a CBA is inferred automatically, so employers do not need to bargain away their unilateral rights to obtain this benefit.

In theory, labor–management relations need not be limited to the struggle characteristic of adversarial collective bargaining. The Korean labor law framework explicitly provides for various channels of cooperative employee representation. The most important formal channel is the Labor Management Council (LMC) system. The Labor Management Council Law requires that a LMC must be established in all firms except those with under 50 employees who have not had a labor union or a labor dispute within the past few years. Consultation is required in the LMC on various non-adversarial issues, but resolutions cannot be made without a two-thirds majority. (In the absence of a resolution, management retains its unilateral authority.) Korean scholars, managers and union representatives are virtually unanimous in discounting the significance of the LMC system and viewing the hype surrounding it with a good deal of scepticism.[33] Where there is no union, labor activists complain that LMCs are used to preempt union organizing, that employers completely dominate the sessions, or that the employers fail to meet in good faith. On the other hand, where strong independent unions are in place, managers complain that LMC sessions are as adversarial as collective bargaining, and that the atmosphere is invariably stressful and non-productive. The employee representatives to the LMC in unionized workplaces lack sufficient leverage to win meaningful concessions from management through the LMC, so they would be suspected of selling out their constituents if they agreed to any management initiatives. This pattern could change if the employers were willing to grant certain benefits in exchange for the employees' cooperation, but Korean observers acknowledge that this type of give-and-take bargaining very rarely occurs in LMCs.

Labor's brief interlude of freedom from hostile government intervention came to a gradual end beginning in late 1989.[34] In the next few years the dissident labor movement was severely weakened by the arrest and imprisonment of the leaders of many dissident unions as well as many rank and file labor activists.[35] The Ministry of Labor, and other government offices, attempted to take most of the contentious issues outside the scope of permissible collective bargaining. The number of union members has declined significantly, and the independence and potency of the remaining unions was severely abridged. It is safe to conclude that the decline in labor disputes that occurred in this context can more reasonably be attributed to union suppression or a decline in union power than to the peaceful resolution of all employee concerns.

When former opposition leader Kim Young-Sam won a free and fair election and was inaugurated President of Korea in February, 1993, it marked the end of the military's long domination over the Korean government. In terms of political processes and individual liberties, the transition away from authoritarianism has been impressive, and the new administration has taken courageous steps to eliminate the tradition of corrupt influence peddling. In the area of labor policies, however, far less has changed. The government still gives priority to holding down labor costs, and it is still unwilling to legalize the dissident labor unions. In a move that was reminiscent of earlier administrations, the Kim Young-Sam administration even authorized the use of paramilitary troops to break up a strike and enforce an emergency mediation decree at a Hyundai Heavy Industries plant in Changwon (*Korea Economic Report*, August, 1993).[36]

The record of Korean labor relations shows that if the primary basis for labor peace is governmental intervention to suppress union organizing and collective action, any slippage in the government's ability or willingness to maintain its hard-line position could lead to another upsurge in labor conflict. On the other hand, it is now evident that the surge of labor conflict and the alleged breakdown of labor discipline between 1987 and 1989 (which at the time were widely reported as threatening the entire Korean economy with collapse) did not prevent the economy from enjoying fantastic growth and did not prevent even many of the companies that suffered strikes from attaining record profits. Even in that 'worst case', most employers were able to weather the storm without any serious damage, and to emerge with most of their authority intact. The fact that the new government has not fundamentally abandoned the old anti-labor policies, and that most employers have failed to give any meaningful role to the various possible channels for the peaceful expression and resolution of employee concerns, suggests that they have all quietly decided that the risk of overt conflict is not sufficiently serious to induce them to forego the advantages of reduced labor costs and the maintenance of unilateral prerogatives.

The lack of trust, loyalty and commitment engendered by the antagonistic labor relations system may emerge as a more serious problem than the occasional risk of disruptive collective action. As might be expected in a society where the traditional mass production model is predominant, government and business elites do not seem to consider the benefits of cooperative labor–management relations to be worth the costs in terms of higher wages or reduced managerial prerogatives. The behavioral patterns and expectations that arise in this context may prove to be a serious handicap for employers that are attempting to move into more advanced industries and to adopt production systems that depend on the cooperation and initiative of employees whose work cannot be subjected to direct supervision.

HRM practices and work systems

The HRM policies and practices that are said to contribute to the cooperative involvement of highly skilled, loyal and committed employees in achieving a flexible quality-oriented operating system include: careful selection, extensive socialization and continuous training in technical and interpersonal skills, broad job classifications and team-oriented assignments, measures to increase employment stability, and contingent compensation that reinforces cooperation and goal congruence (Kochan and Dyer, 1993). The pages that follow show that the HRM policies applied by elite Korean firms in advanced industries to their most valued employees do approximate that package, but it is much more common for employers to adopt policies that are designed to maximize output through standardized tasks at the lowest possible cost.

Recruitment and training The recruitment, selection, orientation, training and career development patterns for production workers of most Korean firms, and particularly in small and medium-sized enterprises (SMEs) and firms in labor-intensive industries, generally conform to the traditional mass production model.[37] Once hired, new production workers receive very little orientation or formal training, they are typically assigned to simple jobs that they can learn with only a few days of on-the-job training, and they are rarely rotated or given an opportunity to learn new jobs (Cho, 1987; K.C. Lee, 1990; O.J. Lee, 1990; Rodgers, 1993). The opportunities for internal promotions are very limited and labor turnover rates are very high.

At the opposite end of the spectrum, large corporations affiliated with the major *chaebol* apply HRM practices that conform, in some respects, to the Japanese-style lean production model to managerial employees and professionals (virtually all men with degrees from top-ranking universities).[38] Applicants are subjected to a rigorous competitive selection process. Those who are hired receive several weeks of orientation (primarily socialization into the corporate family), and then on-going training (in class rooms and/or on-the-job), mentoring, job rotations and systematic career development. Though the ideal is not always realized in practice, members of this elite core are expected to remain with the firm or with other affiliates of the same *chaebol* throughout their working careers, and to give the *chaebol* their intense loyalty and dedicated service.

Between the two extremes, there is an array of intermediate positions ranging from unskilled male production workers in marginal SMEs to skilled workers and technicians in sophisticated industries. Employers are looking for higher educational qualifications in their new recruits, and they are particularly anxious to hire graduates of vocational/technical high schools and two-year colleges. Employees who start out with higher technical qualifications are then given many opportunities for additional training from the employers which will qualify them for promotions into positions that had been traditionally reserved for college graduates.

Compensation policies Employers who wish to encourage long-term employment stability are often advised to adopt a compensation system that gives a heavy weight to seniority. In the Korean case, however, labor turnover rates have always been very high[39] despite the prevalence of a strong seniority wage system.[40] A closer examination of the data reveals why. Korean employers do indeed continue to give substantial seniority-based wage increases to professional and managerial personnel year after year until they retire. On the other hand, employers have not been willing to apply a full-fledged seniority-wage system to production workers to achieve a turnover inhibiting effect. The substantial wage increases given to production workers after their first and second years subsequently level off when their productivity ceases to improve (S.K. Kim, 1982; Bae and Form, 1986). In any case, there are virtually no production workers who attain high levels of seniority.

A related aspect of the Korean-style seniority-wage system is the 'living-wage' system whereby employees are granted many allowances that do not necessarily correspond to their relative productivity levels so that they will be able to meet their family obligations. Where in practice almost all production workers are young men or women (of any age) whose family obligations are (often unrealistically) deemed to be minimal, this system results in a discriminatory wage policy that has the actual effect of holding labor costs down. By basing a major portion of total compensation on family obligations (rather than work responsibilities or productivity), employers can pay employees with smaller family obligations less than their productivity levels would warrant.

The opposite of a seniority-based compensation system is one whereby pay increases, bonuses and promotions are effectively linked to individual merit, whether it be productivity, demonstrated competence or effort. Ironically, most Korean firms also fail to effectively implement individual merit-based reward systems. As a result, management experts argue that they do not attain the legitimizing and motivating effects that such a system would bring (S.K. Kim, 1982; T.K. Kim, 1991). Some claim that the reason why few Korean employers attempt to distinguish between members of the same cohort groups on the basis of individual merit is the scarcity of professional managers who know how to develop and administer valid performance appraisals (S.I. Park, 1988), but there may also be a more fundamental reason. It appears that Korean workers are even more opposed than workers in other countries to a compensation system that allows managers to distinguish, possibly on a discriminatory basis, among members of the same cohort groups. Korean managers also generally concede that a reward system that emphasizes distinctions between members of the same work group is inconsistent with the most basic principles of human relations.

In contrast to the Western idea that an individual should be accountable only for his/her own performance, Koreans are brought up to identify closely with, and share the fate of, the groups to which they belong (Brandt, 1987). Building on this cultural norm, most Korean employers encourage the formation of close relationships between members of the same work group. This is thought to enhance the employees' identification with the company, reduce turnover, and improve teamwork. As long as all members of a cohort group are treated equally, close personal and social relations develop that contribute to cooperation and informal learning of efficient work techniques. If an individual merit system could be administered fairly (no easy task!) it could have positive motivation and control effects, but these would still probably be outweighed by the negative effects; resentment, envy and suspicion among co-workers, a breakdown of teamwork, and general outrage against management. Most employers who have attempted to implement appraisal systems that differentiate among cohorts have had to contend with mutually antagonistic divisions in the workforce. Additionally, all except the most favored workers are likely to unite in their opposition to management (K.C. Lee, 1990).

Compensation systems that include a substantial contingent element payable in accordance with the achievement of certain designated criteria have been widely praised as a means of stimulating diligence and teamwork, reducing the uncertainty and contentiousness of wage bargaining, and increasing flexibility (Weitzman, 1984; Blinder, 1990; Y.V. Kim, 1991). Almost all large Korean companies include 'bonuses' as a substantial part of total compensation, but since the amounts to be paid are almost invariably fixed in advance, these 'bonuses' generally lack the virtues of contingent payments (Ito and Kang, 1989; Y.V. Kim, 1991; Kochan, 1991). The Korean Employers' Federation and the Ministry of Labor have recently been encouraging firms to adopt a genuinely contingent payment system, but employees are naturally unwilling to see conditions attached to what they have always received automatically. Some progressive employers have, therefore, attempted to introduce an additional contingent bonus on top of the existing automatic one. Even in this case, the contingency principle has not caught on because after the extra bonuses have been paid for several years the employees view them as fixed entitlements that can never be eliminated or reduced (Y.V. Kim, 1991).

There are several reasons why it has proven so difficult to implement contingent bonus systems in Korea. From the general literature on bonuses it is clear that for productivity bonuses to function effectively, the affected employees (1) should clearly understand and accept the conditions that must be met for bonuses to be paid, (2) they should understand how their own performance, and that of their co-workers, can contribute to meeting those conditions, and (3) they should be able to unequivocally verify whether the conditions have been met and whether the earned bonuses have been fully paid. Due to the typically antagonistic labor–management relations in Korea, and the absence of effective bilateral channels of communications, it is difficult for Korean employers and employees to agree on objective standards that can be attained by the employees' own performance. Perhaps most importantly, employees' representatives are invariably denied any means of independently verifying the company's financial reports so employees have learned not to believe claims that poor financial performance prevents the employer from paying. The net result is that Korean firms are rarely able to either effectively link individual performance to rewards (as explained above) or to introduce a genuinely contingent element into the overall compensation system.

Work organization and production processes   There is ample evidence that Korean firms in labor-intensive industries that are pursuing low-cost mass production strategies typically have hierarchical, non-participatory management structures and fragmented, low-skilled production processes (T.K. Kim, 1991; Kearney, 1991; K.C. Lee, 1990). According to the critics, tasks are deliberately simplified and subdivided so they can be performed by workers who have learned only a narrow range of specific tasks. Job rotation is rare and there is almost no coordination across functions. Technology is selected and utilized in a way to reduce labor costs and maximize control rather than to achieve greater flexibility. The work flow is irregular and unevenly distributed, and workers are often compelled to work in reckless disregard for quality or safety in order to compensate for continuous interruptions. Managers and engineers are usually completely separated from the shop floor and lack any understanding of the actual production processes.

Firms that conform to the above pattern are easy to criticize, and most researchers assume that the international competitiveness of such firms in Korea must be plummeting. That assumption is not correct. By introducing relatively simple labor-saving equipment and eliminating various forms of 'X-inefficiency', Korean firms in labor-intensive industries have been able, in recent years, to achieve tremendous improvements in productivity,[41] in product quality, and in the variety and technological sophistication of their product lines. These incremental improvements have been made without fundamentally altering the hierarchical management structure or the Taylorist form of work organization. Particularly in industries where the direct production workers are virtually all women, technical training programs are almost non-existent and there is almost no role for employee involvement in improving the production processes. Since improvements have still been possible, and since it appears that they have been sufficient (at least in the short run) to keep the firms viable, the mass production model may remain dominant for some time to come.

In capital/technology/knowledge intensive industries, a different pattern is emerging. There has traditionally been a wide gap in heavy industries between the predominantly male production workers and college-educated salarymen, but the gap is rapidly narrowing. There are still many workers in semi-skilled positions who receive little training and whose skills and productivity levels remain low, but most new recruits start out with higher qualifications and they receive much more advanced training from their employers. The militancy of the young workers has prompted many companies to go beyond what is economically rational in their haste to introduce expensive capital equipment that will reduce their need for skilled labor,[42] but still the demand for more and more highly skilled workers continues to grow.

The relatively greater demand in industry for young men with manual and technical (as opposed to academic) qualifications is cutting away at the traditional preference for college graduates. The shift to computer-assisted production processes is also causing the distinction between manual/technical skills and cognitive skills to disappear. Many salarymen with college degrees in engineering are being assigned to production facilities to set-up and maintain automated equipment, while some employees who have only graduated from vocational/technical high schools or two-year colleges are receiving training that enables them to step up to the level of regular college graduates. In a few continuous process industries (notably steel and petrochemicals) the high wage, continuous training and long-term employment policies apply to all regular employees, and the problems of adversarial labor–management relations have largely been avoided.

IR/HRM in the Korean Auto Industry

Labor–management relations in the major Korean auto companies

Having described the prevailing institutions and business norms in the ROK, we may now turn to the experience of the major firms in the auto industry. Prior to 1987, Hyundai Motors, Daewoo Motors and Kia Motors were about as different as three large companies in the same industry could be in their labor-relations postures. By its vigorous opposition to any sign of union organizing, Hyundai Motors was able to prevent a union from being established. A union had been organized in Daewoo Motors, but it was weak and compliant until 1985, at which time workers repudiated the union leaders and successfully waged a major strike. Since that time, labor–management relations have been consistently adversarial and the company has not been able to bring the union under its control. In Kia Motors, by contrast, a strong independent labor union was well-established but labor relations had been unusually harmonious since the early 1980s when labor and management were forced into a cooperative partnership as the only way to save the company from bankruptcy.

When the tumultuous labor struggle swept across the Korean economy in 1987, Hyundai Motors still attempted to prevent the formation of a union. As a result, it was engulfed in a particularly bitter and prolonged conflict until it reluctantly recognized a union. Since that time, Hyundai Motors has suffered a series of strikes. The climax came in January, 1992, when the company refused to distribute a portion of its higher than expected earnings to the workers in the form of an extra bonus. The company was unwilling to yield anything to resolve the strike, and the government ultimately sent paramilitary troops in to disperse the strikers. The union completely lost the strike, but the company has still not realized its hope of being able to control its operations without union interference. Daewoo Motors was also hit by repeated strikes and an endless string of minor confrontations with the union at its own plants, and it suffered further set-backs due to strikes in its affiliated suppliers. Only Kia Motors was able to maintain generally positive labor relations between 1987 and 1989. When Kia employees suspected that they were falling behind the other auto companies in wages in 1991 they also called a strike. The union's militant bargaining posture won a substantial wage increase for the workers, but cooperative operations were subsequently resumed.

The harmful effects attributable to negative labor relations in the Korean auto industry are emphasized in a case study based on Hyundai Motors (Kim and Lee, 1992). Hyundai has invested heavily in advanced capital equipment and it is struggling obsessively to increase its output, so the costs of lost production directly attributable to the strike were enormous. Aside from the strike itself, the company's calculations indicate that in the period leading up to the 1992 strike, sabotage and refusals to work overtime accounted for over 80 per cent of the shortfall of actual production below potential production. Even if Hyundai Motors has been able to beat the union into submission, its hard-line position may aggravate other subjective or less easily quantifiable problems.[43] Though the direction of causation is unclear, Hyundai Motors' antagonistic labor relations are linked to its continued adherence to a Fordist/Tayloristic production system, its inadequate training program (see below), and its lack of operational flexibility. Kim and

Lee also consider the company's efforts to implement a just-in-time production system to have been ineffective,[44] and they attribute the shortcomings to insufficiently skilled and poorly motivated employees and a general lack of trust between labor and management. They blame similar problems for what they consider the poor performance of the company's quality circles.[45] In the same vein, they report that Hyundai Motors is unable to realize the full benefits from the new technology that it has introduced because it uses it primarily to decrease the required labor input and to increase managerial control rather than to increase quality and flexibility. All these problems, say Kim and Lee, have contributed to Hyundai Motors' continuing inability to meet the rising world standards for quality.

Daewoo Motors has the same types of labor-relations problems that Hyundai Motors has experienced, with the added problem that it has been far less successful at maintaining effective managerial control.[46] Things are very different at Kia Motors, however.[47] In contrast to the family-owned conglomerates (*chaebol*), Kia Motors is run by a professional manager (Kim Seon-Hong) who claims to explicitly take the interests of the employees into account in determining corporate policies. Indeed, Kia's employees comprise the single largest block of shareholders. Survey evidence cited in Jo (1992) suggests that the employees at Kia trust their union more than the employees at Hyundai or Daewoo, but the union is also able to work more constructively with management. Kia's efforts to implement the 'best practice' techniques it learned from Mazda, including just-in-time operations, total quality control, quality circles and flexible modular production, are considered very successful, and it has consistently achieved very positive quality ratings. It is still too early to evaluate the labor-relations record at the Daewoo (Ship-Building) Tico factories, but it does not appear that they are plagued by the same problems as Daewoo Motors. All early reports of their operations are highly positive.

HRM practices in the Korean auto industry

The Korean auto industry occupies an intermediate position between the labor-intensive industries that depend on low-cost female workers and the capital/technology intensive continuous process industries in which labor costs are relatively insignificant. Since labor costs in the auto industry are a significant portion of the total cost of production, the companies must be concerned about holding down labor costs.[48] Due to the introduction of new technology and the increased emphasis on flexibility and product quality, however, Korean auto companies recognize that cultivating a highly skilled, committed work force capable of working cooperatively in integrated operations is more important than marginally reducing labor costs. The total compensation rates in all the Korean auto companies are very similar (Korea Labor Institute, 1989). It is difficult to evaluate the record of the companies in terms of long-term employment stability because the entire industry has expanded so much in recent years, but it appears that Kia Motors places greater emphasis than Hyundai Motors or Daewoo Motors on long-term employment and training, and it certainly has more integrated production processes (Jo, 1992). The auto industry faces the same difficulties that other industries face in relation to contingency payment schemes or individual merit-based wage and promotion schedules. In conformity with the national norms, all the companies pay substantial 'bonuses' with the amounts and the dates of payment fixed in advance, but as of 1992 none of them had yet implemented genuinely contingent profit-sharing plans. Insofar as many employees of Kia Motors have been granted shares of the company's stocks, however, they have an additional stake in its profitability. By way of contrast, Hyundai Motors chose to withstand a major strike in early 1992 rather than to grant larger bonuses based on higher than expected profits. Both Daewoo Motors and Kia Motors include an individual merit component in their pay and promotion programs, but first-line supervisors are said to submit uniformly positive performance appraisals that provide little basis for distinguishing among employees in order to avoid conflict (author interview with a Daewoo executive). The individual performance appraisal scheme used by Hyundai provoked serious conflict, and after the union was established it succeeded in forcing the company to abandon that program (Korea Labor Institute, 1989).

Information reported by Kim and Lee (1992) shows that Hyundai Motors relies primarily on traditional Fordist production processes characterized by a continuous assembly line rather than modular manufacturing and semi-autonomous work teams. Production workers at Hyundai reportedly do not ordinarily learn multiple skills. Though the company boasts elaborate educational facilities, only about 15 per cent of the employees receive systematic training each year. Kim and Lee argue that lack of 'know-how' acquired through long-term continuous service may be an even more serious problem, and they cite company data showing that more than 75 per cent of the Hyundai employees have remained at the company for less than five years (see Table 4.2).[49]

Table 4.2   Long-term employment among Hyundai
Motors production workers

Years	Number	Per cent
< 2 yrs	5 889	27.9
2–5 yrs	10 020	47.5
5–10 yrs	2 411	11.4
> 10 yrs	2 774	13.2

Source: Kim and Lee (1992) based on 1989 data
provided by Hyundai Motor Company.

Kim and Lee also cite comparative data to show that Korean auto companies provide fewer hours per year of training to their employees than their counterparts in other countries (see Table 4.3).

Table 4.3   Comparative data on employee training in the auto industry

	ROK (unit: hours/year)	Japan	USA	Europe
Production workers	33.3	108.0	31.8	115.1
Engineers	50.0	159.8	85.2	44.9
Line supervisor	67.3	123.5	84.0	57.6

Source: Hyun (1991) as cited by Kim and Lee (1992).

Though there are gaps and inconsistencies in the information on HRM practices and the production systems in the Korean auto companies, a few conclusions are warranted. In relation to production workers, the predominant practices of the Korean companies still seem closer to the traditional mass production model than to Japanese-style lean production; and they are even further removed from the flexible specialization or diversified quality production models. As noted earlier in this chapter, the Korean auto companies are attempting to move up-scale in their production and marketing strategies, so we might eventually expect IR/HRM policies designed to facilitate more cooperative and integrated operations. Until now, however, movement in that direction has been very uneven.

CONCLUSIONS AND IMPLICATIONS

The preceding pages show the labor relations and human resource management practices of Korean auto companies in the context of the national institutions and economy-wide norms. This final section will examine the extent to which the predominance of the traditional mass production paradigm inhibits firms from pursuing alternative strategies, and then, somewhat speculatively, will explore the prospects of the Korean auto industry in the light of the strategies that are realistically available to the major companies.

In the area of labor relations, institutions and expectations that grew up around the traditional low-cost mass production paradigm constitute a serious obstacle for firms that might wish to enlist labor unions as active partners in a mutually beneficial endeavor to raise skills, improve working conditions and boost quality and productivity. The harsh tactics used by the government and business elites in Korea to suppress independent labor unions and collective action may have been consistent with the needs of firms in labor-intensive industries whose competitiveness depended on a well-disciplined low-cost labor force, but they have contributed to the nearly universal distrust between labor and management. The prospects for labor–management cooperation suffered another set-back in the years since 1990 when the Korean Ministry of Labor returned, at least partially, to its traditional anti-labor policies. Labor unions now may be coopted and/or impotent, or they may be fiercely antagonistic, but it is very unusual for unions to play a meaningful role as partners who are able to generate the employees' cooperation by ensuring that their interests will be protected.

The preceding paragraph probably represents the most plausible interpretation of the evidence, but it is necessary to point out that another interpretation is possible. The record of Hyundai Motors is mixed, and a more positive labor-relations climate has emerged in some of the other auto companies (especially Kia Motors). Some reports indicate that the strong independent labor union in Kia Motors is helping in the transition to more integrated production processes. Insofar as Kia Motors has also achieved superior performance on many criteria, it is likely that the other companies will try to follow its example.

The prevailing norms and expectations probably do not limit the choices effectively available to firms in their HRM policies as narrowly as in their labor-relations policies. The most common pattern in Korea is undoubtedly that of firms in labor-intensive industries that are pursuing a strategy of low-cost mass production. By consistently implementing various HRM policies in a way that neglects all other objectives in order to maintain unilateral control and minimize labor costs, these firms have failed to promote employment stability, skill formation or positive employee involvement. At the opposite extreme, large Korean firms typically adhere to a pattern of benevolent paternalism that contributes to the internal skill formation, loyalty and commitment of professional and managerial employees. Though they are still the exception rather than the rule, some firms in capital and technology-intensive industries that compete more on the basis of quality and flexibility than on price are now also beginning to apply relatively similar HRM policies to their skilled production workers as well.

The record of firms throughout the Korean economy, and particularly those in the auto industry, allows us to evaluate which of the three models discussed earlier could be applied in Korea. It is evident that the traditional mass production model is still predominant in most industries. The ubiquitous criticism of the mass production paradigm in current academic literature should not blind us to the accomplishments of many Korean firms who continue to pursue mass production strategies. By introducing advanced capital equipment in new, large-scale facilities, and by producing in large volume to achieve optimum economies of scale, they have reached the world frontier in efficiency in many industries (Amsden, 1989; Porter, 1990; Ernst and O'Connor, 1992). The huge *chaebol* have kept pace with the nation's shifting comparative advantage away from labor-intensive industries that depend primarily on low labor costs to capital and technology-intensive industries that depend on a well-educated workforce capable of rapidly absorbing foreign-based technology. In most cases, however, they have not fundamentally revised their basic corporate strategy of competing in goods of acceptable quality produced in massive volume at a low per-unit cost. The auto companies may be trying harder than firms in other industries to overcome the limitations of traditional mass production, but they are trying to do so through incremental improvements without abandoning their basic cost-leadership strategy.

A system conforming to the diversified quality production (DQP) model would be difficult to implement in the Korean environment. As described earlier, DQP depends on a web of social and political institutions that effectively obligate all firms to adopt an array of practices that individual firms would be neither willing nor able to choose on their own initiative. Given the very different social and political institutions in the ROK (including the historical opposition of the military dictatorship to the labor movement and the continuing exclusion of labor from politics) and the virtual absence of effectively enforced regulations to protect workers and to ensure a meaningful role for strong, independent labor unions, any version of DQP that could be implemented in the ROK would deviate drastically from the North-West European model.[50]

The Korean environment offers much more fertile ground for lean production modelled after the leading Japanese firms. The experience of the Japanese transplants around the world show that the key elements of this system can be successfully transferred to diverse environments. Even many aspects of Japanese-style management practices that are often considered culturally based, and thus non-transferrable to the West, would be very familiar to Korean firms. Indeed, as noted above, the system of benevolent paternalism that virtually all large Korean firms apply in relation to their core white-collar personnel is very similar to the Japanese model. Many authors have also noted many parallels between the current legal and social institutions in the ROK (including the labor union struggle and the prevalence of enterprise-based unions) and those in Japan in earlier years (S.K. Kim, 1983; Kang, 1989; D.O. Kim, 1992). Most importantly, the most successful Korean auto companies all explicitly acknowledge the Japanese lean production model to be the most appropriate model for upgrading their own operations, and they have entered into close relationships with Japanese companies for assistance in making the transition.

The Korean auto companies still fall far short of the standards achieved by the leading Japanese firms, and it appears that several American auto companies have made more progress than any Korean company in adopting the essential aspects of lean production. The standards are continually rising, so newcomers such as the Korean companies will have to make rapid progress just to keep from falling behind. It is possible that the Korean companies' inability or unwillingness to fundamentally move beyond their mass production strategies, which is itself partially determined by national institutions and norms oriented around the mass production paradigm, will prevent them from catching up. Insofar as the leading Japanese companies developed lean production on the basis of their proficiency in mass production, however, it would not be prudent to conclude that Korean firms will not be able to do the same.

EPILOGUE

When the first draft of this article was written, most auto industry analysts dismissed the expansion plans of the Korean automobile manufacturers as absurdly grandiose. Since that time, the apparently reckless expansion has continued apace and it is now clear that the Republic of Korea will, for the foreseeable future, be one of the world's leading auto producing nations. There has been a steady advance, marked by the continuous introduction of new models, a higher proportion of locally designed and manufactured components, and less dependence on foreign technology. Furthermore, the recorded levels of labor productivity and product quality have continued to improve. The significance of such improvements is overwhelmed, however, by external factors favorable to the old cost-based competitive strategies, such as the opening of non-traditional markets (Eastern Europe, China, Southeast Asia) with price-sensitive consumers, and the price advantages handed to the Koreans by the exceedingly strong Japanese Yen. Whether the Koreans have substantially improved their international competitiveness on factors other than price remains an open question.

Turning to industrial relations institutions and human resource management practices at the enterprise level, the developments of the past few years have generally been favorable for some movement away from the exclusive emphasis on minimizing costs while maximizing hierarchical control (associated with standardized low-cost mass production), to a form of work organization that depends more on the cooperative involvement of highly skilled workers. Throughout the Korean economy, the number of labor disputes in 1993 and 1994 fell below the numbers that had prevailed even in the years before the 1987–89 surge of labor conflict, but wage rates have continued to rise dramatically. The particularly large rise in per-unit labor costs for blue-collar workers in the auto industry has only been partially offset by the rising skill and productivity levels, and reductions in labor turnover rates. Meanwhile, the traditionally antagonistic labor relations climate in Hyundai Motors and Daewoo Motors has given way to a much greater willingness of both labor and management to pursue mutual gains through increased productivity.

While the facts are clear regarding the expansion and market strategies of Korean auto manufacturers, and the improvements in industrial relations and work organization, any attempt to attribute the former to the latter would not be reasonable. There are many reasons unrelated to the level of skills or the prevailing form of work organization why it makes sense for the Korean auto makers to pursue a strategy of large-scale production of low-cost vehicles of acceptable quality, rather than a differentiation strategy focusing on limited scale production of premium-quality vehicles. External factors such as access to foreign markets and international exchange rates are probably more vital to the continued success of the Korean producers than further marginal improvements on the shop floor. What has set the Korean auto industry apart from anything in other developing or newly industrialized countries where foreign multinationals predominate is not the industrial relations institutions, business norms or forms of work organization at the shop floor. Instead, the decisive difference is probably the ability of the top managers in the huge Korean conglomerates (who are motivated more by their long-term ambitions than by any rational calculation of an acceptable rate of return on investments) to pour an enormous quantity of resources into the industry so that they will be ready to reap the benefits when favorable external conditions emerge.

Notes

1. In support of their argument that the automobile industry is being trans-
    formed from a traditional industry to a high-technology industry, Kenney
    and Florida (1993, p. 304) note that the leading producers must be able to
    'produce software, integrated circuits, programmable logic controllers, ad-
    vanced robotics and machine tools, and the artificial intelligence and soft-
    ware programs that run those various machines, tools and pieces of
    equipment'.
2. A lively debate has arisen as to whether there is any such thing as 'best prac-
    tice' which is applicable to all industries or to any specific industry (that is,
    the auto industry), and, if so, whether optimum performance for all firms in
    all countries may be achieved by implementing approximately the same
    package of technology and management practices (Piore and Sabel, 1984;
    Dertouzos, Lester and Solow, 1989; Womack, Jones and Roos, 1990; Mac-
    Duffie and Krafcik, 1992; Berggren, 1992 and 1993; Kenney and Florida,
    1993). While some scholars believe that the only firms in any country that
    will be able to maintain international competitiveness (at least in the auto
    industry) are those that conform closely to one particular best practice
    model, others insist that the practices associated with the currently fashion-
    able 'best practice model' are culture bound and that there is no generally
    applicable formula for superior performance. This article is written with
    that debate clearly in mind, but suggests that the experience of the Korean
    auto industry does not lend unequivocal support for either position.
3. A negative answer to the first question would give rise to several follow-up
    questions: First, is it absolutely impossible for Korean auto producers to
    achieve satisfactory performance if they do not make the transition from
    traditional mass production to a fundamentally different type of produc-
    tion system? Second, is it realistically possible for individual companies, in
    the Korean economic, social and political environment, to make the types
    of changes in their IR/HRM practices that would pave the way for a flex-
    ible quality-oriented production system? To anticipate what will be pre-
    sented below, Korean auto producers have been able to make sufficient
    improvements in productivity and quality to substantially increase sales
    even though they have not abandoned their predominantly mass produc-
    tion orientation. On the other hand, those who contend that flexible
    quality-oriented production systems depend on progressive IR/HRM
    institutions and norms can also find support for their views from the Kor-
    ean experience. As the Korean auto industry has advanced, changes have
    begun to appear in the national institutions and the practices of several
    auto manufacturers that are consistent with the requirements of a flexible
    quality-oriented production system.
4. While one cannot safely attribute the economic performance of the leading
    Korean auto companies to the type of IR/HRM practices the firms have
    implemented (because it is not possible to isolate the impact of such prac-
    tices from the impact of many other factors), data on the firms' economic
    performance does at least support a negative conclusion: the national and
    enterprise-level IR/HRM institutions and norms have not prevented the

leading Korean auto companies from achieving respectable results in terms of the traditional economic criteria.

5. Most of the information on the history of the Korean auto industry is taken from N.Y. Lee (1994), and from two shorter papers (N.Y. Lee, 1991; Lee and Cason, 1993). Additional information may be found in Green (1992), Amsden and Kim (1989), and Chang (1985).

6. By the late 1970s, the excessive and/or premature 'Big Push' into capital intensive industries had already lead to high inflation, a scarcity of investment capital for labor intensive industries, and a slow-down in economic growth. The situation was severely aggravated by the second oil shock, rising interest rates, a global recession and the political chaos surrounding the assassination of President Park. The domestic demand for autos plummeted, causing the overall capacity utilization ratio to drop to 26 per cent and forcing the three automobile manufacturers to the verge of bankruptcy (Green, 1992, p. 415). The technocrats who were elevated to prominence under Chun Doo-Hwan were determined to stabilize the economy along neo-classical lines. Some argued that Korea lacked any comparative advantage in manufacturing complete automobiles so it should concentrate first on an auto components industry. The policy-makers who ultimately prevailed tried to salvage the existing industry by merging the companies into a single dominant firm that would be able to achieve economies of scale. In the end two firms emerged: Hyundai Motors and the Daewoo–General Motors joint venture. Kia Motors was prohibited from making passenger cars until 1986.

7. The Korean auto industry was not able to climb back to its peak in exports until 1993, by which time it had widely diversified its export markets.

8. There has been much debate on whether the domestic markets can continue to absorb the expanding output of Korean auto companies. With only 80 cars per thousand people, the Korean markets would hardly seem saturated by international standards. Some auto industry representatives have suggested that the ratio could rise to 150 cars per thousand. On the other hand, to anyone who confronts the congested traffic in Seoul or Pusan, the thought of so many more cars in such a small crowded country is a horrible nightmare.

9. In their enthusiastic response to the rising competition among domestic auto companies, Korean consumers are becoming much more knowledgeable and demanding, with the result that all the firms are being pushed to upgrade the quality and technological sophistication of their products without increasing prices.

10. A *Wall Street Journal* article (2 March 1990) on the grandiose expansion plans of Korean auto producers reported a projected total capacity of 5 million vehicles by 1996 if the major Korean auto companies' plans (as of the time of writing) were realized. While that figure will have to be scaled back considerably, there is now no denying the rapid expansion that is actually underway.

11. The most remarkable new auto maker may be the subsidiary of Daewoo Ship-Building that produces the mini-car called the 'Citizen's Car', or Tico, which currently claims about 5 per cent of the Korean markets. In establishing this company, Daewoo entered into a comprehensive

technology transfer agreement with Suzuki for extensive assistance in installing an operating system very similar to what exists in Suzuki's Japanese facilities.

12. Hyundai Motors is the leader in research and development. It has major research centers near its production facilities in Ulsan, another research center near Seoul, and a third one in Ann Arbor, Michigan. Its expenditures on research and development in 1992 amounted to about US $311 million, approximately 4 per cent of its sales revenues (*Korea Economic Report*, September 1993).

13. Clifford (1992) reported that the amount of direct labor required to assemble the Elantra was from 16 to 17 hours. A conflicting figure appeared in a *Business Korea* article (November 1993) which reported a study (without any citation) indicating an average of 30.3 hours of labor to assemble a Hyundai car.

14. For comparative purposes, Jo reports that the defect rates in 1989 in General Motors, Ford and Toyota were 169, 149 and 117, respectively per 100 vehicles. The *Business Korea* article reported the defect rates in Ford and Toyota as 112 and 74, respectively.

15. It appears from some literature that a 'lean production' system is any one that has achieved a high degree of efficiency, but in other literature the appellation applies only to firms that have adopted a specific package of production processes. If a lean production system is simply one that is highly efficient, it is tautological to argue that lean production offers the key to increased efficiency. The lean production model, as discussed in this article, entails a rather large package of production processes and a corresponding set of IR/HRM practices (see below).

16. Williams *et al.* (1992) sharply criticize the methodology and conclusions in Womack *et al.* about the universal superiority of lean production. Berggren (1992a and 1992b) also criticizes the universalist claims for lean production and suggests that alternative production systems are superior in terms of important social criteria.

17. Streeck (1989; 1991a and 1991b) explains that though this type of production system is desirable for employers as well as for workers, it would not be viable without 'hard' social and political institutions that are able to effectively impose compulsory obligations on all employers.

18. Noting the difficulties that non-Japanese companies are encountering in their attempts to adopt lean production, Womack *et al.* wrote (p. 12), 'The companies that first mastered this system are all headquartered in one country – Japan.' In a later passage (p. 87), however, they insist that lean production is not the same as Japanese production because not all Japanese firms conform to the model and some non-Japanese firms do.

19. A portion of the immense literature on Japanese industrial relations, particularly as it relates to 'Japanese-style lean production' is reviewed in Rodgers (1993, pp. 142–65).

20. Employers that adhere to the lean production model do typically have relatively low labor costs per unit of output, and they do maintain an extremely effective form of labor control; but the mechanism of control is factors other than harsh supervision, extrinsic rewards, or machine pacing.

21. The literature on the foreign affiliates of Japanese multinationals, their ability to implement Japanese-style management practices, and their influence on host-country firms, is reviewed in Rodgers (1993, pp. 243–300).

22. Trevor (1983 and 1991) notes that Japanese managers often believe that Japanese management practices are superior to those in other countries, but that they are not transferrable to countries where employees lack a highly contextual system of shared values and close identification with the firm. See also Yoshino (1976).

23. Authors who assert that specific practices conforming to this model can be selectively adopted by Western firms include Taira (1990), Ouchi (1981) and Womack *et al.* (1990).

24. A rather thick assortment of statutes, regulations, decrees, ordinances and guidelines has accumulated over the years to govern various aspects of the employment relationship, but these regulations are not effectively enforced and/or they are interpreted in a way that falls so far below the industry norms that they have almost no practical effect (Rodgers, 1990).

25. The continuing antipathy of Korean employers to labor unions is evident from the results of a survey of 725 firms in various industries conducted by the Korea Chamber of Commerce and Industry, as reported in the *KEF Quarterly Review* (first quarter, 1990). The respondents indicated that the positive effects of labor unions in terms of employment stability and improved working conditions and communications between labor and management were more than offset by a decline in management authority, conflict between workers and their superiors, declining productivity, a drop in the affected firms' reliability and corporate reputation, and an overall decline in profits.

26. Between 1971 and 1981, government officials had referred all labor disputes in which the parties were unable to reach an agreement to mandatory arbitration, and until 1987 mandatory arbitration had remained the dominant dispute resolution procedure. Throughout that time, the low-wage policies promoted by the government were a major influence on the arbitrators' decisions.

27. The officially recorded number of labor disputes in 1960 jumped up to 256 from an annual average of 43 during the preceding five-year period; the peak in 1980 was 405 after an average in the preceding five-year period of 72; and the peak in 1987 was 3749 after an annual average in the preceding 5 years of 168.

28. The ILO Yearbook of Labour Statistics, 1993, gives the following official Ministry of Labor statistics showing the number of strikes and working days lost due to strikes:

Year	1987	1988	1989	1990	1991	1992
Strikes:	3749	1873	1616	322	234	235
Days lost (1000)	6946.9	5400.8	6351.4	4487.2	3257.6	1527.6

29. It would not be safe to conclude from Song's study that Korean labor unions will henceforth be able to drive compensation levels for their members above the levels of comparable non-unionized workers. The information presented in F.K. Park (1993) shows that the only official labor confederation (the Federation of Korean Trade Unions) has been quite moderate in their recommended wage demands since 1990. As it has turned out, the actual wage increases in the years 1989–91 have exceeded the bargained outcomes by almost 7 per cent per year. Where employers have to pay substantially above the amounts agreed upon in collective bargaining to attract the kind of employees they need, the wage effect of collective bargaining is minimal.

30. Using Freeman and Medoff's terminology, a significant union-wage effect would indicate that Korean unions have a 'monopoly face', but the lack of effective grievance procedures suggests that their 'voice face' is limited.

31. In theory, employees whose legal or contractual rights had been violated can seek redress through the Labor Committees (a form of labor courts), the civil courts, or the prosecutors' office. In practice, such institutions are so ineffective and inaccessible that employers can safely ignore their existence.

32. The only company that the author is aware of that has a disciplinary committee made up of an equal number of representatives of labor and for management is Kia Motors, but even in that case management has retained ultimate tie-breaking authority.

33. The conclusions in this paragraph are based primarily on questionnaires distributed to a small sample of personnel managers, supplemented by detailed interviews with scholars, consultants, managers, and labor activists conducted by the author between July and November, 1991.

34. The government's partial reversion to its traditional hard-line anti-labor stance coincided with the merger of opposition leader Kim Young-Sam and his supporters into President Roh Tae-Woo's party to form a ruling party with a solid majority.

35. Support for this conclusion may be found in Asia Watch, 1990; Kochan, 1991; Ogle, 1990, *KRIC Monthly Newsletter* (various issues); and *Hankyoreh Shinmun* (various issues). The author also benefited from conversations with Harry Kamberis (AAFLI representative in Seoul), Choi Jang-jip (Korea University professor), Phi Jung-sun (editor of the *KRIC Newsletter*), and many others between May and November, 1991.

36. Though this labor dispute did not directly involve Hyundai Motors, labor relations in all the member companies in the Hyundai Group are coordinated by top management in the Group's central offices. Similarly, a dissident labor council coordinates the activities of the member companies' unions.

37. Though these categories do not represent the glamorous side of the Korean economy, their role should not be under-estimated. Traditional labor-intensive industries such as textiles, garments, footwear and simple consumer electronics are still the most important industries in terms of employment and sales revenues (Porter, 1990; Young, 1990); and they

have consistently met or exceeded the national averages both in productivity increases and profitability. Women constitute over a third of the employed workforce in Korea, and employers are increasingly looking to married women for a solution to their acute labor shortages. And with the growing tendency of large corporations to out-source sub-assemblies and components, and to sub-contract labor-intensive functions, firms with under 300 employees (SMEs) have come to account for over two-thirds of the total manufacturing workforce (Small and Medium Industry Promotion Corporation, 1988).

38. Insofar as full conformity to the lean production model implies vertical and horizontal integration encompassing the entire workforce, and a high degree of involvement for employees at all levels, the Korean version that applies only to the elite core deviates substantially from the ideal.

39. Data presented by Y.V. Kim (1991, Table 3) shows that in 1989, 61.6 per cent of all private-sector male employees in Korea had been with their employer for less than five years, whereas in Japan and the USA (in 1982 and 1979) only 27.3 per cent and 50.0 per cent, respectively, of private-sector male employees had been with their present employers for such a short time. For employees with at least 20 years of seniority with the same employer, the percentages were 1.8 per cent in Korea, 25.1 per cent in Japan and 12.4 per cent in the USA. Ministry of Labor statistics show a recent decline in the labor turnover rate, however. Whereas the aggregate labor turnover rates had ranged from 4.0 per cent to 6.5 per cent per month in earlier years, they have dropped in recent years to between 2.5 per cent and 4 per cent per month.

40. Survey evidence indicates that Korean personnel managers consistently rate seniority as the most important factor in determining individual wage rates (S.K. Kim, 1982), and the wage differential between new recruits and employees with at least 20 years seniority is even higher in Korea than in Japan (S.I. Park, 1980).

41. The quintessential female-dominated labor-intensive industries in the ROK are garments and footwear. Though they account for a declining portion of total employment, the index of labor productivity for production workers in the two industries rose from 100 in 1981 to 211 and 395, respectively, by 1990. The six-fold expansion of output of Korean electronics manufacturers in the same period was aided by an increase in the index of productivity for production workers from 100 to 470 (Rodgers, 1993, Table 2.5, calculated from Korea Productivity Center data).

42. Labor unions in Korea have rarely objected to the introduction of labor-saving technology. Indeed, labor leaders generally say that this is not an issue that concerns them because the demand for labor (and especially skilled labor) in manufacturing industries has always exceeded the supply (Kim and Lee, 1992).

43. Kim and Lee's negative evaluation of Hyundai Motors' attempt to implement advanced production processes, and their attribution of the poor outcomes to antagonistic labor relations, is inherently subjective. Where they do make explicit comparisons, the standard usually is the world leader (Toyota Motors) rather than the local or global industry norms. As noted below, the operations or Kia Motors were evaluated much more

positively by different authors, but this may reflect the different authors' perspective as much as the objective differences among the companies.

44. There are actually two distinct aspects to a 'just-in-time' production system; internal and external. Kim and Lee's criticism relates primarily to the internal processes within the final assembly plant. In the cultivation of suppliers who reliably supply components that meet the very high quality standards that it requires directly to the work stations where they are needed on a just-in-time basis, Hyundai is far ahead of the other Korean auto companies (author interviews with an executive in Hyundai affiliate that supplies components to Hyundai Motors and with Nae-Young Lee). On the role of Hyundai Motors in building up the suppliers and sub-contractors, see also Amsden (1989).

45. Not everyone agrees with Kim and Lee's negative assessment of Hyundai's quality circles. In an interview with the author of this article, the managing director of a joint venture between Hyundai Motors and a major American company that produces state-of-the-art components for the auto industry said that the effective quality control circles program introduced by Hyundai was a model for the American parent company.

46. This conclusion is based on the author's interviews in 1991 with Oles Gadacz (staff writer for *Automotive News*), and with anonymous officers of Daewoo Motors and an affiliated supplier of Hyundai Motors.

47. The information about Kia Motors comes from the Korea Labor Institute (1989), Kim and Park (1992), and Jo (1992).

48. The Korean Labor Institute study (1989) presents data showing that labor costs amounted to only 5.1 per cent of the total cost of production at Hyundai, 11.4 per cent at Daewoo and 8.9 per cent at Kia, but it does not give detailed information of the basis of the calculation. It is likely that these unusually low numbers primarily reflect the low degree of vertical integration by the final assemblers. The share going to labor would obviously be higher if the labor costs of components suppliers were also taken into account. Aggregate data published by the Korean Ministry of Labor show that nominal compensation levels in the transport equipment manufacturing sector as a whole more than doubled between 1987 and 1990, and they continue to rise at a rapid rate.

49. The average length of service has evidently increased since 1989. Company data (also cited by Kim and Lee) show that as of April, 1992, the average length of service was 5.3 years. The high proportion of employees in the 1989 table who had been with the company only a short time reflects the recent expansion, and is not direct evidence of high turnover rates.

50. The flexible specialization model does not seem to depend as heavily as DQP on a thick web of German or Swedish-style social and political institutions, but it would also be difficult to implement in the Korean environment. Firms pursuing the flexible specialization model must be able to draw on a vibrant craft tradition. Prior to its industrialization, Korea was a non-mechanized agricultural society with only a very minimal indigenous craft tradition, and it still lacks a well-developed vocational training and apprenticeship system. Manual and technical skills are accorded low social prestige, and the tradition of independent craftsmen motivated by an intense pride in workmanship receives little recognition.

References

Abo, Tetsuo (1990) 'New Technology and Manpower Utilization in Japanese Automobile Firms in Japan and their Plants in the United States'. Paper presented at a conference on 'Technology and Labor in the Automotive Industry', Korea Automobile Manufacturers' Association, Seoul.

Amsden, Alice (1989) *Asia's Next Giant: South Korea and Late Industrialization* (New York: Oxford University Press).

Amsden, Alice and Linsu Kim (1989) 'A Comparative Analysis of Local and Transnational Corporations in the Korean Automobile Industry', in Dong-Ki Kim and Linsu Kim (eds), *Management Behind Industrialization: Readings in Korean Business* (Seoul: Korea University Press).

Asia Watch (1990) *Retreat from Reform: Labor Rights and Freedom of Expression in South Korea* (Washington, DC: Asia Watch Committee).

Asia Watch (1986) *Human Rights in Korea* (Washington, DC: Asia Watch Committee).

Bae, Kyu-Han and William Form (1986) 'Payment Strategy in South Korea's Advanced Economic Sector', *American Sociological Review*, 5, p. 1.

Berggren, Christian (1992) *Alternatives to Lean Production: Work Organization in the Swedish Auto Industry* (Ithaca, NY: ILR Press, Cornell University).

Berggren, Christian (1993) 'Lean Production – The End of History?' in *Work, Employment and Society*, 7:2, pp. 163–188.

Blinder, Alan (ed.) (1990) *Paying for Productivity: A Look at the Evidence* (Washington, DC: Brookings Institute).

Bognanno, M.F. (1988) 'Korea's Industrial Relations at the Turning Point'. Seoul: Korea Development Institute, working paper no. 8816.

Bognanno, M.F. and S.K. Kim (1981) 'Collective Bargaining in Korea'. Industrial Relations Research Association, Proceedings of the 34th Annual Meeting.

Brandt, V.S.R. (1987) 'Korea', in George C. Lodge and Ezra Vogel (eds), *Ideology and National Competitiveness: An Analysis of Nine Countries* (Boston, MA: Harvard Business School Press).

Chang, Dal-Joon (1985) *Economic Control and Political Authoritarianism: The Role of Japanese Corporations in Korean Politics, 1965–1979* (Seoul: Sogang University Press).

Cho, Soon-Kyung (1987) 'How Cheap is "Cheap Labor?" The Dilemmas of Export-Led Industrialization', Ph.D. dissertation, University of California at Berkeley.

Clifford, Mark (1994) *Troubled Tiger: Businessmen, Bureaucrats, and Generals in South Korea* (Armonk, New York: M.E. Sharpe).

Clifford, Mark (1992) 'Can-do, Make-do: Hyundai Motors Pins Hopes on Automation', *Far Eastern Economic Review*, 5 March, p. 53.

Dertouzos, Michael, Richard Lester and Robert Solow (1989) *Made in America: Regaining the Productive Edge* (New York: Harper Perennial).

Dore, Ronald (1990) 'Two Kinds of Rigidity: Corporate Communities and Collectivism', in Renato Brunetta and Carlo Dell'Aringa (eds), *Labor Relations and Economic Performance* (Basingstoke: Macmillan).

Ernst, Dieter and David O'Connor (1992) *Competing in Electronics: The Experience of Newly Industrializing Economies* (Paris: Organization for Economic Cooperation & Development).

Freeman, Richard and James Medoff (1984) *What Do Unions Do?* (New York: Basic Books).

Fucini, Joseph and Suzi Fucini (1990) *Working for the Japanese: Inside Mazda's American Auto Plant* (New York: Free Press).

Green, Andrew (1992) 'South Korea's Automobile Industry: Development and Prospects', *Asian Survey*, 32(5) pp. 411–28.

Gwynne, Robert (1991) 'New Horizons? The Third World Motor Vehicle Industry in an International Framework', in Christopher Law (ed.), *Restructuring the Global Automobile Industry: National and Regional Impacts* (London and New York: Routledge).

Hirschman, Albert O. (1970) *Exit, Voice and Loyalty: Responses to Decline in Firms, Organizations and States* (Cambridge, Mass: Harvard University Press).

Humphrey, John (1982) *Capitalist Control and Workers' Struggle in the Brazilian Auto Industry* (Princeton: Princeton University Press).

Itagaki, Hiroshi (1989) 'Application–Adaptation Problems in Japanese Automobile and Electronics Plants in the USA', in Kazuo Shibagaki, Malcolm Trevor and Tetsuo Abo (eds), *Japanese and European Management: Their International Adaptability* (Tokyo: University of Tokyo Press).

Ito, Takatoshi and Kyoungsik Kang (1989) 'Bonuses, Overtime and Employment: Korea vs. Japan', *Journal of Japanese and International Economics*, 3, pp. 424–50.

Jo, Hyung-Je (1992) 'A Study of the Production System of the Korean Automobile Industry', Ph.D. dissertation, Seoul National University (in Korean).

Jones, Daniel T. and James P. Womack (1985) 'Developing Countries and the Future of the Automobile Industry', *World Development*, 13(3) pp. 393–407.

Kang, T.W. (1989) *Is Korea the Next Japan? Understanding the Structure, Strategy and Tactics of America's Next Competitor* (New York: Free Press).

Kearney, Robert P. (1991) *The Warrior Worker: The Challenge of the Korean Way of Working* (New York: Henry Holt).

Kenney, Martin and Richard Florida (1993) *Beyond Mass Production: The Japanese System and its Transfer to the US* (New York & Oxford: Oxford University Press).

Kim, D.O. (1993) 'Analysis of Labor Disputes in Korea and Japan: The Search for an Alternative Model', *European Sociological Review*, 9:2, pp. 139–54.

Kim, Hwan-Suk and Young-Hee Lee (1992) 'Korea's Labor Relations and Technology Change: A Case Study of Hyundai Motors'. Korea Advanced Institute of Science and Technology, working paper (in Korean).

Kim, Kihwan and Danny Leipziger (1993) 'Korea: The Case of Effective Government-Led Development', in Peter Petri (ed.), *The Lessons of East Asia: Common Foundations of East Asian Success* (Washington, DC: The World Bank).

Kim, S.K. (1989) 'Societal Changes and New Labor–Management Relations.' Paper presented at the Korea Development Institute Policy Forum on 'Private–Public Interaction Toward Economic Development', Seoul: 10–17 April 1989.

Kim, S.K. (1988) 'Labor–Management Relations in Korea'. East Asia Economics Policy Studies No. 4 (Honolulu: East–West Center).

Kim, S.K. (1983) 'Is the Japanese System of Lifetime Employment Applicable to a Developing Country Such as Korea?' Seoul: Korea Development Institute, working paper series, 82–03.

Kim, S.K. (1982) 'Employment, Wages and Manpower Policies in Korea: The Issues'. Seoul: Korea Development Institute, working paper series, 82–4.

Kim, Tai-Ki (1991) 'Production and Human Resource Management: The Case of Production Workers in Large Companies'. Seoul: Korea Labor Institute, mimeograph (in Korean).

Kim, T.K. and J.S. Park (1992) *Case Studies on Labor Relations in Large Manufacturing Companies*. Seoul: Korea Labor Institute (in Korean).

Kim, Young-Vae (1991) 'Several Issues to Promote Sound Labor Relations in Korea: Current Situation and Prospects'. Paper presented on 25 March, at an International Labour Office Conference.

Kitschelt, Herbert (1991) 'Industrial Governance Structures, Innovation Strategies, and the Case of Japan: Sectoral or Cross National Comparative Analysis?' *International Organization*, 45(4) pp. 453–93.

Kochan, Thomas A. (1991) 'Industrial Relations and Human Resource Policy in Korea: Options for Continued Reform'. Paper presented in Honolulu at the East–West Center Conference on political economy and public policy in Korea.

Kochan, Thomas and Lee Dyer (1993) 'Managing Transformational Change: The Role of Human Resource Professionals', *The International Journal of Human Resources Management*, 4(3) pp. 569–90.

Korea Employers' Federation (1990) *KEF Quarterly Review*, First Quarter.

Korea Labor Institute (1989) *Labor Relations in the Auto Industry*. Seoul (in Korean).

Krafcik, John (1989) 'A First Look at Performance Levels at New Entrant Assembly Plants', Cambridge, MA, MIT International Motor Vehicle Program (MIT: IMVP International Policy Forum working paper).

Lee, K.C. (1990) 'Labor Control of Female Production Workers: Case Study Research of a Company in the Electronics Industry', M.S. thesis, Ehwa Women's University, Seoul (in Korean).

Lee, Ok-Jie (1990) 'Labor Control and Labor Protest in the South Korean Textile Industry, 1945–1985', Ph.D. dissertation, University of Wisconsin, Madison.

Lee, N.Y. (1994) 'The Politics of Industrial Restructuring: A Comparison of the Auto Industry in South Korea and Mexico.', Ph.D. dissertation University of Wisconsin, Madison.

Lee, N.Y. (1991) 'The Politics of Industrial Restructuring: The Case of the South Korean Auto Industry'. Paper prepared for the Annual Midwest Political Science Association Meeting, Chicago, 18–20 April 1991.

Lee, N.Y. and Jeffrey Cason (1993) 'Automobile Commodity Chains in NICs: A Comparison of South Korea, Mexico and Brazil', In Gary Gereffi and Miguel Korzeniewicz (eds), *Commodity Chains and Global Capitalism* (Westport, Conn: Greenwood Press).

MacDuffie, J.P. and J. Krafcik (1992) 'Integrating Technology and Human Resources for High Performance Manufacturing: Evidence from the International Auto Industry', in Thomas Kochan and Michael Useem (eds), *Transforming Organizations* (New York: Oxford University Press).

Mishel, Lawrence and Paula Voos (eds) (1991) *Unions and Economic Performance* (Washington, DC: Economic Policy Institute).

Ogle, George (1990) *South Korea: Dissent within the Economic Miracle* (New Jersey: Zed Books).

Oliver, Nick and Barry Wilkinson (1988) *The Japanization of British Industry* (New York: Basil Blackwell).

Ouchi, William (1981) *Theory Z: How American Business Can Meet the Japanese Challenge* (Reading, Mass: Addison-Wesley).

Park, F.K. (1993) 'Industrial Relations in Transition: Recent Developments and Prospects', in Lawrence Krause and Fun-Koo Park (eds), *Social Issues in Korea: Korean and American Perspectives* (Seoul: Korea Development Institute).

Park, S.I. (1988) Case studies on Korean companies appearing in Barry Wilkinson (ed.), *Technical Change, Work Organization and Pay: Lessons from Asia* (Geneva: ILO).

Park, S.I. (1980) 'Wages in Korea: Determination of the Wage Levels and the Wage Structure in a Dualistic Labor Market', Ph.D. dissertation, Cornell University.

Park, Young-Ki (1991) 'South Korea', chapter to be published in *Law and Practice of Industrial Relations in East and South East Asia* (Melbourne, Australia: University of Melbourne Press).

Piore, Michael and Charles Sabel (1984) *The Second Industrial Divide: Possibilities for Prosperity* (New York: Basic Books).

Porter, Michael (1990) *The Competitive Advantage of Nations* (New York: Free Press).

Rodgers, R.A. (1993) 'Industrial Relations Policies and Practices in the Republic of Korea in a Time of Rapid Change: The Influence of American and Japanese Invested Transnational Corporations', Ph.D. dissertation, University of Wisconsin, Madison.

Rodgers, R.A. (1990) 'An Exclusionary Labor Regime Under Pressure: The Changes in Labor Relations in the Republic of Korea since mid-1987', *UCLA Pacific Basin Law Journal*, 8(1) pp. 91–162.

Shaiken, Harley (1990) *Mexico in the Global Economy: High Technology and Work Organization in Export Industries*. Center for US –Mexican Studies, Monograph Series, 33: University of California, San Diego.

Small and Medium Industry Promotion Corporation (1988) 'An Overview of Small and Medium Industry in Korea', Seoul.

Song, Ho-Kun (1991) 'What Do Unions Do in Authoritarian Korea? Union Effects on the Quality of Working Life'. Paper presented at an international conference on the role of labor in 21st Century Korea, Sungshil University, Seoul.

Sorge, Arndt (1991) 'Strategic Fit and Societal Effect: Interpreting Cross-National Comparisons of Technology, Organization and Human Resources', *Organization Studies*, 12, pp. 161–90.

Streeck, Wolfgang (1991a) 'On the Institutional Conditions of Diversified Quality Production', in Egon Matzner and Wolfgang Streeck (eds), *Beyond Keynesianism: The Socio-Economics of Production and Full Employment* (Brookfield, Vermont: Edward Elgar).

Streeck, Wolfgang (1991b) 'Industrial Relations in a Changing Western Europe'. Paper presented at the Plenary Session of the Third European Regional Congress of the International Industrial Relations Association, Bari and Napoli, Italy (23–26 September).

Streeck, Wolfgang (1989) 'Skills and the Limits of Neo-Liberalism: The Enterprise of the Future as a Place of Learning', *Work, Employment and Society*, 3, pp. 90–104.

Streeck, Wolfgang (1987) 'Industrial Relations and Industrial Change: The Restructuring of the World Automobile Industry in the 1970s', *Economic and Industrial Democracy*, 8.

Taira, Koji (1990) 'From Americanization of Japan to Japanization of America in HRM/IR'. *Proceedings of the Forty-Third Annual Meeting*, Industrial Relations Research Association Series (Madison, Wisconsin: IRRA).

Trevor, Malcolm (1991) 'The Overseas Strategies of Japanese Corporations', *Annals of the American Academy of Political and Social Sciences* (January).

Trevor, Malcolm (1989) 'Japanese Managers and British Staffs: A Comparison of Relations and Expectations in Blue Collar and White Collar Firms', in Kazuo Shibagaki, Malcolm Trevor and Tetsuo Abo (eds), *Japanese and European Management: Their International Adaptability* (Tokyo: University of Tokyo Press).

Trevor, Malcolm (1983) *Japan's Reluctant Multinationals* (London: Francis Pinter).

Weitzman, Martin (1984) *The Share Economy: Conquering Inflation* (Cambridge, Mass: Harvard University Press).

White, Michael and Malcolm Trevor (1983) *Under Japanese Management* (Oxford: Heinemann).

Williams, K., C. Haslam, J. Williams, T. Cutler, A. Adcroft and S. Johal (1992) 'Against Lean Production'. Polytechnic of East London Occasional Papers on Business, Economy and Society.

Womack, James, Daniel Jones and Daniel Roos (1990) *The Machine that Changed the World* (New York: Rawson Associates).

Womack, James and Daniel Jones (1989) 'The New Entrants: Searching for a Role in the World', Cambridge, MA: MIT, International Motor Vehicle Program. International Policy Forum (working paper).

Young, Soo-Gil (1990) 'New Challenges to the Korean Economy and their International Implications'. Paper presented at an Asia Forum Researchers Conference, Tokyo (Korea Development Institute, working paper No. 9004).

Yoshino, Michael Y. (1976) *Japan's Multinational Enterprises* (Cambridge, Mass: Harvard University Press).

News Sources

Automotive News (various issues).
Business Korea (various issues).
Far Eastern Economic Review (various issues).
Hankyoreh Shinmun (various issues).
Korea Economic Report (various issues).
Korea Labor (Korea Research and Information Center Newsletter).

5 Competition, Flexibility, and Industrial Ascent: The Thai Auto Industry[†]

Frederic C. Deyo

INTRODUCTION

Late twentieth-century global industrial restructuring poses new challenges to developing countries seeking upward mobility in the global economy. This is particularly true of middle-income countries where rising labor costs are no longer competitive in global markets as lower-cost producers like Indonesia and China enter export markets. The developmental imperative for semi-industrial countries such as these is to restructure into higher-value-added market niches where competitiveness derives as much from process efficiences, product flexibility and quality as from low labor costs. The relative stability of country rankings in the international division of labor may in part be understood as a consequence of the difficulty in realizing this imperative.

A confluence of recent changes in the global political-economy has made the transition doubly difficult. First, the globalization of neoliberal trade and investment regimes intensifies global competitive pressures facing local firms by opening domestic markets to foreign competition and deregulating foreign investment. At the same time, heightened pressures for a reduced state economic role have placed new constraints on the ability of states to lead the process of restructuring through industrial policy.

In addition, the global ascendancy of post-Fordist industrial production systems creates new requirements for improved internal flexibility in order to foster higher levels of quality and process efficiencies, rapid product development and product diversification. As noted in the Introduction to this volume, this change calls into question the possibilities for continued industrial ascent by developing countries. First,

† This research was supported by grants from the Thailand–US Educational Foundation (The Fulbright Program) and from the Social Science Research Council. The paper has benefited from helpful suggestions by Rick Doner and Steve Frenkel.

flexible production greatly increases requisite demands for close proximity to a dense supplier base, a good transportation and communications infrastructure, and a highly educated workforce, particularly in technical and engineering areas. Such requisites are infrequently achieved in developing countries. Second, the literature on flexible production suggests a very close linkage between flexibility on the one hand, and human resource practices and labor relations on the other (Kochan and Katz, 1988, pp. 46, 469). Inasmuch as flexible production demands involvement of shopfloor employees in inspection, training and quality improvement, it is argued, employment practices must foster trust, cooperation, commitment and identification with the firm and its success. Such employee attitudes, and the employment practices which encourage them, are often difficult to achieve in the context of low-trust, authoritarian industrial relations climates so common in developing countries.

To the extent such requisites place developing countries at a relative disadvantage in attracting new investment and in competing in world markets, the increasing dominance of flexible production practices might be expected to consign those countries to stagnant, standard-production industrial niches in global markets (Hoffman and Kaplinski, 1988; Womack, Jones and Roos, 1990). But it is clear that the auto industries of a number of developing countries, including Mexico, South Korea and Thailand, have continued to prosper and grow in recent years. The following case study of the Thai auto industry helps to explain this counter-intuitive finding.

THE THAI CASE

The Thai economy has grown rapidly over recent years, averaging around 10 per cent during the late 1980s. Much of this growth derived from dramatic gains in manufacturing output, which expanded at roughly 15 per cent during this period. Pursuant to a strategy of export-oriented industrialization, light manufacturing has been the pace-setter for economic growth. This sector, led by textiles, wearing apparel, jewelry, toys and electronics assembly, has until now competed successfully in world markets on the basis of low domestic production costs (Bank of Thailand, 1992). Rapid growth in light manufacturing exports during the second half of the 1980s derived in part from an inflow of Japanese direct foreign investment following rapid appreciation of the Yen during 1985–88. An additional impetus to growth was loss of eligibility on the part of the East Asian NICs for preferential tariff treatment under the Generalized System of Preferences (GSP) in OECD countries, and a resultant outflow of investment from those countries to South-East Asia to take advantage of continued eligibility there.

But as new lower-cost producers have emerged as strong world market competitors, Thai manufacturers find themselves in what might be termed a 'sandwich trap'. Pushed out of cheap labor export niches from below by the next wave of industrial exporters, manufacturers find it necessary to move up to higher-technology, higher-value-added niches. At the same time, however, such a shift is impeded by strong competition from above, particularly from South Korea, Taiwan, Hong Kong and Singapore, countries whose industries began this transition during the 1970s.

Thai industry faces other impediments to restructuring as well. First, both domestic and international pressures have induced dramatic liberalization of trade and domestic economic policy. Indeed, the very choice of an export-oriented-industrialization development strategy encourages trade liberalization both to increase competitiveness in local industry and to gain access to foreign markets.

Liberalization has in turn dramatically boosted Thailand's trade dependency and competitive vulnerability. Between 1986 and 1991, trade as a percentage of GDP rose from 60 per cent to 80 per cent (*The Nation* 29 September 1992). International trade liberalization, associated especially with the General Agreement on Tariffs and Trade (GATT) and the ASEAN Free Trade Agreement (AFTA), has further intensified international competitive pressures.

Second, increasing labor costs have reduced the competitiveness of manufactured exports. Between 1980 and 1988, the real earnings of manufacturing employees increased by 6.4 per cent per year, with continuing rapid gains in the 1990s (World Bank, 1991, cited in Brown and Frenkel, 1993). While labor cost increases have stemmed mainly from growing shortages, particularly for skilled workers, these pressures have been further exacerbated by a number of politically-driven legislative enactments beginning in the early 1970s. During the 1973–76 period of popular political mobilization and collapse of military rule, minimum wage and liberal labor legislation imposed new costs on employers while at the same time encouraging the formation of trade unions in large firms. As employers struggled to resist unionization and to postpone compliance with wage and benefit legislation, strikes escalated, increasing from 19 903 working days lost in 1972 to 425 430 in 1974. Even after reversion to military rule in 1976, minimum wage and employee benefits requirements, culminating in 1990 in a new Social Security Act which codified and expanded a number of state-mandated work benefits and programs for employees, are widely seen by employers as further impediments to success in global markets.

Finally, liberalization pressures, including demands for privatization of state enterprise, have diminished the possibilities for extensive reliance on state-led industrial restructuring through selective trade protection, promotional industrial targeting, labor market intervention, state enterprise, and other instruments of state strategy which played so important a role in the older NICs. This undercutting of state developmental capacity has occurred at precisely a time when new pressures for industrial restructuring may impose new tasks on states to support firms in their efforts to enhance flexibility and absorb new technology.

In response to these heightened competitive pressures, employers have more often adopted cost-cutting measures than longer-term programs to restructure into higher-value-added, skill and technology-intensive activities. The latter alternative is clearly essential for the long term. More immediate considerations, however, have encouraged cost-cutting measures which often impede productivity and quality-enhancing enterprise reforms. These include the competitive disadvantage facing firms which take on long-term investments in human resource, technology and other areas in contrast to other firms which do not; the possibility of appropriation of the benefits of those investments by competing firms which, for example, hire away newly-trained workers and thus acquire not only their training but the technological innovations they have learned as well; and the difficulties in adopting participatory shop-floor practices in the context of low-trust and confrontational labor–management relations.

The welfare consequences of cost-cutting strategies are most immediately seen in trends toward labor casualization, sweat-shop subcontracting, and widespread violation of minimum wage and social security laws, especially in light, labor-intensive export industries (Sussangkarn, 1990; Yosamornsunton, 1986). There are indications that both casualization and subcontracting have increased in recent years (Arom Pongpa-ngan Foundation, 1988 and 1991; Zuesongham and Charoenloet, 1993; Brown and Frenkel, 1993). Survey data collected for the Thai Development Research Institute show that the ratio of temporary and contract workers outside the Bangkok area has increased significantly over the 1980s (Charsombut, 1990, p. 19). A 1988 labor survey in the Bangkok area found that about 19 per cent of factory workers were employed on a temporary basis (Samakkitham 1990,

p. 32). A more focused survey of four industrial areas near Bangkok showed a rapid increase in the number of firms employing at least 20 per cent of their workforce on a temporary basis between 1983 and 1988. In one industrial area, over 60 per cent of all workers were employed on a temporary basis in 31 surveyed factories (Piriyarangsan and Poonpanich, 1992). In many cases, the decision to make increased use of temporary workers has followed labor disputes or worker efforts to establish labor unions. Whether or not processes of informalization and casualization have actually deepened in recent years (see Brown and Frenkel, 1993 regarding earlier years), it is clear that such strategies remain the predominant response to growing competitive pressures.

Casualization and short-term cost-cutting strategies are not particularly surprising in wearing apparel, toys, electronics assembly and other labor-intensive standardized-production industries. But what of more capital and technology-intensive industries where immediate cost pressures are accompanied by other, sometimes competing, requirements for costly reforms supportive of flexible, high-quality production? An examination of competitive pressures and responses in the auto industry suggests how and with what degree of success managers in such industries have sought to balance sometimes divergent competitive demands.

INDUSTRIAL UPGRADING IN THE THAI AUTO INDUSTRY

The expansion and development of automobile and other engineering-based industries plays an important role in industrial restructuring. In the past, these industries have not been directly supportive of export-development. Indeed, they have often required continuing import protection, a carry-over from earlier import-substitution periods. Rather, their importance has derived from their multiple beneficial linkages to a large number of other industries, their attractiveness to foreign investors, and their capacity to act as conduits for foreign technology with subsequent spin-offs to local supplier and other firms.

In addition, regional trade liberalization has led to growing realization of the potential role of automotive exports as part of more general industrial restructuring. Thai-Hino Industry Co., an assembler and distributor of buses and trucks, seeks to export vehicle components to ASEAN countries within three years (*The Nation*, 17 February 1993), while Opel, Toyota and Mitsubishi plan to increase auto exports to other countries in the region (*Bangkok Post*, 28 August 1993; 11 September 1992; 18 February 1993). For these varied reasons, the Thai government has promoted the vehicle industry, which now employs tens of thousands of people in assembly and supplier plants.

Under liberalization, the Thai auto industry has faced growing international competition in both export and domestic markets. Beginning in 1991, auto import tariffs were substantially reduced. Similar tariff reductions were effected for completely knocked down units (CKDs). And a previous decision to incrementally increase required domestic content for locally assembled cars was rescinded, although suppliers of auto parts continue to enjoy moderate protection under existing domestic-content regulation. As a result, both auto assemblers and suppliers have faced increased trade pressure during recent years as seen in rising imports and declining exports (*The Nation*, 31 October 1992; 7 December 1992; *AsiaWeek*, 24 February 1993, p. 58).

Even before trade liberalization, the Thai auto industry faced a highly fragmented market, with many import-sheltered assemblers producing several vehicle models each for a small market (at 323 961 total vehicles in 1993; Far Eastern Economic Review, *Asia 1994 Yearbook*), thus boosting relative production costs (for discussion, see Doner, 1991, Chapter 8; also *The Nation*, 5 April 1993). Despite rapid expansion in the domestic auto market, this problem may increase under recent proposals to permit entry of additional assemblers in Thailand (*The Nation*, 5 April 1993). Consequently, production runs tend to be small, and economies of scale minimal.

The net impact of import liberalization on assembler companies is not yet clear. On the one hand, these firms experience intensified competition especially in up-scale auto niches, thus further reducing attainable economies of scale. But on the other hand, several important opportunities present themselves. First, trade liberalization presents an opportunity for increased economies of scale through greater concentration on a few product models, relying on imports of other models to fill out local sales offerings. Second, Thailand's rapidly expanding domestic auto market, which grew at 36 per cent during 1991–92, along with increasing export possibilities, opens up further potential for longer production runs. Third, under pressure of Yen appreciation, the need for assured access to ASEAN domestic markets, and increasing labor costs in South Korea and Taiwan, Japanese companies are increasingly transplanting integrated production systems and recently-developed technologies to South East Asia. This process of 'global localization', (Hill and Lee, forthcoming) which recreates within regional markets the tight systems of interfirm cooperation previously confined to Japan, is in part compromised by a 1988 ASEAN regional 'complementarity' scheme under which auto and other companies are encouraged to manufacture major components and parts for all their regional production in single countries (thus dispersing production across the region), and then export them to assembly sites in other ASEAN countries without incurring substantial tariffs. This scheme, already utilized by Toyota and Mitsubishi, complements the ASEAN Free Trade Agreement (AFTA) in permitting enhanced economies of scale through the consolidation of regional production activities. Under both global localization and regional complementation scenarios, opportunities present themselves for continued development of national automobile industries.

Parts suppliers are more directly affected by trade liberalization. First, increasing imports reduce the potential for rapid growth in local assembly operations, the primary source of demand for original equipment. Second, the freezing and probable future relaxation of domestic content requirements, enables and encourages assemblers to purchase OEM parts regionally, thus increasing quality pressure on local suppliers. This possibility is reinforced by the regional complementation scheme. Third, a proliferation of vehicle models, both imported and domestic, further fragments the market for replacement parts, thus reducing economies of scale among parts manufacturers. The complementation scheme may be expected to alter these possibilities in two ways; first by further heightening regional competition in parts manufacture, and second by enhancing economies of scale on the part of firms which increasingly serve the regional auto industry.

Trade liberalization, market fragmentation, local globalization and regional production complementarity have pushed local auto companies into head-on regional competition to attract or retain high-value-added production. Countries which are able to meet the stringent human resource, R&D, infrastructural and other requirements of flexible production will be able to take advantage of new opportunities created by the dispersion of Japanese auto production to South East Asia. Losers in this competition will probably, under complementation, remain producers of standardized low-value-added parts alongside inexpensive vehicles for domestic markets.

Assemblers

The assembly industry comprises 13 auto and pick-up producers, most of which retain equity or technology-licensing relationships with Japanese auto companies. While the assemblers have sought to meet

foreign competition through organizational and operational upgrading, such reforms have been uneven in depth and effectiveness. Without
exception, the reforms have included human resource innovations in
the areas of worker training and shopfloor problem-solving and improvement.

Toyota Motor Company (Thailand) has been perhaps the most aggressive of the Thai auto assemblers in upgrading domestic operations
both to maintain its premier position in the domestic auto market and
to expand exports. Following successful reduction of defects per vehicle
from 14 in 1990 to only two in 1992 (*Bangkok Post*, 21 February 1993,
Motoring, p. 8), the company was designated by Toyota (Japan) as the
second-highest-quality Toyota international affiliate, after Toyota
USA. Most recently, Toyota announced establishment of a new 1.7 billion Baht (approx US $68 million) Technical and Service Training Cen-
ter along with future plans to set up a research and development center
for product development in Thailand. Such upgrading has been reflected as well in human resource policy. A close look at personnel policy at a progressive company like Toyota suggests what may be the
upper limit to near-term human resource restructuring in Thai industry.

As Toyota has sought aggressively to improve production efficiency
and quality, it has continued to develop many of the human resource
practices utilized by the parent company in Japan. Like several other
auto assemblers, Toyota helps fund public and community educational
and training programs. Toyota's most visible commitment in this regard is its support for a large training program for automotive engineering and research at Chulalongkorn University's Engineering
School. In addition, the company has established an Automotive Vocational Development Center to train workers in production processes
and auto technology. Within the company's plants themselves, shopfloor quality circles meet at least weekly to deal with production problems. A very active suggestion system, butressed by generous awards,
produces about 200 useable ideas per month. Worker appraisals, the
basis for year-end bonus determination, give 30 per cent weight to *kaizen* activities for constant improvement. Workers are responsible for
in-process inspection, and are expected to stop the line if problems cannot be resolved immediately. Toyota regularly rotates workers among
jobs and production lines as requirements dictate, although the requisite multiskilling for such flexible deployment is greatly reduced under
Toyota's continuing efforts at job simplification.

* * *

The literature on flexible production suggests that shop-floor flexibility of the sort found at Toyota requires substantial workforce commitment, cooperation and involvement and that these, in turn, presuppose progressive, trust-engendering employment practices and harmonious industrial relations. In part, Toyota does conform to the expected pattern. Once part of the 'Toyota Team', regular workers and skilled workers above them enjoy at least limited promotional opportunities. For these workers, wages and benefits are substantially better than those enjoyed in other companies. And the company provides a wide range of recreational, educational and other facilities and programs offered at the parent company in Japan.

But this is not to say Toyota labor relations are entirely harmonious. Indeed, rather serious problems arise from other employment practices at this company. Following 1989 legislation which restricted the use of temporary labor, Toyota turned to contract labor mainly to provide a full year's probation before upgrading workers to regular status. The shorter four-month legal maximum for retaining workers in temporary status, it was felt, did not permit adequate time for careful worker screening and assessment. Toyota, like most other companies, uses temporary contract workers for a large number of entry-level production jobs. These workers, who usually have some experience in the industry, often with suppliers, are hired for a fixed term to do specific jobs, and receive little on-the-job training. At the end of their contract, they may or may not be hired as permanent Toyota workers. Reliance on contract labor for many of the lesser skilled assembly jobs accomplishes several things. First, it reduces labor costs. Contract workers are obtained from an independent placement company through which Toyota pays referred workers. This company provides inferior work benefits and pays Toyota's contract workers less than regular Toyota workers. Second, use of contract labor fosters external (numerical) flexibility to meet market fluctuations. But third, contract labor supports internal flexibility as well insofar as it permits careful selection of regular workers, creates strong motivation to work hard to earn permanent status, and yields moderately strong skills among entry-level workers without requiring substantial company training. This is an important consideration in view of relatively high rates of labor turnover and correspondingly high training costs.

The use of contract workers, who account for around 25 per cent of the workers on most lines, has produced conflict and divisions in the workforce as contract workers have sought wage and benefit parity with regular workers. And it has been opposed by regular workers and their union as a threat to their own job security and wages. To Toyota's credit, it must be noted that the morale problems created by reliance on contract labor has prompted plans to reduce and ultimately eliminate the contract labor system. Following the 1995 opening of Toyota's new Gateway City assembly plant in Chachoengsao, most contract workers will either be terminated or given regular status, despite the higher costs in wages and benefits such a move will entail, and despite the fact that the other companies will continue to enjoy the cost advantages of contract labor.

A further problem is that rapid company growth has forced Toyota to resort to external hiring of large numbers of workers at technical, engineering and managerial levels, thus compromising the motivational benefits of internal labor markets and corporate socialization.

In addition, corporate loyalty and identification is undercut by Toyota's foreign ownership and top management, as well as by the relatively short reward-time-horizon of many Thai workers, engineers and managers for whom slow, seniority-based career increments up the promotional ladder do not adequately compensate for immediate deprivation. Partly for this reason, Toyota Thailand offers higher starting pay and a shorter pay ladder than does its parent company in Japan.

Finally, preservation of payroll flexibility through the use of large, variable bonuses creates a continuing potential for labor conflict and mistrust. Given Toyota's somewhat acrimonous relations with its union, which it fought strenuously to avoid at the outset of the initial unionization drive, this potential is further increased.

Given these various morale-compromising problems, it is not surprising that Toyota's workforce turnover rate, although low by Thai standards, is relatively high. While much of this instability is accounted for by temporary and contract workers, quit rates among engineers and middle-level management have become a concern as well.

But having said all this, it is important to note that despite an industrial relations climate marked by some degree of conflict and mistrust, Toyota has achieved national and regional recognition for its high quality, flexible production. We return to this important point below.

Mitsubishi

Perhaps more typical of the difficult transition to flexible, quality production among Thai auto assemblers is the case of MSC Sittipol (hereafter referred to as Mitsubishi), manufacturer of Mitsubishi cars, pick-ups and trucks. With the exception of the Lancer, exported to

Canada as the 'Colt', Mitsubishi's vehicles are sold primarily in the domestic market. Like Toyota, Mitsubishi has sought to become more productive in domestic and export markets through improved quality and productivity, and has sought to introduce new training programs, quality circles, suggestion systems and other supportive human resource practices.

The company's successes have been mixed. On the one hand, Toyota now views Mitsubishi as a credible threat to its own fledgling export program, given Mitsubishi's diversified and integrated Thai operations. And, indeed, the Lancer/Colt is Thailand's most successful export model.

On the other hand, Mitsubishi has faced some important problems in its upgrading efforts. At the Lat Krabang plant outside Bangkok, where Galants, pick-ups and large trucks have been assembled, large numbers of vehicles have in past years been routinely diverted from production lines for correction of paint and trim defects. Indeed, at a second Thai Mitsubishi plant, quality problems at one time forced a halt in Colt exports to Canada. Quality circles were instituted in the truck plant, but were abandoned in the auto and pick-up plant because of lack of worker cooperation. And an extensive training program for new engineers is undermined by high quit rates among engineers, a very large per cent of whom leave the company within two years.

In part, these problems are attributable to Mitsubishi's more traditional personnel practices than those found at Toyota. A somewhat larger proportion of production workers are contract workers, hired 'on loan' from suppliers. More middle-level staff are externally hired, with a corresponding de-emphasis on internal promotions. Status distinctions, displayed by elaborate hat and uniform color coding, are especially sharp and tend to inhibit joint problem-solving in quality circles. Beyond midday meals, transportation and uniforms, few non-mandatory employee benefits or social programs are provided.

* * *

The experience at Toyota and Mitsubishi suggests several tentative conclusions. First, major assembly firms have made substantial efforts to meet new competitive pressures through improved quality, efficiency and flexibility. As part of their efforts to achieve these goals, they have introduced corresponding reforms in human resource efforts.

More uneven and less successful, however, have been efforts to introduce employment practices in areas of worker welfare and security often assumed to be important for flexibility reforms. But it is important to note that resulting morale problems, union conflict, and even high turnover rates have not seriously undercut efforts to enhance flexibility and quality. Toyota, after all, has received international recognition for quality and efficiency. For its part, Mitsubishi has been relatively successful in exporting economy cars to North America. At Mitsubishi, however, conflict and low morale, eventuating in somewhat higher quit rates than at Toyota, have undercut efforts to improve flexibility and quality. It may be that in this case a critical threshold was reached beyond which lack of trust and low morale do begin to compromise flexibility. We return to this question below.

Suppliers

As in Japan, Thai auto assemblers outsource a very large percentage of their parts and components. This means that a weakness in the supplier base will have very serious consequences for assemblers. Mitsubishi, for example, has had to abandon its just-in-time supplier delivery system for many locally sourced parts and components because of poor supplier reliability. The company will try to reduce this problem through relocation of 12 of its parts and components supplier companies to its new engine and auto assembly location in Chon Buri.

By and large, Japanese firms dominate supplier niches for complex, high-value-added parts and components, while Thai firms are more often in lower-level supplier niches. The explicit tiering of suppliers by assembler firms is seen most clearly at Toyota. Firms participating in Toyota's supplier 'Cooperation Club' are assigned to one of two tiers. Tier-A suppliers, which produce complex or safety-related parts and components, are generally Japanese or Japanese joint-venture firms. Tier-B suppliers, more often Thai, produce simpler parts. The initial consignment of Thai firms to tier-B reflects the need on the part of assemblers to quickly meet domestic content requirements without sacrificing quality. The easiest way to do this is by assisting established Japanese supplier companies to produce parts in Thailand. Thai government encouragement for Japanese auto parts suppliers to establish operations in Thailand (*The Nation*, 20 February 1993) further exacerbates this problem.

A related explanation for the over-representation of Thai firms among tier-B suppliers is the vicious cycle associated with the initial relegation to low-end supplier niches. Assembler pressures for flexibility and innovation are moderated among tier-B firms. Minimal economies of scale, a product of market fragmentation and relatively small parts orders from assemblers, have led suppliers to seek supply relations with more than one assembler, a practice that is encouraged by the assemblers themselves in recognition of this problem. In many cases, the parts supplied to various assemblers are very similar, thus enhancing economies of scale. Where parts interchangeability is not possible but where greater economies of scale are present, assemblers are assigned dedicated production lines, thus reducing the need to cross-train line workers. To the extent that Japanese auto firms have helped to upgrade technical capability among supplier firms, such efforts have been limited to simple skills relating to instrument reading, welding, lathe operations and the like (interview with Director, Mitsubishi Training Center, 1992).

In part too, however, lack of participation by Thai firms in Tier-A activities reflects the difficulty of instituting comprehensive training and participation schemes in the context of capital scarcity and severe status differentiation in small Thai firms, alongside a general lack of government support for small and medium-sized enterprise. The tendency in such firms to continue to focus on cost-cutting through low wages and minimum benefits to at least a partial exclusion of investments in human resource development may well consign these firms to lower rungs in the auto industry for some years to come.

CONTENDING COMPETITIVE DEMANDS AND MIXED STRATEGIES

It was noted earlier that competition places multiple demands on companies, and that these various demands push in sometimes very different directions. Immediate pressures encourage short-term cost-cutting through casualization, labor-law evasion, efforts to cut wages and benefits, and sweat-shop outsourcing. Pressures for internal flexibility and improved quality highlight the need for increased investments in human resource, technology and organizational reforms, along with technology assistance to suppliers. Such reforms may be appropriate and even superior in the long term, but are costly and risky in the short run.

It is clear that firms in fact must and do simultaneously pursue several seemingly discordant strategies in meeting the diverse competitive pressures they face. But do these strategies conflict? More specifically, do cost-cutting strategies which create conflict and mistrust undermine flexibility-enhancing measures which would seem to require cooperation and high morale?

The resolution of this dilemma is fourfold. First, it should not be immediately assumed that these different strategies cannot be combined in mutually complementary ways. Second, it may be that reliance on seemingly incompatible competitive strategies may be facilitated by processes of institutional segregation which permit their simultaneous operation. Third, internal flexibility strategies may not in fact require high levels of morale, and may not be entirely incompatible with harsh employment practices, authoritarian management and low-trust industrial relations. And related to this third possibility is a fourth: that there may be subtypes or hybrids of internal flexibilization which have not been noted in a flexible production literature centering largely on Japan, Europe and North America, but which are likely to occur in more authoritarian political systems such as those in East and South East Asia.

The first of these alternatives, that seemingly incompatible strategies can sometimes be combined, is most readily suggested by the use of skilled contract labor. Contract workers, after all, comprise a temporary workforce with generally varied experience and skills in the industry, thus providing both internal and external flexibilities.

The second alternatives, that of the institutional segregation of diverse strategies, is suggested by the parallel and simultaneous existence within larger firms of multiple labor systems as well as by tiered subcontracting. Casual, contract and regular employees work together on the shop floor under quite different employment conditions. At the outset of employment, new workers are made aware of the tenure, conditions and security of their employment as well as differences among the three categories of employment. Demarcation among the categories is further reinforced by differences in cap color codes, extent of participation in quality circles and other work activities, and types of assigned duties. Whether this instance of institutional segregation has been entirely successful, given Toyota's decision to phase out contract work in the face of morale problems and conflict, is uncertain.

Perhaps a better example of institutionally segregated multi-strategies is provided by parts subcontracting chains. Tier-A suppliers are given strong encouragement to develop in-house design capabilities, high quality standards, and a highly trained workforce required for flexible production. Lower-tier suppliers, while encouraged to improve quality, are pushed to a relatively greater extent to reduce costs. This difference in the nature of supplier assistance and support by assembly companies like Toyota tends to reinforce existing differences in competitive strategies across supplier chain tiers.

The third alternative, that internal flexibility does not in fact require the degree of morale and commitment hitherto assumed in much of the literature, is in part challenged by the abandonment of contract labor at Toyota and by the training and quality circle difficulties at Mitsubishi. On the other hand, the very fact that Toyota and, to a lesser degree, Mitsubishi are internationally competitive despite extensive reliance on temporary labor and fairly autocratic management suggests that internal flexibility may not in fact place as stringent demands on industrial relations systems and employment practices as one might infer from the literature on Japanese and European industry.

This consideration brings us to the fourth alternative: that of hybrids or subtypes of flexibility. If existing models of internal flexibility presuppose substantial pro-active participation on the part of shopfloor workers, other flexibility models may not. To this possibility we now turn.

Autocratic Flexibility and Industrial Ascent

Work reforms in the auto industries of Germany and Sweden have fostered high levels of quality, shopfloor innovation and product flexibility (see Streeck, 1991; Turner, 1991). In many cases, such flexibility has been accompanied by substantial pro-active shopfloor participation in production decisions and trouble-shooting, extending even to direct business dealings with suppliers. In the case of Japan, more circumscribed forms of participation flowed from managerial success in containing worker militancy in the 1950s and in encouraging the subsequent emergence of more enterprise-focused company unions. In both cases, the early necessity for management to accommodate labor demands in developing strategies to meet increasing competitive pressures precluded simple cost-cutting responses and pushed companies toward progressive human resource strategies and participative forms of flexible production.

But what of Thailand and other developing countries which have lacked the democratic traditions and strong unions which have encouraged participative flexibility in the industrialized countries? Union density in Thailand's private enterprise sector is roughly 3 per cent (Brown and Frenkel, 1993). Where private sector unions do exist, as at major auto assemblers like Toyota, their weakness and exclusion from participation in decision-making render them unable to play the role of Japanese enterprise unions in supporting participatory flexible production systems (Poonpanich, 1991).

Labor's weakness outside the state enterprise sector is in part a consequence of political exclusion, discouragement and occasional repression (Satitniramai, 1992). In part, too, it flows from employer strategies of casualization in many industry sectors. To the extent that workers have been successful in pushing for improved wages, benefits and work conditions, their successes have been confined to the political arena. The legislative victories they have won in that arena, however, have brought few substantial improvements at their places of work in the face of a lack of managerial compliance or of effective government enforcement. Indeed, such victories have only provided further impetus to casualization and other cost-cutting strategies. Where unions have played an effective role, as in the state enterprise sector, the government has acted directly to contain them.

In such a context, management has substantial discretion in determining appropriate responses to intensified competition. In most instances, this response has been one of cost-cutting in labor and other areas. To the extent that internal flexibility and innovation-fostering subcontracting have been instituted, their form has been determined less by labor politics than by competitive requirements themselves. By consequence, inclusion of workers in decision-making and in the sharing of material benefits has been far more limited. In the case of the auto industry, contract and regular workers participate in quality circles and other deliberative fora for improving quality and productivity. But observation of the discussion that occurs in these meetings suggests more a process of question-and-answer than of joint problem-solving. Similarly, the wage and benefits gap separating production workers and managers in these firms is far wider than that obtaining in European or Japanese firms.

The rather top-down model of flexibility obtaining in Thai auto firms shares with its more participatory counterparts in Europe and Japan multiskilling, in-process inspection, just-in-time production and delivery, and constant improvement in process and product. It differs substantially, however, in its internal politics, in that the exclusionary internal flexibility of Thai firms favors management autocracy over worker participation in 'flexibly' organizing work and deploying labor.

Is such exclusionary, autocratic flexibility less competitive than more participatory forms found elsewhere? Perhaps not. First, it may well be that managerially-imposed flexible production systems which attend mainly to the dictates of market competition and only minimally to social and political considerations, is highly competitive. This possibility strongly suggests itself in the context of increasing economic pressures and Japanese competition in European automobile markets, where employers are now seeking to rescind some of their earlier concession in matters of employment security, worker participation and human-centered work organization (Rehder, 1992; *Wall Street Journal*, 4 November 1993). A second consideration relates more specifically to developing countries like Thailand. Following Amsden (1989), one may distinguish between cases of industrial advance based on continued product and process innovation in industrially advanced countries and firms, and other cases in which such advance is rooted in local adaptation and implementation of technologies and processes developed elsewhere. While Amsden argues that the latter case centers competitive success on shopfloor implementation, she suggests that the major role is played by engineers, rather than by production workers *per se*. And, indeed, it may well be that the international transfer and adoption of already debugged product and process technology is less dependent on pro-active problem-solving and involvement on the part of production workers than would be the case for innovation in new products and processes. From this it follows that factories in developing countries relying mainly on technologies developed abroad, say in Japan, may require less of their shopfloor workers and for this reason find it less necessary to institute the sorts of trust and commitment-supporting employment practices associated with more innovative flexible-production systems found elsewhere.

Of course, there may well be a critical threshold beyond which autocracy, mistrust and conflict vitiate efforts to introduce the degree of participation and job involvement required by all variants of flexible production, as seen especially in the failure of quality circles and the continuing loss of trained engineers at Mitsubishi. Short of this threshold, however, autocratic low-trust flexibility may provide an adequate basis for competitive success in the second-tier technology-dependent automotive industries of developing countries.

The Role of the State in Industrial Restructuring

Even if flexible production in Thailand assumes a truncated autocratic form, its successful diffusion may, in the absence of the dense private-sector governance network of organizations and associations found in Taiwan, presuppose government support. Such support must, at a minimum, include provision of a supportive educational and physical infrastructure. In addition, it should discourage self-defeating cost-cutting labor strategies by establishing for all firms a minimal set of requirements relating to wages, benefits and work conditions. It should provide substantial encouragement for flexibility-enhancing long-term company investments in training, technological development, process flexibility and necessary work reforms. And it should give added support for the development of a high-quality, flexible domestic supplier base serving auto and other key industries.

Most of these forms of support were evident during the period of rapid industrial restructuring in South Korea and Singapore during the 1970s. This was especially true in the area of human capital investments in education and training, and, in Singapore, in that of housing and public health. In addition, discouragement of continued cost-cutting strategies took a rather dramatic form when the Singapore government urged major wage increases in 1979–81 precisely to discourage further investment in labor-intensive production in favor of investment in higher-value-added, high-skill activities (Deyo, 1989, pp. 140–2). At the same time, the government provided incentives for company training programs, vigorously supported quality circles, works' councils and worker-involvement programs, encouraged loyalty-enhancing personnel policies, and instituted a wide range of state-supported technical education and training activities. In many cases, Singapore has systematically controlled and utilized trade unions in support of such productivity, quality enhancement and other industrial improvement campaigns. While tight government controls over unions has somewhat reduced their legitimacy among rank and file workers, they have also served to reduce labor turnover (thus encouraging training) through joint-provision of a wide range of employee benefits and welfare programs with government and employers.

While Singapore's restructuring programs have not been uniformly successful, the contrast with the relative passivity of the Thai government in this area is striking. Especially apparent is the Thai failure to actively encourage human resource development. In 1990, 42 per cent of Thai production workers lacked more than an elementary education (Labor Department, 1991), thus substantially reducing the ranks of middle-school graduates, the backbone of productivity and skill enhancement programs in Singapore, Taiwan and South Korea. Indeed, the percentage of secondary-school-aged youth actually enrolled in secondary school is the lowest in the region, lower even than in China or Indonesia (*The Economist*, 16 November 1991, p. 18). A new program to extend mandatory education from the current six years to nine years will be helpful, although there is little evidence of a significant shift in priorities toward vocational education.

In the area of training, there have been some important initiatives. In response to repeated calls from the Thai Garment Manufacturers' Association (TGMA) (*The Nation*, 22 February 1993), the Ministry of Industry is considering the establishment of a textile industry development institute to assist in technology and human resource development (*Bangkok Post*, 22 February 1993, B-26). In addition, modest government support will be offered to the TGMA for research and training activities for member firms and to assist in the creation of four textile training institutes outside Bangkok to accomodate firms wishing to locate in upcountry provinces.

Somewhat better has been government support for local supplier firms in auto and other industries. Under a program (BUILD) instituted in 1989, incentives and support have been provided both directly to local supplier companies, and indirectly through efforts to persuade contracting firms to provide greater technical assistance to their subcontractors.

But, more generally, provision and support for training has been inadequate. Under the major national vocational training program, operated by the Department of Labor's Institute for Skill Development, only 24 000 workers received government-sponsored vocational training in 1990, much of it in non-technical areas (Labour Department, 1991). And research and development expenditures in Thailand are substantially lower than corresponding levels in such countries as South Korea and Taiwan (*The Nation*, 28 November 1992).

Similarly inadequate has been state planning and investment in physical infrastructure. Poor quality telephone and telecommunications services, and an extremely over-burdened transportation system in particular, impede efforts to enhance supplier–contractor communications and just-in-time delivery practices.

Cost-cutting labor strategies have been encouraged by lack of enforcement of existing labor legislation, alongside public commitment to a labor policy emphasizing cost-restraint and anti-unionism while often neglecting organizational and work reforms needed for improved quality and flexibility.

In part by consequence of a general lack of state support for industrial restructuring, effective flexible production systems have thus far been confined primarily to large, resourceful, and mainly foreign companies like Toyota, Thai-Hino, Sony and Mitsubishi (see Siengthai, 1988). These companies, along with a few exceptional domestic firms such as those in the Siam Cement group, have been able to absorb the short-term competitive disadvantages of increased expenditures in training, research and development, and work reorganization. And indeed in some instances, as in the case of Toyota's funding of the automotive engineering program at Chulalongkorn University, these firms have taken a lead role in investing in industrially supportive public infrastructure. The very exceptionality of these programs points to the inability of most firms to assume the burden of such public investments and to the corresponding need for far greater government assistance.

More generally, lack of systematic and sustained government encouragement for the upgrading of industry has led to growing pessimism among government, international and academic specialists regarding possibilities for a high-tech industrial future for Thailand.

References

Amsden, Alice (1989) *Asia's New Giant: South Korea and Late Industrialization* (New York: Oxford University Press).
Arom Pongpa-ngan Foundation (APF) (1991) 'Temporary Employment After the Ministry of Interior Decree No. 11' (Bangkok: APF). (in Thai).
——(1988) 'Labour Relations Strategies and Short-Term Employment', manuscript (Bangkok: APF).
AsiaWeek, published in Hong Kong.
Bank of Thailand (1992) *Quarterly Bulletin*, 32 (1) (March) p. 23.
Bangkok Post (various issues), published in Bangkok, Thailand.
Brown, Andrew and Steve Frenkel (1993) 'Union Unevenness and Insecurity in Thailand', in S. Frenkel (ed.), *Organized Labour in the Asia–Pacific Region: A Comparative Analysis of Trade Unionism in Nine Countries* (Ithaca: ILR Press).
Charsombut, Pradit (1990) *Provincial Industry Labor Market* (Bangkok: Thailand Development Research Institute Foundation).
Deyo, Frederic (1989) *Beneath the Miracle: Labor Subordination in the New Asian Industrialism* (Berkeley: University of California Press).
Doner, Richard (1991) *Driving a Bargain: Automobile Industrialization and Japanese Firms in Southeast Asia* (Berkeley, CA: University of California Press).
The Economist, November 1991: 18 (London).
Far Eastern Economic Review (1994) *Asia 1994 Yearbook*, 35th edn.
Hill, Richard Child and Yong Joo Lee (forthcoming), in Leslie Sklair (ed.), *Capitalism and Development* (London: Routledge).
Hoffman, Kurt and Raphael Kaplinsky (1988) *Driving Force: The Global Restructuring of Technology, Labour, and Investment in the Automobile and Components Industries* (Boulder, CO: Westview Press).
Kochan, Thomas A. and Harry C. Katz (1988) *Collective Bargaining and Industrial Relations: From Theory to Practice* (Homewood, Ill: Irwin).

156   *The Thai Auto Industry*

Labour Department, Thailand (1991) *Yearbook of Labour Statistics, 1990.*
The Nation (various issues), published in Bangkok, Thailand.
Piriyarangsan, Sangsit and Kanchada Poonpanich (1992) 'Labour Institutions in an Export-Oriented Country: A Case Study of Thailand'. Paper presented at the International Workshop on Labour Institutions and Economic Development in Asia, Bali, Indonesia, 4–6 Feb.
Poonpanich, Kanchada (1991) 'Employment Promotion and Workers' Participation', cited in Piriyarangsan and Poonpanich.
Portes, Alejandro and Richard Schauffler (1993) 'Competing Perspectives on the Latin American Informal Sector', *Population and Development Review*, 19 (1) (March) pp. 33–60.
Samakkhitham, Somsak (1990) 'Economic Life of Low-Level Workers', (Bangkok: Arom Pongpa-ngan Foundation) (in Thai).
Satitniramai, Apichat (1992) 'The Formation of Labor Movements in [the] Textile Industry'. Master's Thesis, Economics, Thammasat University, Bangkok, Thailand.
Siengthai, Sununta (1988) 'Thai-Hino Industry Co., Ltd', International Labour Office *Case Studies in Labour–Management Cooperation for Productivity Improvement* (Bangkok: ILO) pp. 265–308.
Standing, Guy (1989) 'The Growth of External Labour Flexibility in a Nascent NIC: Malaysian Labour Flexibility Survey (MLFS)'. World Employment Programme Research Working Paper No. 35 (November).
Streeck, Wolfgang (1991) 'On the Institutional Conditions of Diversified Quality Production', in Egon Matzner and Wolfgang Streeck (eds), *Beyond Keynesianism: The Socio-Economies of Production and Full Employment* (Brookfield, VT Edward Elgar).
Sussangkarn, Chalongphob (1990) 'Labour Markets in an Era of Adjustment: A Study of Thailand'. Thailand Development Research Institute Foundation, Bangkok.
Thailand Development Research Institute (1992) 'Managing the Urban Informal Sector in Thailand: A Search for Practical Policies Based on the Basic Minimum Needs Approach'. Bangkok.
Turner, Lowell (1991) *Democracy at Work: Changing World Markets and the Future of Labor Unions* (Ithaca: Cornell University Press).
Wall Street Journal (various issues), New York.
Womack, James, P., Daniel T. Jones and Daniel Roos (1990) *The Machine that Changed the World* (New York: Rawson Associates).
Yosamornsunton, Amphan (1986) 'Wages and Working Conditions in the Garment Industry'. Master's Thesis, Economics, Thammasat University, Bangkok, Thailand.
Zuesongham, Sakool and Voravidh Charoenloet (1993) 'Fragmentation of the Trade Unions: Inevitably or Not?' Paper presented at a conference organized by the Friedrich-Ebert-Stiftung (foundation) on 'NICs in Asia: A Challenge to Trade Unions', Singapore, 30 March–1 April.

Part III
Labor's Response

6 Change, but in what Direction?[†] Divergent Union Responses to Work Restructuring in the Integrated North American Auto Industry

Pradeep Kumar and John Holmes

The internationalization of production and the emergence of Japan as the leading efficient producer of high-quality motor vehicles have created a 'competitive crisis' for the North American automobile industry.[1] In the past three decades its share of world production has declined from more than one-half to about one-quarter. Japan's share of global production over the same period has risen from less than three per cent to 31 per cent. The deterioration in the competitive position of the traditional North American manufacturers (General Motors, Ford and Chrysler) has been even more dramatic in the domestic market. In a short span of a dozen years, between 1979 and 1992, their share of total retail sales in Canada and the United States slipped from nearly 80 per cent to 64 per cent largely due to the popularity of vehicles produced by Japanese auto makers. Japanese transplants (a term used for plants in North America owned by foreign-based companies) accounted for over 15 per cent of North American sales in 1992 compared to only one per cent in 1979. The competitive advantage enjoyed by the transplants in labor costs and superior productivity and quality performance[2] have raised serious questions about the future survival of the traditional segments of the North American auto industry. If the trans-

† The question in the title is taken from a recent speech by Buzz Hargrove (1993), the President of the CAW – Canada. The paper is part of a research study of diversity and competitive efficiency focusing on divergent labor relations responses to workplace flexibility, conducted by the two authors and funded by the Social Sciences and Humanities Research Council of Canada.

plants continue to erode the Big Three's share of sales, there are fears that the industry may be changed in ways which will create serious risks to workers and their unions.

The Big Three have responded to this competitive crisis by revamping their production, supply and management systems to enhance efficiency, flexibility and product quality and by focusing on rationalization and cost-cutting. A key element of this 'lean production' strategy[3] is experimentation with Japanese style work organization, human resource practices and enterprise unionism. Typically, the workplace changes sought by employers have included flexible work rules and work arrangements, fewer job classifications, variable compensation, team work, multi-tasking, and employee and union involvement in shopfloor decision-making to foster a 'participatory' enterprise culture.

The attempts by management to restructure work and reward systems, in line with the principles of lean production, have had numerous effects on workers and their unions including an increase in insecure and stressful jobs, the erosion of worker rights and union institutional security, and the breakdown of labor solidarity. Thus, the competitive strategy being pursued by management has threatened to undermine the long-established system of labor relations in the industry. This system was linked with the rise of industrial unionism in North America in the mid-1930s and based on multi-year contracts which contained a wage-setting formula designed to ensure annual increases in real wages, pattern bargaining to ensure inter-company and inter-plant uniformity in wage rates and work rules, and a job control focus which linked individual worker rights to narrowly defined job classifications. This industrial relations system, developed out of hard bargaining between the Big Three and the United Auto Workers union (UAW) in the late 1940s and early 1950s, has been a source of stability in the industry and has produced many significant gains for workers in the form of high wages, better working conditions, employment security, and a strong and independent role for the union at the workplace level.

The Big Three's restructuring strategy also produced, indirectly, the split in the UAW which led to the formation of the Canadian Auto Workers union (CAW) in 1985. Prior to the split, the UAW was a model international union representing workers in both Canada and the United States and championing cross-border wage parity, uniform working conditions, and progressive legislation on worker rights and social and economic security. The split, therefore, has been a serious blow to continental union solidarity, providing, as it did, an added stimulus to the diminishing role of international unions in Canada.[4] The break-up occurred largely because the American and Canadian wings of the UAW responded quite differently to the restructuring strategy being advanced by management. In an effort to preserve auto industry jobs in the United States, the UAW leadership generally accepted and even became active partners in implementing the contractual and workplace changes being advocated by management. They accepted management demands for variable compensation in the form of lump-sum payments and profit-sharing bonuses in lieu of contractually guaranteed real wage increases and for a transformation of union–management relations from an adversarial relationship to one characterized by partnership and jointness between management and the union. The leadership of the Canadian Region of the UAW was critical of what it saw to be a change in strategic direction by the union, being sceptical of management motives and convinced that partnership with management was not in the long-run interest of workers and the union. It firmly believed that management's preoccupation with reducing costs and efforts to reorganize work would jeopardize worker rights, undermine working conditions and erode the independence of the union.

The divisions within the UAW came to a head during the negotiations for a new collective agreement with General Motors in 1984. GM demanded a fundamental revision of the traditional collective agreement including a shift to lump-sum payments and profit sharing, flexible work rules and work arrangements, and a new system of workplace governance built around the concept of 'jointness' between the union and management. While the UAW leadership acceded to management's bargaining agenda, the Canadian leadership refused to comply and struck General Motors of Canada in open defiance of the International. Following a two-week strike, the Canadian workers were successful in negotiating a traditional collective agreement without lump sums, profit sharing or jointness with management. The event precipitated the split and the formation of the Canadian Auto Workers union. Since the split, while the UAW has continued to follow the new direction set by the 1984 agreement and has become even more deeply committed to partnership with management, the CAW has grown even more resolute in its opposition to partnership with management, articulating an alternate and independent labor vision of industry restructuring.

Espousing the traditional UAW philosophy of social unionism and political activism through coalition building with community and social groups, the CAW, in the decade years since the split, has shown remarkable bargaining and organizational strength and dynamism. The union membership has grown through mergers and aggressive new organizing and the CAW now represents workers in a diverse range of industries.[5] The union has passed through a transition in leadership, and has continued to innovate in organizational structures, policies and practices to better serve its changing membership. It has achieved a number of significant gains for workers both at the collective bargaining table and outside. The union, despite its militant stance and hard bargaining, has also developed a strong working relationship with employers, helping the Big Three to improve productivity and product quality performance in their Canadian plants.

Thus, the CAW's strategic response to work restructuring apparently has been very different than that of the UAW. Underlying and shaping these differences are the environmental contexts of the two countries, the two unions' relative bargaining strength, their internal decision-making structures, and vastly different visions of labor–management relationships. The CAW vision, centered around an independent labor agenda and a philosophy of a 'working relationship' with employers within an adversarial framework, is fundamentally at odds with the UAW orientation towards a partnership with management. Moreover, empirical evidence suggests that the CAW approach, favoring incremental, evolutionary and informal change, is not incompatible with the goal of competitive efficiency being sought by the auto-makers.

The theme of this chapter is to explore the development of the different responses towards industry restructuring followed by the UAW and the CAW. It also addresses the strategic implications of this development for auto workers and their unions in the context of the increasing economic integration of automobile production and trade within the North American trade bloc. The chapter begins with an overview of the uniform system of labor relations in the Canadian and US auto industries which served as a source of stability in the industry for nearly four decades. It then traces, for the 1980s, the significant events and root causes of the divergent union responses which arose in the two countries and led to the split in the UAW. The second section analyzes the growing divergence between Canada and the United States in collective bargaining approaches and outcomes, and labor–management relations. The third section focuses on the CAW vision of work restructuring and explains how and why it differs fundamentally from the UAW response. The final section draws implications from the analysis for the future shape of lean production in the industry. It also identifies the particular challenges that confront attempts to build international solidarity and a strong and independent labor movement in an integrated auto industry which spans three countries – the United States, Canada and Mexico – with different and distinctive industrial relations institutions and political cultures.[6]

THE SYSTEM OF LABOR RELATIONS IN THE NORTH AMERICAN AUTO INDUSTRY

Perhaps the single most important element of the Fordist mass production model in the North American auto industry was the development of a unique labor relations system which governed collective bargaining and labour–management relations in the industry in the United States and Canada from the 1940s through to the early 1980s.[7] The establishment of this system was linked to poor conditions of work in the depression era and the subsequent rise in the late 1930s of industrial unionism. The UAW, a pioneer industrial union, organized virtually all American and Canadian workers in the vehicle assembly sector and in the automaker's 'captive' component plants, as well as a substantial majority of workers in the independent parts sector. This enabled the union to establish uniform pattern contracts across the industry.

The model for postwar labor contracts in the industry was set by the 1948 collective agreement between General Motors and the UAW in the United States (which was replicated in Canada in 1953) which quickly spread to other companies in the auto industry (and ultimately to other industries). There were a number of key features of these multiyear agreements (after the early 1950s the contracts were usually of three-year duration) and the bargaining process that produced them, which resulted in uniform pay and working conditions across the industry.

The first of these was the *pattern bargaining process* itself which produced *uniformity between companies*. The expirations of contracts with each of the major auto makers in both countries were timed to occur in the same year, and, at times, even in the same month. As contract renewal time approached, the union, after a period of initial negotiations, would select a target company for bargaining based on strategic and market considerations – the company from which it thought it could wrest the best contract to set the pattern. Once agreement had been reached with that company, with or without a strike, the other auto makers quickly settled for almost identical contracts thus establishing a uniform pattern across the industry. During the 1960s and 1970s the US contracts were always settled prior to the Canadian contracts.

Thus, *de facto*, the American contracts largely established the pattern for the Canadian contracts, except for particular local issues.

The second was the *connective bargaining* structure which defined the relationship, or 'connection', between enterprise and plant-level bargaining and facilitated the achievement of *inter-plant uniformity* in wages and general contract provisions. Through collective bargaining at the company level, the union set the general wage increases and formulated the general principles and rules governing seniority, union representation and security, hours of work, overtime, holidays and vacation pay, the treatment of the skilled trades, and the mechanisms for resolving grievances. Each union local negotiated the detailed job classifications and seniority provisions for the plants it represented and administered the collective agreement. The national office of the union, however, played an active role in plant-level bargaining and contract administration, requiring, in pursuit of inter-plant uniformity, that local agreements received its approval. This connected system of enterprise and local bargaining between companies and the union effectively separated work-rule bargaining from wage determination and meant – particularly in a period of general growth and expanding markets such as existed in the 1950s and 1960s – that there was little pressure on unions at the local level to agree to the relaxation of work rules in order to save jobs.

In the agreements, wages were determined through formula-like *wage rules*. Annual wage increases, which were negotiated in 'national' collective agreements with each company, consisted of two components; a cost of living escalator (COLA) designed to protect real wages against price inflation, and an annual improvement factor (AIF), linked explicitly to expected long-term rates of productivity growth.[8] With only very minor exceptions, this formula was used to set wage increases among the major car makers and parts producers from 1948 to 1979 and, once set, the national contract wage increases could not be modified in local bargaining. Monitoring by both the companies and the union ensured the convergence toward identical wage rates between plants for any one job classification.

These methods for determining wage increases and wage rates 'took wages out of competition' (Kochan, 1988, p. 285) by effectively eliminating variations in wage rates between companies, and between plants within the same company. Initially, wage rates in Canada were lower than in the United States as a reflection of the lower productivity rates in Canada. However, following the signing of the Auto Pact by the two countries in 1965, the UAW pressed hard for, and in 1973 achieved, nominal wage parity between Canadian and American autoworkers.[9] The integration of collective bargaining between the two countries was further underscored by the fact that from 1968–81 there was simply one international collective agreement between the UAW and Chrysler which covered all Chrysler workers irrespective of whether they worked in the United States or Canada.

Another important element of these contracts, which is important for an understanding of the nature and implications of some of the changes in work practices and work rules demanded by management during the 1980s, was their 'job-control focus'. This refers to the very formalized and detailed nature of the collective agreements which linked workers rights and obligations to a set of highly articulated and sharply delineated jobs and tasks. Central to this system was an elaborate job classification scheme that formed the core of each local (or plant) collective agreement and was built around narrowly defined jobs which, in turn, were grouped into job ladders such that the mastery of one task ideally prepared the worker for a slightly more demanding one. Workers moved up the job ladder according to seniority and, similarly, during downturns, layoffs were in reverse order of seniority. Base pay was determined by attaching a wage rate to the specific job being performed rather than to the qualifications or characteristics of the workers undertaking it.

The job-control focus of contracts provided the union with a significant degree of control over the internal labor market and was the primary source of union power on the shopfloor. While the system made it relatively easy to lay off and re-hire workers, it made it extremely difficult for management to re-deploy workers within a plant: in other words, it resulted in a flexible external labor market but a very rigid internal one (Katz, 1985).

Under this system, the day-to-day operation of production was left to management discretion. There was an explicit agreement, formalized in a management rights clause,[10] that it was the job of management to organize and direct work, the employees' obligation to follow instructions, and the unions' role to ensure that management carried out its function in a fair and just manner and in accordance with the literal interpretation and administration of the rules contained in the contract. Thus, from the late 1940s through until the late 1970s there was a well-functioning labor-relations system within the North American auto industry, consistent with the general Fordist principles of mass production and Taylorist principles of job design, that provided significant benefits to both workers and employers. Worker gains came in the form of rising real wages, continuous improvements in non-wage benefits, employment security, and a strong union presence at the workplace-level to defend worker rights. Employers benefitted through higher production and sales, productivity and profits. In this sense, it was a central element of the hegemonic structure of postwar Fordism (Jessop, 1992).

During the late 1970s and early 1980s, however, the system began to show signs of instability as the Big Three experienced a significant erosion of their share of the domestic market due both to increased competition for that market from Japanese-based auto makers and a decline in their own competitive position due to escalating production costs. Japanese competition initially came in the form of increasing import penetration into the North American market of vehicles built in Japan, but by the late 1980s it was being driven by Asian direct investment into North American based assembly and component production facilities – the so-called 'transplants'. The escalation in Big Three production costs during this period can be explained as follows. Throughout the 1950s and 1960s, the annual increases in base wage rates and improvements in employee benefits had been financed out of sustained increases in labor productivity. Labor productivity growth, however, stagnated in the early 1970s and showed no signs of significant recovery for over a decade. Coupled with the contractual annual real wage increases, which had become an entrenched feature of postwar pattern bargaining in the auto industry, the poor productivity performance led to rapidly escalating unit production costs, further weakening the international competitiveness of North American auto makers (Holmes, 1987; Fuss and Waverman, 1992).

It was this unprecedented sea-change in trade, investment flows and international labor-cost competitiveness that both forced and shaped the restructuring of the North American auto industry during the 1980s through a wave of new investment in both the construction of 'greenfield' plants and in the 'modernization' of existing Big Three facilities. Much of this investment was tied to the introduction of advanced forms of automation and the reorganization of work and production both within the individual plant and across the wider production system.

At the heart of the restructuring lay the need to lower production costs and increase productivity, and this placed heavy demands on the industrial relations system. After an initial phase of concession bargaining at the beginning of the 1980s, during which management simply sought a reduction in nominal wages, deferment of scheduled

COLA increases, and roll-backs on benefits such as holiday entitlements, pressure mounted to restructure the whole compensation system and, particularly, to reorganize work and construct a more
cooperative shopfloor and plant-level relationship between labor and
management.[11] Kochan, Katz and McKersie (1986) suggest that during the 1980s the traditional Fordist labor relations system was transformed to produce a 'new industrial relations system' that, in the auto
industry at least, was fashioned around lump-sum payments and profit-sharing schemes instead of regular annual increases in base wage
rates, and the redesign and broadening of jobs to allow management
more control and flexibility in the deployment of the workforce. Also,
as part of the 'transformation', the UAW was pressed to give up the adversarial 'job control system' in favor of a new 'high trust' or 'cooperative' relationship built around variants of the 'team concept'. While
the traditional system assumed that workers had no personal responsibility for efficiency or productivity, in the 'new' system workers are
expected to participate in groups in order to pool and apply their
knowledge and tacit skill to improve productivity and quality.

The memorandum of understanding (and subsequent collective
agreement) signed by the UAW with GM for the new greenfield Saturn
production facility in Springhill, Tennessee incorporated virtually all
of these elements (Katz, 1987). By the end of the 1980s, many other
plants, particularly in the United States, embodied at least some of
these practices and the Big Three regularly used phrases such as 'World
Class Contracts' (GM) and 'Modern Operating Agreements' (Chrysler) to describe the package of new work and industrial relations practices that they were seeking. A World Class Contract, according to a
1987 Company memorandum, includes: a joint statement of commitments and responsibilities, fewer job classes (two to nine for skilled
and one to two for non-skilled), flexibility in skilled trades utilization,
increased management rights and flexibility with regard to such things
as overtime use, simplified seniority group definition, improved layoff
and recall provisions, reduction in transfer activity, fewer restrictive
work practices, joint commitment on quality, training and operational
effectiveness, separate progressive discipline procedures for absenteeism, and provision for a 'living agreement' with no expiry date. Similarly, Modern Operating Agreements (MOA) also include a statement
of mutual goals and commitments, a pledge to work together and forge
a labor–management relationship based on mutual trust and understanding and a working environment based on progressive change,
pride in workmanship, team effort and shared responsibilities and

decision-making. The MOAs also provide for team concept, capability progression pay, a collegial relationship and a participatory style of operating (Lovell, 1991).

The transition from the stable Fordist labor relations system couched within the framework of adversarial labor–management relationships, to a new system based on partnership and jointness with management was far from smooth, however. The UAW, and ultimately the workers, paid a heavy price through the fracturing of labor solidarity as reflected in the oppositional movement within the UAW to lump sums, profit sharing and work reorganization around team concepts led by the New Directions Movement[12] and, more significantly, by the split between Canadian and American workers which arose from similar opposition by the leadership of the Canadian wing of the industry. The latter ended cross-national pattern bargaining and four decades of close and intimate institutional links between the Canadian and American labor movements.

FROM UNIFORMITY TO DIVERGENCE: COLLECTIVE BARGAINING APPROACHES AND OUTCOMES BETWEEN CANADA AND THE UNITED STATES

A comparison of auto industry labor contracts negotiated in both the United States and Canada since 1979 reveals a growing divergence in the content of agreements between the two countries (see Kumar and Meltz, 1992, for a detailed analysis of the divergence in contract provisions). The first signs of divergence appeared in the union's response to management's demand for concessions on wages and benefits during the early 1980s when company restructuring strategies were firmly centered on cost-cutting. The 1984 round of contract negotiations, which saw the establishment of a new 'pattern' contract in the United States that changed the traditional rules for wage formation in the industry, led to further divergence. Although these events are now reasonably well known in the literature (Gindin, 1989; Yates, 1990; Herzenberg, 1990 and 1991; Holmes and Rusonik, 1991; Kumar and Meltz, 1992) it is useful to briefly review and contextualize them in order to provide a backdrop to the later analysis of the contrast between Canadian and US auto workers' responses to the key question of work reorganization and the union's role in workplace governance.

A self-conscious choice of different strategic directions by the two sections of the union, which, in turn, were related to differences in political and economic environment between the two countries, clearly underlay the divergence in collective bargaining approaches and outcomes. In the United States, the UAW leadership, confronted with huge losses of jobs and consequent union membership on account of a series of plant closings and large numbers of workers on temporary or permanent layoff, made job security its number one bargaining priority. In pursuit of this goal, the union agreed to concessions on wage increases and work rules and to actively promote a more 'cooperative' relationship with management in order to achieve some measure of future employment security. The union in Canada, on the other hand, which experienced far fewer layoffs and plant closings and had been more aggressive than its American counterpart in new organizing to bolster its membership,[13] rejected concession bargaining, continued to press for long-term income security through improved wage and benefit settlements using the traditional formulae, and resisted management's efforts to transform the traditional shopfloor relationships between workers, their union representatives and management.[14]

The choice of different strategic directions followed by the two sections of the union must be understood in the context of two key environmental factors. The first is the geographically uneven development of the North American auto industry which produced an absolute and relative expansion of the industry in Canada during the 1980s and, thus, placed the Canadian wing of the union in a far stronger bargaining position than its American counterpart. The second factor is the fundamental differences in political ideology between the Canadian and American sections of the union with regard to concessions specifically, and the future strategic trajectory of the labor movement more generally.

The performance indicators of output, employment, plant capacity utilization rates and trade under the Auto Pact all reveal that although the North American auto industry as a whole experienced considerable difficulties, the Canadian portion of the industry has fared much better than its American counterpart since 1980 (Holmes, 1991). While the industry in the United States failed to regain the levels of employment and production attained in the late 1970s, the industry in Canada not only staged a rapid recovery from the deep recession at the beginning of the last decade, but continued to prosper throughout the 1980s registering record levels of output of assembled vehicles (10 per cent higher in 1990 than the previous peak in 1978) and employment (over 25 per cent higher in 1990 than the 1978 peak), and racking up significant new capital investment (over $13 billion between 1985 and 1990) and huge annual surpluses on its automotive trade with the United States (over $14.5 billion on motor vehicles and $8.7 billion on total automotive trade in 1990).[15] Although Canada's share of the total North American market for vehicles remained at around 8–9 per cent, its share of both total North American vehicle production and industry employment rose to over 15 per cent in 1990.

By far the most significant factor underlying the stronger perform-ance of the industry in Canada during the 1980s was the real labor-cost advantage enjoyed by the Big Three in Canada. This advantage, which by the mid-1980s was of the order of 30 per cent (or over US $7.50 per hour worked), was related to (a) the lower value of the Canadian dollar against the US dollar, and (b) the lower cost of employee benefits, particularly the health insurance costs (estimated at $30 per vehicle compared to over $600 in the US) which are subsidized in Canada through universal medical care. Taking into account that productivity and efficiency in Canadian assembly plants are generally judged equal to or greater than the plants in the United States (Katz and Meltz, 1989; Economic Strategy Institute, 1992; Harbour 1990, 1992) these labor-cost savings were both substantial and significant.

The differences in ideology and political culture between the labor movements and their relative strengths in Canada and the United States also shaped the strategic choice of the union in the two countries. With regard to union density, political influence and labor solidarity, the labor movement was far stronger in Canada than in the US during the 1980s (Kumar, 1993a). While the differences in ideology and politi-cal culture had relatively inconsequential effects on bargaining out-comes during the 1960s and 1970s when employment and real wages were rising steadily on both sides of the border, they suddenly assumed a new significance in the recessionary climate of the early 1980s. For ex-ample, the Canadian UAW's opposition to management's demands for concessions was part of the general campaign by the Canadian la-bor movement against concession bargaining and was very much shaped by a particular understanding of the fundamental nature and purpose of trade unionism. The Canadians feared that irreparable da-mage would be done to the longer-term commitment of the rank-and-file membership to the union if they followed the lead of the UAW lea-dership in the United States and granted uncritical support to conces-sions. As Gindin (1989, p. 81) argues, 'the fight *against* concessions was therefore a fight *for* the continued health of the trade union move-ment'. The debate about concessions that occurred at a special 1981 meeting of the Canadian Council of the UAW and which led to the adoption of an official anti-concessions position by the union, and later at the Canadian Labour Congress convention in 1982, focused on:

> ... why they [concessions] were disastrous for working people; why they would not bring job security to workers; how they would divert attention from real alternatives; how they would fragment workers; why accepting them would be to argue that unions had bargained 'too well' in the past and should, therefore, forever be weakened; and why in general acquiescence to their logic would eventually destroy the lifeblood of unions.

> (Gindin, 1989, p. 73)

The Council's 'no concessions resolutions' prohibited union locals in Canada from deviating from the wage scales and work practices specified in the Master Agreement. The debate on concessions did not have the same intensity in the United States. A weak labor movement also implied that the UAW could muster little support to fight the management agenda in the United States. The CAW was able to withstand the pressure, in part, because of the strength and solidarity of the Canadian labor movement.

The Significant Events in Divergence: Chrysler and GM Negotiations

Most commentators view the 1979 negotiations between Chrysler and the UAW as the beginning of the 'era of concession bargaining' in the North American auto industry. Chrysler claimed that if the Company were to be saved from bankruptcy, workers would not only have to accept massive lay-offs, but would also have to make major concessions on wages and benefits. For the first time in the union's history, the UAW negotiated a contract which included no wage increase. In addition, Chrysler workers agreed to forego six days of personal paid holidays (PPHs) a year and made other concessions with respect to pensions and sickness and accident benefits. Since there was a single international collective agreement covering Chrysler workers in both the United States and Canada, Canadian Chrysler workers had to accept the package of concessions, in the interest of preserving trans-border uniformity in contracts that had existed for so long.

However, when Chrysler demanded further concessions, and won them in the United States, the Canadian leadership, backed by the mandate provided by the Canadian Council's official rejection of concession bargaining, refused to either reopen contracts or to recommend to its membership the granting of further concessions. In retrospect, it is plain that the 1982 round of contract negotiations with Chrysler was a milestone in the development of the distinct path that Canadian Autoworkers later decided to pursue, independent of the union in the United States. In 1982, Canadian auto workers not only opposed profit sharing and rejected concessions on job classifications made by the union in the United States, but after a five-week strike against Chrysler Canada they won a wage increase that for the first time established the 'pattern' for the United States as well. The Chrysler strike demonstrated to Canadian auto workers that not only could they win a difficult strike on their own, but also that their leadership's analysis, '. . . that management's strategy of restructuring through concessions was not the *only* one available', was sound and viable (Yates, 1990, p. 100).[16]

The 1984 round of collective bargaining negotiations between the UAW and General Motors in the United States was another significant event in the development of the divergence in union responses between the United States and Canada. The UAW in the United States entered the 1984 contract negotiations with GM committed to a strategy of trading off concessions on wage increases for improved employment security provisions, having already accepted a wage freeze and profit sharing in 1982. The union finally settled for a contract that surrendered the traditional 3 per cent AIF and COLA in favor of a 2.25 per cent wage increase in the first year, lump-sum payments in the next two years of the contract, profit sharing, extended SUB and an innovative Job Opportunity Bank fund; in contrast to the old AIF increases, lump sums were not to be folded into the base rate.[17] The leadership also advised their Canadian counterparts to accept the pattern in the interests of the industry.

The Canadians rejected the new pattern for wage determination set by the GM contract in the United States and instead concentrated on re-establishing the traditional contract model through the restoration of wage increases determined by COLA and AIF, and the maintenance of wage uniformity between companies and plants. They continued to reject on principle the concept of profit sharing. Partly because of their victory at Chrysler in 1982, and the fact that General Motors' sales and profit were far healthier in Canada than in the United States, the Canadian leadership was confident that they could adhere to their traditional bargaining goals. After a twelve and a half day strike in late October 1984, the Canadians obtained a contract on their terms. This contract, however, was only won after an intense struggle which pitted the Canadian wing of the UAW not only against GM, but also against the leadership of the International union. The strain within the UAW proved too great, and in 1985 the Canadian region left the International UAW to form the autonomous CAW (see Gindin, 1989; Holmes and Rusonik, 1991; Friedman, 1989; and Perusek, 1989, for various analyses of the split). Following the break-up, the CAW successfully negotiated with Chrysler in 1985 a restoration of the AIF, parity with Ford and General Motors by the end of the contract, and a two-year contract term to synchronize contract renewal with other auto makers in 1987 to re-establish pattern bargaining. The UAW again followed the Canadian pattern, but was unable to obtain a two-year term to facilitate synchronization with GM and Ford contracts. In the 1987, 1990 and 1993 contract negotiations, the CAW was again able to retain the traditional AIF and COLA and made a major breakthrough by negotiating pension indexing (1987) and a new worker security program (1990). The UAW similarly continued to follow its new pattern, strengthening its partnership with management (for example, through the memoranda on jointness included in GM contracts and the new style labor contract at GM's Saturn facility), and employment security provisions.

Table 6.1 highlights key areas of growing divergence in collective bargaining outcomes at the Big Three in Canada and the United States. These include wages, employment/income security, paid time off, work practices and work organization, training, and the nature of union–management relations – areas where differences in union responses and approaches to industry restructuring have made the most impact. The different outcomes demonstrate that the CAW, by adhering to its role as an independent voice of workers and building on its past collective bargaining achievements, has been able to secure significant gains to workers in the form of higher wages, more paid time off, more realistic income and job security, and a strong collective voice at the workplace. While defending workers' rights and improving workers' economic and social well-being, the union has also been sensitive toward management needs to enhance production flexibility to regain competitiveness and effectively respond to the changing market and technology. Without giving management a *carte blanche* to restructure work and reward systems, it has provided flexibility in work scheduling and work arrangements whenever needed. As Katz and Meltz (1989) have noted, although the nature of changes have been more informal and incremental, Canadian auto plants provide considerable flexibility in work rules and an input in decision-making through informal participation and communication on productivity and quality improvement related issues. Whether or not this informal and evolutionary approach is a more stable and effective response to restructuring than the more formal and instantaneous change approach adopted by the UAW is still an open question. However, as evidence of its viability, it is noteworthy that the Canadian plants of the Big Three continue to be rated high in both quality and productivity, leading Ford and Chrysler to substantially increase capital investment in Canada. An important factor behind the Big Three's improved plant performance is that despite the CAW's adherence to the view that the labor–management relationship is fundamentally an adversarial one, it has developed a strong and mutually beneficial working relationship with management. While cooperating with management in their drive to become competitive, the union has also pursued its social unionism goals by negotiating human rights and literacy training, the right to refuse work on the grounds of harassment, and innovative provisions such as a social justice fund to provide financial assistance for international development and relief projects as well as contributing resources to deal with domestic situations such as food banks and national disasters. The UAW, once a champion of such social causes, appears to have overlooked its responsibility in these areas because of its preoccupation with saving jobs and helping the industry to achieve competitive advantage.

Table 6.1   Key areas of US–Canada divergence at the Big Three

Wages	In 1978, base wage rates for assemblers were almost identical at the Big Three in both Canada and the United States. By the end of the last contract in 1993, however, base wage rates in Canada were $2.88 an hour higher than in the United States. Unlike the Canadian contracts which provide for annual increases in base rates, the American contracts at General Motors, Ford, and Chrysler include a base rate increase in the first year, lump sum payments in the second and third years, and profit sharing bonuses in lieu of base rate increases. However, profit sharing bonuses vary by company and have not totally compensated for the loss of earnings due to abandonment of annual wage increases. Although wage rates in Canada are higher, total compensation per hour (in US dollars) continues to be less than in the United States due to the lower cost of employee benefits.
Paid time off	Canadian contracts provide for more holidays and vacations (through higher paid absence allowance) in pursuit of the CAW goal of reducing annual hours of work. While the US collective agreements provide for less holidays and vacation, they include two weeks of summer shutdown.

Employment security	American contracts include more emphasis on job security provisions such as 'Expanded Job Opportunity Bank' and 'Secure Employment Levels' while Canadian contracts contain income security programs (e.g. indexed pensions, expanded supplementary unemployment benefits and severance pay plans for voluntary termination of employment). In Canada, employers are required to give up to one-year advance notice for plant closure, while in the US there are strong provisions for the placement of workers affected by closures.
Work practices and work organization	American contracts have fewer job classifications, more team concept/employee involvement provisions and provide for greater management flexibility in work scheduling, shift work, job rotation, multi-tasking and work assignments. Canadian contracts allow less management discretion, but changes in work scheduling and work arrangements are negotiated as need arises. There are far fewer formal contractual provisions for team work and employee involvement in Canada, although as Katz and Meltz (1989) have shown there is considerable *informal* employee participation and communications on productivity and quality issues.
Training	In the United States, training in all areas is conducted jointly by both union and management. In Canada, training is provided by the union in consultation with management. Both countries have an extensive array of training programs.
Union–management relations	American contracts, both at the national level and in many cases locally, provide for a formal pledge of union–management cooperation, jointness and partnership in shopfloor governance, productivity and quality initiatives, outsourcing decisions and in-training and education activities. The CAW is opposed to cooperation and partnership with management although a few local contracts (e.g. Ste Thérèse plant of General Motors and Chrysler's Bramalea plant) include a formal pledge of cooperation and commitment to 'working together'.

Source: Kumar and Meltz (1992), and *Contract Highlights*, CAW and UAW.

DIFFERENT UNION VISIONS OF WORK REORGANIZATION AND LABOR–MANAGEMENT RELATIONS: THE ROOT CAUSES OF DIVERGENCE

At the heart of the divergence in collective bargaining approaches and outcomes between the CAW and UAW lies the different strategic responses chosen by the two unions with regard to work restructuring generally, and to management's lean production strategies in particular. What accounts for the divergent responses and why? The different environmental and institutional contexts faced by the industry in the two countries is without doubt a critical factor shaping both management's approach to work organization and the union's response. As suggested earlier, the industry in Canada has been relatively healthy in comparison to the United States due to lower labor costs, a favorable product mix and protections afforded by the Auto Pact. Canada also has a more facilitative public labor policy environment reflected in its expanded labor legislation and an extensive array of labor market adjustment programs (see Kumar, 1993a; Lecki, 1993). The better protection afforded to workers in Canada has made it possible for the Canadian union to be less preoccupied with job security issues. The facilitative public policy environment also acts as a constraint on management's ability to force concessions.

The relative strength of the Canadian labor movement, particularly its more solidaristic orientation, and the organizational dynamism of the CAW have also been critical factors shaping the union and management response. The CAW membership, in the auto industry and outside, has been rising steadily as a result of both aggressive new organizing and mergers, while the UAW has experienced a marked decline in its organizational strength. The CAW has also been able to withstand management pressures to comply with its competitive agenda on account of its more democratic internal decision-making structures which encourage local autonomy and promote debates and discussions on critical issues through a network of consultative councils at the national, regional, industry and enterprise level. Through these councils, the rank-and-file and their elected officials are able to wield greater influence on union decision-making, 'providing opposition caucuses with an organizational structure through which to mobilize and coordinate the activities of supporters'. These structures tend to reduce 'the union leadership's capacity to impose strategic solutions' on workers, and at the same time enable the national leadership to feel the pulse of the membership on such critical issues as concessions and management-designed and controlled work organization and help to mobilize the rank-and-file behind a course of action arrived at by consensus (Yates, 1992, pp. 120–1). The UAW in the United States does not have such structures of interest representation. Although district councils once existed throughout the union, by 1945 most of these bodies were disbanded in the United States (Yates, 1992, p. 121). The absence of such open forums for regular consultation and discussions has been a source of cleavage between the union bureaucracy and the membership on the one hand, and between the national leadership and local leaders on the other on issues relating to work rules and partnership with management (Herzenberg, 1990; Perusek, 1988). These conflicts within the union have strengthened management bargaining power, leading to management's use of the practice of whipsawing, and weakened the UAW in its ability to oppose the management agenda and to articulate an independent and alternate course of action.

Although differing environmental contexts, relative organizational and bargaining strength, and the internal decision-making structures of the two unions are critical factors shaping the divergent CAW vs UAW response, the root cause of the different paths taken by the two unions is their fundamentally different vision of work restructuring and union–management relations. Whereas the CAW has succeeded in articulating its own independent vision, centred around 'a democratic and dynamic unionism' and an alternate worker agenda, the UAW, at least since the early 1980s, has become deeply committed to the idea of 'jointness' and partnership with management to 'save jobs and preserve them for the future' and to 'improve the quality of life in the plants through participatory efforts'. The UAW orientation is evident in various memoranda on 'jointness' included in Big Three contracts and in its involvement in the conceptualization, development and administration of Saturn, a recent greenfield General Motors plant, 'a joint effort of both union and management' with a new style labor contract incorporating team work and full participation by the union in a 'consensus decision-making' process (UAW, 1987). While endorsed by the national leadership, the new direction is not universally shared by the rank-and-file and many local union officials. Indeed, not only are there wide plant-level variations in the extent of 'jointness', but the union's decision to participate with management in joint decision-making is itself a source of serious conflict within the union. The union strategy, according to Turner (1991, pp. 47–99) has been largely defensive rather than pro-active. He further notes that while the union has 'embarked on the laborious process of developing its own concepts of work organization', it has yet to produce a 'consistent strategy of its own for responding to management initiatives' (p. 49). The *Collective Bargaining Program* prepared for the UAW's 1993 bargaining convention held in Detroit, still only contained a relatively innocuous one-page statement regarding 'new methods of work organization'. In contrast, the CAW position, formulated after extensive debate and discussions in 1988–

89, is clear and well-articulated in its 1989 *Statement of Work Re-organization* and further refined in the *Report* to the national collective bargaining and political convention held in Toronto on 4–7 May 1993 (CAW, 1993).

The CAW's View of Itself

The CAW, following the goals and traditions of the CIO unions (Taylor and Dow, 1988), considers itself a social union subscribing to a form of 'unionism which is rooted in the workplace, but understands the importance of participating in, and influencing, the general direction of society' (CAW, 1993, p. v). Its leadership is dedicated to the preservation and promotion of a tradition of union democracy and union dynamism. This includes, according to a recent union document, *Hard Times and New Times: Fighting For Our Future*, 'widespread opportunities for discussion, debate and influence ... equality within the membership ... developing the capacities of individual members and activists ... empowering workers collectively ... and avoiding bureaucratization ...' (CAW, 1993, p. 25). The union believes that 'democracy is not something to announce but something that has to be built and continuously rebuilt', particularly in the context of the changing nature of the union and the move 'from "hard times" to redefining what "new times" can mean'. In pursuit of these goals, the union is actively involved in an ongoing assessment of its own role, functions and organizational structures while following a strategy of innovative collective bargaining, political action, coalition-building with social and community groups, and labor solidarity based on close relationships and alliances with unions at home and abroad.

While these goals and strategies are not unknown to the UAW – they have been an integral part of its organizational purposes since the inception of the union – they appear to have been relegated to secondary importance over the past decade. In fairness, it must be acknowledged that the favorable economic conditions enjoyed by the auto industry in Canada have afforded the CAW the 'luxury' of being able to assume and maintain a tough militant stance. It should also be noted that this stance has led to significant and increasing ideological friction between the CAW and some other powerful industrial unions in Canada, and it would be false to see the CAW positions on labor–management relations and the appropriate union response to work reorganization as positions widely held within the broader Canadian labor movement.

The CAW Vision of Labor–Management Relationships

The CAW adheres to the position that the nature of the union–management relationship is fundamentally an adversarial one. While recognizing the need for a 'working relationship' with employers, with many of whom it has a sound relationship based on many common interests and, at times, similar objectives, the union stresses that 'the role of the union is to pursue the goals of workers, including more democratic workplaces with more worker involvement and control, better wages, hours of work and benefits. Many times these goals conflict with employer interests' (CAW, 1989). As a recent CAW report explains:

> Relationships in the workplace include a basic conflict between labour and management. Our income is their costs. And, since selling labour is different than selling other things like a washing machine or a car – the 'sale' of labour can not be separated from the human being that accompanies it – there is a conflict over how the labour is used. Management wants the flexibility to use what they bought as they see fit, while we want to retain some control over what happens to our bodies and minds: the environment in which we work, how we are used or abused, how our skills are developed or wasted.
>
> (CAW, 1993, p. 4).

The union rejects the notion of 'partnership' with management, arguing at the same time the need for a closer working relationship. The present CAW President explains the difference as follows:

> One difference is that partnership assumes common goals, while 'working relationship' implies some overlap in goals, but also *differing interests*. Another is that partnership implies some equality in regard to power, while 'working relationship' recognizes the reality of *who owns the factories we work in*. A third is that partnership downplays the need for an independent workers organization while 'working relationships' – based on different interests and unequal power – emphasizes the importance of an independent base for *negotiating* with management.
>
> (Hargrove, 1993)

He believes that labor and management have different interests, different constituencies and unequal power, pointing out, however, that strong unions are not inconsistent with better economic performance, and that 'to run complex workplaces in a single way, a measure of cooperation over and above any technical language in a collective agreement is absolutely essential'. Citing the excellent productivity and quality performance of Big Three plants in Canada, and lower Canadian average hourly labor costs in the industry, Hargrove maintains that 'we have the potential to develop an excellent relationship based not on any superficial partnership but on negotiated compromises that address both corporate and worker concerns' (Hargrove, 1993, p. 4).

Aside from the deep-rooted conviction that the interests of labor and management are not inherently the same, the CAW leadership believes, based largely on the US experience, that the management's call for a new partnership is designed to transform the role and functions of the union from a 'management watchdog' and an independent voice of workers, to an enterprise union, another transmission belt for achieving management goals. The management objective, a CAW document stresses, is to replace worker solidarity with the goals of the company:

> This partnership and its promises are false. For all the talk about jointness and worker control, employers are certainly not putting true equality between themselves and their employees on the agenda. Management will continue to jealously guard the management's rights clause and to unilaterally decide when to modernize, how much to invest, what to produce, with what kind of technology and so on. The truth is that management's agenda is not about surrendering its power, but of finding sophisticated ways to extend it.
>
> (CAW, 1989)

Thus, suspicious of management motives, the union is adamantly opposed to jointness and partnership and rejects 'management efforts, under whatever name, which jeopardize worker rights, undermine workplace conditions, and erode the independence of the union' (CAW, 1989).

The CAW Vision of Work Reorganization

The CAW, over the last few years, has been engaged in articulating an independent, alternate labor agenda on work reorganization, based on its experience with QWL experiments in the 1970s and the workplace changes introduced by the Big Three in its Canadian plants since the mid-1980s. The agenda is both defensive and pro-active (pro-active in the sense defined by Turner (1991, p. 49) of taking the initiative, proposing alternatives and negotiating for them) and reflects a culture of resistance and change within an adversarial framework of union–management relations.[18] Its purpose is to 'oppose lean production from a position of engagement and work to change it through negotiations' (CAW, 1993). The key elements of the agenda include (1) challenging 'the ideology of lean production, both in terms of its structures for partnership and its underlying logic of competitiveness', (2) a focus on the changes to jobs and production systems, and (3) responding to 'new managerial techniques and workplace structures (teams, rotation, etc.)'.

In response to the Big Three's attempts to whipsaw locals to adopt changes in work organization, in 1989 the CAW was the first national union in Canada to issue a national policy statement on work reorganization (CAW, 1989). Following extensive consultation and debate with the local leaderships and activists, the Statement reaffirmed the adversarial nature of labor–management relationship based on conflicting goals and a mutual 'commitment to building quality products and services'. The Statement made clear that while 'there is nothing inherently bad about working together and there may be some advantages', the union 'will not support management attempts to use the team concepts or quality circles, to manage the workplace by stress, to introduce speed up or to encourage workers to discipline each other'. It also rejected the inference that workers are part of the management team, arguing that 'true partnership means a measure of equality. None of the examples of work organization promoted by management includes workers or their union in any meaningful way in the decision-making process'. However, while the union pursued 'ideological resistance' to new forms of work organization that management sought to introduce using the stick and carrot of 'the threat of competitiveness and the promise of a new "partnership" between workers and management', it did not rule out what the union termed 'positive changes in the workplace' that 'use workers' experience, knowledge and skills to produce good quality products and quality services in well-designed workplaces equipped with the proper tools and equipment'.

This pragmatic orientation to workplace changes in the framework of ideological resistance to any form of 'concessions and structures that undermine union solidarity' led the union to participate in a number of work reorganization experiments (for example, at the Ste Thérèse and Oshawa plants of GM, Chrysler plants in Bramalea and Windsor, Ford plants in Oakville, and at CAMI, a greenfield joint venture of GM and Suzuki in Ingersol, Ontario) with a view to learn 'whether they can have input into the changes that actually improve the life of workers and their working conditions'.[19] It appears that both the companies and the union have benefitted from the experiments. The companies on their part have realized that they can work around 'the labels' and still improve their productivity and quality performance. As Katz and Meltz (1989) discovered in their 1987 survey of auto assembly plant practices, even though Canadian plants do not have formal team concepts or employee involvement programs, management has been able to considerably increase flexibility in work rules. The incidence of informal employee participation and communication on productivity and quality issues has been on the increase resulting in substantial improvements in productivity and product quality. Consequently, Canadian plants are rated high in both economic performance and industrial relations climate (see Kumar and Meltz, 1992, for details). Indeed, almost all Ford and Chrysler assembly and parts plants in Canada have won numerous internal and external awards for quality. Anecdotal evidence also suggests that despite the militancy of the union and its flat rejection of any form of partnership with management, the Big Three have engaged in considerable information sharing and communications with the union. The positive 'working relationship' was an important factor in securing the substantial new investments announced by Ford and Chrysler recently, and by GM in the mid-1980s. For its part, the union has learned that it can effectively pursue its goals and objectives, and through participation and discussion based on a strong independent stance can change production and work methods to the benefit of workers. Following the first ever strike against a transplant, the CAW success in persuading the Japanese management at CAMI to modify team concepts and practices and accept union input to setting production standards has been a big source of optimism and support for those in the union who favor positive intervention in work reorganization (CAW, 1992).

Based on the positive, but 'uneven', experience with these experiments the union has been able to articulate a convincing independent worker agenda on work reorganization. The fresh strategy, adopted at the bargaining convention in May 1993, 'is to oppose lean production from a position of engagement and to work to change it through negotiations'. The strategy is inspired by the philosophy of a 'working relationship' based on different interests and unequal power, and emphasizing the importance of an independent base for negotiating with management. The new CAW agenda stresses the importance of negotiating access to company information, to resources, and for the right to have input into, and influence over, the reorganization of work and the negotiation of specific training/education time to upgrade and develop worker skills, understanding and capabilities. The union believes that if there is involvement (in work reorganization efforts) it can not be passive; the 'participation is premised on advancing the interests of workers and strengthening the union as an organization capable of advancing those interests' (CAW, 1993).

The CAW sees union intervention in workplace changes, not only as a way of defending working conditions by seeking 'to make jobs more rewarding and workplaces more democratic', but also as an 'opportunity to develop a new activism in the workplace, an opening to mobilize ... members around new – or at least previously underemphasized needs'. The union believes that union intervention can lead to greater worker control, an improved work environment, and expanded job mobility for both skilled trades and production workers. The union agenda emphasizes that along with teamwork, job rotation, greater employee involvement and responsibility and broader jobs, work reorganization needs to encompass good job designs and extensive training and retraining opportunities. According to the CAW National President (Hargrove, 1993), 'workers should have more authority and not just added responsibility, opportunities to learn new skills not just to perform additional tasks, more mobility in the workplace rather than just being moved around'. The recent CAW (1993) document notes that:

Developing good job design means:

- Jobs which are not only safe but healthy.
- Jobs which are constructed on the basis of deepening skills and expanding discretion rather than the reverse.
- Workplaces that have a mix and range of jobs and not a regulated way of getting to them.
- Workplaces that accommodate injured workers so that there would be no additional pressures on other workers.

The union's work reorganization agenda also incorporates expanded employment equity and flexibility provisions for workers. The CAW believes that equity measures including equal opportunities in hiring, transfers, promotions and training, physical access to the workplace, flexibility to combine work and family demands, and the elimination of workplace harassment should be a part and parcel of workplace change programs. The union seeks greater union input with regard to the 'conception, development and implementation of any work reorganization initiative and desires expanded opportunities to discuss production issues from a union perspective'. It advocates:

> ... training committees to assess training needs and develop training programs; ergonomics committees to improve the design of work stations and the design of jobs; technology committees that focus on the design, implementation and the effects of new technology; and environmental committees which discuss environmentally sound products and production methods.
>
> (CAW, 1993).

However, while favoring participation and involvement, the union document states bluntly:

> ... we are not interested in becoming junior partners in production, but we want to develop an effective relationship with management which improves the conditions of work for our members as well as the productive capacity of the workplace.
>
> (CAW, 1993)

THE CAW vs THE UAW RESPONSE: A SUMMARY

The preceding analysis unambiguously suggests that the CAW vision of work reorganization and the union–management relationship is fundamentally at odds with the UAW position. The CAW, by adopting both defensive and pro-active strategies, has been able to articulate its own independent agenda, based on its view of different interests and different constituencies but stressing the importance of developing a working relationship with management. Conversely, the UAW has remained preoccupied with preventing job losses and preserving future jobs and, in the process, by accepting jointness and partnership with management in shopfloor governance and lacking a consistent strategy of its own for responding to management initiatives, has become a hostage to management's competitive agenda. There are two key questions to explore. The first is which of the two responses is stable in the long run? The second is which of the two union strategies, the CAW strategy to oppose and modify lean production from a position of engagement and to work to change it through negotiation, or the UAW's accommodative strategy of cooperation and partnership with management, is the most effective for protecting worker interests and for maintaining a strong union presence at the workplace? A partial answer lies in the effects of the CAW and UAW responses to management-inspired initiatives for work reorganization on workers and on the organizational and bargaining strength of the union.

A key reason for the UAW's decision to accept jointness and participation with management was to prevent job losses and preserve future jobs. In pursuit of this goal, the union in 1984 and in subsequent bargaining rounds with GM and Ford 'emphasized job security in the form of a significant new commitment not to lay off any worker with a year or more of seniority as a result of outsourcing, new technology, or other actions under control of corporations' (Friedman, 1989; and Friedman and Fischer, 1989), and provided for Job Banks to handle the relocation and retraining of displaced workers, union involvement and participation in managerial decision-making, and jointness in training and other activities.[20] Turner (1991) and Herzenberg (1991) have pointed out that the UAW, despite the contractual guarantees and influence on management decisions, has been unable to protect workers against the effects of corporate rationalization and cost cutting through productivity-enhancing technological change and work reorganization. Herzenberg (1991) shows that although employment at the Big Three increased by around 10 per cent between 1982 and 1987, it declined by over 16 per cent between 1987 and 1990. The unionized workforce at component-parts operations has been declining steadily since the early 1980s.[21] Herzenberg also notes that there is evidence to indicate that injury and illness rates have also gone up following the diffusion of lean production. Turner (1991, pp. 87–8), following a review of the UAW accomplishments, concludes that there are important limitations to contractual forms of employment security for protecting the workforce. He, and Perusek (1988), also suggests that despite the development of cooperative models:

> ... whipsawing has become a standard practice, as managers pressure UAW locals and workforces to grant concessions on work organization. And the danger of an American version of enterprise unionism can not be discounted as locals and different firms and plants go their own, joint productivity-enhancing way.
>
> (Turner, 1991, p. 89)

Perusek (1988, pp. 346–7) concludes that since individual locals' ability to resist work-rule concessions has weakened, the work-rule changes now underway promise to destroy the system of job control, a characteristic of the postwar labor relations system in the industry. In addition to the effects of these developments on workers, the UAW's organizational and bargaining strength has weakened as a result of declining membership and internal dissentions within the union over the UAW national leadership's orientation toward cooperation and partnership with management.

In contrast to the experience in the United States, the Canadian workers have enjoyed greater job and income security, partly due to a more favorable economic environment and partly as a result of the CAW's emphasis on income security. The CAW has always maintained that it was difficult to provide guarantees against job losses in a cyclical industry undergoing restructuring. Canadian workplaces also appear safer, judging by the unpublished data from Statistics Canada which show that injuries in the industry have declined substantially between 1987 and 1991. Canadian workers are also better protected against management whipsawing due to the strong union presence and representation. There is considerable solidarity within the union on account of forums for expression of dissent and an emphasis on consensus decision-making.[22] The union has gained membership through new organizing and mergers. The success in winning new membership is attributed to its reputation of being a strong, dynamic union with innovative collective bargaining and organizational and political strategies responsive to the changing needs and aspirations of workers. Moreover, the union, with its combined strategy of resistance and change has effectively limited the wide discretion traditionally enjoyed by management in the American auto industry with regard to introducing new work rules and production standards, insisting instead on informal and incremental changes as needed. However, while the restructuring of work and the reward system has proceeded more slowly in Canada than the United States, Big Three plants in Canada have continued to show significant improvements in productivity and product quality.

Turner (1988) has identified three possible outcomes of the drive for work reorganization and a corresponding new form of industrial relations in the United States auto industry:

1.   The marginalization of union influence and the imposition of Nissan and Honda-type solutions;
2.   An enterprise unionism model characterized by the spread of the team concept with well-integrated unions and consensual industrial relations, in which local unions play a decidedly subordinate role in managerial decision-making – the NUMMI model;

3. A homegrown version of team organization resulting from prolonged discussion, negotiation and conflict between labor and management in which the union would play a more assertive and independent role.

Whereas in the United States, option (2) has increasingly become the preferred outcome for management and has, in part, either deliberately or by default, been endorsed by the union leadership, in Canada the union has explicitly rejected options (1) and (2) and, therefore, option (3) is the more probable outcome.

CONCLUSIONS

Workers and their unions in the integrated North American automobile industry face hard and difficult choices and challenges in the 1990s. After more than a decade of adjustment and restructuring, the industry is still in a state of flux. The Big Three, in an effort to maintain, and if possible regain, their market share have embarked upon a mix of lean production strategies. Their aim is to achieve competitive cost efficiency by reducing costs and improving productivity and product quality through rationalization of the workforce and work reorganization to enhance managerial discretion and flexibility in the deployment of the workforce. The workplace changes, largely modelled on Japanese practices, pose a serious challenge to unions, threatening their traditional role of safeguarding worker rights and promoting equity and fairness.

The Big Three's attempts to restructure work and reward systems and the nature of union–management relationships has led to an increasing diversity in work practices between companies and plants, and between Canada and the United States. The cross-border divergence in collective bargaining approaches and outcomes has been the most notable feature of contemporary industrial relations in the industry. The latter, for the first three decades of the postwar period had been characterized by uniform wages and similar contract provisions. The divergence between the United States and Canada, which along the way precipitated a split in the international union and the formation of the CAW, is principally attributable to the different responses of the unions in the two countries toward managerial strategies to transform the industrial relations system and reorganize work. Whereas the Canadian union, the CAW (a UAW region from its creation in 1935 until 1985), has successfully opposed management efforts to transform work organization, the wage-structure, and union–management relationships, in the United States the UAW has traded off annual increases in wages and work-rule concessions for the promise of job security and an involvement in managerial decision-making. The divergent responses have not only damaged the unique and unprecedented cross-border labor solidarity that existed in the auto industry, but have also led to serious internal divisions within the UAW, encouraging management to whipsaw locals to grant further concessions. While the UAW leadership has yet to produce a consistent counter-strategy to provide an effective response to management initiatives,[23] the CAW in Canada has taken a bold and innovative step by articulating an independent agenda centered around a strategy of resistance and change, emphasizing different interests and constituencies of labor and management but stressing the importance of a close working relationship. The CAW remains opposed to jointness and partnership, initiatives supported by the UAW, and is dedicated to opposing lean production from a position of strength and engagement and to work toward changing it through negotiations. Paradoxically, while the economies of Canada and the United States became even more interdependent with the signing of the Canada–US Free Trade Agreement in 1989, and the NAFTA in 1994 which, in turn, has generated pressures for the creation of a 'level playing field' and the harmonization of social and economic policies, a 'continental divide' has emerged in the goals, priorities and strategies of the two unions operating in the highly integrated auto industry and between the two labor movements more generally.

The divergent responses of the CAW and the UAW raise a number of questions regarding the future shape of the management's lean production strategies and the implications for the economic and political well-being of workers, particularly in the context of the widening of the free-trade bloc under the NAFTA to incorporate Mexico.[24] Key questions are, which of the two union responses are stable in the long run, and which of the two has the greatest potential for humanizing the lean production system and for maintaining a strong union presence at the workplace to protect and safeguard worker interests? The evidence to date, in the form of differentials in wages, working conditions, employment security, worker control over work practices and union democracy, favors the CAW response. The Canadian response appears even more viable in view of the impressive improvements in productivity and product quality of Big Three plants in Canada, leading the Big

Three to significantly increase investment in plant modernization. The UAW gains in the areas of employment security and involvement in management decision-making, despite contractual guarantees and innovative new styles of labor contracts at NUMMI and Saturn, remain spotty. Moreover, in the absence of a consistent consensus-based independent vision of work reorganization and the labor–management relationship, the risks of the emergence of a culture of enterprise unionism in US plants remain high, as Turner (1991) and Herzenberg (1990) have noted.

The CAW experience confirms the conclusions reached by Middlebrook (1991, pp. 276–7) that workers' organizational and bargaining strength is 'the central factor determining variations in the character of the restructuring process and its political and economic consequences for labor in different countries and production sites'. The Canadian response further demonstrates that strong unions, with an independent worker agenda of resistance and change and rank-and-file solidarity based on opportunities for debate, discussions and dissent, are better able to defend workers' rights and mobilize workers' support to shape the character of the lean production process. Unions, therefore, have the option of either simply acquiescing to the management agenda or devising their own strategies for, what Berggren has called, the 'selected synthesis of both lean and human-centered practices' (Berggren, 1992, p. 255). The choices they make have important consequences for workers' well-being and the survival of unions as an independent voice.

The different strategic paths chosen by the CAW and the UAW have critical implications for workers in view of the NAFTA. Whereas the CAW resistance has forced managers to reassess their workplace change agenda, the UAW's 'cooperatist' response has permitted the Big Three to exploit the vulnerabilities inherent in plant-level unionism to push for greater management discretion in work organization and to transform the role and functions of the union in the US. Similarly in the case of Mexico, Middlebrook (1991, pp. 292–3) argues that:

> ... the absence of a democratically organized national automobile workers' union has permitted transnational firms to exploit the vulnerabilities inherent in enterprise and plant level unionism and reduce wages and fringe benefit levels, cut employment, rewrite contracts, and redefine workplace relations. The geographical dispersion of automobile workers resulting from industry reorganiza-

tion in the 1980s and political divisions among labor organizations have precluded effective long-term political action by workers.

Furthermore, Middlebrook believes that the managerial flexibility built into the contracts negotiated with CTM-affiliated unions, particularly in the recently built export-oriented vehicle assembly and engine plants in northern Mexico, give the transnational auto makers, including the Big Three, an additional negotiating advantage in bargaining with automobile workers in Canada and the United States. Thus, the extension of the current North American free-trade bloc to Mexico is likely to further strengthen management ability to whipsaw workers and their unions to grant wage and work-organization concessions under the threat of the reassignment of work to Mexico.

To prevent competition on the basis of wages, which in Mexico are about 10 per cent of the level in Canada and the US, and being played-off against each other over work reorganization concessions, Canadian, American and Mexican workers need to fashion a *labor* vision of economic development and continental integration and push for a harmonization of labor standards and industrial-relations practices that protect workers' interests across the continent, preferably using Canadian standards as a benchmark. While the negotiation of parallel side agreements on labor and environmental issues under the NAFTA is an important and defensive first step, the development by labor of a much broader and historically progressive strategy is required if the consolidation of a segmented pattern of continental economic development is to be prevented. Without a solidaristic stand, the NAFTA may further erode not only wages, working conditions and union influence in the United States (and ultimately in Canada), but could also have a dampening effect on Mexican automobile workers' struggle for improvements in their economic well-being and a meaningful control over the production process. Only a strong union movement, with an independent labor agenda, emphasizing, among other things, alliances, coalition-building and international solidarity can change the corporate lean production agenda, promote workers' interests, and effectively defend workers' rights. The big question is, can the CAW and the UAW learn from each other's experience, as well as from the labor relations developments in Mexico over the last decade, and coordinate their activities with Mexican unions in the spirit of international solidarity to provide a potent, progressive response to the restructuring of the North American automobile industry to ensure an enhanced quality of work life for workers in an expanded free-trade bloc?[25]

Notes

1. The North American automobile industry here refers to auto (passenger car and trucks) assembly and parts manufacturing in Canada and the United States. The industry includes the three traditional manufacturers (General Motors, Ford and Chrysler), the focus of this paper, as well as Asian transplants and independent parts suppliers. It is a highly integrated industry characterised by common employers in both countries, workers who from the 1930s to 1985 were represented on both sides of the border by a single international union, the UAW, and governed, since 1965, by a sectoral free-trade agreement, called the Auto Pact. The Big Three operate 10 car and truck plants and 12 component parts manufacturing facilities in Canada. There are five transplants, three Japanese, one South Korean, and one Volvo plant. See Kumar and Meltz (1992) and Holmes (1993) for an analysis of the evolution of the industry in Canada.

2. A recent study by the Economic Strategy Institute (1992, p. 16) reveals that while Japanese transplants' non-labor costs exceed the Big Three, due largely to higher costs of purchased components and materials, transplants enjoy a significant advantage in labor costs and also had superior productivity performance.

3. Lean production, according to the MIT study in which the term was coined, *The Machine that Changed the World: The Story of Lean Production*, is a method of production that 'uses less of everything compared with mass production – half of the human effort in the factory, half of the manufacturing space, half the investment in tools, half the engineering hours to develop a new product in half the time' (Womack, Jones and Roos, 1990, p. 13). The MIT study believes that lean production is a superior system of production that will ultimately become standard best practice throughout the global auto industry. For a critique of the system see Berggren (1992), Williams *et al.* (1992), and Wood (1991). For a Canadian perspective on the application of lean production in a unionized setting see Robertson *et al.* (1992). For a critical perspective on how lean production has changed American industry see Applebaum and Batt (1994). European unions' responses to the challenge posed by lean production are summarized in Hans Böckler Foundation (1992).

4. International unions were a major factor in the development of the Canadian labor movement, accounting for between one-half to over four-fifths of total union membership in Canada during the period 1911–75. Their relative strength has been declining over the past three decades, reaching a historic low of 31 per cent in 1992. See Kumar (1993a) and Arrowsmith (1992). This decline is even more significant when viewed in the context of the seemingly irreversible move toward continental economic integration under the free-trade regime.

5. CAW membership stood at 170 000 in 1993, compared to 120 000 in 1984, a year before the split. The motor vehicle industry accounted for about 55 per cent of the membership (24 per cent in assembly, 13 per cent in captive parts and 18 per cent in independent parts). Of the 50 000 increase in membership, about 60 per cent has come from mergers with unions in fisheries, rail, mining, airlines and electrical industries; the remaining

40 per cent was from net additions due to new organizing (CAW 1993, pp. iii–iv).

6. Most observers agree that even before the signing of the formal NAFTA between the United States, Mexico and Canada, the auto industry was set on an irreversible course toward continental integration. The implications of the NAFTA for the auto industries in Canada and the United States are discussed in Holmes (1992 and 1993), Eden and Molot (1993), Molot (1993) and Herzenberg (1991).

7. According to Turner (1991, p. 37), when viewed from a comparative perspective the critical elements of the postwar industrial relations system in the US auto industry included: (1) adversarial, arm's-length relationships between labor and management; (2) a centralized union, the UAW, with an emphasis on pattern-setting bargaining; (3) active, democratic local unions (within the UAW), that negotiated and administered local contracts in a framework of job control unionism; and (4) the union's broader pattern-setting role in the economy and society. While the system constrained management's ability to set work rules, it gave management a free hand with regard to technological change and the organization of production and work. One of the major differences between the postwar 'Fordist' collective bargaining system that emerged in North America and that which developed in other OECD countries was the decentralized and 'localized' nature of bargaining in Canada and the United States (see Lewchuk, 1987; Clark, 1986; and Boyer, 1988).

8. During the late 1960s and 1970s the AIF was usually set at 3 per cent. For a history of the AIF see Bluestone and Bluestone (1992, pp. 44–6).

9. Nominal wage parity refers to wages rates that are equal when measured in national currencies, such that if an assembler in Detroit, Michigan was paid US$5.12/hour (the rate in 1973), an assembler in Windsor, Ontario would be paid CAN$5.12/hour.

10. A typical management rights clause reads as follows:

> The Union recognizes the right of the company to hire, promote, transfer, demote and lay-off employees, and to suspend, discharge or otherwise discipline employees for just cause subject to the right of any employee to lodge a grievance in the manner and to the extent as herein provided.
>
> The Union further recognizes the right of the company to operate and manage its business in all respects, to maintain order and efficiency in its plants, and to determine the location of its plants, the products to be manufactured, the scheduling of its production and its methods, processes, and means of manufacturing. The union further acknowledges that the company has the right to make and alter, from time to time, rules and regulations to be observed by employees, which rules and regulations shall not be inconsistent with the provisions of this agreement (Master Agreement between General Motors of Canada and the CAW, 1993:5).

The clause has remained almost unchanged since the first agreement was signed in 1953. Similar clauses are included in Ford and Chrysler agreements in both Canada and the United States.

11. See Katz (1988a) for a critical analysis of the General Motors Corporation's business and labor-relations strategies. He argues that auto companies in general, and GM in particular, have employed two basic strategies for restructuring: (1) the downsizing strategy to cut costs; and (2) the reorganization strategy to change production and labor-relations practices.

12. For a discussion of internal divisions within the UAW, reasons for defections and the challenges mounted by the dissenting groups under the banner of the New Directions Movement see *Labor Notes* (monthly), Herzenberg (1990) and Perusek (1988). A chronology of the conflict is provided in Katz and Kochan (1992, p. 159). See also Katz (1988b) who argues that much of the debate within the UAW has involved an argument between those led by Don Ephlin, the former UAW vice-president who favored trading-off wage concessions for job security and involvement in decision-making, and the militants under the New Directions banner, who oppose concessions on the grounds that they create divisive splits across workers and are a step toward company unionism (in the pejorative sense). The two groups, cooperatists and militants as Katz calls them, differ sharply in their views on work reorganization. While cooperatists favor reorganization, militants oppose team systems and related committee and pay structures associated with work reorganization (see Parker and Slaughter, 1988, for a detailed exposition of the militant position).

13. Herzenberg (1990) points out in his study of the North American auto industry that the CAW (and the Canadian region of the UAW prior to 1985) has always been very active in new organizing. His calculations show that while Canadian membership from new organizing has been stable, the UAW organizing peaked in 1966–67 and has been declining ever since. The Canadian region of the UAW received special mention for its organizing successes throughout the President's Report to the UAW constitutional conventions throughout the 1960s and 1970s (Herzenberg, 1990, p. 185, ft. 129). Also see note 5 above.

14. The emphasis placed on wages and benefits by the Canadians is also explained by three other income-related factors. First, there is more protection in Canada afforded against the consequences of layoff by government legislation and programs such as unemployment insurance and laws governing plant closure and severance pay. Second, higher rates of inflation in Canada in the early 1980s as compared with the United States meant that wage restraint of the kind accepted by the American union would have had a more serious impact on real wages in Canada. Third, there is a much larger differential in the US than in Canada between auto industry wages and the average manufacturing wage, which means that American auto workers could afford to make significant concessions on earnings and yet still earn substantially more than the average industrial worker (Gindin, 1989, p. 85).

15. During the recession of the early 1990s, Canada's trade balances under the Auto Pact and the Canadian shares of North American vehicle production and employment in the assembly sector all continued to increase. However, employment in the Canadian automotive parts sector fell by around 20 per cent between 1988 and 1992.

16. The 1982 Chrysler Canada strike also provided a dramatic example of how the integration of the North American automobile industry, which had begun with the Auto Pact and was further cemented by technological change and the development of just-in-time production methods, provided Canadian auto workers with a powerful lever. It demonstrated that strike action by a relatively small number of workers in Canada (or the United States for that matter) could now cripple auto production throughout North America.

17. In the United States, wages were frozen and profit sharing introduced, first by Chrysler in 1980, and then by Ford and GM in 1982. However, on those occasions the traditional Fordist wage rules of AIF and COLA were viewed as being temporarily suspended rather than superseded. The significance of the 1984 UAW–GM contract was that it established a new pattern for the setting of wage increases in the United States auto industry, a pattern that was quickly incorporated into contracts with Ford and Chrysler and subsequently reaffirmed in the 1987, 1990, and 1993 contracts.

18. An adversarial culture of resistance and change is not unique to the CAW but a characteristic of the Canadian labor movement generally. See Kumar (1993b) for an analysis of the positions on work restructuring adopted by the CAW, Steel Workers, and Communications, Energy and Paper Workers–the three leading private-sector unions in Canada.

19. To gain a more systematic understanding of the Japanese-style lean production system, how it operates, and what kind of effects it has on workers and the role of the union, the CAW negotiated in 1989 the provision for a longitudinal two-year investigation of work practices at CAMI to be conducted by a CAW national office research team (Robertson *et al.*, 1992).

20. According to Katz and MacDuffie (1994), the job-security measures serve two purposes: (1) they function as a partial compensation to the union and workers for the pay concessions and reduced worker resistance to plant closures; and (2) they provide direct assurance to the workers that pay and work-rule concessions will, in fact, lead to an improvement in their job security. They also point out, however, that the effects of the income and job security are very unclear, vary substantially across plants, and are closely linked to the dynamics of labor–management relations at the plant level.

21. Herzenberg (1991) suggests that UAW representation at independent parts suppliers in the United States has declined from over one-half of the workforce in the early 1970s to between one-fifth and one-third, depending on the estimation methods used. Using UAW membership data he shows a decline from 60 per cent in 1976–78 to 23 per cent in 1988–90. The Canadian union coverage of independent parts, according to Herzenberg, has remained stable at over 50 per cent.

22. Herzenberg (1990) argues that while 'UAW leaders' ability to incorporate dissent and their confidence in and capacity for pursuing mobilization strategies gradually declined ... within the Canadian union, quarterly meetings of a rank and file elected Canadian Council helped sustain traditions of internal debate, limited the extent to which leaders could ignore

rank-and-file pressure, and enhanced the union's ability to mobilize workers' (Herzenberg, 1990, pp. 13–14).

23. Herzenberg (1990, p. 44) observes that 'with union coverage shrinking, with the decline of union presence on the shopfloor in organized factories, and with US labor's invisibility in national politics, forging an inclusive auto sector pattern of development in the US will require regenerating rather than simply redefining the role of industrial unions in plants and in society'.

24. For discussions of the implications of the NAFTA specifically for the automobile industry see Eden and Molot (1993) and several of the essays in Molot (1993). Throughout the 1980s there was a progressive integration of Mexican automotive production into the rest of the North American automobile industry and, with or without the formal signing of the NAFTA, it was likely that such integration would have continued apace during the 1990s (Holmes, 1993).

25. An important first step in this regard was taken by the two unions when the UAW President, Owen Bieber, was invited to speak to the CAW political and bargaining convention in May 1993, the first such invitation since the split. Bieber, in his address, reaffirmed 'the intertwined interests of US and Canadian workers', 'the two unions' history, tradition and perspective', the fact that they 'bargain with many of the same employers' and the two unions' 'desire to win for working people a better life – on the job and off'. He underscored the necessity of working 'even more closely to *coordinate* our campaigns to educate our members and our fellow citizens on this vital issue [the NAFTA]'. The UAW President suggested that 'transnational corporations *must* be met with *united worker power* that also transcends national boundaries' (Bieber, 1993).

References

Applebaum, Eileen and Rosemary Batt (1994) *The New American Workplace* (Ithaca, New York: ILR Press).

Arrowsmith, David (1992) *Canada's Trade Unions: An Information Manual* (Kingston, Ontario: IRC Press, Queen's University).

Berggren, Christian (1992) *Alternatives to Lean Production* (Ithaca, New York: ILR Press).

Bieber, Owen (1993) 'Remarks of UAW President, Owen Bieber, at Canadian Auto Workers Convention, Toronto, Canada, 6 May 1993', *UAW News*. Detroit, MI: Solidarity House, United Automobile Workers of America.

Bluestone, Barry and Irving Bluestone (1992) *Negotiating the Future: A Labor Perspective on American Business* (New York: Basic Books).

Boyer, Robert (1988) 'Wage/Labour Relations, Growth and Crisis: A Hidden Dialectic', in Robert Boyer (ed.), *The Search for Labour Market Flexibility* (Oxford: Clarendon Press).

Canadian Auto Workers (1989) *CAW Statement on the Reorganization of Workers* (North York, Ontario: CAW).

Canadian Auto Workers (1991) *Departmental Reports*, 3rd Constitutional Convention (North York, Ontario: CAW).

Canadian Auto Workers (1992) *CAW-Canada/CAMI Report: Highlights of the Tentative Agreement Between CAW-Canada and CAMI* (North York, Ontario: CAW).

Canadian Auto Workers (1993) *Hard Times, New Times: Fighting for our Future.* Report to the National Collective Bargaining and Political Action Convention (North York, Ontario: CAW).

Clark, Gordon (1986) 'Restructuring the US Economy: The NLRB, the Saturn Project, and Economic Justice', *Economic Geography*, 62(4), pp. 289–306.

Economic Strategy Institute (1992) *The Future of the Auto Industry: It Can Compete, Can It Survive?* (Washington, DC: Economic Strategy Institute).

Eden, Lorraine and Maureen Appel Molot (1993) 'The NAFTA's Automotive Provisions: The Next Stage of Managed Trade', *C.D. Howe Institute Commentary*, No. 53 (Montreal: C.D. Howe Institute).

Friedman, Sheldon and Lydia Fischer (1989) 'Collective Bargaining and Employment Security', in *Proceedings of the Forty-First Annual Meeting, December 28–30, 1988, New York* (Madison, WI: Industrial Relations Research Association).

Friedman, Sheldon (1989) 'Discussion: IR Developments in US and Canada', in *Proceedings of the Forty-First Annual Meeting, December 28–30, 1988, New York* (Madison: WI: Industrial Relations Research Association).

Fuss, Melvyn A. and Leonard Waverman (1992) *Costs and Productivity in Automobile Production: The Challenge of Japanese Efficiency* (Cambridge: Cambridge University Press).

Gindin, Sam (1989) 'Breaking Away: The Formation of the Canadian Auto Workers', *Studies in Political Economy*, 29, pp. 63–89.

Hans Böckler Foundation (1992) 'Industrial Democracy in the Modern Workplace', *Die Mitbestimmung*, special 1992 English edition (Düsseldorf, Germany: Hans-Böckler Foundation).

Harbour and Associates (1990) *The Harbour Report: A Decade Later. Competitive Assessment of the North American Automobile Industry 1979–1989* (Troy, MI: Harbour and Associates).

Harbour and Associates (1992) *The Harbour Report: Competitive Assessment of the North American Automobile Industry, 1989–1992* (Troy, MI: Harbour and Associates).

Hargrove, Buzz (1993) 'Labour Relations: Change, But in What Direction?' Notes for an Address to the Financial Post Conference on Canada's Auto Industry: North Americanization (North York, Ontario: CAW).

Herzenberg, Stephen (1990) 'Towards a Cooperative Commonwealth? Labor and Restructuring in the US and Canadian Auto Industries', Ph.D. dissertation, Department of Economics, Massachussets Institute of Technology.

Herzenberg, Stephen (1991) *The North American Auto Industry at the Onset of Continental Free Trade Negotiations.* Economic Discussion Paper No. 38, US Department of Labor, Bureau of International Labor Affairs.

Holmes, John (1987) 'The Crisis of Fordism and the Restructuring of the Canadian Auto Industry', in John Holmes and Colin Leys (eds), *Frontyard/Backyard: The Americas in the Global Crisis* (Toronto, Ontario: Between the Lines Press).

Holmes, John (1989) 'New Production Technologies, Labor and the North American Auto Industry', in Godfrey J.R. Linge and Bert van der Knaap (eds), *Labour, Environment and Industrial Change* London: Routledge.

Holmes, John (1991) 'The Globalization of Production and Canada's Mature Industries: The Case of the Auto Industry', in Daniel Drache and Meric Gertler (eds), *The Era of the New Competition* (Kingston: McGill/Queen's University Press).

Holmes, John (1992) 'The Continental Integration of the North American Automobile Industry: From the Auto Pact to the FTA and Beyond', *Environment and Planning A*, 24, pp. 95–119.

Holmes, John (1993) 'From Three Industries to One: The Integration of the North American Automobile Industry', in Maureen Appel Molot (ed.), *Driving Continentally: National Policies and the North American Auto Industry* (Ottawa: Carleton University Press).

Holmes, John and Anthony Rusonik (1991) 'The Break-Up of an International Labour Union: Uneven Development in the North American Auto Industry and the Schism in the UAW', *Environment and Planning A*, 23, pp. 9–35.

Industry, Science and Technology Canada (1992) *Statistical Review of the Canadian Automobile Industry: 1992 Edition* (Ottawa: Supply and Services Canada).

Jessop, Bob (1992) 'Post-Fordism and Flexible Specialization: Incommensurable, Contradictory, Complementary, or Just Plain Different Perspectives', in H. Ernste and V. Meier (eds), *Regional Development and Contemporary Industrial Response* (Aldershot: Belhaven Press).

Katz, Harry C. (1985) *Shifting Gears: Changing Labor Relations in the US Automobile Industry* (Cambridge, MA: MIT Press).

Katz, Harry C. (1987) 'Collective Bargaining in the US Automobile Industry', in D. Lipsky and C. Donn (eds), *Collective Bargaining in American Industry* (Lexington, MA: D.C. Heath).

Katz, Harry C. (1988a) 'Business and Labor Relations Strategies in the US Automobile Industry: The Case of the General Motors Corporation', in Ben Dankbaar *et al.* (eds), *Die Zukunft der Arbeit in der Automobilindustrie* (Berlin: Ed. Sigma)

Katz, Harry C. (1988b) 'Policy Debates Over Work Reorganization in North American Unions', in Richard Hyman and Wolfgang Streeck (eds), *New Technology and Industrial Relations* (Oxford: Basic Blackwell).

Katz, Harry C. and John Paul MacDuffie (1994) 'Collective Bargaining in the US Auto Assembly Sector', in Paula Voos (ed.), *Contemporary Collective Bargaining in the Private Sector* (Madison, WI: Industrial Relations Research Association).

Katz, Harry C. and Noah M. Meltz (1989) 'Changing work practices and productivity in the auto industry: a U.S.-Canada Comparison'. Proceedings of the 26th Conference of the Canadian Industrial Relations Association, Industrial Relations Issues for the 1990s. (ed.) Michel Grant, Quebec City: CIRA Université Laval, 388–396.

Katz, Harry C. and Thomas A. Kochan (1992) *An Introduction to Collective Bargaining and Industrial Relations* (New York: McGraw-Hill).

Kochan, Thomas A., Harry C Katz and Robert B. McKersie (1986) *The Transformation of American Industrial Relations* (New York: Basic Books).

198   *Change, but in what Direction?*

Kochan, Thomas A. (1988) 'Adaptability of the US Industrial Relations System' *Science* (15 April), 240, pp. 287–92.

Kumar, Pradeep (1991) 'Labour Market Adjustment Issues in Canada: An Industrial Relations Perspective', *Queen's Papers in Industrial Relations 1991–6* (Kingston, Ontario: School of Industrial Relations, Queen's University).

Kumar, Pradeep (1993a) *From Uniformity to Diversity: Industrial Relations in Canada and the United States* (Kingston, Ontario: IRC Press, Queen's University).

Kumar, Pradeep (1993b) 'Canadian Labour's Response to Work Reorganization', *Queen's Papers in Industrial Relations 1993–6* (Kingston, Ontario: School of Industrial Relations, Queen's University).

Kumar, Pradeep and Noah M. Meltz (1992) 'Industrial Relations in the Canadian Automobile Industry', in Richard P. Chaykowski and Anil Verma (eds), *Industrial Relations in the Canadian Industry* (Toronto, Ontario: Dryden).

Lecki, Norman (1993) 'An International Review of Labour Adjustment Policies and Practices', Queen's Papers in Industrial Relations 1993–15 (Kingston, Ontario: School of Industrial Relations, Queen's University).

Lewchuk, Wayne (1987) *American Technology and the British Vehicle Industry* (Cambridge: Cambridge University Press).

Lovell, Malcolm R. (1991) *Making It Together: The Modern Operating Agreement Between Chrysler Corporation and the United Auto Workers* (Springfield, VA: National Technical Information Service, US Department of Commerce).

MacDuffie, John Paul (1991) *Beyond Mass Production: Flexible Production Systems and Manufacturing Performance in the World Auto Industry*, Ph.D. dissertation, Sloan School of Management, Massachusetts Institute of Technology.

Middlebrook, Kevin J. (1991) 'The Politics of Industrial Restructuring: Transnational Firms' Search for Flexible Production in the Mexican Automobile Industry', *Comparative Politics* (April), 23 (3) pp. 275–97.

Molot, Maureen Appel (1993) *Driving Continentally: National Policies and the North American Auto Industry* (Ottawa: Carleton University Press).

Parker, Mike and Jane Slaughter (1988) *Choosing Sides: The UAW and the Team Concept* (Boston: South End Press).

Perusek, Glenn W. (1988) *The International Politics of the United Automobile Workers, 1967–1985*, Ph.D. dissertation, Department of Economics, The University of Chicago.

Perusek, Glenn W. (1989) 'The U.S.-Canada Split in the United Automobile Workers' in *Proceedings of the Forty-First Annual Meeting, December 28–30, 1988 New York* (Madison, WI: Industrial Relations Research Association).

Robertson, David, James Rinehart, Christopher Huxley, Jeff Wareham, Herman Rosenfeld, Alan McGough, Steve Benedict (1992) *Japanese Production Management in a Unionized Auto Plant* (North York, Ontario: CAW Research Department).

Taylor, Don and M. Bradley Dow (1988) *The Rise of Industrial Unionism in Canada: A History of the CIO*, Research and Current Issues Series No. 56 (Kingston, Ontario: Industrial Relations Centre, Queen's University).

Turner, Lowell (1988) *Are Labor–Management Partnerships for Competitiveness Possible in America: The US Auto Industry Examined*, BRIE Working Paper No. 36 (Berkeley: University of California).

Turner, Lowell (1991) *Democracy at Work: Changing World Markets and the Future of Labor Unions* (Ithaca, New York: Cornell University Press).

United Auto Workers 1987, '1987 Contract Proposals: UAW-GM National Negotiating Committee', Detroit, MI: Solidarity House, United Automobile Workers of America.

Williams, Karel, Colin Haslam, John Williams, Anthony Cutler, Andy Adcroft, and Sukhdev Johal(1992) 'Against Lean Production', *Economy and Society*, 21 (3) pp. 321–54.

Womack, James., Daniel Jones and Daniel Roos (1990) *The Machine that Changed the World* (New York: Rawson Associates).

Wood, Stephen (1988) 'Between Fordism and Flexibility? The Case of the US Automobile Industry', in Richard Hyman and Wolfgang Streeck (eds), *New Technology and Industrial Relations* (Oxford: Basil Blackwell).

Wood, Stephen (1991) 'Japanization or Toyotism?' *Work, Employment and Society*, 5 (4) pp. 567–600.

Yates, Charlotte (1990) 'The Internal Dynamics of Union Power: Explaining Canadian Autoworkers' Militancy in the 1980s', *Studies in Political Economy*, 31, pp. 73–106.

Yates, Charlotte (1992) 'North American Autoworkers' Response to Restructuring', in Miriam Golden and Jonas Pontusson (eds), *Bargaining for Change: Union Politics in North America and Europe* (Ithaca, NY: Cornell University Press).

7 The Politics of Industrial Restructuring: Transnational Firms' Search for Flexible Production in the Mexican Automobile Industry[†]

Kevin J. Middlebrook

The emergence of a highly competitive world automobile industry and the internationalization of automotive production in the 1970s and 1980s intensified transnational firms' search for new corporate alliances, innovative production technologies, and more flexible labor relations. The global transformation of automotive manufacturing has produced broad challenges for workers because in many countries the process of industrial restructuring has resulted in lower employment levels, reduced wages and fringe benefits, and other economic disruptions. Moreover, in their drive to achieve higher levels of production efficiency and quality control, many US and West European automobile companies have also re-examined the long dominant Fordist–Taylorist model of workplace organization in which relatively unskilled workers perform repetitive, narrowly defined tasks in a hierarchically organized, fragmented (assembly line) work process dedicated to the mass production of standardized products.[1]

Many of these firms (often consciously mimicking their very successful Japanese competitors) have instead adopted post-Fordist labor-relations arrangements that typically feature flexible work rules and job rotation, broadly defined job classifications, work teams, 'quality circles', and other measures designed to defuse labor–employer tensions

---

[†] This essay, based on field research conducted in Mexico in the late 1980s, was first published in *Comparative Politics* in April 1991 (vol. 23, no. 3). The concluding section has been revised to reflect recent developments potentially affecting the Mexican automobile industry.

and further motivate workers.[2] This new managerial approach challenges such mainstays of traditional industrial unionism as seniority, contractually specified job definitions designed to protect the rights of individual workers, and union representatives' role in the resolution of workplace grievances. As a consequence, the struggle over flexible production arrangements has become a central element in labor–employer negotiations in the automobile industry.

Because of transnational firms' vigorous competition for international market share, restructuring in the automobile industry is fundamentally a global process. Nevertheless, the political character of this process and its consequences for automobile workers vary greatly both from one country to another and among different firms.[3] In Mexico, transnational firms adopted two main strategies in their efforts to institute more flexible production arrangements capable of responding to the trend toward globally integrated production and the sudden decline in domestic demand following the country's 1982 financial crisis. First, they shifted the principal focus and location of automotive production by constructing export-oriented manufacturing facilities in central and northern Mexico in the early 1980s. By doing so, company managers sought to capitalize on the country's potential as a low wage base for manufactured exports and the Mexican government's export promotion program in the automobile industry. Equally important, the movement of automotive production away from established sites in Mexico City and surrounding areas (where, in several instances, democratic labor unions had won highly beneficial contract terms and broad influence over the production process) offered firms an opportunity to redefine labor relations in the new plants so as to lower labor costs and limit unions' influence in the manufacturing process. Company managers sought to ensure more docile labor relations by negotiating for workers at each of the new plants to be unionized under the auspices of the Confederation of Mexican Workers (CTM), the governing Institutional Revolutionary Party's labor sector, whose dependence on the Mexican state for financial and political subsidies and whose internal organizational weaknesses place it in a reactive position *vis-à-vis* government labor authorities and many large companies. Although a similar 'green field' strategy has sometimes been employed by automobile companies in other countries, the characteristics of state–labor relations in the Mexican authoritarian regime make this approach particularly attractive to firms seeking production flexibility.

Second, several transnational firms have introduced post-Fordist labor-relations measures in an attempt to increase managerial control, lower production costs, and improve product quality at their Mexican facilities. These arrangements have been used most extensively in the new export production plants, but wherever they have been tested, company managers conclude that these innovations improve workplace communications and quality control. However, this strategy has been less important in Mexico than in the United States and some West European countries because firms have been able to achieve production flexibility through other means.[4] The absence of a unified national automobile workers' union capable of enforcing uniform working conditions in different manufacturing plants and CTM affiliates' ready acceptance of employer preferences permitted firms to negotiate extremely favorable contracts at export production facilities. When concessionary bargaining with unions at older manufacturing plants has failed to produce comparable results, company managers have cut employment at these sites and shifted production to facilities where labor costs are lower. Thus, transnational firms have relied primarily on flexible labor contracts to win broad control over promotion procedures and policies affecting employment security, the disposition of personnel on the shop floor, and other aspects of the production process in order to respond to changing market conditions. Their pursuit of production flexibility has been facilitated by the de la Madrid (1982–88) and Salinas de Gortari (1988–94) administrations' active support for broad industrial restructuring and increased export production, although the restructuring process has mainly involved bilateral negotiations between different transnational firms and enterprise- or plant-specific automobile workers' unions.

Diverse factors may shape the character of transnational automobile firms' efforts to achieve production flexibility, including strategic choices by companies in response to labor market conditions[5] and the tactics adopted by unions. However, an analysis of the Mexican case and a review of other national studies of automobile industry restructuring suggest that workers' bargaining power is the central factor determining variations in the character of the restructuring process and its political and economic consequences for labor in different countries and production sites. The extent of labor's bargaining leverage in this process depends principally on three factors: (1) automobile workers' organizational strength in the workplace, which requires institutionalized procedures for local union participation in shop floor decisions, the democratic accountability of union officials to the rank and file, and, where industry federations or national confederations are not responsive to rank-and-file interests, sufficient organizational autonomy to permit the local union to strike or otherwise mobilize its members in support of collective demands; (2) automobile workers' organizational strength at the national level, which chiefly depends upon whether automobile workers are united nationally in a single industrywide union, grouped in different national level craft organizations, or organized only in enterprise- or plant-specific unions; and (3) the overall extent of organized labor's influence in national politics, which depends in large part on the organized labor movement's autonomy *vis-à-vis* the state and the nature of labor's linkages to political parties and on whether the political regime is democratic or authoritarian.[6]

This analysis of industrial restructuring in the Mexican automobile industry begins with an overview of key developments in the industry from the 1960s through the early 1980s. The emergence of democratic automobile workers' unions in the 1960s and 1970s, the consequent (although temporary) decline in CTM influence, and the response by automobile companies to more conflictive industrial relations established the context for subsequent management restructuring strategies. The second and third sections discuss the political and economic consequences for labor of transnational firms' shift toward export production in newly constructed plants in central and northern Mexico and company managers' implementation of post-Fordist labor-relations arrangements in their drive for production flexibility. The conclusion places this discussion in comparative perspective by examining the factors that distinguish industrial restructuring in the Mexican automobile industry from parallel processes in the United States, Canada, and western Europe. This comparative analysis shows the significant contribution the Mexican case makes to an understanding of labor's bargaining power as the central factor shaping the character and consequences of industrial restructuring in the global automobile industry.

THE MEXICAN AUTOMOBILE INDUSTRY IN TRANSITION

The Mexican automobile industry was founded in the 1920s and 1930s when Ford, General Motors and Fábricas Auto-Mex (a Mexican firm assembling Chryslers) established assembly facilities in the Mexico City area as part of their international expansion programs or in response to tariff protection offered to local assembly operations. However, no significant automobile manufacturing was performed in Mexico before 1962, when a government decree required firms to increase sharply the nationally produced share of components. Manufacturing activities expanded dramatically as a result, with transnational firms holding a predominant position in the production of finished vehicles. Virtually all blue-collar workers in the terminal (vehicle manufacturing) industry were organized in enterprise- and plant-level unions, nearly all of which were affiliated with the Confederation of Mexican Workers.[7] Workplace relations in the industry were structured in accordance with conventional Fordist–Taylorist principles.

The transformation of the Mexican automobile industry in the 1960s and 1970s sparked widespread sociopolitical change as workers at Diesel Nacional (DINA, a state-owned firm), Nissan, Volkswagen, and Ford overthrew entrenched labor leaders and instituted more democratic forms of union governance. Worker challenges to incumbent CTM leaders and established union organizations resulted primarily from structural changes in workplace relations, demands for greater worker control over internal union decision-making and increased union autonomy in negotiations with management, and the breakdown of labor control mechanisms characteristic of traditional Mexican unionism.[8] By 1975, workers in five of the seven principal vehicle manufacturing firms (the four firms named above plus General Motors, where a democratic union had been active since the 1940s) had won control over the selection of union leaders and other aspects of union decision-making.

Union democratization in the automobile industry had important consequences for workers. Union statutes were substantially revised (or new ones adopted) to provide for the regular election of union officers and their accountability to members, improve procedural safeguards on workers' union rights, increase rank-and-file participation in general assemblies, and expand the general assembly's role in internal union decision-making. These reforms significantly enhanced opportunities for members' participation in union affairs. Moreover, the election of departmental delegates produced a differentiated representational structure that greatly increased the union's mobilization capabilities in negotiations with management.

Once elected, democratic union leaderships usually acted quickly to redefine the character of local union ties to state and national labor organizations. Between 1961 and 1975, four automobile workers' unions either broke their ties with the CTM (DINA, 1961; Volkswagen, 1972; Nissan, 1972) or substantially redefined this relationship (Ford, 1975) in an effort to increase local union autonomy. Although the DINA, Volkswagen and Nissan unions subsequently joined the Independent Worker Unit (UOI) in order to increase their bargaining leverage *vis-*

à-vis employers, the character of such external linkages remained a source of intense union debate. Indeed, political divisions between democratic unions and undemocratic CTM affiliates precluded effective labor collaboration at the industry level. The International Metalworkers' Federation had failed to establish an industrywide automobile workers' council in the mid-1960s because of personal and political rivalries among CTM federation leaders,[9] but the decision of several democratic unions to break ties with the CTM and the emergence of the UOI as a rival organization made collective action even more problematic.

Despite these difficulties, democratic unions acted energetically to protect workers' interests, both in the resolution of individual and collective conflicts at the enterprise level and in grievance proceedings before such government agencies as the national social security administration and labor conciliation and arbitration boards. Over time, automobile workers in democratic unions won significant control over the production process (especially union participation in the determination of production rates, work force distribution within a plant, and occupational health and safety measures), promotion procedures and employment security (including union participation in the elaboration of the personnel hierarchy and in workplace promotions and the progressive reduction of temporary employees in the work force). The DINA, General Motors, Nissan and Volkswagen unions were more likely to strike than CTM affiliates, although their more assertive conduct in labor–management negotiations did not always produce larger wage increases.

These developments posed significant challenges for employers. More frequent strikes and democratic unions' assertiveness in collective bargaining made their conduct of labor relations much more difficult. Even more important, however, increased union control over the work process and limitations on the flexible movement of workers among different work areas constrained company managers' ability to respond to day-to-day shifts in production requirements. Similarly, the reduction in the proportion of temporary workers (those workers hired for less than 60 days or for a specific task) reduced firms' capacity to respond quickly to changing market conditions by dismissing redundant workers without paying costly separation indemnities. These issues were particularly significant because the ministry of industry and commerce administered both production quotas and price controls on finished vehicles from 1962 to 1977.[10] As a result, wage and fringe benefit costs and control over the disposition of workers within the workplace were of central importance to management. Managers in automobile manufacturing firms with democratic unions responded to these problems by vigorously contesting worker demands for increased wages and fringe benefits, employment security (especially the automatic promotion of temporary workers to permanent positions), and union control over promotions and the production process. But, over time, assertive union bargaining generally compelled firms to make important concessions in these areas.

However, General Motors and Nissan management sought to regain lost production flexibility through a different strategy: opening new manufacturing facilities in which the work force was affiliated with the Confederation of Mexican Workers, whose close ties to the government and generally cooperative attitude toward management permitted these firms to restore control over plant-level labor relations. In what became an important precedent in the industry, General Motors founded a motor manufacturing plant in Toluca in 1965 and negotiated with the CTM to unionize the new labor force. By doing so, General Motors took advantage of government investment incentives for manufacturing operations constructed outside the highly congested Mexico City area, and it was able to hire workers at the lower wage levels prevailing in the region. Even more important, company management eliminated union control over various aspects of the production process, regained flexibility over the movement of workers among different work areas and the use of temporary workers, and sharply reduced seniority-based labor costs by hiring a new work force. Although the union at General Motors' Federal District facility (affiliated with the Revolutionary Confederation of Workers and Peasants, CROC) went on strike to prevent company managers from abrogating a contractual guarantee that it would have legal representation of workers in any new manufacturing plant established in the country, the firm won a union concession on this key point and settled the strike after only two days by offering to increase the number of permanent workers at the Federal District plant.[11] In 1978, Nissan replicated General Motors' stratagem by establishing a CTM-affiliated plant in Lerma, thus removing the labor force at its foundry operations from the legal control of the democratic union at its assembly plant in Cuernavaca. Both the General Motors and the Nissan work forces have since remained under tight CTM control, and neither plant has experienced serious labor conflict.[12]

Despite gains by democratic unions and a recession in 1975–76, the Mexican automobile industry generally prospered during the 1970s.

The value of automobile industry production grew at an average rate of 10.3 per cent per year during 1975–81, and over the same period the automobile industry's share of gross domestic product in manufacturing (including auto parts) increased to 7.5 per cent (at constant 1970 prices).[13] The total production of cars and trucks rose to 587 460 vehicles in 1981.[14] The Mexican automobile industry remained a comparatively high cost, inefficient producer because of the number of firms producing a wide range of models destined primarily for a restricted national market, but the 1978–81 petroleum-led economic boom greatly expanded domestic demand and temporarily masked these problems.

However, the onset of economic crisis in 1982 struck the industry hard. Total production of cars and trucks fell by 51.6 per cent between 1981 and 1983, and despite a partial recovery thereafter, the level of production in 1987 (395 258 vehicles) remained only slightly above that achieved in 1975.[15] Total employment in the seven principal terminal industry firms fell from 60 388 persons in 1981 to 51 676 persons in 1986, a decline of 14.4 per cent; blue-collar employment (*obreros*) fell almost as sharply (by 12.5 per cent) over this same period.[16] The dramatic contraction of the domestic market forced Ford to close two of its three plants in the Mexico City area between 1983 and 1986, and Renault ended its vehicle manufacturing operations in Mexico in 1986.

EXPORT PROMOTION AND INDUSTRY REORGANIZATION IN THE 1980s

The crisis in the national automobile market after 1982 compelled both the Mexican government and transnational firms to reassess the future of the domestic automobile industry. In September 1983, the de la Madrid administration issued a decree designed to improve industry efficiency by sharply limiting the number of permitted makes and models (beginning in 1987 each firm was limited to a single make and five models), increasing the domestic content for all automotive vehicles (to 60 per cent for the 1987 model year), and encouraging exports.[17] Transnational firms had long resisted constraints on the number of makes and models produced, but they had begun export production (especially motors and other automotive parts) in the late 1970s.[18] With the domestic market in crisis, these companies aggressively expanded automotive exports. Annual exports of finished vehicles rose from 15 819 to 155 983 units between 1982 and 1987, and exports of engines increased from 320 301 to 1 431 733 over the same period.[19] By the late

1980s companies were firmly committed to export production; indeed, 34.9 per cent of the 290 476 vehicles produced between January and July 1988 were exported.[20]
The shift toward export production was accompanied by a significant spatial reorganization of the automobile industry. Chrysler (Ramos Arizpe, 4-cylinder engines), General Motors (Ramos Arizpe, 6-cylinder engines and automobiles), and Nissan (Aguascalientes, 4-cylinder engines) opened new plants in central and northern Mexico in 1981. In some cases these facilities had originally been planned when hope for increasing domestic automobile sales was bright, but after 1982 they were dedicated primarily to export production. Ford (Chihuahua, 4-cylinder engines, 1983; Hermosillo, automobiles, 1986) soon followed with its own export production plants.[21] These northern sites were chosen mainly because of their geographical proximity to the United States, the intended export market, and the investment incentives available for locating new manufacturing facilities outside the Mexico City metropolitan area. For example, Ford received large subsidies from both federal and state governments for its Hermosillo plant,[22] and several firms used debt-equity swaps to finance their new operations.[23] Equally important, however, the construction of these plants in central and northern Mexico offered automobile companies important political advantages.

The Restoration of CTM Preeminence

By negotiating for the CTM to represent workers at these plants, transnational firms won far-reaching managerial control over labor relations and the production process, and they placed democratic unionism in the industry on the defensive. Chrysler's Ramos Arizpe labor force became part of the National Union of Automotive Industry Workers (the union formed to represent all three Chrysler plants in Mexico), while Ford's Chihuahua and Hermosillo work forces were organized as local sections of the National Union of Ford Motor Company Workers. Neither Chrysler nor Ford managers had any incentive to seek alternatives to their established CTM-affiliated unions to organize the new northern plants; the Chrysler union (whose general secretary had previously been the company's chief production manager) had never permitted an outbreak of rank-and-file discontent after 1969, and despite the Ford union's success in winning very favorable contract benefits, Ford management saw important advantages in preserving unified union representation of its workers.[24] General Motors management, on the other hand, was determined that its engine and automobile manufacturing plants at Ramos Arizpe would have no organizational ties to the democratic, assertive union at its Federal District facility. In 1980 the Federal District union fought a bitter 106-day strike (the longest in the history of the Mexican automobile industry) for legal control of the General Motors sites in northern Mexico, but management eventually prevailed, and the regional federation of Saltillo unions (affiliated with the CTM's Coahuila state federation) organized workers in the two facilities as separate plant-level unions.[25] Similarly, Nissan's labor force at its Aguascalientes plant was organized as part of the CTM's Aguascalientes state federation.

The ability of CTM-affiliated unions to maintain control over workers is due primarily to the national confederation's close political ties to the post-revolutionary Mexican state, federal and state governments' willingness to defend incumbent union leaders against rank-and-file challenges when they occur, and union shop provisions in federal labor law that grant a union a representational monopoly in the workplace once a labor force is unionized. However, the effectiveness of CTM control also depends on the character of plant-level labor-relations arrangements. Following its loss of influence in the automobile industry in the 1970s, the CTM's national leadership reformulated its approach to local level labor relations in the new plants established in central and northern Mexico. The CTM made a concerted effort to upgrade the quality of its representatives; its local union advisers in these plants are often graduates of CTM leadership training schools in Saltillo and Cuernavaca, where they received instruction in economics, labor law, negotiating strategies, and the leadership skills required to manage a more educated labor force.[26] Moreover, the CTM's national leadership recognized the importance of establishing formal representational structures at the plant level, including elected union executive committees. Elected union representatives may demonstrate considerable autonomy from the CTM in internal decision-making, but they enjoy much greater legitimacy *vis-à-vis* the rank and file than the appointed plant delegates traditionally in charge of local affairs in CTM-affiliated unions. Thus the national CTM leadership's clear preference was for local union structures that permitted the effective representation of workers' economic interests while preserving overall CTM influence.[27]

Nevertheless, the CTM's national leadership is not always able to impose its views on the confederation's heterogeneous constituent organizations, and in practice there is considerable diversity in union structures at the new export production automobile plants. At all four Ford and General Motors northern plants, workers enjoy important opportunities to participate in local union affairs.[28] There is a regular turnover in elected union officials, competing slates of candidates often contest union elections, and general assemblies are commonly held. Workers at all four plants receive copies of the labor contract for their inspection. On several occasions in the early 1980s the executive committees at the General Motors Ramos Arizpe engine and automobile manufacturing plants were overturned by internal opposition movements in disputes over the incumbents' conduct of union business. In addition, a system of departmental delegates was created at both General Motors plants in 1986 to give the rank and file a larger role in union affairs. Rank-and-file opponents also succeeded in overthrowing the local executive committees at Ford's Chihuahua and Hermosillo facilities when the union leadership failed to respond to workers' economic and personnel concerns.[29]

Local unions at all four Ford and General Motors plants also exercise a degree of autonomy *vis-à-vis* their respective enterprise union or state level federation, although state and national CTM leaders have succeeded in maintaining strict control over the labor contract terms most important to employers. In each case, the firm provides paid full-time leave for several executive committee members (ranging from two in the General Motors plants to three at Ford-Chihuahua and four at Ford-Hermosillo) to facilitate union work. Although the enterprise union takes a leading role in contract and wage negotiations at the Ford plants, local union representatives are also involved; indeed, the labor contract at Ford-Chihuahua provides three local representatives (in addition to three local executive committee members) paid full-time leave during contract revisions. At General Motors' Ramos Arizpe facilities, the state CTM federation is represented by trained union advisers, who take part in contract and wage negotiations with the local executive committee.

In contrast, the CTM maintains tight control over workers at the Chrysler Ramos Arizpe and Nissan Aguascalientes plants through more traditional means.[30] Plant delegates appointed by the enterprise union serve as the principal intermediaries between workers and company managers at Chrysler-Ramos Arizpe, and the head of the Aguascalientes state federation also serves as secretary general of the Nissan-Aguascalientes union. Local union representatives are not involved in contract and wage negotiations at either plant. Nor are labor contracts distributed to workers. In short, the CTM has reproduced in these two plants the traditional control mechanisms that served CTM and employer interests so well before democratization movements swept the industry in the 1960s and 1970s. At least in Chrysler-Ramos Arizpe and Nissan-Aguascalientes, these arrangements have not yet been challenged by a serious rank-and-file protest movement. Despite this diversity in local union structures, state and national CTM leaders are united in their opposition to worker dissent. The 'exclusion clause' (cláusula de exclusión) provisions generally included in Mexican labor contracts provide union officials with a strong defense against rank-and-file challenges: the employer is legally required to dismiss any worker who is expelled from the officially recognized union. In the history of the Mexican automobile industry, union leaders – whether they were democratically elected or not – have frequently used this mechanism to suppress internal dissent. Union leaders at the new export production plants have not departed from this tradition. CTM officials and management colluded to fire the entire union executive committee at General Motors' Ramos Arizpe engine plant in 1985 when these local leaders aggressively pressed economic demands. Similarly, incumbent union leaders at Ford's Hermosillo plant compelled management to dismiss four activist workers in 1987.[31]

There is, then, a strategic convergence of interests between company management and CTM officials in maintaining control over workers in these export production plants. For management, the unionization of a labor force under CTM auspices offers greater stability in day-to-day labor relations and fewer political risks than does an unorganized work force. The representational monopoly that federal labor law confers on an officially recognized union makes it more difficult for rival labor and political groups to establish a presence in the workplace, and incumbent union leaders can readily use the exclusion clause to defend their position against internal challengers. For CTM leaders, especially in less industrialized states such as Aguascalientes, representation of an important industrial labor force constitutes a major political and economic resource. Workers at automobile plants often constitute a significant proportion of a state federation's total membership, and a larger membership base increases the federation's political influence at state and national levels. In addition, the CTM derives important economic benefits from the automatic deduction of workers' union dues. In some cases, CTM affiliation offers federation leaders special opportunities for financial gain; for example, labor contracts at all three Chrysler plants in Mexico require that workers' life insurance policies be subscribed from a firm selected by the leadership of Section 23 of the CTM's Federal District Workers' Federation.[32]

The Economic Consequences of Industry Reorganization

In addition to construction subsidies and reliable control over labor relations under CTM auspices, transnational firms gained other important economic advantages by founding new manufacturing facilities in central and northern Mexico. Because these plants are often located in low-wage areas without significant concentrations of heavy manufacturing, companies have been able to hire workers at wages substantially below those in established automobile plants in and around Mexico City. For example, in April 1987 workers at Ford's recently inaugurated plant in Hermosillo earned an average of 945 pesos per hour, while workers at Ford's Cuautitlán facility earned an average of 1 355 pesos per hour.[33] Because seniority-based fringe benefit payments are smaller for newly hired labor forces, firms' total labor costs are also lower than in older manufacturing facilities. Moreover, the work week is from one to eight hours longer in export production plants than in a given firm's facility in central Mexico.

Workers at both Ford's and General Motors' export production plants have lobbied strenuously to reduce disparities in wage and benefit levels between new and old manufacturing facilities.[34] Wage and contract negotiations at these plants are normally accompanied by formal strike petitions, and workers at Ford-Chihuahua (in 1983, 1986, and 1988), Ford-Hermosillo (in 1987), and General Motors-Ramos Arizpe (automobiles and engines in 1982 and automobiles in 1986) have struck for periods ranging from 11 to 39 days in support of their economic demands.[35] But because workers at these plants were originally hired at wage and benefit levels far below those prevailing at older manufacturing facilities, this gap will close only gradually even if workers enjoy some success in bargaining with employers. Moreover, local unions had little opportunity to overcome these historical disparities between 1986 and 1988 because wage increases in the automobile industry were generally tied to national emergency increases in minimum wages.

For these reasons, wages and fringe benefits at export production plants have continued to lag behind those in older manufacturing facilities. In March 1988 average daily wages at the Chrysler-Ramos Arizpe, Ford-Chihuahua, General Motors-Ramos Arizpe (automobiles and engines), and Nissan-Aguascalientes plants were all substantially lower than those at the same firms' established facilities in central Mexico (see Table 7.1).[36] This also was the case for Ford's Hermosillo plant until October 1987, when wage and benefit levels at Ford-Cuautitlán were cut sharply at the end of a bitter strike. A similar pattern holds for fringe benefits: both the range and the level of fringe benefits normally available to individual workers have been more favorable in older plants in Mexico City and surrounding areas than in the new export production plants.[37] The only partial exception is again Ford-Cuautitlán after October 1987.

Table 7.1   Worker's daily wages in Mexican automobile firms, 1988 (in pesos)

	High wage	Low wage	Average wage*
CHRYSLER			
Federal District			
(1 March 1988)	$26 947	$11 401	$21 188
Toluca			
(1 March 1988)	28 200	9 900	20 010
Ramos Arizpe			
(1 March 1988)	23 300	9 000	14 833
FORD			
Cuautitlán			
(1 March 1988)	31 176	14 594	22 553
Chihuahua			
(1 March 1988)	24 770	11 455	17 029
Hermosillo			
(1 March 1988)	34 048	18 950	26 520
GENERAL MOTORS			
Federal District			
(1 March 1988)	32 343	16 968	25 041
Toluca			
(1 March 1988)	31 311	10 620	20 350
Ramos Arizpe (Autos)			
(4 March 1988)	20 894	8 965	15 043
Ramos Arizpe (Engines)			
(4 March 1988)	21 376	9 557	14 806
NISSAN**			
Cuernavaca			
(1 April 1988)	30 371	14 492	22 204
Aguascalientes			
(1 March 1988)	16 939	8 287	12 931
VOLKSWAGEN			
Puebla			
(1 March 1988)	35 388	13 648	22 789

* Average of wage categories; 2278 pesos = US$1.00 in March 1988.
** Data not available for Nissan's Lerma plant.
Note: Data do not include the value of fringe benefits, which significantly increase total earnings.
Source: Author's calculations based on automobile industry labor contracts and Junta Federal de Conciliación y Arbitraje internal documents.

Equally important, company managers have successfully used these differences in wage and fringe benefit levels to their advantage in contract negotiations with unions in older, less technologically advanced manufacturing plants. They argue that if the plant in question is to remain competitive in national and international markets, the union must make economic concessions and accept changes in work rules designed to increase productivity. When Ford's Cuautitlán union vigorously resisted such demands in July–September 1987, company managers ended a bitter 61-day strike by liquidating the entire work force, temporarily closing the plant (with the tacit support of the CTM's national leadership and the de la Madrid government, which permitted this politically sensitive action in the name of greater industry efficiency), and then rehiring 2 500 of its original workers under terms that were very favorable to management. Ford was able to implement contract modifications that greatly increased production flexibility and permitted it to recover its considerable liquidation costs in a single year. After October 1987, wage and benefit levels at Cuautitlán were much closer to those at Ford's northern export production plants.[38]

The Volkswagen union successfully waged a 57-day strike in June–August 1987 against the firm's call for major contract concessions, but the results of the Cuautitlán strike starkly revealed the potential vulnerability of unions at older manufacturing facilities in central Mexico. The 'solidarity pact' signed in January 1988 by delegates representing local unions at Ford's three plants, Diesel Nacional (the state-owned truck and bus manufacturer in Ciudad Sahagún), General Motors-Federal District, Nissan-Cuernavaca, and Volkswagen-Puebla sought to unite workers so as to resist more effectively employer demands for wage cuts and contract concessions.[39] By exchanging data on wage and fringe benefit levels and by amassing a large strike fund, these unions were able to offer valuable support to fellow automobile workers during contract negotiations at DINA's affiliated enterprises and at General Motors' Federal District plant. However, a similar initiative in support of Ford-Chihuahua's 1988 strike was blocked when Fidel Velázquez, the CTM's long-time general secretary, forced the local union executive committee to reject external assistance or risk losing CTM support. The Ford-Cuautitlán union later withdrew from the pact for similar reasons, and the alliance lost its momentum. This experiment in labor solidarity established a valuable precedent in the industry, but it also revealed the difficulties of collective action among unions that are geographically dispersed and divided by ties to rival labor organizations.

POST-FORDIST LABOR RELATIONS AND THE SEARCH FOR
FLEXIBLE PRODUCTION

Since the early 1980s, Ford, General Motors, Nissan, Volkswagen and
Chrysler have implemented post-Fordist labor relations arrangements
at their production facilities throughout Mexico. The initiative for this
new approach to industrial relations in the Mexican automobile industry usually came from each transnational firm's home office. However,
local managers perceived such mechanisms as quality circles and work
teams to be important elements in their campaign to maximize flexibility in the production process, defuse labor–employer tensions by improving communications and increasing worker participation in the
organization of production, and achieve internationally competitive levels of production efficiency and quality control in export programs.
This new approach to workplace relations was particularly attractive
to company managers confronting an experienced industrial labor force
with a long tradition of union militancy because such arrangements as
quality circles and work teams might progressively undercut the position of union representatives on the shop floor. This section examines
different firms' use of post-Fordist strategies, their relative significance
in the managerial drive for more flexible production, and their potential
impact on democratic unionism in the automobile industry.

Individual firms have introduced post-Fordist arrangements in different combinations at their various manufacturing facilities.[40] For example, Ford first established quality circles at its Cuautitlán plant in
1981–82 as part of its 'integral participation program'; work teams
were introduced in the mid-1980s. Ford-Chihuahua has employed
work teams, quality circles, and worker rotation among different production areas since the plant opened in 1983.[41] General Motors introduced work teams (with eight to twelve workers in each one) and
quality circles at its Ramos Arizpe automobile and engine plants in
1985; similar measures were adopted at its Toluca and Federal District
plants later the same year. Nissan created quality circles at its Aguascalientes, Lerma, and Cuernavaca plants in 1983 as part of its 'shopfloor
management reform program'. Work teams (with six to eight persons
in each team) followed in 1987–88. By 1987, Volkswagen also had
adopted work teams and quality circles. Chrysler implemented both
work teams and quality circles at its Toluca facility in the mid-1980s,
but only work teams at its Ramos Arizpe plant.[42]

In contrast to the partial utilization of post-Fordist concepts at most
production facilities, Ford created an innovative labor-relations sys-

tem at its Hermosillo plant that enhanced management flexibility while redefining the traditional structure of labor–management relations in assembly line work. The system features flexible work rules, regular job rotation, broadly defined job classifications, work teams, and quality circles. Promotions are based, not on seniority, but on demonstrated technical proficiency and proven versatility at different tasks. Satisfactory completion of requirements at each job level includes mandatory rotation among specified production areas, and an individual's work team, area supervisor, union representative, and training coordinator (in this order) all must approve a promotion.[43] A worker must first attempt to resolve a grievance through his or her work group and production specialist before taking the problem to a union representative.[44] Management's goal is to reduce workplace tensions and motivate workers so that they function well in a state-of-the-art manufacturing environment, maintaining internationally competitive productivity and quality levels.

The ease with which firms have been able to implement post-Fordist arrangements in different manufacturing plants depends mainly on the political orientation and workplace organizational strength of the local union, although workers' industrial experience and the physical characteristics of different production facilities may also be important considerations.[45] General Motors faced no resistance to such mechanisms at its Ramos Arizpe facilities, where a comparatively inexperienced labor force is organized by CTM-affiliated unions. These are the only General Motors plants in Mexico where management has introduced 'pay by knowledge' compensation arrangements and a nonseniority promotion system. In marked contrast, the more experienced labor force at General Motors' Federal District plant has resisted management efforts to redefine work rules and downplay the established role of seniority. The local union also perceives work teams and quality circles to be a threat to its own authority. As a result, General Motors management has been unable to introduce compensation and promotion systems like those in place in Ramos Arizpe. Similarly, Nissan managers encountered no serious obstacles to the introduction of post-Fordist mechanisms at either its Aguascalientes or Lerma plants where workers are organized by the CTM, but a combative, independent union representing an experienced work force at the company's Cuernavaca plant has vigorously resisted the adoption of flexible work rules and the creation of work teams since 1987. When company managers proposed a Japanese-style program of thirteen physical exercises before work each morning, the union demanded that attendance be voluntary and that participating workers be paid overtime. During the 1980s persistent union resistance also limited the adoption of post-Fordist arrangements at Volkswagen's Puebla plant.[46]

Where they have been implemented, company managers are convinced that post-Fordist industrial relations arrangements contribute to increased communications on the shop floor and improved quality control, and the fragmentary evidence that is available suggests that some workers may view favorably such innovations as work teams and quality circles.[47] For example, Ford managers argue that a new approach to industrial relations was necessary at the Hermosillo facility because extensive automation and the complexity of computer-assisted technologies demand more cooperative, flexible workplace relations. The use of post-Fordist arrangements helped Ford's Chihuahua plant win the company's coveted 'Q1' award for quality control in 1987.[48] In the case of General Motors, this approach has helped the Toluca engine plant and the Ramos Arizpe automobile plant achieve the highest levels of quality control in the company's global network of manufacturing facilities.[49] The use of post-Fordist mechanisms also remedied specific problems at General Motors. The introduction of work teams at the Ramos Arizpe automobile and engine plants in 1985 led to a sharp decline in industrial accidents and substantially reduced personnel turnover. As a result, the team concept was welcomed by workers.[50]

However, the principal source of managerial flexibility in organizing the production process lies in the labor contracts negotiated with CTM-affiliated unions rather than in post-Fordist arrangements such as work groups. Table 7.2 presents a content analysis of labor contracts for the five principal transnational firms now operating in the Mexican automobile manufacturing industry. Contracts are a generally reliable indicator of labor-relations practices, especially the extent of union involvement. The central question to be examined here is whether (and to what degree) labor unions exercise influence over three key areas of industrial relations: promotion procedures and policies affecting employment security, rules governing the production process, and plant-level conflict resolution procedures.

The absence of a unified national automobile workers' union in Mexico and the heterogeneity of CTM affiliates permit considerable variation in labor contracts both among different firms and among a single firm's separate production facilities. However, the data presented in Table 7.2 indicate that only democratic unions affiliated with labor organizations other than the CTM enjoy generally favorable contractual terms. Unions at General Motors-Federal District, Nissan-Cuernavaca,

Table 7.2 Comparative evaluation of workplace relations in Mexican automobile firms

| | Chrysler | | Ford | | | General Motors | | | Nissan | | | Volkswagen |
	Toluca Federal District	Ramos Arizpe	Cuautitlán	Chihuahua	Hermosillo	Federal District Toluca	Ramos Arizpe (Autos)	Ramos Arizpe (Engines)	Cuernavaca	Lerma	Aguascalientes	Puebla
Promotion procedures and employment security												
Union participation in hiring and promotions	0	0	3	0	1	4	2	1	4	0	0	3
Specification of promotion criteria	0	0	0	2	4	4	2	2	4	0	0	4
Automatic promotion of temporary workers or other limitations on their number	0	0	1	0	0	4	0	1	4	0	0	2
Other job security provisions	1	1	1	1	0	4	2	2	4	0	0	2
sub-total	1	2	5	3	5	16	6	6	16	0	0	11
Production process												
Union participation in determination of work rhythm, production rate	0	0	1	0	1	3	1	1	4	0	0	2
Union control over workforce distribution within plant	0	0	0	0	0	4	2	2	2	0	0	4
Equalization of wage categories	1	1	4	1	1	3	1	1	3	1	1	3
Union participation in occupational health and safety measures	0	0	3	1	0	4	0	0	4	0	1	4
sub-total	1	1	8	2	2	14	4	4	13	1	2	13

Conflict resolution procedures

Specification of procedures,
labor-management
authorities, time periods
for resolution of

workplace conflicts	0	0	0	4	1	2	3	1	1	1	4	1	1	4
TOTAL	2	3	2	17	6	9	33	11	11	11	33	2	3	28

The numerical values listed in the table refer to the following code:

0 = No special benefits or provisions beyond those set by federal labor law

1 = Very limited measures

2 = Moderate protection or union participation

3 = Extensive protection or active union participation

4 = Very extensive protection or active union participation in formal institutional mechanisms or specified procedures

Source: 1988 labor contracts for Chrysler-Ramos Arizpe, Ford-Hermosillo, General Motors-Toluca, General Motors-Ramos Arizpe (both automobile and engine plants), Nissan-Cuernavaca and Nissan-Aguascalientes;

1987 labor contracts for Chrysler-Federal District, Chryster-Toluca, Ford-Cuautitlán, General Motors-Federal District;

1986 labor contracts for Ford-Chihuahua and Volkswagen-Puebla;

1985 labor contract for Nissan-Lerma.

and Volkswagen-Puebla play a very active role in hiring and promotion decisions. At Nissan's Cuernavaca plant, the sons and brothers of union members receive preference in hiring, while at Volkswagen no hiring is permitted unless the union is notified in advance and given the opportunity to identify possible candidates. In all three cases, union delegates have equal representation with management on the commission that supervises promotions; seniority is the principal criterion affecting promotion decisions. At General Motors' Federal District plant, the union has won contractual terms that specify the percentage of the work force in different skill classifications and wage levels, thus guaranteeing regular promotion for workers and preventing management from holding employees at low-level classifications.[51]

Similarly, unions at General Motors-Federal District and Nissan-Cuernavaca have won job security provisions for workers that are far more favorable than the separation benefits provided by federal labor law. At General Motors' Federal District facility, for example, the contract imposes heavy financial penalties on the company if managers close the plant, and management can not reduce the number of permanent (*planta*) positions during the life of the contract. A worker whose employment at the plant is interrupted for up to 90 days can return to his or her former job without loss of seniority.[52] Unions at all three plants are also actively involved in protecting workers' occupational health and safety, and they have succeeded in creating institutionalized plant-level conflict resolution procedures (workers' rights, time periods for grievance resolution, and other issues are clearly defined) in which union representatives are fully involved.[53]

Even more important, these democratic unions have used their organizational strength in the workplace to win broad influence over the production process itself. Over time, unions at the General Motors–Federal District and Nissan-Cuernavaca plants have imposed contractual restrictions on management's use of temporary workers by limiting the permitted number of *eventuales*, by requiring their automatic promotion to *planta* positions after a specified period, or both. These restrictions simultaneously increase a union's bargaining leverage *vis-à-vis* a firm by limiting its flexible use of labor and prevent managers from manipulating *eventuales'* job insecurity to their political advantage in negotiations with the union.[54] In addition, the General Motors and Nissan unions participate extensively in decisions affecting work rhythms and production rates. The General Motors–Federal District contract requires that one meter be maintained between units on the assembly line, and any changes in the work pace require advance approval from the union. At Nissan-Cuernavaca, union representatives meet regularly with company managers on a special commission that oversees a 'normal' work rate, and management is required to train union representatives in time-and-motion procedures to allow them to make informed judgments in this area. Although the Volkswagen contract does not provide union representatives extensive influence in this area, it does allow union participation in the elaboration of annual and monthly work schedules, and it restricts overtime work.[55] Finally, all three unions exercise considerable influence over the movement of workers among different production areas, thus limiting managerial discretion in the organization of production. Contracts at these plants stipulate the conditions under which such transfers are permitted (generally limiting them to one to three days) and guarantee workers the wage corresponding to the new position.[56]

Unions at all other terminal industry plants in Mexico exercise considerably less influence in these areas. Indeed, the contracts at Chrysler's three production facilities and Nissan's Aguascalientes and Lerma plants provide company managers with virtually unrestricted control over hiring and promotions, the use of temporary workers, the determination of work rhythms and production rates, and the movement of employees among different departments on the shopfloor. Even though the CTM's reformulated approach to labor relations at the Ford and General Motors northern export production plants permits workers new opportunities to participate in union affairs, local unions have little control over promotion procedures and employment security, the production process, or conflict resolution procedures. Of course, workers in these plants may eventually win contract concessions that increase their negotiating leverage *vis-à-vis* management, but this is unlikely as long as the CTM maintains tight control over contract negotiations. Company managers and CTM federation leaders have preserved a labor contract highly favorable to management interests at General Motors' Toluca facility for over 25 years.

Contract flexibility of this kind offers firms two other major advantages. First, the absence of contractually-specified union participation in decisions affecting the production process greatly simplifies company managers' work and significantly increases the opportunity costs of collective worker resistance to managers' day-to-day actions. In firms with little union influence over workplace relations, supervisors need not negotiate with union representatives on such issues as the movement of personnel on the shop floor, the hiring of temporary workers, and the introduction of new technologies or other changes in the production process. Second, contract-based managerial flexibility may be even more important than low wages to production efficiency in highly automated plants. This is especially important in the capital-intensive, technologically advanced export production automobile plants in central and northern Mexico. Labor costs generally represent a low proportion of total manufacturing value-added in these facilities, yet high depreciation and start-up costs make it imperative that managers avoid work stoppages or other labor disruptions that reduce the productivity of capital.[57] Flexible contract conditions increase managers' ability to utilize labor fully in these plants. Indeed, the importance of contract flexibility to efficient production may in the near future encourage firms to exert greater pressure on democratic unions at General Motors-Federal District, Nissan-Cuernavaca, and Volkswagen-Puebla, where labor contracts are now out of step with new industry norms.

Shaiken's exhaustive study of Ford's Chihuahua engine plant offers the best available test of the relative importance of post-Fordist arrangements and labor contract terms in providing flexible managerial control over the production process. In planning the Chihuahua facility, Ford managers carefully studied Japanese automobile firms' manufacturing techniques and adopted from them such concepts as broadly defined job classifications, job rotation, and promotion based on the mastery of specified tasks rather than seniority.[58] However, when asked to assess the factors that account for the facility's high efficiency and internationally-competitive product quality, plant supervisors emphasized the great flexibility that the existing contract provided to management to control the production process and move employees among different work areas as needed. One industrial-relations manager even argued that the contract provided the plant 'more flexibility than any other [company] plant in the world.'[59] When negotiating the work agreement, Ford's CTM-affiliated union had accepted the company's calls for far-reaching managerial flexibility in the new plant, and the union has had only a limited presence on the shop floor, prompting one plant manager to remark that, 'as far as I'm concerned there is no union here.'[60] Ford managers clearly understood the potential advantages in establishing a new plant outside the Mexico City area with an inexperienced labor force, and they made every effort to avoid contact between the Chihuahua work force and the employees at the company's Mexico City facilities. Workers hired at the Chihuahua plant had no previous experience in the automobile industry, and even though an inexperienced work force caused delays and other start-up problems, Ford imported no workers or managers from Mexico City in order to keep the Chihuahua plant free of traditional work roles and attitudes toward management. One measure of the success of this strategy is Ford supervisors' praise for Chihuahua workers' positive, flexible attitudes toward automation and management.[61]

Automobile firms' success in achieving broad production flexibility through labor contracts may have implications extending beyond the Mexican case. Some analysts argue that developing countries' comparative advantage in automobile manufacturing will decline as the use of advanced manufacturing techniques (including robotic assembly technologies, computer-assisted design, and new approaches to production management) becomes more common in industrialized countries, thereby reducing firms' incentive to locate labor-intensive tasks in areas where wage rates are relatively low.[62] However, the combination of significant (and, in all likelihood, persistent) hourly wage differentials between the United States and Mexico[63] *and* extensive managerial flexibility through contracts negotiated with CTM-affiliated unions may considerably extend Mexico's competitive edge in the global automobile industry. To the extent that the characteristics of state–labor relations in other newly-industrialized countries offer comparable benefits to management, transnational firms may find that there are long-term, non-wage advantages to locating automobile manufacturing in these areas. At a minimum, the availability of such flexible contract conditions in Mexico gives these firms an additional negotiating advantage in bargaining with automobile workers in industrialized countries.

It remains to be seen what impact the introduction of work teams and quality circles might have on union democracy in the Mexican automobile industry. By providing opportunities for increased communications among workers, such structures might facilitate the emergence of new union leaders with close ties to the rank and file. Workers' enhanced access through quality circles to information concerning management policies might also lead to broad support for an expanded union presence on the shop floor. If this occurs, then post-Fordist arrangements of this kind might progressively undermine the position of CTM-designated union leaders at Chrysler-Ramos Arizpe, Nissan-Aguascalientes, and elsewhere. However, it is also possible that these structures will obstruct the emergence of rank-and-file protest movements by defusing employee discontent with working conditions. Work teams make the individual employee's performance the object of peer group pressure and lower the supervisor's profile on the shop floor. Moreover, some analysts have suggested that, because departmental union representatives sometimes serve as work team or quality circle leaders, they become partly integrated into production management, thereby compromising their legitimacy as worker representatives. Quality circles might also emerge as alternative representational bodies that undercut the union's traditional role in the workplace. Thus in some cases post-Fordist arrangements might challenge the position of established democratic union leaders.[64]

THE MEXICAN CASE IN COMPARATIVE PERSPECTIVE

The global transformation of automotive manufacturing has produced significant challenges for workers throughout the industrial world. In many countries, the last decade has witnessed increased unemployment, reduced wages and fringe benefits, and other economic disruptions that have placed organized labor on the defensive as new competitive pressures in the industry forced rapid adaptation by transnational firms. However, in the United States, Canada and some West European countries (particularly the Federal Republic of Germany and Sweden), democratically organized national unions have frequently succeeded in modifying the effects of automobile firms' restructuring programs. These unions differ in their specific organizational characteristics and in the nature of their ties to political parties, but they all have centralized decision-making structures that permit national union representatives to negotiate with firms regarding the content of restructuring measures and the rate at which they are implemented. Although their overall bargaining position was weakened in the 1980s by the internationalization of automotive production, these unions have often won enhanced employment security in exchange for concessions on wages and modifications in work rules, job classifications, and so forth.[65] Strong union defense of wage and employment levels has in some cases shaped even companies' decisions regarding the automobile models they produce.[66] Moreover, the presence of institutionalized representational structures in the workplace has allowed workers themselves to monitor the restructuring process and influence its impact.

The Mexican case provides new insight into the global process of automobile industry restructuring because Mexican workers lack similarly effective negotiating leverage at the national level and because wide intra-industry variations in the political character and organizational strength of local unions underline the importance of democratic representational structures as a prerequisite for workers' capacity to influence industrial change in the workplace. The absence of a democratically organized national automobile workers' union has permitted transnational firms to exploit the vulnerabilities inherent in enterprise- and plant-level unionism and reduce wage and fringe benefit levels, cut employment, rewrite labor contracts, and redefine workplace relations. The geographical dispersion of automobile workers resulting from industry reorganization in the 1980s and political divisions among rival labor organizations have precluded effective long-term collective action by workers. Some democratic unions have successfully used their organizational strength in the workplace to resist employers' demands for contract concessions and a restricted union presence on the shop floor, but they ultimately lack the resources and negotiating leverage necessary to influence the overall character of restructuring in the industry and thereby win concessions in areas such as employment security.

Because post-Fordist labor-relations arrangements have generally proved most effective from management's perspective where employment guarantees, muted hierarchical divisions between workers and employers, and other limitations on company managers' traditional prerogatives contribute to a sense of collective responsibility in the workplace, this very lack of national level negotiating effectiveness by Mexican automobile workers' unions might work to transnational firms' long-term disadvantage if rank-and-file discontent with post-Fordist measures becomes a serious issue. One Ford worker pointedly observed, 'As they say on the assembly line, you can't eat [*no me hago un "taco"*] motivation and quality.'[67]

The Mexican case also illustrates the significance of regime type and organized labor's overall position in national politics for the character and consequences of automobile industry restructuring. The Confederation of Mexican Workers is unable to play a role in the restructuring process comparable to that of national unions in many industrialized countries. Because of its dependence on state-provided political, financial, and legal subsidies to insure its dominance in the organized labor movement, the CTM has had little incentive to develop an organizational structure that would permit it to negotiate effectively with individual private sector firms on a continuing basis. Indeed, many CTM leaders have been more intent on controlling workers for political purposes than on developing an institutionalized presence in the workplace that would permit them to resolve day-to-day worker grievances or mediate the impact of industrial restructuring. Because of the constraints inherent in the structure of state–labor relations in the Mexican authoritarian regime and organized labor's reduced bargaining leverage during a period of rapid economic reorganization, the CTM's national leadership has been reluctant to challenge the government's policy of supporting automobile industry restructuring as part of its national economic recovery strategy. In any event, individual CTM leaders have been more inclined to seek private gain through a de facto alliance with transnational automobile firms than to challenge their drive for production flexibility.

It remains to be seen whether future political developments in Mexico enhance automobile workers' ability to shape the course of industrial restructuring. At present, despite the growing prominence of opposition political forces in Mexico, ties between unions and opposition parties remain weak. This situation is the result of company managers' and state labor officials' enduring hostility to such linkages, the reluctance of some democratically-organized unions to compromise their hard-won autonomy by establishing affiliations with groups whose agendas might expose them to new risks, and some opposition parties' decisions to emphasize electoral activities rather than organizational work in the workplace. A more competitive national political environment would perhaps encourage labor organizations to form closer ties to parties, and linkages of this kind might increase automobile workers' capacity to influence the legal norms and government policies that condition the restructuring process. For the foreseeable future, however, Mexican automobile workers' struggles for improved wages and fringe benefits, union democracy, and greater control over the production process will almost certainly be fought plant-by-plant on the shop floor rather than in a larger political arena.

Over the longer term, the North American Free Trade Agreement (NAFTA) might also create political conditions that increase Mexican automobile workers' bargaining leverage *vis-à-vis* transnational firms. Mexican workers are in the short run likely to face additional managerial pressures as automobile companies move aggressively to promote export production for an expanded North American market. However, their economic and political demands may also have greater resonance than in the past because of heightened international attention to the issue of labor rights in Mexico. Moreover, debate concerning NAFTA and its consequences increased Canadian, Mexican and US trade unionists' awareness of the common problems facing North American workers, and the challenges posed by on-going processes of industrial restructuring and the internationalization of production may stimulate transnational cooperation among automobile workers' unions. The multiple obstacles to such collaboration (language barriers, opposition from company managers, political divisions among different labor organizations, and so forth) will not be easily overcome. Nor will the availability of international labor allies necessarily lead to the creation of more effective forms of plant-level worker representation or a nationally-organized automobile workers' union in Mexico, although expanded contacts with Canadian and US automobile workers might well encourage reform initiatives in these areas. Whether creative leadership and innovative strategies can, in time, promote effective forms of cross-national labor cooperation is one of the principal challenges confronting North American automobile workers.

Notes

A preliminary version of this essay was presented at the Bildner Center for Western Hemisphere Studies, City University of New York, and the Kellogg Institute for International Studies, University of Notre Dame, in 1989. I wish to thank seminar participants for their valuable suggestions. I am also grateful to Arnulfo Arteaga, Gustavo del Castillo, Alfred Diamant, Harley Shaiken, and anonymous reviewers for insightful comments on this project. The Howard Heinz Endowment provided generous financial support for field research conducted in Mexico in October–November 1987 and October 1988.

1. This summary of Fordism–Taylorism draws on John F. Krafcik, 'A New Diet for US Manufacturing', *Technology Review*, 92 (January 1989), p. 32, and Michael J. Piore and Charles F. Sabel (1984) *The Second Industrial Divide: Possibilities for Prosperity* (New York: Basic Books) pp. 111–15.
2. For a discussion of the post-Fordist model of labor relations, see Martin Kenney and Richard Florida, 'Beyond Mass Production: Production and the Labor Process in Japan', *Politics and Society*, 16 (March 1988), 121–58; Knuth Dohse, Ulrich Jürgens, and Thomas Malsch (1985) 'From "Fordism" to "Toyotism"? The Social Organization of the Labor Process in the Japanese Automobile Industry', *Politics and Society*, 14, pp. 115–46; Charles F. Sabel (1982) *Work and Politics: The Division of Labor in Industry* (Cambridge: Cambridge University Press) pp. 209–16.
3. See, for example, Harley Shaiken, Stephen Herzenberg, and Sarah Kuhn, 'The Work Process under More Flexible Production', *Industrial Relations*, 25 (Spring 1986), 167–83; Wolfgang Streeck (1987) 'Industrial Relations and Industrial Change: The Restructuring of the World Automobile Industry in the 1970s and 1980s', *Economic and Industrial Democracy*, 8, pp. 437–62; Harry C. Katz (1985) *Shifting Gears: Changing Labor Relations in the US Automobile Industry* (Cambridge, Mass.: The MIT Press) chaps. 3–4: Leon Grunberg, 'Workplace Relations in the Economic Crisis: A

Comparison of a British and a French Automobile Plant', *Sociology*, 20 (November 1986), 503–29; Jonas Pontusson, 'The Micro and Macro Politics of Industrial Innovation: A Comparison of Volvo and British Leyland' (Department of Government, Cornell University, August 1989); Richard M. Locke, 'In Search of Flexibility: Industrial Restructuring and Industrial Relations in the Italian Auto Industry', paper presented at the 1988 meeting of the American Political Science Association; Kathleen Thelan, 'Union Structure and Strategic Choice: The Politics of Flexibility in the German Metalworking Industries', paper presented at the 1988 meeting of the American Political Science Association; Ben Dankbaar, 'New Technologies, Management Strategies, and the Quality of Work' (Berlin: International Institute for Comparative Social Research/Labor Policy, IIVG/dp 86–211, November 1986); Ulrich Jürgens, Knuth Dohse, and Thomas Malsch (1987) 'New Production Concepts in West German Car Plants', in Steven Tolliday and Jonathon Zeitlin (eds), *The Automobile Industry and Its Workers* (New York: St Martin's Press) pp. 258–81.

4. I am not aware of any comparable studies of automobile industry restructuring in other newly industrializing countries with an important automotive export sector. Research on such cases would further increase our understanding of this process.

5. Pontusson, 'The Micro and Macro Politics of Industrial Innovation' (note 3 above) pp. 7–8, argues that differences in the 'industrial innovation' approaches pursued by Volvo and British Leyland were due primarily to variations in labor-market conditions. He concludes that Volvo's more collaborative approach *vis-à-vis* workers resulted from company managers' need to reduce labor turnover.

6. This analysis focuses principally on the political and organizational bases of automobile workers' bargaining power. The proportion of the work force that is unionized at the national, industry, and enterprise or plant level is, of course, an important foundation of labor's negotiating leverage. For a more general discussion of the bases of labor power, see David R. Cameron (1984) 'Social Democracy, Corporatism, Labor Quiescence, and the Representation of Economic Interest in Advanced Capitalist Society', in John H. Goldthorpe (ed.), *Order and Conflict in Contemporary Capitalism* (New York: Oxford University Press) pp. 164–65.

7. Kevin J. Middlebrook (1989) 'Union Democratization in the Mexican Automobile Industry: A Reappraisal', *Latin American Research Review*, 24, pp. 71–73.

8. *Ibid.*, pp. 72–85, provides a detailed analysis of this process.

9. See Kevin J. Middlebrook (1982) 'International Implications of Labor Change: The Automobile Industry', in Jorge I. Domínguez (ed.), *Mexico's Political Economy: Challenges at Home and Abroad* (Beverly Hills: Sage Publications) pp. 133–70.

10. Production quotas were intended to preserve a minimum market share for firms with Mexican capital, and price controls were designed to encourage firms to control costs and achieve greater production efficiency. See Douglas C. Bennett and Kenneth E. Sharpe (1985) *Transnational*

Corporations versus the State: The Political Economy of the Mexican Auto Industry (Princeton: Princeton University Press) pp. 117, 149, 210.

11. Jorge Carillo V. and Patricia García, 'Etapas industriales y conflictos laborales: La industria automotriz en México', *Estudios Sociológicos*, 5 (May–August 1987), 325.

12. Workers at Nissan's Lerma plant staged a six-day wildcat strike in 1979 to protest union leaders' actions. See Ian Roxborough (1984) *Unions and Politics in Mexico: The Case of the Automobile Industry* (Cambridge: Cambridge University Press) p. 48.

13. Author's calculations based on data presented in Asociación Mexicana de la Industria Automotriz (AMIA), *La industria automotriz de México en cifras: Edición 1986* (Mexico City: 1986), p. 6.

14. *Ibid.*, pp. 54–55.

15. *Ibid.*, and AMIA, *Boletín*, 265 (January 1988), 23. The 1987 production figure includes tractor-trailers and passenger buses.

16. AMIA internal documents.

17. 'Decreto para la racionalización de la industria automotriz', *Diario Oficial de la Federación*, 15 Sept. 1983, pp. 3–9. The decree permits firms to produce an additional model only if half its production is exported and if the model is self-sufficient in foreign exchange terms, which became the legal basis for much export production from new plants in central and northern Mexico. The decree also barred eight-cylinder engines and required that one-fourth of each firm's production be 'austere' cars not equipped with extras.

18. See Bennett and Sharpe, *Transnational Corporations versus the State*, chaps. 7–9, for an analysis of earlier government efforts to restructure the industry. Rainer Dombois, 'La producción automotriz y el mercado de trabajo en un país en desarrollo: Un estudio sobre la industria automotriz mexicana' (Berlin: International Institute for Comparative Social Research/Labor Policy, IIVG/dp 85–206, July 1985), pp. 48–50, discusses initial export promotion efforts in the late 1970s.

19. Keiichi Tsunekawa (1989) 'Dependency and Labor Policy: The Case of the Mexican Automotive Industry' (Ph.D. diss., Cornell University) p. 82, Table 2.13.

20. AMIA, *Boletín*, 272 (August 1988), 1.

21. Renault constructed a 4-cylinder engine plant at Gómez Palacio in 1985. This article focuses on Chrysler, Ford, General Motors, Nissan and Volkswagen because of their greater importance in the Mexican automobile industry.

22. Jorge Carrillo V., 'Reestructuración en la industria automotriz en México: Políticas de ajuste e implicaciones laborales' (mimeograph, El Colegio de la Frontera Norte, Tijuana, Mexico, January 1989), p. 8.

23. *South*, 84 (October 1987), 7; AMIA, *Boletín*, 253 (January 1987), 1–2.

24. Author's interview with Ford labor relations manager, 25 October 1988, Mexico City.

25. Author's communication with Arnulfo Arteaga, 18 October 1988.

26. Tsunekawa, 'Dependency and Labor Policy', p. 286; author's communication with Arnulfo Arteaga, 16 October 1987.

27. Author's interview with former Secretaría del Trabajo y Previsión Social official, 2 October 1987, Mexico City.

28. This discussion is based on an analysis of Junta Federal de Conciliación y Arbitraje (JFCA) internal documents and the author's communications with Arnulfo Arteaga, 16 October 1987, and 18 October 1988.
29. Carrillo, 'Reestructuración en la industria automotriz en México', p. 24; *La Jornada*, 21 Oct. 1988, p. 10.
30. This discussion is based on JFCA internal documents and Tsunekawa, 'Dependency and Labor Policy', p. 284.
31. Author's communication with Arnulfo Arteaga, 18 October 1988, and Tsunekawa, pp. 276, 286.
32. See Chrysler labor contracts for its Federal District (1987, clause 60), Toluca (1987, clause 60), and Ramos Arizpe (1988, clause 45) plants.
33. These are averages of wage categories, calculated by the author on the basis of labor contracts for the two plants and JFCA internal documents.
34. Author's interview with Ford labor relations manager, 25 October 1988, Mexico City; author's communication with Arnulfo Arteaga, 18 October 1988.
35. Tsunekawa, 'Dependency and Labor Policy', pp. 276–78; *La Jornada*, 21 Oct. 1988, p. 10; JFCA internal documents; author's communication with Arnulfo Arteaga, 16 October 1987. No strike has yet occurred at either Chrysler-Ramos Arizpe or Nissan-Aguascalientes.
36. The data necessary for a detailed comparison between wage rates and costs of living at different automotive production sites are not available.
37. The fringe benefits that firms regularly provided to individual workers during the 1986–88 period included a Christmas bonus, seniority-based paid vacations and a vacation bonus, paid legal holidays, life insurance, cost-of-living and punctuality bonuses, subsidies for transportation and children's education, and contributions to a worker savings fund. For data on benefit levels in different plants, see Kevin J. Middlebrook, 'Organized Labor and the State in Postrevolutionary Mexico' (manuscript in preparation), Table VIII, 2.
38. Author's interviews with Ford labor relations manager, 6 November 1987, and 21 October 1988, Mexico City.
39. This discussion is based on the author's communications with Arnulfo Arteaga, 11, 14 October 1988; *La Jornada*, 31 Jan. 1988, p. 9, and 10 Feb. 1988, pp. 7, 9; *Excélsior*, 31 Jan. 1988, p. 6.
40. This discussion is based on the author's interviews with Ford (25 October 1988), General Motors (28 October 1988), and Nissan (27 October 1988) labor relations managers, Mexico City; Carrillo, 'Reestructuración en la industria automotriz en México', Table 9; *La Jornada*, 28 July 1987, p. 13.
41. Harley Shaiken (with Stephen Herzenberg) (1987) *Automation and Global Production in Mexico, the United States, and Canada* (La Jolla: Center for US–Mexican Studies) pp. 59, 63.
42. No information is available for Chrysler's Federal District plant.
43. Ford-Hermosillo labor contract, 1988, clause 12. Ford received assistance from its Japanese partner, Mazda, in the creation of this labor relations system.
44. *Ibid.*, clause 9.
45. It is possible that the physical layout of traditional assembly line manufacturing facilities such as General Motors' Federal District plant might

hinder the efficient operation of work teams and quality circles, whereas technologically modern plants specifically designed to incorporate post-Fordist labor relations concepts (for example, Ford's Hermosillo plant) might facilitate their functioning.

However, developments at Volkswagen's modern Puebla facility, where stiff worker resistance has prevented management from making much headway in introducing post-Fordist arrangements, suggests that the union's political character and bargaining strength are the most important determinants in this process. This discussion is based on the author's interviews with General Motors (28 October 1988) and Nissan (27 October 1988) labor relations managers, Mexico City, and internal Nissan documents.

46. Yolanda Montiel, 'Volkswagen: Un triunfo significativo', *La Jornada*, 28 Aug. 1987, p. 12.
47. See Jorge Carrillo V., 'Calidad con consenso en las maquiladoras: ¿Asociación factible?' (mimeograph, El Colegio de la Frontera Norte, Tijuana, Mexico, 1989), Table 2, for survey data on workers' attitudes toward work teams and quality circles in two Ford plants. The impact of political culture on workers' attitudes toward post-Fordist arrangements remains an unexplored subject.
48. Author's interview with a Ford labor relations manager, 25 October 1988, Mexico City; Carrillo, 'Reestructuración en la industria automotriz en México', p. 501.
49. Author's interview with General Motors labor relations manager, 28 October 1988, Mexico City.
50. Author's communication with Arnulfo Arteaga, 14 October 1988.
51. General Motors' 1987 Federal District labor contract, clauses 4, 9, 10; Nissan's 1988 Cuernavaca labor contract, clauses 7, 12, 62, 86; Volkswagen's 1986 Puebla contract, clauses, 14, 19, 28, 33–37.
52. General Motors-Federal District (1987), clauses 5, 10(e), 19bis, 27; Nissan-Cuernavaca (1988), clauses 14, 16. Although the Volkswagen contract is less favorable in this regard, the union has won legal control over the work force at any new plant established in Mexico, and it has an opportunity to negotiate labor force reductions with management (1986 labor contract, clauses 2, 92).
53. For details, see General Motors-Federal District (1987), clauses 19bis, 30, 49, 50, 62, 75, 81; Nissan-Cuernavaca (1988), clauses 1, 50, 54–60, 95, 96, 103, 106; Volkswagen-Puebla (1986), clauses 6, 7, 9, 10, 74, 76, 88–90.
54. General Motors-Federal District (1987), clauses 10(e), 20, 31, 33; Nissan-Cuernavaca (1988), clauses 7, 20, 21, 23, 24. The Volkswagen union has not been able to impose such stringent limitations, but over time it has gradually limited managerial flexibility in this area by requiring that the company pay a bonus to temporary workers who are not rehired (1986 labor contract, clause 24). The union also won significant numbers of *planta* positions for temporary workers in contract negotiations in the 1980s; see JFCA internal documents and Rainer Dombois, 'La producción automotriz y el mercado del trabajo en un país en desarrollo: Los mercados internos del trabajo y las relaciones industriales' (Berlin: International Institute for Comparative Social Research/Labor Policy, IIVG/dp86–216, 1986), p. 68.

232   *The Politics of Industrial Restructuring*

55. General Motors-Federal District (1987), clauses 80, 85; Nissan-Cuernavaca (1988), clauses 13, 17, 18, 101; Volkswagen-Puebla (1986), clauses 44, 45, 50, 60.
56. General Motors-Federal District (1987), clauses 18, 85; Nissan-Cuernavaca (1988), clause 13; Volkswagen-Puebla (1986), clause 65.
57. Shaiken, *Automation and Global Production*, pp. 25–26, 42; author's communication with Shaiken, 14 October 1988; author's interview with Nissan labor relations manager, 27 October 1988, Mexico City; Karl H. Ebel, 'Social and Labour Implications of Flexible Manufacturing Systems', *International Labour Review*, 124 (March–April 1985), 134.
58. Shaiken, pp. 45, 49, 59, 61–63. Ford's Chihuahua facility is not identified by name in this study.
59. *Ibid.*, p. 48.
60. *Ibid.*, p. 61; see also pp. 22, 42, 44, 47, 48.
61. *Ibid.*, pp. 22, 43, 45, 47, 51, 52, 62, 67.
62. See James P. Womack, 'Prospects for the US–Mexican Relationship in the Motor Vehicle Sector', in Cathryn L. Thorup (ed.), *The United States and Mexico: Face to Face with New Technology* (Washington, DC: Overseas Development Council, 1987), pp. 101–25, and Daniel T. Jones and James P. Womack, 'Developing Countries and the Future of the Automobile Industry', *World Development*, 13 (1985), 404–5.
63. Shaiken, *Automation and Global Production*, p. 42, states that in the mid-1980s the hourly wage differential (including fringe benefits) between the United States and Ford's Chihuahua plant was about 17:1. A study undertaken by the Mexican government and private US consultants indicates that in 1987 this differential ranged from 20:1 to 10:1 across the whole Mexican automobile industry; see Secretaría de Comercio y Fomento Industrial and Banco Nacional de Comercio Exterior, *Industria de autopartes* (1987), p. 81.
64. See Wolfgang Streeck, 'Editorial Introduction', *Economic and Industrial Democracy*, 9 (1988), 308, and Keith Bradley and Stephen Hill, ' "After Japan": The Quality Circle Transplant and Productive Efficiency', *British Journal of Industrial Relations*, 21 (November 1983), 291–311.
65. See, for example, Michael J. Piore, 'Perspectives on Labor Market Flexibility', *Industrial Relations*, 25 (Spring 1986), 149, 160; Harry C. Katz and Charles F. Sabel, 'Industrial Relations and Industrial Adjustment in the Car Industry', *Industrial Relations*, 24 (Fall 1985), 298–99; Charles F. Sabel, 'A Fighting Chance: Structural Change and New Labor Strategies', *International Journal of Political Economy*, 17 (Fall 1987), 46–50; Paul Windolf, 'Industrial Robots in the West German Automobile Industry', *Politics and Society*, 14 (1985), 459–95; Stephen J. Silvia, 'The West German Labor Law Controversy', *Comparative Politics*, 20 (January 1988), 156–58, 170 n. 50; Charlotte Yates, 'New Directions for the Canadian Labour Movement: The UAW and Beyond', paper presented at the 1986 meeting of the American Political Science Association.
66. Streeck, 'Industrial Relations and Industrial Change', p. 449.
67. Quoted in Carrillo, 'Reestructuración en la industria automotriz en México', p. 26.

8 A Diversity of New Work Organization: Human-centered, Lean and In-between[†]

Lowell Turner and Peter Auer

INTRODUCTION

In response to changing world markets, intensified competition, new technologies and worker demands, managers everywhere are required to reorganize work in important and sometimes profound ways. Such innovation, part of larger processes of industrial restructuring and production reorganization, is one of the central features of the modern workplace. But the new processes and impacts of work reorganization can be interpreted in different ways.

In one prominent contemporary view, Japanese firms have reinvented production and all others will have no choice but to follow. For Womack, Jones and Roos (1990), for example, the Toyota production system is paradigmatic. 'Lean production', based on innovations such as just-in-time supply networks and shopfloor production teams, has proven its superiority and will now replace mass production and 'change the world'. Work will be (or at least should be) reorganized everywhere based on superior Japanese methods; the outcome, in time, should be cross-national convergence along with more interesting, challenging and team-based work as the superior techniques spread.

Another view agrees that managers everywhere, in the auto industry but in other industries as well, are pushing new team systems of work organization on the Toyota model; but they are doing so to speed up and tighten control over their workforces, pushing toward an increasingly nightmarish outcome for shopfloor workers. Thus, Parker and Slaughter (1988) also see potential convergence for new systems of

[†] This paper has also been published in the German journal *Industrielle Beziehung*, vol. 1, no. 1, 1994, pp. 39–61.

234   *A Diversity of New Work Organization*

work organization, in this view around a more intense version of Taylorism that they call 'management by stress'. The saving grace in this view is that workers can and will rebel. Parker and Slaughter thus project a picture of converging managerial initiatives to promote oppressive new work organization systems such as the 'team concept', accompanied by increasing shopfloor resistance and conflict.

Our view is that both of these analyses, in spite of the substantial contributions of each, are flawed in their general orientations. The research we have done on the US, German and Swedish auto industries (the paradigmatic industry both for Womack, Jones and Roos and for Parker and Slaughter) shows that not only are there different roads to new work organization, but there are distinctly different outcomes as well. We see not convergence around a single model but considerable diversity; and this diversity is not only nationally based but is apparent in considerable variation of plant-level outcomes within each nation. This diversity, we believe, is not a transitory phenomenon but an enduring one, as new and distinct contending models of production and work organization take root in contemporary processes of industrial restructuring.

The driving forces for organizational change are similar across and within nations: changing world markets, intensified competition, the rise of successful Japanese production models, the spread of new microelectronic technologies, and new worker demands for more interesting and varied work. But outcomes vary in different political, economic and social contexts. The mistake that analysts such as Krafcik (1988) and Womack, Jones and Roos (1990) make is to downplay the importance of these contexts. We argue, by contrast, that the political, economic and social contexts are crucial in determining outcomes, both for the shape of new work organization systems and the accompanying prospects of 'new industrial relations' (see also Jürgens, Malsch and Dohse, 1989; and Dankbaar, 1990). We find no persuasive empirical grounds for the view that contemporary globalization means the dominance of and convergence around one model of production organization (see also BRIE, 1991). On the contrary, we find significant cross-national variation, with distinct national patterns that are strongly influenced by the institutions of industrial relations, the role of organized labor, and national labor-market characteristics. And not only do we find national patterns, we find as well considerable diversity within the national range of choice for particular plants, dependent on the local institutions, preferences and political interactions of employers, unions and governments.[1]

It is not true, of course, that all things are possible. Japanese lean producers have reached levels of productivity, product quality and flexibility of product offering that are forcing others to respond. Western managers, for good reason, are adopting many new Japanese techniques. Japanese firms, especially in the auto industry, have made a major contribution by developing and showing the possibilities of highly efficient new work organization. Womack, Jones and Roos have provided an important service in analyzing and calling attention to the elements of one prominent Japanese firm's success.

But convergence, we argue, will be limited by national and local institutions and circumstances; patterns of diversity in production and work organization will persist, even as successful Western producers reach Japanese levels of efficiency.

SOURCES OF DIVERSITY

Why do we find such cross-national, cross-firm, and intra-national differences in contemporary work reorganization? The answer is that politics, industrial relations institutions, union and firm strategies, and labor-market conditions all matter. This is a perspective that has informed much of the best recent work on industrial relations and new work organization (such as Sabel, 1982; Katz and Sabel, 1985; Kochan, Katz and McKersie, 1986; Jürgens, Malsch and Dohse, 1989; Pontusson, 1990; Locke, 1990; and Thelen, 1991). It is a perspective that is worth re-emphasizing as we enter a post-Fordist era in which the natural inclination for researchers and analysts may be to seek to define a sweeping new paradigm of 'best practice'.

If one accepts the conclusion that contrasting political, economic and social contexts lead to different shopfloor forms of organization, the next and more difficult step is to specify the particular factors leading to particular outcomes. In other words, how do we explain the differences? We need testable propositions that specify interrelationships and that can be applied broadly, across nations and industries. A full set of hypotheses is beyond the scope of this article; but the following are examples of propositions, suitable for wider testing, that are supported by the evidence presented here.

1. Where unions are integrated in management decision-making processes through legal or bargained institutions of codetermination, unions in the current period of work reorganization develop proactive strategies to influence the shape of new organization. The result is negotiated solutions: new shop floor organization takes shape

in a bargaining process between labor and management. One can expect in these cases that while some aspects of lean production will be adopted for efficiency purposes, other human-centered concerns that are not part of the lean system (such as longer cycle times, more autonomy for work groups, and elected group leaders) will also be incorporated. This pattern can be seen in Sweden and Germany.

2. Where unions have long-established arm's-length relations with employers and no formal rights in management decision-making, unions face a choice between collaboration and opposition but are unable to play a pro-active role in the shape of new work organization (at least until the arm's-length relation is substantially changed). Management will push for implementation of its own team concepts (heavily influenced by Japanese/lean models). The transition to new work organization will be rocky as management encounters a patchwork pattern of acceptance and rejection within the workforce, as the US experience indicates.

3. The specific form and implementation of new work organization is linked not only to industrial relations but to other factors such as national and local labor-market conditions. The drive to implement human-centered forms of work organization is stronger in tight labor markets, where competition for labor is based not only on wages but on the quality of jobs. In loose, low-skilled labor markets, new forms of work organization are less necessary to attract labor, leaving room either for lower skilled, traditional work organization or for lean production.[2]

4. There is a link between labor-market incentives for work reorganization and the national (and local) vocational training system. If such a system produces high skills as a 'public good', the spread of human-centered work organization based on high skills content becomes more probable. Contemporary Swedish and German experience provides evidence for this claim.

These propositions emphasize both institutional and economic variables (see also Cole, 1985, who identifies organized labor and labor-market circumstances as key variables in determining the success of 'small group activities'). Indeed, we argue that both markets and established institutions are critical in determining the shape of new production and work organization systems in this period of major transition and restructuring.

As evidence both for our general argument and specific hypotheses, we present summaries of our case studies of organizational innovation in the US, German and Swedish auto industries.[3] To provide focus for this chapter, we emphasize the path-breaking arrival, at auto plants of all three of these countries, of team and group forms of shopfloor organization, where the isolated, individual regimentation of traditional mass production once held sway.

JAPANESE-STYLE TEAMS AND HOMEGROWN SOLUTIONS IN THE UNITED STATES

The early groundwork for the coming of team organization in the US auto industry was laid at GM in the 1970s, through widespread Quality of Working Life experiments and in efforts by GM to introduce team organization at non-union plants in the South (Katz, 1985, pp. 73–104). Both initiatives represented efforts to resolve shopfloor worker discontent, to improve labor–management relations (in an industry notorious for relations of 'armed truce'), and to tap shopfloor workers' ideas and thereby improve workforce morale, productivity and product quality. But the big push came in the 1980s. The GM–Toyota joint venture in Fremont, California, known as NUMMI (New United Motor Manufacturing, Inc.), proved that the introduction of Japanese-style teams was possible in an American setting, even with an established American workforce and union (the United Auto Workers).

The plight of the US auto industry in the wake of the 1978–79 oil shock and 1980–82 recession is well known (Altshuler *et al.*, 1984; Quinn, 1989). Market shares of Japanese firms rose rapidly while the sales of US firms dropped, plants closed and employment in the industry plunged. Japanese firms, it turned out, had developed enormous cost advantages (for cars of similar or superior quality) over US firms, advantages which to a significant degree could be traced to innovations in production organization. It was in this context, as US managers sought to imitate just-in-time, outsourcing and quality circle (among other) strategies, that they were suddenly presented, in 1984–85, with the successful 'demonstration plant' NUMMI model.

NUMMI is a Toyota-run plant from which GM has made a major effort to learn.[4] There are many aspects of NUMMI's success (just as there are for the Toyota production system from which NUMMI is derived), but a key ingredient is the thorough-going organization of the plant workforce into shopfloor production teams. At NUMMI, workers are organized into teams typically composed of four members and a team leader. Although jobs are enriched through the teams for workers where the technology is most advanced (as in the stamping plant), most workers, especially in final assembly, do repetitive, routine and highly standardized work in short cycles (about one minute). They rotate jobs within the teams, include inspection and some minor repair and machine maintenance within the teams, and meet every two weeks for half an hour to discuss production problems and suggest improvements. Although the system has been referred to as 'team Taylorism' (Wood, 1986) and 'management by stress' (Parker and Slaughter, 1988), union election results from 1986 to 1990 favored the cooperation-oriented incumbent leadership. The local UAW, in fact, led by former union militants from the earlier GM plant at the same site, has been well integrated into a new system of consensual labor–management relations; workers received employment security in return for new functional flexibility and the elimination of most job classifications.

But NUMMI is no workers' nirvana: in 1991 elections, opposition candidates won several top local union positions. Even supporters of the (former) opposition, however, who criticize the constant pressure to work harder and faster, claim to prefer NUMMI to the highly adversarial, low morale, work-fragmented GM system in which most NUMMI employees formerly worked. In the years following those elections, the cooperative, integrated labor–management relationship has persisted. An accurate evaluation of NUMMI should therefore be two-sided: on the positive side, high productivity and product quality, employment security for the workforce, and work that on the whole is probably more satisfying and equally apportioned than before; on the negative side, very limited team autonomy (at least in production), short cycle times composed largely of repetitive tasks, and constant 'no buffer' pressure on the workforce.

But NUMMI, although it may be the model to which many managers aspire, is far from the whole story of new work organization in the US auto industry. Big Three auto firm management has been notoriously slow and only occasionally successful at spreading the lessons of NUMMI. Katz, Kochan and Keefe (1988), for example, found no positive correlation between team organization at US auto plants and good performance (such as productivity). Managers have often avoided the risks of change, even when prime opportunities have presented themselves; and when they have initiated major team organization campaigns, they have often pursued counterproductive implementation strategies that have resulted in failure.

At an assembly plant in Van Nuys, California, GM made a major effort to transfer the lessons of NUMMI.[5] Management, however, pursued reorganization in a typically old-fashioned, heavy-handed way which polarized the workforce and undermined the possibility of new labor–management trust and successful teamwork. The plant manager negotiated a local 'team concept' agreement in 1986 with the cooperative wing of the local union leadership. But the agreement was rejected by the workforce; only after heavy pressure and threats of plant closure did the workers finally ratify the agreement on a later vote. Team organization on the NUMMI model was then implemented throughout the plant in 1987 in a polarized atmosphere; and management wasted the opportunity and support it did have by its own failure to live up to promises of a new and more humane management style. The experiment struggled gamely along, supported by many but undermined as well by others within the ranks of both management and workforce, until the announcement was finally made in 1991 that the plant was scheduled for permanent closure.

In 1984, GM opened its Hamtramck flagship plant in Detroit to great fanfare about the revolutionary combination of new work organization (shopfloor teams, new human relations) and advanced assembly technology. Although all workers received some training in the new system and at least enough 'organizational development' to raise their hopes, expectations were soon dashed when production pressure mounted in the early months. Managers reverted to their old ways, sacrificing new concepts such as job rotation, pay-for-knowledge, and substantial team participation in the push to produce. By 1989, a union opposition group was strong enough to ride the crest of disillusionment and anger into office. Hard negotiations followed, centered around union demands that management fulfill human-side promises of the new system; by 1990, prospects improved for a team system that included short cycle times and limited team autonomy on the one hand, but job rotation, team meetings and improved worker input and labor–management relations on the other hand.

The variety of outcomes for innovation at GM plants remained wide throughout the 1980s and into the new decade. At plants in Lansing and Lordstown, for example, management and labor initiated wide-ranging 'joint' cooperative processes that included grouping workers into teams. Although cycle times remained short and team autonomy limited, these new processes showed promise for shopfloor innovations such as job rotation and worker involvement while protecting traditional union bases of influence (such as seniority rights – in contrast to NUMMI). Workers at Lordstown called their teams 'groups', to emphasize that this was not the Japanese or NUMMI team concept but rather a distinct and evolving 'homegrown' solution to the need for new work organization and engaged labor–management relations. And at Saturn, labor and management collaborated from the start in the conceptual and physical building of a new plant, to establish yet another, more thorough-going model of distinctly American work reorganization and labor–management partnership.

Diversity is even greater within the US auto case when we consider Chrysler, Ford and the Japanese transplants. At Chrysler, management has implemented 'modern operating agreements', including team organization, at some plants but not at others (depending in part on workforce/union resistance). Ford had the best production results of the Big Three in the mid-to-late 1980s, but moved slowly in the introduction of teams (wisely seeking to avoid the problems associated with GM's often rushed implementation). And the Japanese transplants, except for the joint ventures, have stayed non-union and have implemented team organization throughout their plants, with positive results for productivity and product quality (Florida and Kenney, 1991).

In the US auto industry, therefore, the most obvious fact concerning new work organization is the great diversity of plant-level outcomes. In spite of widespread initiatives on the part of management and a general willingness on the part of the national union and many local unions to cooperate, the overall picture for the Big Three is of a very rocky transition that has yet to yield consistently successful results. Traditional ways die hard, and innovation failure has probably been more widespread than innovation success. Milkman (1991) argues persuasively that the failure to move decisively toward a 'new social contract' that would include appropriate work organization is rooted above all in management's bureaucratic inertia. US auto industry management has on the whole failed to reform itself adequately for the tasks at hand, while the UAW, still a strong union but within a seriously declining labor movement, has so far shown a limited capacity to develop its own concepts and push management toward successful work reorganization.

Of the three country cases we consider, however, the US has moved the farthest toward Toyota-style lean production.

THE COMING OF GROUP WORK IN THE GERMAN AUTO INDUSTRY

In comparison to the US case, the coming of new work organization, including the current move toward *Gruppenarbeit* (group work), has been slow, smooth and fairly regularized throughout the German auto industry. In response to economic recession, intensified competition and the export challenge of Japanese firms, German managers since the 1970s have moved to rationalize production. In so doing, they have introduced new technology and work organization that has included speed-up and de-skilling for some production workers as well as 'new production concepts' for others (Jürgens, Malsch, and Dohse, 1989). The latter is especially associated with advanced technology, and in many cases has meant a reintegration of tasks and a shift away from assembly-line fragmentation to more conceptual work such as machine monitoring (Kern and Schumann, 1984; 1987).

At the same time, building on the union/SPD campaign for the 'humanization of work' in the 1970s, the German metalworkers' union (IG Metall) since the early 1980s has developed and actively negotiated for its own concepts of group work (Muster, 1988; Roth and Kohl, 1988; Turner, 1991, pp. 111–17). In the auto industry, this union campaign accelerated after 1985 and has laid the basis for labor–management negotiation and the contemporary spread of group work at major assembly plants. In contrast to both the US and Swedish cases, workers' interest representation (IG Metall and works councils) in the German auto industry has played a leading role in designing group work concepts and promoting their implementation.[6]

The core ideas of union-promoted group work were developed at IG Metall headquarters in Frankfurt in the early-to-mid 1980s. Building on past research and experiments from the humanization campaign, union representatives and researchers developed group work concepts in response to works council and local union and member complaints about the effects on the workforce of management's rationalization drive. In a back-and-forth dialogue between union and works councils of the major auto assembly plants, union thinking crystallized around 1986–87 in the following 12 principles of group work:[7]

1. A broad assignment of varying tasks for the group (including long cycle times);
2. Group competence and authority in decision-making in such areas as job rotation, division of work, quality control and training needs;
3. Decentralization of the plant decision-making structure;
4. Selection of production organization and technology suitable for group work (based on decentralized technology and production concepts);

5. Equal pay for group members;
6. Equal opportunity for all, including special training where necessary for the disabled and the socially disadvantaged, to participate in group work ('group work as solidaristic work organization');
7. Support for the personal and occupational development of individuals and the group;
8. Regular group meetings, at least one hour per week;
9. Representation of group interests within the established plant system of interest representation;
10. Voluntary participation in the groups;
11. Pilot projects to test the functioning of group work before broader implementation;
12. A joint steering committee at the firm level, with equal labor and management representation, to oversee and coordinate the implementation of group work and the activities of the groups.

IG Metall argued that group work could serve management interests in cutting costs and raising productivity while at the same time raising skill levels and making work more interesting and 'human'. High skill levels in the German workforce, promoted by an extensive national vocational education system already in place, would make possible the widespread introduction of skilled group work. By 1987, works councils at most of the West German auto assembly plants had adopted statements of policy endorsing group work, based on the twelve principles or something similar, and had entered into negotiations with management to establish pilot projects and prepare for broader implementation. Management, for the most part, disregarded works council suggestions on group work until around 1986, when NUMMI and other examples (such as the Austrian GM plant at Aspern) began to drive home the potential contribution of shopfloor teamwork. In a reverse situation to the US case, managers just beginning to develop their own thinking found union group work concepts already on the bargaining table. As negotiations proceeded and pilot projects spread in the late 1980s, the actual shape of new group or team organization emerged from processes of compromise between the union's maximal position and developing employer notions (favoring a more NUMMI-style approach with, for example, less autonomy for the groups).

At VW, for example, substantial pilot projects were established at the Emden and Salzgitter plants as well as at the VW subsidiary Audi.[8] In 1988, the VW general works council at Wolfsburg endorsed group work as its vision of future work organization in the auto industry, a vision addressing both production needs (flexibility, productivity and a highly skilled workforce) and a union-backed democratic workplace culture (Riffel and Muster, 1989). In 1989, negotiations with management began in earnest for the establishment of new pilot projects and the gradual spread of group work throughout the VW plants. Both works council and management faced problems in this effort, both in their relations with each other (and their contending, if in some ways overlapping, viewpoints) and in their attempts, especially by the works council, to elicit shopfloor support.

But management, union and works council are all strong and well organized at VW. One can predict (and already see the outlines of) lengthy processes of negotiation accompanied by fairly smooth and gradual implementation of group work at the VW plants. The works council won't get all that it is asking for in the design of new work organization. But it does speak with a consistent and pro-active voice, backed by formal rights (in the Works Constitution Act) to information, consultation and participation in management decision-making.[9] The works council will get some of what it seeks, including the preservation of its own important position at VW, and the path will be cleared for implementation. Group work, we predict, will be quite different at VW from teamwork at NUMMI or the other American plants considered above, and will include more 'human-centered' features such as longer cycle time and more group autonomy.[10] One can see the outlines of such innovative work organization emerging at the new VW plant at Mosel in the eastern state of Saxony.

Similar processes are underway at Ford and Opel in Germany. At Ford, for example, the works council countered management plans to strip labor from a new advanced technology installation (in the tool-and-die plant) with its own proposal for group work. After hard bargaining, management accepted the plan in 1987 and set up a group work experiment that became a model for the integration of computer room programming and shopfloor machine monitoring. And at Opel, the first German auto industry agreement for the firm-wide implementation of group work was signed in early 1991 between management and the general works council.[11] Building on pilot projects that included 1700 Opel workers, labor and management agreed to full implementation of group work by 1993 in all Opel plants. The design of the groups is based to a significant degree on IG Metall concepts, including 8–15 members at varying skill levels, considerable group autonomy in job design and the organization of assigned work, a major commitment to training within the groups, pay raises for all (3 per cent on the average along with this agreement), elected group leaders, and group meetings for one hour per week. Opel management expects that the added costs of group work will be more than offset by the gains in productivity. And Mercedes Benz announced the implementation of negotiated group work for 10 000 workers in 1992, to expand to include half the workforce by 1995.

In contrast to the US case, processes and outcomes for group work appear fairly regularized throughout the German auto industry. The relatively narrow range of outcomes results above all from the IG Metall's coordinating role in the development and promotion of group work concepts and bargaining strategies. The works councils at most German auto assembly plants adopted the concepts and put them on the bargaining table around the same time. And everywhere in the auto industry, management is restricted in what it can do unilaterally given substantial works council co-determination rights. We can expect that the 1991 agreement at Opel will be followed by similar agreements at VW and Ford, and that group work in the German auto industry will continue to be implemented in comparatively smooth processes based on negotiated labor–management agreement.[12]

A LONG HISTORY OF GROUP WORK IN THE SWEDISH AUTO INDUSTRY

As in Germany and the US the current Swedish experience with work reorganization has a history that stretches back two decades or more.[13] Until the 1970s, Swedish industrial relations were based largely on a broad agreement between the social partners; with the Saltsjöbaden agreement of 1938, unions and employers each recognized the other's legitimacy and agreed to strive for the peaceful settlement of industrial conflicts, with employers retaining the exclusive right to organize production at the workplace. Wage bargaining occurred at the central level, while a 'hands-off' approach for government in industrial relations prevailed. The first attempts at fundamental work reorganization came from certain managers who adopted 'social-technical system analysis' ideas in order to reduce high turnover and absenteeism rates.[14]

Organized labor, however, considered the early management approach too individualistic, preferring a more collective concept of industrial democracy. During the 1970s, unions thus engaged in a broad 'legal offensive' which left Swedish industrial relations more extensively regulated by the early 1980s. Included in the new legislation was the law on co-determination, passed in 1976, which established union rights to information, consultation and participation in management decision-making at the plant and firm levels. A central-level collective bargaining agreement in 1982, between LO (the blue-collar federation), TCO (white-collar) and SAF (the employers' association), established a framework for the implementation of co-determination, which was then supplemented by specific union–employer agreements such as the one at Volvo in 1984.

The union legal campaign brought the movement for new work organization to a slowdown by the late 1970s. Although the experiences of that first period did not spread, some of them, such as innovations at the Volvo Kalmar plant beginning in 1974, nonetheless set the pace for further developments.

After a period of turmoil in industrial relations, brought on in part by the union legal offensive and the campaign for wage earner funds (interpreted by many as the end of the 'Swedish model' of peaceful bargaining for structural change; Auer, 1983), a new period of work reorganization began around the mid-1980s.

The new drive for changes in work organization was again initiated by management. This time, however, the changes were founded less on humanization-of-work than on efficiency concerns, aimed at reforming a bureaucratic, centrally controlled organization. Although changes were now legitimized on efficiency grounds, they were not opposed by the unions. Labor's new approach was based in large part on the success of the legal offensive and the new union rights to full information and consultation on all shopfloor matters. The metalworkers' union (including the auto workers) began to develop labor strategies for organizational change, which by the mid-1980s led to proposals for 'good work' which included group-work (Svenska Metalarbetareförbundet, 1985). Union group work concepts paralleled the basic group work plans already developed by management, which had continued to discuss and implement changes even during the period of the legal offensive. Work groups were designed to execute regular production work in reorganized plants, based on ideas of product shops, flow groups and the general notion that 'small is surveyable' (Agurén and Edgren, 1980). Such planning aimed at creating highly integrated teams of production workers engaged in job rotation, enlargement and enrichment. Production groups of the Swedish kind, in addition to direct production work, take on extensive tasks such as maintenance of equipment and tools, material planning, 'housekeeping' of the group area, distributing work assignments among the group members, and vacation planning. Usually a group leader is elected, and leadership can rotate among group members. Wage incentives (pay for knowledge of tasks within the group and performance pay based on group or plant performance) as well as flatter hierarchies accompany the new forms of work organization.

A study conducted at ten plants of the Swedish car producer Volvo (Auer and Riegler, 1990b), as well as other research (Berggren, 1991), shows the diversity of group work forms. At the new plant in Uddevalla, highly integrated teams each assembled a whole car; in other plants, however, a team may only be a group of workers executing specialized tasks under the control of a foreman selected by management. But in most plants there is a constant effort to push group work concepts further.

Plant-level diversity in the Swedish auto industry is even greater if one takes into account the changes in work organization at the second Swedish car manufacturer, Saab. Although group work was introduced there as well, Saab never developed a broad strategy to diffuse the innovations as Volvo did. Some of the changes (as in engine production at Södertälje) have been discontinued; and the new assembly plant in Malmö never represented as clear a departure from the assembly line as Volvo's Uddevalla plant, built around the same time (Berggren, 1991). When GM took over Saab in 1990, management decided to close the new Malmö factory, believing both that capacity at the principal Saab site in Trollhättan was sufficient for the future and that car assembly in the new plant was too costly.

Different companies, but also different plants within a company (which are usually run on a profit center basis and therefore have considerable autonomy concerning issues such as work organization) exhibit considerable diversity of implementation in the forms of group work. It is astonishing, for example, that Womack, Jones and Roos (1990, pp. 101–2) put on the same level of 'neocraftmanship' two very different Volvo plants, Uddevalla and Kalmar, when the latter is much closer to 'lean production' than the former.

Although at Kalmar a new assembly technique (carriers on magnetic tracks) was developed and the plant was divided into small workshops (group areas of 15–20 workers each), the factory did not represent a radical departure from the assembly-line principle. The carriers' pace was centrally set; and earlier possibilities of variation afforded by buffers and dock assembly (working at stationary platforms) were restricted by new requirements such as just-in-time parts delivery.

Uddevalla, by contrast, started production 15 years after Kalmar and afforded a radical departure from the assembly line. The entire car was assembled on a stationary platform by a work group of around ten members; without centrally controlled pacing, there was more autonomy for the groups and more scope to vary production speeds. For the first time, assembly work, typically low-skilled in auto assembly plants, was upgraded: workers had to complete 16 months of training before becoming fully-fledged assembly workers at Uddevalla.[15]

A close look at work organization in the Swedish auto industry thus shows very different forms even at plants considered innovative within the same firm. The form of implementation appears to depend on a variety of factors such as available skills in local labor markets. Restrictions or incentives for implementation, for example, are set by the availability of both skilled labor and alternative jobs in the area, with important effects on turnover rates.

In comparison to the other countries in our study, the following national pattern of work reorganization in Sweden emerges. Changes are mainly management driven, with extensive diffusion channels (through the strong employer federation) to spread information and facilitate broader implementation of change. Management sees working groups as one element of a larger strategy of organizational change, to delegate responsibility for profits, costs and 'total quality' as far down as the shopfloor level.

The attitude of Swedish unions has changed over time from resistance to support for change, in part because co-determination rights were enacted in law. The metalworkers union in particular has in recent years developed pro-active policies for work reorganization. Given high Swedish rates of unionization (90 per cent or more) and broad union influence in the political economy, union work organization strategies provide an effective channel for the diffusion of group work. The union goal is the realization of principles of 'good work', combining stable, well paid jobs with challenging, skills-developing assignments.

Although goals are not the same on both sides, there is enough overlap between the designs of labor and management for a 'modernization agreement' to have taken hold. A cooperative way of implementing change has developed which has contributed to the diffusion of experiences and new forms.

Volvo's decision to close Uddevalla in 1993 and Kalmar in 1994 cuts the ground from under proponents of Swedish-style group work. But according to Volvo management, the decisions to close resulted not from weak performance but from overcapacity. It makes sense to close small final-assembly plants (lacking body and paint shops and stamping plants) and consolidate production at the larger Torslanda plant and the Skövde engine plant, where group work innovations will continue. Just as we have seen the influence of industrial relations in the development of Swedish work organization, so industrial relations also played a role in recent decisions. The union understood the overcapacity problem and preferred closing the smaller plants to cuts in the large union stronghold at Torslanda. Managers and unionists alike are emphatic that the remaining plants will survive and thrive with variations of Swedish group work rather than lean production.

CONCLUSION

The overall picture that emerges from these national stories, based on empirical studies of the politics of new work organization systems at numerous auto plants, is one of rich diversity. The isolated work stations of traditional mass production are giving way everywhere to new forms of team or group-based work organization. But the politics and processes of change as well as the specific shape of the outcomes vary considerably within and across both nations and firms. Although plant-level variation is important within each national case, there do appear to be distinct national patterns for the processes and outcomes of contemporary work reorganization.

- *In the US*, we see the broadest diversity of plant-level outcomes. The drive toward team forms of organization is management-led, inspired by a Japanese 'team concept'; but management has often pushed its programs onto reluctant and divided workforces and above all has failed to adequately reform itself, to play a less authoritarian, a more cooperative, facilitative and inspirational role. The official union response has been to collaborate with management on new work organization, although at the plant-level local union responses range from collaboration to opposition. The union has played only a minimal proactive role of its own, one that would promote an independent vision of the shape of new work organization. The overall pattern has been one that includes both widespread failure to reorganize successfully, especially at the dominant firm, GM, and a rocky transition toward Japanese-style team organization. The US case provides evidence for the second hypothesis: that arm's-length labor–management relations result in employer dominance of work reorganization and a very rocky transition toward variations of lean production.

- *In Germany*, progress toward group work in the auto industry has been slower and more deliberate. Here, the union has played a strong pro-active role in developing and promoting its own concepts of new work organization. There has been a relatively narrow range of plant-level outcomes, marked by group work negotiations and pilot project implementation, although labor and management at Opel have signed a breakthrough agreement that calls for broad group work implementation. As employers have become more interested in team forms of organization since the mid-1980s, labor (through the works councils) and management have been negotiating the substance of group work, including some elements that could be considered 'lean' and others that come from the union's 'humanization' orientation. The German case provides evidence for the first and fourth hypotheses: that institutions of co-determination facilitate pro-active union strategies which result in negotiated work reorganization; and that extensive vocational training promotes human-centered work organization.

- *In Sweden*, the overall move toward group work began early, in the 1970s, and has progressed through a variety of forms at various plants. The drive toward new work organization has for the most part been management led, as part of a drive to attract workers and reduce absenteeism and turnover in a full employment economy. Backed by new co-determination legislation and bargaining agreements, the union in recent years has moved toward its own engaged, pro-active stance on group work, and has tipped the balance within management toward more autonomous, 'human-centered' forms of organization that are quite different from Japanese team concepts. There is in effect a 'modernization agreement' between labor and management to promote both the introduction of advanced technology and new forms of group work designed to be both human-centered and efficient. The Swedish case therefore provides evidence for the first, third and fourth hypotheses: that institutions of co-determination facilitate pro-active union strategies which result in negotiated work reorganization; and that tight labor markets and extensive vocational training promote human-centered work organization.

Our hypotheses on work reorganization are not intended to be exhaustive, but rather to illustrate the importance of industrial relations and labor-market circumstances for variations in new work organization. Although the evidence is richly suggestive we have not proven these hypotheses, which require further testing in other industries and industrial societies coping with the challenges of work reorganization. If valid, these claims should be widely applicable in Western Europe and North America, and not just in the automobile industry.

The Japanese case, by contrast, is unique as an important driving force for change in other countries. Although analysis of work organization in Japan is beyond the scope of this article, it is nonetheless clear that firms such as Toyota display great strengths in productivity and product quality. But Toyota is not the only Japanese way; there is considerable diversity within Japan, even within the auto industry (between, for example, Toyota and Honda). In addition, there is mounting evidence that contemporary work organization in Japan is changing; several analysts have claimed that on the shopfloor, the lean model even at Toyota is beginning to loosen up in response to the demands of Japanese workers and the need to make factory work more attractive to young workforce entrants (Nomura, 1992).[16] And Japanese work organization in all its varieties is very much a product of its own institutional, historical and labor-market context. Enterprise unions grease the wheels of cooperative labor–management relations and team-based work organization; and enterprise unionism itself is based in part on past union demands for employment security and seniority-based rewards (Kenney and Florida, 1988, pp. 127–9).

In their seminal study of lean production, Womack, Jones and Roos mention in passing that there may be many aspects of Japanese society that others will not want or need to adopt (1990, p. 9). One of these, which they do not mention and about which they say almost nothing in their book, may be Japanese industrial relations, in which the subordinate enterprise union functions in many cases as a virtual arm of management. This is in fact the biggest mistake that Womack, Jones and Roos make: the failure to acknowledge that the Toyota production system which they laud was founded in part on the defeat of independent unionism in the 1950s, and that industrial relations is always an important part of the development of new work organization.[17] And other important factors influencing work organization are beyond the decision range of individual firms: labor laws, for example, that allow generous leaves of absence or reduce working time, making it necessary to put additional personnel on the books; and tenure and mobility patterns, which may result in high turnover rates and in any case leave their mark on productivity and cost. It is precisely for reasons such as these that production organization will continue to look different in different national and local settings.

Although it is true that extraordinarily efficient Japanese production models are driving much change in work organization practices in other countries, it is wrong to judge others by how closely they approximate the ideal type of lean production. Because political, economic and social contexts matter so importantly, there will be enduring and substantial cross-national and sub-national variations in new work organization, as the evidence presented here on team and group work makes apparent. And there is no more apparent reason now than there has been in the past to assume that there is 'one best way', that one way will in the long run necessarily prove far superior in productivity, product quality and worker satisfaction. Even at its high point of worldwide diffusion, Fordism had widely varying local forms of implementation, as comparative studies of factory organization have made apparent (Lutz, 1976; Maurice, Sellier and Sylvestre, 1986). And in an interesting counterpoint to the image of inexorably spreading lean production, Ruth Milkman has shown that even most Japanese producers in the US continue to use traditional methods and have chosen not to make use of innovative NUMMI-style ways of organizing their workforces (Milkman, 1991).

If it is true, as we argue, that there is not necessarily one best way, alternative models must nonetheless successfully compete. In this essay, we have juxtaposed Toyota's lean production, which we believe includes human downsides such as intensive work pace, high stress, long hours, short cycle times, limited worker independence and an absence of truly independent employee representation, against more human-centered German and Swedish group work.[18] But while Toyotism has emphatically proven itself in competitive terms, the same is not yet true for German or Swedish group work. We think it is too soon to evaluate the latter nascent efforts and other current attempts at synthesis; but we do acknowledge, as do the relevant practitioners from both management and labor, that Japanese levels of productivity must be approached if German or Swedish group work is to succeed.

In this regard, the building of a new VW plant at Mosel (Saxony) in eastern Germany is an important case. Here, VW management aims to match Japanese levels of productivity by combining elements of lean production with union group work concepts, the terms of which are negotiated and overseen by an elected, union-dominated works council. Managers and unionists alike are excited about the development of innovations that could be spread throughout Germany.

The important point here is that while elements of lean production are arriving in Germany (and many other countries as well), new work organization looks different in many ways from Toyotism, especially in the emphasis on human-centered design. Elements of new work organization – just-in-time, job rotation, skills training, elected group leaders, decision-making capacities – can in fact be developed and combined in different ways, resulting in more or less individual and group autonomy.

Convergence theories were dominant in the social sciences in the 1950s and 1960s, spearheaded as they were by the 'industrialism' perspective of Kerr, Dunlop, Harbison and Myers (1960). These theories captured part of the truth: that industrialized societies contain many common economic, political, social and organizational aspects. But the predictive power and credibility of these theories were soon swamped by persistently distinct structures of political economy, even within the ranks of the advanced industrial democracies (Dore, 1973; Schmitter, 1974; Wilensky, 1976; Zysman, 1983). Even the dominant mass production paradigm for industrial organization always contained within it important cross-national (and other) variations, which became increasingly important with new markets and technologies since the 1970s (Piore and Sabel, 1984).

Now, with the collapse of the communist regimes of Eastern Europe, economic integration in Western Europe, and the contemporary dominance of free-market ideology, new convergence theory becomes tempting. But entrenched national institutions and particular market circumstances make national and local diversity as important now as ever. This is especially true for production organization, in spite of the obvious success of lean production and the current widespread interest of Western managers in Japanese forms of organization. Firms, it is true, that cannot respond to Japanese levels of productivity, quality and flexibility will decline or die out altogether. Nonetheless, the evidence presented here indicates that although Japanese practices such as the team concept are widely promoted by employers in North America and Europe, the specific shape of new work organization will be significantly determined by national and local institutions, circumstances and negotiations.

Notes

1. We are not arguing that organizational transfer is impossible. NUMMI and other Japanese transplants have shown that transfer is indeed possible, especially when Japanese management is part of the transfer (Florida and Kenney, 1991). As a general rule, however, we argue that national and local contexts will shape distinctive national and local patterns.
2. Successful Japanese transplants in the US make it clear that labor markets with abundant skills are not necessary for the success of Toyotism/lean production.
3. Although our case studies are of the auto industry, the hypotheses are of a general nature and should apply across a range of industries. We look here at the auto industry as one important test of our claims.
4. Case study research on NUMMI and the other US auto plants mentioned below is based on intensive interviews conducted at each plant between 1987 and 1989 (see also Turner, 1991, pp. 31–90).
5. For more on the introduction of teams at Van Nuys, see Mann 1987, pp. 219ff; and Turner 1991, pp. 62–70. For a comparison of NUMMI and Van Nuys, see Brown and Reich, 1989.
6. In contrast to both the US and Sweden, Germany has a 'dual system' composed on the one hand of 16 major industrial unions, engaged in regional bargaining with centralized employer associations, and on the other hand a separate structure of legally mandated works councils, with information, consultation and co-determination rights in the workplace. Although works councils are elected by the entire workforce, blue and white collar, at each workplace and have no formal relationship to unions, most works councilors are union members. The tight linkage between union and works council is especially pronounced in the auto industry.
7. Based on a summary translation of Muster and Wannöffel, 1989, pp. 39–54. See also Turner, 1991, pp. 113–14. For an updated version and general discussion, see Hans-Böckler Stiftung/IG Metall, 1992.
8. Case study presentations of VW, Ford and Opel in Germany are based largely on interviews conducted at the plants in 1988–89. For more detail see Turner, 1991, pp. 117–48.
9. For more detail on the specific nature of these rights, see Turner 1991, pp. 98–99.
10. Negotiations for group work at Wolfsburg in the early 1990s took a back seat to other issues (such as employment security, VW investment in eastern Germany and, elsewhere in eastern and central Europe, a shorter working week, and the building of a cross-national Euro-works council at VW). Wolfsburg works councillors, nonetheless, are working closely with and watching carefully the more advanced efforts to build plant-wide group work both at VW-Salzgitter and at Mosel.
11. *European Industrial Relations Review*, 210, July 1991, pp. 11–12; 'Betriebsvereinbarung Nr. 179: Gruppenarbeit', Adam Opel A.G. and the Opel General Works Council, Rüsselsheim.
12. Economic recession and the continuing crisis of German unification, however, may well speed up processes of work reorganization. Just as

VW looks at Mosel, so Opel looks at its innovative 'lean' plant at Eisenach for clues about how to promote reform.

13. The material in this section is based on intensive interviews and other research at Swedish auto plants since the mid-1980s. For more detail, see Auer and Riegler, 1990a and 1990b.

14. These ideas were developed by experts at the Tavistock Institute in Britain (Trist and Bamforth, 1951) and then elaborated by Scandinavian researchers such as Thorsrud (1972). Until the 1970s, Swedish industrial relations were based largely on the Saltsjöbaden agreement of 1938, in which employers and unions agreed to strive for the peaceful settlement of industrial conflicts and employers retained the exclusive right to organize production at the workplace. There was no German-style dual system and no co-determination until the 1970s.

15. For more on Kalmar and Uddevalla, see Auer and Riegler, 1990a, 1990b.

16. And at the new Honda plant in Tochigi, Siegfried Roth reports, 'a production system was introduced which for the first time did not include an assembly line and which was strongly influenced by the skilled worker orientation found in Germany and Scandanavia' (Roth, 1992, p. 19).

17. Womack, Jones and Roos present detailed discussions of the relations and tensions between firms and suppliers and between firms and dealers, but unaccountably omit any substantive discussion of the relations and tensions between firms and their own employees and unions. This omission is all the more glaring because the predecessor to this book, the first volume produced by the MIT International Motor Vehicle Program which they co-authored (Altshuler *et al.*, 1984), was quite explicit in according a primary importance to contrasting cross-national industrial relations.

18. A more useful conceptualization would be a continuum between the two, and the ideal version would probably contain a synthesis of lean and human elements

References

Agurén, Stefan, and Jan Edgren (1980) 'Job Design through Factory Planning in Sweden' (Stockholm: SAF).

Altshuler, Alan, Martin Anderson, Daniel Jones, Daniel Roos and James Womack (1984) *The Future of the Automobile.* The Report of MIT's International Automobile Program (Cambridge, MA: MIT Press).

Auer, Peter, Boris Penth and Peter Tergeist (1983) *Arbeitspolitische Reformen in Industriestaaten: Ein Internationaler Vergleich* (Frankfurt: Campus Verlag).

Auer, Peter and Claudius H. Riegler (1990a) *Post-Taylorism: The Enterprise as a Place of Learning Organizational Change* (Stockholm and Berlin: Arbetsmiljöfonden and Wissenschaftszentrum).

—— (1990b) 'The Swedish Version of Group Work – The Future Model of Work Organizational in the Engineering Sector?' *Economic and Industrial Democracy*, 11, pp. 291–9.

Berggren, Christian (1991) *Von Ford bis Volvo: Automobilherstellung in Schweden* (Berlin: Springer).

BRIE (Berkeley Roundtable on the International Economy) (1991) 'Globalization and Production'. BRIE Discussion Paper, University of California at Berkeley.

Brown, Clair and Michael Reich (1989) 'When Does Union–Management Cooperation Work? A Look at NUMMI and GM-Van Nuys', *California Management Review*, 31(4) pp. 26–44.

Cole, Robert E. (1985) 'The Macropolitics of Organizational Change: A Comparative Analysis of the Spread of Small-Group Activities', *Administrative Science Quarterly* (December), 30(4) pp. 560–85.

Dankbaar, Ben (1990) 'International Competition and National Institutions: The Case of the Automobile Industry', in C. Freeman and L. Soete (eds), *New Explorations in the Economics of Technological Change* (London: Pinter).

Dankbaar, Ben, Ulrich Jürgens and Thomas Malsch (eds) (1988) *Die Zukunft der Arbeit in der Automobilindustrie* (Berlin: Edition Sigma).

Dore, Ronald (1973) *British Factory–Japanese Factory: The Origins of National Diversity in Industrial Relations* (Berkeley: University of California Press).

Florida, Richard and Martin Kenney (1991) 'Organization vs Culture: Japanese Automotive Transplants in the US', *Industrial Relations Journal* (Autumn), 22(3) pp. 181–96.

Hans-Böckler Stiftung/IG Metall (eds) (1992) *Lean Production* (Baden-Baden: Nomos).

Jürgens, Ulrich, Larissa Klinzing and Lowell Turner (1993) 'The Transformation of Industrial Relations in Eastern Germany' *ILR Review* (January), 46(2), pp. 229–44.

Jürgens, Ulrich, Thomas Malsch and Knuth Dohse (1989) *Moderne Zeiten in der Automobilfabrik: Strategien der Produktionsmodernisierung im Lnder- und Konzernvergleich* (Berlin: Springer-Verlag).

Katz, Harry (1985) *Shifting Gears: Changing Labor Relations in the US Automobile Industry* (Cambridge, MA: MIT Press).

Katz, Harry C., Thomas A. Kochan and Jeffrey Keefe (1988) 'Industrial Relations and Productivity in the US Automobile Industry'. *Brookings Papers on Economic Activity*, 3, pp. 685–715.

Katz, Harry and Charles F. Sabel (1985) 'Industrial Relations and Industrial Adjustment in the Car Industry', *Industrial Relations*, 24(3) pp. 295–315.

—— (1987) 'Limits of the Division of Labour. New Production and Employment Concepts in West German Industry', *Economic and Industrial Democracy* (May), 8(2) pp. 151–70.

Kern, Hurst and Michael Schumann (1984) *Das Ende der Arbeitsteilung* (Munich: C.M. Beck)

Kerr, Clark, John Dunlop, Frederick Harbison and Charles Myers (1960) *Industrialism and Industrial Man* (Cambridge, MA: Harvard University Press).

Kochan, Thomas A., Harry C. Katz and Robert B. McKersie (1986) *The Transformation of American Industrial Relations* (New York: Basic Books).

Krafcik, John (1988) 'Comparative Analysis of Performance Indicators at World Auto Assembly Plants'. Master's thesis, Sloan School of Management, MIT, January.

256   *A Diversity of New Work Organization*

Locke, Richard M. (1990) 'The Resurgence of the Local Union: Industrial Restructuring and Industrial Relations in Italy', *Politics and Society*, 18(3) pp. 347–79.

Lutz, Burkhart (1976) 'Bildungssystem und Beschäftigungsstrukturen in Deutschland und Frankreich', in ISF München (ed.), *Betrieb-Arbeitsmarkt, Qualifikation* (Frankfurt: Campus Verlag).

Mann, Eric (1987) *Taking on General Motors: A Case Study of the UAW Campaign to Keep GM Van Nuys Open* (Los Angeles: Institute of Industrial Relations Publications, UCLA).

Maurice, Marc, Francois Sellier and Jean-Jacques Silvestre (1986) *The Social Foundations of Industrial Power* (Cambridge, MA: MIT Press).

Milkman, Ruth (1991) 'Labor and Management in Uncertain Times: Renegotiating the Social Contract', in Alan Wolfe (ed.), *The Recentering of America: American Society in Transition* (Berkeley: University of California Press).

Mishel, Lawrence and Paula Voos (eds) (1992) *Unions and Economic Competitiveness* (Armonk, NY: M.E. Sharpe).

Muster, Manfred (1988) 'Zum Stand der Gruppenarbeit in der Automobilindustrie in der Bundesrepublik', in Roth and Kohl (eds), pp. 259–81.

Nomura, Masami (1992) 'Farewell to Toyotism? Recent Trends at a Japanese Auto Company'. Manuscript, Department of Economics, Okayama University.

Parker, Mike and Jane Slaughter (1988) *Choosing Sides: Unions and the Team Concept* (Boston: South End Press).

Piore, Michael J. and Charles F. Sabel (1984) *The Second Industrial Divide: Possibilities for Prosperity* (New York: Basic Books).

Pontusson, Jonas (1990) 'The Politics of New Technology and Job Redesign: A Comparison of Volvo and British Leyland', *Economic and Industrial Democracy*, 11(3) pp. 311–36.

Quinn, Dennis (1989) 'Dynamic Markets and Mutating Firms: The Changing Organization of Production in Automotive Firms'. BRIE Research Paper #1, Berkeley Roundtable on the International Economy, University of California, Berkeley.

Riffel, Michael and Manfred Muster (1989) *Bericht über das Planungsseminar 'Neue Lackiererei Wolfsburg' vom 16.01–20.01.1989 in Hustedt/Celle* (Wolfsburg: Betriebsrat der Volkswagen AG, Wolfsburg).

Roth, Siegfried (1992) 'Japanisation, or Going Our Own Way? New Lean Production Concepts in the German Automobile Industry' (Frankfurt/Main: IG Metall).

Roth, Siegfried and Heribert Kohl (eds) (1988) *Perspektive: Gruppenarbeit* (Kln: Bund-Verlag).

Sabel, Charles F. (1982) *Work and Politics: The Division of Labor in Industry* (Cambridge: Cambridge University Press).

Schmitter, Philippe C. (1974) 'Still the Century of Corporatism?' *Review of Politics*, 39. Reprinted in Schmitter and Lehmbruch (eds), 1979.

Schmitter, Philippe C. and Gerhard Lehmbruch (1979) *Trends Toward Corporatist Intermediation* (Beverly Hills: Sage).

Svenska Metallindustriarbetareförbundet (1985) *Det goda arbetet*. Huvudrapport fran programkommitten om industriarbetets vrd och villkor (Stockholm: Metallindustriarbetareförbundet).

Thelen, Kathleen A. (1991) *Union of Parts: Labor Politics in Postwar Germany* (Ithaca, NY: Cornell University Press).

Thorsrud, Einar (1972) 'Job Design in the Wider Context', in Louis E. Davis and James C. Taylor (eds), *Design of Jobs* (Hammondsworth: Penguin).

Trist, Eric L. and Bamforth (1951) 'Some Social and Psychological Consequences of the Longwall Method of Coal-Getting', *Human Relations*, 4.

Turner, Lowell (1991) *Democracy at Work: Changing World Markets and the Future of Labor Unions* (Ithaca: Cornell University Press).

Wilensky, Harold L. (1976) *The 'New Corporatism', Centralization, and the Welfare State* (London: Sage).

Womack, James P., Daniel T. Jones and Daniel Roos (1990) *The Machine That Changed the World* (New York: Rawson Associates).

Wood, Stephen (1986) 'The Cooperative Labour Strategy in the US Auto Industry', *Economic and Industrial Democracy*, 7, pp. 415–7.

Zysman, John (1983) *Governments, Markets, and Growth: Financial Systems and the Politics of Industrial Change* (Ithaca, NY: Cornell University Press).

Part IV
Policy Alternatives and Social Outcomes

9 Regulatory Frameworks and Development in the North American Auto Industry

Stephen Herzenberg

INTRODUCTION[1]

A full account of the social and economic consequences of the restructuring of the North American auto industry requires raising the analytical focus above work reorganization in individual plants and companies (and even assembly companies taken as a group) to development in the industry as a whole. This sectoral perspective suggests that two distinct patterns of development could result from economic integration of the United States and Canadian auto industries with that of Mexico.[2] In one scenario, the auto industry would enjoy rapid productivity growth and help develop and deploy new technology, providing a positive example of workforce skill development, cooperation between assemblers and suppliers, and of organizational practice generally. In another scenario, high productivity, new technology and human resource development would be confined to portions of the operations of major assembly companies and first-tier suppliers. Even in these industry segments, the weakness of worker representation and high levels of work intensity would place limits on worker commitment to corporate goals. Outside the industry core, competition would be driven more by a search for low-wage, non-union workers.

After a review of trade rules and trade patterns, this chapter reviews the institutional evolution of the US and Canadian auto industries. It then characterizes the Mexican industry, with an eye to understanding its likely future interaction with the US and Canadian industries. Given empirical evidence that points toward a segmented pattern of industry development, the last section of the chapter outlines trade, labor market and industrial development policies that might help to generate a less segmented and more productive North American auto industry.

261

TRADE AND THE NORTH AMERICAN AUTO INDUSTRY

The precipitous increase in imports from Japan beginning around 1980 led to the breakdown of the post-World War II mass production institutional structure in the US and Canadian auto industries. The persistence of the trade deficit with Japan, and the growth of trade within North America provide the context for the continued restructuring of the North American auto industry. In light of their significance, this section reviews the trade rules and trade patterns reshaping the North American auto industry.

Existing Trade and Investment Rules

US restrictions on imports of motor vehicles and parts are quite limited. The only significant US restraint is a 25 per cent tariff on imports of trucks. On imported passenger cars, the US tariff is 2.5 per cent. For most auto parts, the US tariff is 3.2 per cent. Most vehicles and original equipment parts from Canada enter the United States duty-free under the US–Canada Auto Pact. Most Mexican parts also enter at preferential rates (under the North American Free Trade Agreement (NAFTA) or other special provisions).

Reflecting their less liberal economic philosophies and the dominant role of foreign investment in their economies, Canada and Mexico have more extensive regulations on auto imports and foreign investment. When the US–Canada Auto Pact was implemented in 1965, Canada obtained commitments from the Big Three to maintain their current ratio of the value of vehicle sales in Canada to the value of vehicles produced in Canada (0.95–1.00 for cars); and to maintain a Canadian value-added (CVA) to Canadian sales ratio of 60 per cent.[3] While Canada took steps in the 1980s toward extending these requirements to Asian producers, the US–Canada Free Trade Agreement (US–C FTA) obligated Canada *not* to do this. For companies that meet its 50 per cent rule-of-origin, the US–C FTA eliminates over ten years the 9.2 per cent Canadian tariff on non-Auto Pact auto imports from the United States.[4]

In Mexico, a series of five auto decrees issued between 1962 and 1989 reserved the domestic auto market for domestically produced parts and vehicles. The 1989 Auto Decree included trade balancing rules that required each major auto producer in Mexico to run a trade surplus. In 1994, the Decree permitted companies to import 20 per cent of their car sales in Mexico, but only if they exported $1.75 for each dollar's worth of car imports. The 1989 decree also restricted foreign ownership to 40 per cent in the Mexican auto parts industry and required that assembly companies obtain at least 36 per cent of the value of their parts from Mexican suppliers.

The NAFTA significantly liberalized auto trade within North America. For vehicles meeting a 62.5 per cent North American rule-of-origin, the NAFTA:

- Phases out restrictions on Mexican imports of vehicles from the US and Canada;
- Reduces the Mexican trade balancing rule for vehicles and parts to 0.8 to 1 immediately and 0.55 to 1 by 2003;
- Reduces the required Mexican parts content to the lower of 34 per cent or current levels, and to 29 per cent by 2003; and
- Phases out tariffs over a ten-year period, including lowering the US truck tariff from 25 to 12.5 per cent immediately.

In sum, over a transition period and with the exception of weak performance requirements retained by Canada and Mexico, the NAFTA creates unregulated auto trade within North America. This will reinforce competition among the three countries for investment and the interdependence of the two countries' auto sector labor market and industrial relations.

Trade Patterns

Over the past 15 years, the following trade trends stand out:[5]

1. *Japanese vehicle exports to the United States rose, in units, from close to 0 in 1965 to 1 million by the late 1970s and 3.6 million by 1986. By 1994, vehicle imports from Japan declined to 1.8 million.* Reflecting inflation, Japanese sales of more up-market cars and appreciation of the yen, the 1992 nominal dollar value of US vehicle imports was only 11 per cent below the 1986 peak. Light-truck imports from Japan fell most dramatically from 1986 to 1992; by 82 per cent in units and 74 per cent in value terms.[6] Since rising parts imports (see item 3 below) more than compensated for declining vehicle imports, total US nominal dollar auto imports from Japan peaked in 1993 at $35.6 billion, 6 per cent above the 1987 peak (OAA/DOC). Canadian imports of vehicles from Japan, $2.68 billion (in US dollars) in 1991, have followed patterns similar to US vehicle imports.

2. *As finished vehicle imports from Japan fell, vehicle assembly at Japanese-owned transplants and US–Japan joint ventures expanded to 27 per cent of cars assembled in the United States in 1994, a total of 1.8 million vehicles.* In units, Japanese companies' market share in the car plus light-truck markets equalled 24 per cent in 1993.

3. *US imports of Japanese parts rose steadily to $11.9 million in 1992* (Canadian imports in the same parts categories are roughly 10 per cent of this level). Transplants buy the vast majority of US auto parts imports from Japan. One-third of 1992 parts imports from Japan were drive-train components (engines, transmissions and components). Only 3–5 per cent of Japan's 1992 auto parts exports to the United States were bulky (batteries and glass) and labor-intensive assembly (seats, wire harnesses, windshield wipers and so on) parts.

4. *Exports of vehicles and parts to Japan from the United States have risen in percentage terms in recent years but stood at less that $2 billion in 1993 compared to shipments of $36 billion in the opposite direction.*

5. *Within North America since 1979, Canada has built up a 1.15 million unit and $12.8 billion surplus in vehicles trade with the United States*[7] (for some reasons why, see Kumar and Holmes, this volume).

6. *The bilateral US–Canada auto parts trade balance has shifted since the late 1970s in favor of the United States by roughly $10 billion.* The US had a surplus of $4.6 to $7 billion in 1992 depending on whether one uses Canadian or US statistics. Most of this US surplus stems from parts going north to supply Canada's expanding assembly production; some of the surplus may stem from Canadian firms losing labor-intensive product sales to non-union US firms. In some US suppliers, low wages and benefits may outweigh Canadian plants' advantages due to a cheaper dollar and lower health care costs.

7. *Auto trade between the United States and Mexico mushroomed in the 1980s. In 1993, the US imported 400 000 vehicles worth $4.6 billion from Mexico.*

8. *In 1992, US auto parts imports from Mexico equalled 68.5 per cent of US parts imports from Canada.* US imports of auto parts from Mexico come primarily from six highly automated engine plants and from border *maquiladora* plants. The engine plants were constructed to satisfy the performance requirements of the 1977 Mexican auto decree and in anticipation of rapid growth of the Mexican domestic market. *Maquiladoras* benefitted from exemp-

tions from Mexican import regulations (for parts to be re-exported) and from US laws excluding US value in re-imported goods from duty. Forty-one per cent of Mexican auto parts exports to the United States in 1990 were labor-intensive wire harnesses, seat belts, furniture for automotive use (for example, seats), and windshield wipers, defrosters and demistifiers. Another 16 per cent were auto audio equipment. How quickly and effectively the Mexican parts industry will bridge the gap between labor-intensive *maquiladoras* and high-tech engine and assembly plants remains an open question.

9. *In recent years, US parts exports to Mexico have been growing even faster than imports from Mexico.* As a result, the US auto parts trade deficit with Mexico fell to $0.45 billion in 1992. The increase in US auto parts exports to Mexico from 2.5 to 5.7 billion between 1989 and 1992 took place across-the-board. An estimated 70 per cent of this represents shipments to Mexican *maquiladoras*, engine or assembly plants for re-export back to the United States. The rise in US parts exports also resulted from the expansion of the Mexican market. At most, a small residual reflected rising US parts content in Mexican vehicles sold in Mexico.

THE US AND CANADIAN AUTO INDUSTRIES

The Post-World War II Mass Production Regime

Analyzing the future of the US and Canadian auto industries requires understanding the mass production system that governed the development of the North American auto industry from 1950 to 1980. In this mass production system, the major US auto companies used dedicated capital equipment and narrowly-skilled workers to lower the unit cost of high volumes of standardized products.

Mass production in the post-World War II era was supported by wage rules in union contracts, connective (or pattern) bargaining, and periodic increases in the real minimum wage (Kumar and Holmes). Seniority-based job security and job rights also meshed with mass production; they constrained supervisors from taking arbitrary actions that would prompt work stoppages and impede the efficiency of interdependent assembly lines. As long as market expansion limited layoffs and worker movement among jobs, work rules and narrow classifications did not unacceptably impair efficiency.

With respect to assembler–supplier relations, the postwar era in the US auto industry was distinguished by a high degree of vertical integration and by 'arms-length' relations. Major US assemblers performed their own product engineering for outsourced parts. They sourced components from several firms to reinforce price-based competition.

The US and Canadian government during the postwar period used fiscal and monetary policy, and unemployment insurance, to smooth out macroeconomic fluctuations and enable dedicated mass production machinery to operate at close to full capacity. With the exception of Canadian performance requirements implemented with the Auto Pact, neither the US nor Canadian government developed significant sectoral or technology policies in the auto industry during the late 1940s to the late 1970s.

The events of the 1970s and 1980s destabilized the interdependent mass production institutions that shaped the historical development of the US and Canadian auto industries (see Kumar and Holmes). By 1980, the US assemblers faced pressure from a Japanese production system in which labor–management relations, assembler–supplier cooperation, and a developmental government role all helped generate productivity and quality superior to that of the US mass production model.

In response, as detailed below, US producers sought to depart from many organizational practices of mass production, including the deliberate exclusion of hourly workers from performance improvement efforts. They initiated efforts to develop more cooperative, long-term relations with smaller numbers of first-tier suppliers. Complementing private-sector efforts, auto-dependent state and provincial governments began exploring how they could assist the industry's revitalization.

Industrial Relations

Significant changes in four of the defining features of post-World War II auto industrial relations emerged in the United States and Canada over the 15 years: (1) union coverage; (2) wage rules; (3) the system of pattern bargaining through which the UAW diffused Big Three wages and benefits to auto parts firms; and (4) work rules and job classifications.

Union coverage

Between 1950 and 1980, the United Auto Workers International Union (UAW) represented virtually all production workers at auto assembly companies in the United States and Canada. By the early 1990s, Japanese transplants employed roughly 20 000 non-union production workers in the United States and 3000 in Canada. As a result of a shift of investment to non-union plants which accelerated in the mid-1970s, union coverage in independent parts supplier (IPS) firms in the United States declined from over 50 per cent in the 1970s to less than one-third today (for details, see Herzenberg, 1991b). In Canada, union coverage in parts firms in the late 1980s remained over 50 per cent and roughly as high as in the mid-1970s.

Overall union coverage in the US auto industry declined from about 85 per cent in 1978 to about 60 per cent in 1992, in part due a decrease in Big Three employment of 300 000 since 1978. Employment in the independent parts industry remained around 300 000. The more rapid decline in auto assembly company employment reflects a combination of high productivity growth and increasing outsourcing.

Wage rules at the Big Three

Over the course of the 1980s, the UAW agreed to eliminate annual wage rule increases. In exchange, the union obtained profit sharing, lump-sum bonuses, and more occasional (now every three years) real wage increases. Excluding profit sharing, real wages for production workers in US auto assembly plants (which make up the Standard Industrial Classification, or SIC, category 3711) were only one per cent higher in the first half of 1993 than in 1978.

In exchange for wage moderation and UAW acceptance of elements of the Japanese production system (see below), Big Three workers received progressively stronger income security guarantees. For their three-year term, the 1990 and 1993 agreements with the Big Three guaranteed close to full pay for current employees (subject to spending caps).

In the early 1980s, the Canadian UAW opposed the UAW International's decision to accept lump sums and profit sharing instead of annual improvement factor (AIF) base-wage increases (Kumar and Holmes). This contributed to the mid-1980s secession of the Canadian UAW to form the Canadian Auto Workers (CAW). Continued annual base-wage increases (albeit smaller than before 1980) brought Canadian Big Three base hourly wages for an assembly worker from parity with the United States in 1984 to $2.88 more per hour in 1993.

Wage bargaining at suppliers

At US and Canadian suppliers in the 1950s through the 1970s, contract expiration dates were loosely synchronized with Big Three negotiations. After settling with the Big Three, the UAW sought to win the same wage and benefit gains at parts companies. It bargained one company at a time with parts firms that had national agreements, and one plant at a time with other companies. From the recession of the late 1950s forward, supplier wages established through this decentralized bargaining process fell behind assembler wages by about 1 per cent per year. By the 1980s, pattern wage and benefit bargaining in US independent parts supplier (IPS) firms broke down almost entirely. In unionized parts companies by 1989, hourly wages equalled only 67 per cent of those in assembly firms. Non-union supplier workers earned 51 per cent of assembler wages.

In Canada, wages at unionized parts plants employing over 500 workers remained above 80 per cent of assembly company wages. This stemmed from union opposition to wage concessions, the higher levels of union coverage in the Canadian parts sector, and the absence of downward wage pressure from other parts of the Canadian labor market.[8]

Shop floor relations

Competition from, and the example of, Japanese producers also produced a move away from narrow job classifications and work rules within North American auto plants in the 1980s. At the Big Three as well as the Japanese transplants, management industrial relations strategy has been geared toward importing to North America all or part of what originated as the Toyota production system (now known as 'lean production') (see Florida and Kenney, this volume).

In the Japanese transplants and US–Japan joint ventures, Japanese industrial relations practices have been introduced to North America as part of an integrated system. At most Big Three facilities, the elimination of work rules and introduction of the Toyota production system has taken place more gradually. Reorganization has been slowed down by the opposition of union members who believe that the Toyota system intensifies work and dilutes union independence (Parker and Slaughter, 1988). In addition, Ford only began trying to introduce teams, *per se*, in most of its plants in the early 1990s.

One Big Three exception to the piecemeal approach is GM's Saturn subsidiary. Saturn combines teams that elect their team leaders, with off-line problem-solving groups, joint labor–management committees, and the pairing of union and management officials at each managerial level. The union's input in sourcing, product development, marketing and other management decisions almost certainly exceeds that at US (or Japanese) lean production plants. Training for new production workers, at 350–700 hours, exceeds that at most transplants.

It is too early to tell whether the attempt by Japanese and US companies to transfer the Toyota system to North America will prove economically successful and institutionally stable. Womack *et al.* (1990, p. 85) report that, after correcting for the level of automation and for the number of options per vehicle, five Japanese transplants in 1989 had levels of productivity 16 per cent higher on average than 14 North American Big Three plants. Six transplants achieved quality levels five per cent below the average for auto plants in Japan and about 30 per cent better than the average for 42 Big Three plants.

Alongside reports of harmonious labor relations and high productivity and quality at lean plants has come evidence of labor problems. One reason is the intensity of work, which virtually all analysts agree exceeds that under the traditional US system (Florida and Kenney, this volume; Herzenberg, 1991b). Anecdotal evidence suggests that the intensity of work within the Japanese production system may have contributed to increasing injury rates. Aggregate national statistics offer some support for this view – although US Occupational Safety and Health Administration (OSHA) efforts to increase compliance with reporting requirements make these statistics hard to interpret.[9]

In the US auto assembly industry (SIC 3711), injury frequency and lost workdays due to injury equalled 2.6 to 2.9 times the levels of the late 1970s. The rate of repeat trauma illness in SIC 3711 placed it third behind meat packing and poultry processing in 1988 and 1989. Automotive trimmings, stampings, parts and accessories, and engine electrical equipment joined assembly among the 26 industries with the highest repeat trauma rates. From 1985 to 1988, in partial contrast, repeat trauma workers' compensation disabilities in SIC 3711 in six states for which continuous data were available increased only 12 per cent (Herzenberg, 1991b, Table 36).

In response to the stress that it places on them, workers at transplants as well as Big Three operations have pressured managers into modifying plant practices (Parker and Slaughter, 1993). The Mazda plant in Flat Rock, Michigan, elected a more militant local leadership in 1989 to replace union leaders appointed to oversee the plant launch (Fucini and Fucini, 1990). The local at Mazda has fought successfully to modify the company's absenteeism policy, to restrict the company's use of temporary workers, and to make team leaders subject to recall based on a two-thirds vote of team members, and therefore more sensitive to worker concerns. At NUMMI, in June 1991, a militant slate won the local union presidency, a majority on the local executive board, and several shopfloor elected positions.

In addition to job stress and union independence, another potential source of labor conflict at lean production plants concerns skill development and promotion opportunity. With the exception of small numbers of positions as joint program administrators, and occasional opportunities to work in off-line problem-solving groups, reorganized auto plants offer little prospect of moving beyond standardized assembly work. As carefully screened workers at transplants and the Big Three perceive the possibility of a career on the line, this will reinforce discontent associated with the intensity of work.

Overall, studies of unionized transplants indicate that many workers do not favor a return to the traditional US system and appreciate the opportunity to contribute ideas and learn new skills. Workers believe, nonetheless, that an assertive union and team leaders that are responsive to workers are essential to limit the pace of work, protect health and safety, and pressure employers to live up to rhetoric regarding skill development and participative management (Fucini and Fucini, 1990; Parker and Slaughter, 1983; CAW Research Group, 1993).

In Canada, work reorganization proceeded more slowly than in the United States during the 1980s. The leadership of the Canadian union shared the view expressed by some rank-and-file US UAW members that labor–management cooperation could be a vehicle for persuading workers of the competitive need for wage concessions and higher work standards. In the second half of the decade, the CAW did accept the introduction of work teams in a range of special circumstances (Holmes, this volume). In a 1989 Statement adopted by its rank-and-file Council, the union argued that the critical issue is not teams *per se*, but the implications of new workplace institutions for the strength of the union and its ability to protect workers. A 1993 CAW report outlined a union agenda on four issues within lean workplaces: work pace and production standards; training; job design; and union input (for example, via committees on new technology, ergonomics and training) (CAW, 1993).

The best documented case of lean production in Canada is the GM–Suzuki joint venture, Canadian–American Motors Incorporated (CAMI). A two-year study of CAMI, which included four surveys of the same group of 100 workers six months apart, documented gradual disenchantment with team production as work standards rose and the nature of work failed to live up to expectations raised during recruitment, training and launch (CAW Research Group, 1993). The 1992 CAMI contract modifies lean production in ways similar to the Mazda contract. Team leaders will be elected during a one-year experiment. Production support groups will provide relief for absent or injured workers (CAW Research Group, 1993). The local union at CAMI sees itself as trying to determine how it can sustain a strong union and an identity separate from management within the Japanese production system (CAW Research Group, 1993).

Taken together, the evidence indicates that three ideal types of shopfloor relations can be distinguished based on field research on workplace developments in the United States and Canada (Herzenberg, 1991, Chapter 11; Herzenberg, 1993):

1. The *lean production* alternative would be similar to the Toyota production system as it operates in Japan. High levels of work intensity would result from features such as the lack of absentee replacements, and the peer pressure that this generates to attend work; just-in-time inventory and the premium on solving production bottlenecks quickly; and 'standardized work' and '*kaizen*' problem-solving which translate improved methods into more output, not slack time for the worker. Team leaders and at least some other key workers would cooperate with attempts to improve performance in this model. Workers would not make collective attempts to modify the Toyota system.
2. In the second, or *negotiated flexibility* alternative, workers and unions would force a modification of the Toyota system to relieve the stress it places on workers. The result would nonetheless retain (and even extend) workers' new role in maintaining high quality and other aspects of performance improvement. The transplants with the strongest local unions (Mazda and CAMI) and Saturn represent two distinct variants of negotiated flexibility.
3. In the third, or *autocratic* alternative, the elimination of work rules would lead to the reassertion of unilateral supervisory authority characteristic of non-union mass production. Relations would be adversarial but worker discontent would remain muted.

Among permanent employees in auto assembly companies in the United States and Canada, lean production and negotiated flexibility appear likely to predominate in the future. While less research has been done on suppliers, Luria (1993) concludes on the basis of survey research that roughly half of Michigan suppliers have 'autocratic' (which he calls 'sweating') patterns of shopfloor relations, 15 per cent lean, and one-third negotiated flexibility (which he calls 'American century'). In general, supplier firms face more short-term economic pressure, cannot offer job or economic security to most workers, and have fewer resources to devote to skill development. All of these factors make autocratic patterns more likely than in assembly companies.

Organizing

Faced with non-union assembly transplants and auto parts plants, both the UAW and CAW have attempted to maintain their control over the auto labor market through organizing. To date, no US or Canadian assembly transplants where management sought to avoid unions have been organized. At Nissan, in Tennessee, the UAW campaigned on issues that have arisen in organized transplants: line speed, health and safety, and company failure to fulfill promises of participative management. Workers voted 69–31 against the union. Interviewed afterwards, workers told the *New York Times* 'the union didn't have anything to give me that I don't already have.'

In suppliers, the CAW enjoyed significant organizing success after its formation in 1985. In 1989, about 15 per cent of the 16 000 CAW members in the Ontario auto parts and accessories industry were in units organized between 1986 and 1989 (28 per cent were in units organized since 1977).

Despite limited UAW organizing success in the 15 years after 1978, the recent organization of three Michigan suppliers (two transplants) hints at a new organizing direction that might change this. Mazda assembly plant Local 3000 played a pivotal role in these cases. In 1991, Local 3000 negotiated a contractual letter in which Mazda committed itself not to discriminate against unionized suppliers in sourcing decisions. Mazda workers then participated in the organizing campaigns, emphasizing the positive role union representation can play within lean production. The newly-organized workers amalgamated to Local 3000. These examples suggest the possibility of network unions that span assembly and supplier workers, ameliorating labor-market segmentation, and discouraging the use of low-wage strategies among suppliers.

Assembler–Supplier Relations since 1980

The US assemblers in the 1980s pursued two distinct but overlapping sourcing strategies. On the one hand, they sought to abandon traditional arms-length, 'exit' relations, in which assemblers switched suppliers when sourcing problems surfaced. Particularly in dealings with their own component operations and with suppliers of high-technology products, US companies attempted to establish 'voice' relations characterized by expanded information sharing and attempts to resolve problems that arise. On the other hand, in the context of excess capacity that reduced the leverage of parts companies, US assemblers intensified their search for low cost.

As part of their efforts to establish voice relations, the Big Three substantially reduced the number of first-tier suppliers that they deal with directly. Many of these suppliers have received more long-term contracts and increasing responsibility for quality and engineering. They have also been urged to adopt Japanese labor and organizational practices, including 'just-in-time' delivery systems.

The search for lower costs has been most evident in labor-intensive sourcing trends and among smaller suppliers. Emphasis on low costs has contributed to the de-unionization of the US auto supplier industry and the movement of significant parts production to Mexican maquiladoras. In addition, even first-tier suppliers have faced intensive pressure to reduce prices at the same time as they improve their performance along non-price dimensions. Some suppliers argue that short-term cost pressure deprives them of the financial resources necessary to pursue long-term strategies based on workforce skill development and technology. Suppliers also maintain that demands for price reductions sometimes violate implicit long-term understandings and undermine the relations of trust essential to cooperation with assemblers.

Despite anecdotal evidence of productive restructuring, productivity in captive and independent US auto suppliers stagnated from 1978 to 1988 (Table 9.1). Over the same period, real value-added per worker hour rose 7.5 per cent annually at assembly plants. Despite measurement problems, these data strongly suggest that the Big Three had not, as of 1988, understood how to productively reorganize most of their component plants; and that low-wage strategies may be outcompeting more productive strategies in independent suppliers.

As well as attempts by established suppliers to respond to new sourcing strategies of the Big Three, the restructuring of the US and Canadian auto parts sector has been driven by the construction of new plants by Japanese parts suppliers (Florida and Kenney, this volume). Womack *et al.* (1990) argue that Japanese investment, and emulation of Japanese practices by US suppliers, will lead to the reproduction here of the dynamic, geographically-integrated Japanese production system. Howes (1991) argues, in contrast, that Japanese producers have transferred 'the limbs but not the body' of their integrated assembly–supplier structure. She cites McAlinden *et al.* (1991), who estimated the domestic content of US Honda products (the vehicles thought to have the most North American content) at only 62 per cent (this content figure excludes profits and transportation and marketing costs). Howes also argues, consistent with trade data, that transplants get most engineering-intensive components from Japan. No Japanese companies manufacture transmissions in the United States. While several now assemble engines in North America, only Honda manufactures the most critical engine parts – cranks, cams and blocks – in the United States.

Table 9.1   Annual productivity growth in auto suppliers (in the United States)

Sub-sample	Productivity measure 1972–88 (%)			
	TFP	LP	VTFP	VLP
All SIC 3711	1.3	6.2	5.8	7.4
All SIC 3714	0.0	2.1	– 0.6	0.0
Captive parts suppliers	– 0.5	2.1	– 2.2	– 0.8
Multi-plant independents	1.0	2.0	2.5	1.3
Single plant independents	0.2	1.6	1.1	0.7
OEM independents	0.8	1.9	2.3	1.1

Sub-sample	Productivity measure 1978–88 (%)			
	TFP	LP	VTFP	VLP
All SIC 3711	1.3	5.1	6.6	7.5
All SIC 3714	0.2	2.6	– 0.7	– 0.4
Captive parts suppliers	0.0	3.0	– 2.1	– 0.8
Multi-plant independents	1.0	2.0	2.3	0.4
Single plant independents	0.5	2.2	1.7	1.0
OEM independents	0.6	1.7	1.8	0.1

Sub-sample	Productivity measure 1984–88 (%)			
	TFP	LP	VTFP	VLP
All SIC 3711	2	8.8	9.3	10.3
All SIC 3714	1.1	5	2	2.4
Captive parts suppliers	0.5	5.5	0.9	1.9
Multi-plant independents	2.2	2.9	3.6	2.6
Single plant independents	6.3	9.3	13.7	12.8
OEM independents	1.9	3.1	3.4	2.6

TFP: Total Factor Productivity
LP: Labor Productivity
VTFP: Value-added Total Factor Productivity
VLP: Value-added Labor Productivity
Note: Adjusting for changes in price–cost margins eliminates the systematic difference between captive and independent productivity growth.
Source: Herzenberg and Campbell, 1993, Table 4.

Howes (1993) sees transplant investment as reinforcing labor cost-based competition within North America. Transplant suppliers, almost all non-union, pay several dollars an hour below large UAW IPS (independent parts supplier) firms. Transplants do not have the pension and health benefit costs of older companies with high retiree/active employee ratios. For example, transplant assemblers pay health and pension costs $2.50–$5.50 below the Big Three (*ibid.*, p. 24).

The Role of Government

In the wake of the recession and intensifying international competition of the 1980s, state governments in auto-dependent regions of the United States and Canada began to experiment with *technology and training policies* designed to increase auto industry productivity and quality. State policies focused increasingly on small and medium-sized supplier firms. In aggregate, such firms create as much employment as large ones but do not have the same financial and technological resources. In addition, smaller firms are less mobile and, as a result, states are more likely to appropriate economic gains that result from technical assistance.

With respect to small and medium-sized firms, states and provinces have come increasingly to see their role as catalytic rather than as providing financial support (Sabel, 1990). The critical challenge is seen as establishing a context that leads cooperating networks of firms to produce high quality as well as specialized goods, by combining the inherent flexibility of small organizations with skilled workers and advanced technology. State-catalyzed cooperation among supplier firms is seen as a way of fostering high-skill–high-wage industrial districts (or 'sticky regions') as opposed to more footloose small firms that capitalize on low wages and worker vulnerability. Unlike low-wage producers, small firms that sell in technology-intensive and niche markets are somewhat insulated from competition with low-wage countries.

Examples of state-led network-building efforts in the United States in the 1980s include the Michigan Modernization Service (for details, see Luria, 1989, p. 5). The MMS helped catalyze a labor–management supplier council in part of Michigan that now coordinates cooperation among unionized member firms in technology and training areas (Schippani, 1990). In a related initiative, Wisconsin has established a training consortium for firms in its core metalworking industries (Rogers and Streeck, 1991). The consortium is now exploring cooperative initiatives in the technology extension and development areas.

In Canada, Industry, Science and Technology, Canada (ISTC–Canada's Commerce Department) established the Automotive Components Initiative (ACI) in the 1980s to help small Canadian auto parts firms streamline their operations and adopt new technology and organizational practices. The ACI program provides small Canadian suppliers with up to $10000 in matching funds to hire a diagnostic consultant to help see what methods and technologies they need to modernize their operations. After the diagnostic visit, ISTC will pay up to $100 000 to help firms implement the consultant's recommendations.

The Canadian government has also sought to overcome individual employers' reluctance to provide general training because they cannot capture the returns. Two government-sponsored human resource assessments have led to the creation of a labor–management auto parts sectoral training board (EIC-Canada, 1986; Canada Consulting Cresap, 1991). The council is now establishing a training program for non-apprenticed workers which will be available on company time and lead to an 'auto parts certificate'. In planning this program, management favors joint funding and training targeted at companies' immediate skill needs and at employees who already have good basic skills. The CAW favors universal access, provision of general skills and corporate funding, including time off to take training. In theory, worker certification could relieve individual companies of the need to screen workers extensively and enhance employment security and career opportunities for workers.

INSTITUTIONAL CHARACTERISTICS OF THE MEXICAN AUTO INDUSTRY

Since the early 1980s, the Mexican auto export industry has expanded from less than 10 000 workers to roughly 150 000. This section sketches the evolution of the Mexican auto industry as a prelude to discussion of its future interaction with the United States and Canada. A central question concerns the degree to which low Mexican wages and weak state-controlled unions could reinforce low-wage strategies and lean production or autocratic shopfloor relations in the United States and Canada.

From Import Substitution to Export-Led Growth

Mexico's high tariffs and auto decrees nurtured an auto and auto parts industry that served the domestic market from technologically-obsolete plants operating at below minimum efficient scale. Until the 1960s, the Confederation of Mexican Workers (CTM) – the dominant Mexican labor union federation that is allied with the governing party, the Party of Institutional Revolution (PRI) – represented all workers in Mexican auto assembly companies except at GM (where an independent union established itself in the 1940s). Wage bargaining still took place primarily on a local-by-local basis (and does so today).

On the shopfloor, Mexican auto workers' concerns were initially dealt with by plant delegates appointed from outside the plant by the union federation that gained recognition before operations began (Middlebrook, 1989). In the 1960s and 1970s, workers at the expanding production facilities of the Big Three, Nissan and VW established local autonomy and shopfloor representation more similar to that in the United States and Canada. They did this sometimes by disaffiliating from the CTM and sometimes by gaining more autonomy within the CTM. The strength of local unions at the end of 1970s contributed to decisions by the Big Three and Nissan in the 1980s to locate new plants away from Mexico City in central and Northern Mexico.

In the 1980s, the debt crisis and growing economic integration between the US and Mexican auto industries destabilized labor relations in the Mexican auto industry. The crisis reduced demand for vehicles within Mexico by over one half. Devaluation of the peso, declining real wages, and the availability of excess capacity also made Mexico a more attractive base for low-cost export production to the US market.

Labor Relations in the 1980s

Union coverage

Historically, the major motor vehicle companies in the Mexican auto industry have been 100 per cent unionized. With the exception of some auto parts maquiladoras owned by major assembly companies, this remains true today. Locals affiliated with the CTM or with independent unions represent all workers at the major auto assemblers. Outside the maquiladora sector, in which transportation equipment employment mushroomed from 7500 in 1980 to 135 000 workers in 1992, most large auto parts plants are also unionized. Mexican labor ministry officials place non-maquila overall auto sector union coverage at 40 per cent. The non-union 60 per cent includes 'confidential' employees and large numbers of small auto aftermarket and repair facilities.

Wages

Since 1982, social security institute data indicate that wages in the Mexican transportation equipment sector have fallen more and recovered less than wages generally in Mexican manufacturing. From 1982 to 1988, the average real wages of all workers, including salaried, fell 42.4 per cent. From 1988 to April 1993, real wages rose only 8 per cent, equalling 62.2 per cent of their 1982 level in April 1993. These trends reflect compositional shifts toward maquilas and other northern plants, and wage trends within existing plants. Wages at individual auto assembler plants vary considerably (Middlebrook, this volume). In early 1994, daily wages at a GM-Federal District plant scheduled for closure a year later equalled about $4 per hour worked (this included pay for weekend days not worked); following the establishment of a new contract (see below), wages at VW-Puebla equalled about half of this (author's interviews with local union leaders from the two plants, February 1994). Average hourly compensation (including benefits) in transportation equipment maquiladoras equalled an estimated $1.80 in 1992.

Industrial relations

As in the United States, the 1980s have been a period of substantial change in shopfloor relations at Mexican auto assembly company plants. The most dramatic departures from Mexican shopfloor relations of the 1970s took place at new northern engine and assembly plants. The CTM represents workers at all of the northern and central Mexican plants built by assembly companies since 1977.

Managers in these auto plants have put substantial effort into ensuring that worker militance at Mexico City-area auto plants would not be transplanted north. One US-owned assembly company, for example, decided not to bring skilled workers from Mexico City operations to help train the workers at a new northern engine plant, explaining in a company manual: 'Transfers of hourly personnel and their supervisors from [the company's] Mexico [state] operations were not allowed in order to avoid inflated wages/benefits and old work practices' (Shaiken and Herzenberg, 1987).

In some cases, multinational auto assemblers in new, export-oriented Mexican plants have introduced modern organizational practices such as work teams and continuous improvement *kaizen* problem-solving groups. Managers at one Big Three assembly plant attempted to integrate production and skilled work and rotate employees through skilled positions on a nine-month cycle (Shaiken, 1990). In 1992, after a retooling of the plant for a new model, the company put the rotation experiment on hold (Shaiken, 1992). Nonetheless, the broad distribution of training and experience at the plant may create a workforce with unprecedented potential to participate in improving uptime and quality, and to cooperate with process and product engineers.

Other auto assemblers in Mexico have not sought to widely distribute training and skills. At one Japanese-owned facility that includes an auto engine plant, most workers are incorporated into an autocratic pattern of shopfloor relations (Shaiken, 1992). The CTM, which represents union members, has a reputation for being docile within this state. One manager noted that:

> ... the union exists but if you talk about rights and the law, the union doesn't exist ... The union here doesn't fight for the workers.

The company vests skills and responsibility in the 42 per cent of employees, including indirect and skilled workers, who are not union members, and 50 (earlier 300) Japanese nationals.

In 1988, unionized workers at this plant earned only about half of the GM-Federal District wage in 1988. In the early 1990s, turnover equalled 100 per cent annually (Shaiken, 1992). While new hires receive up to one month's training, at times of high turnover new hires sometime staff the line on their first day. Mexican managers at the plant, their perspective perhaps influenced by resentment of their Japanese superiors, criticized both the pace of work and the pay. Asked why workers quit, one said:

> The pay is poor, the work is heavy, and the company always asks for more ... I think the main reason is the pace of the job. Workers don't have any time to rest, that's why they quit.

The top Mexican manager of the plant said;

> ... basically what we have in this plant is a modern form of slavery; it's a peonage the way people are treated.

Case studies of highly automated Mexican assembly and engine plants reveal comparable productivity and quality to US plants. Womack *et al.* (1990) reported that Ford's Hermosillo plant had the best quality of *any* plant in their sample of 80 plants: that is, better than any of the 20 Japanese plants and six Japanese-owned North American plants in their sample. One of four older Mexican plants studied by Womack (1991) had labor hours per vehicle 25 per cent higher than a 14-plant average for US firms in North America. The Mexican weighted average labor hours per vehicle was 83 per cent higher than the US firms' North American average. Mexican average defects per vehicle were only 10 per cent higher than US levels.

Outside the auto assemblers, Shaiken and Brown (1991) suggest that integrated application of Japanese management practices is not widespread in Mexico. Thirteen Japanese-owned plants that they studied – three of them non-maquila auto plants that produced at least partly for export – did not generally use work teams, just-in-time inventory or lifetime job security. Despite the use of fairly traditional industrial relations practices, these plants achieved quality that managers judged close to and sometimes better than their company's highest quality plant in Japan. Labor productivity was generally somewhat lower than each company's highest productivity plant globally, but only because low Mexican wages made automation unprofitable on some operations.

A number of significant labor conflicts have taken place during the recent restructuring of the Mexican auto industry. In the north, wages have been a central issue. In one northern assembly plant, a 39-day strike took place in March 1987 when workers demanded a 70 per cent wage increase (Shaiken, 1990). They ultimately accepted 34.5 per cent. In 1988, at the same plant, a series of conflicts over working conditions and intra-union politics broke out. The disputes began when the company fired a militant deputy secretary general of the union. This incident led to a four-hour work stoppage two months later and to the subsequent firing of 42 workers, including virtually all union representatives in the plant. Area CTM delegates then selected an interim new local union committee which supported the more conciliatory policies of the national CTM.

Managers in northern plants note the influence of the government in holding down wage increases as part of the government's anti-inflation program. According to a manager at a US-owned assembly plant:

> We even get help from the government making sure that we don't settle too high because of the economic reforms and the fact that we are so visible.
>
> (Shaiken, 1992)

At this and the Japanese facility, even some managers favor paying higher wages. According to one:

You've got only one problem in that plant and that's wages ... We took the cream of the workforce ... and we gave them all this training, and we're just not paying them enough.

In the traditional Mexican industry near Mexico City, there have been two major conflicts originating from a combination of wage, workplace and union representation issues. At Ford-Cuautitlan in 1987 and at Volkswagen-Puebla in 1992, managers sought to reduce wages and make workplace operations similar to flexible northern plants. In both cases, significant parts of the workforce resisted the changes and initiated strikes. Management nonetheless was able to establish a new contract and selectively rehire the workforce. Since the 1987 reorganization of Ford-Cuautitlan, various efforts by elements within the local union to disaffiliate with the CTM, and to maintain more representative local leaders, have been frustrated.

In these cases, government officials and the national CTM may have given corporate managers tacit support (or even, at Ford, pressure). National CTM leaders may have worried that disaffiliation of Cuautitlan, their major foothold in the center of the Mexican auto industry, would have spillover effects at northern auto plants and even outside the auto industry. The government, for its part, may have been reluctant to accept more assertive local unions that could threaten wage control policies and/or the managerially-led redefinition of workplace relations.

These incidents should be understood in the context of broader debates during 1988 about modernization of Mexican labor relations. In this debate, President Salinas spoke about the need for a 'new unionism' based on the maintenance of 'the historic alliance of the worker movement with the state'; more 'representative unions' that have 'interlocution capacity' and political autonomy from the state; and negotiation over workplace reorganization with the active participation of unions.

For two reasons, one might have expected the auto industry to pioneer the modernization of labor relations along the lines of the kind of democratic corporatism suggested by Salinas's rhetoric: the strength (relative to other Mexican sectors) of independent unions in the Mexican auto industry; and the leverage of young, highly trained workers in plants producing at world class quality and productivity levels. To date, however, official union vulnerability, management unilateralism, government ambivalence about an independent union role, and the fragmentation and inexperience of more democratic union forces have prevented the emergence of more negotiated flexibility. To the extent that unilateral variants of lean production and autocratic flexibility predominate in Mexico, this may whipsaw US and Canadian workers into accepting lean production or autocratic flexibility.

THE FUTURE OF THE NORTH AMERICAN AUTO INDUSTRY

Some analysts believe that the current transformation of the auto industry, despite a socially costly transition period, will ultimately benefit North America by leading to the eclipse of mass production by the lean production system developed in Japan (Womack *et al.*, 1990). After the transition, Womack *et al.* (1990) maintain that North America will develop a fully integrated lean production system, including locally-based design and R&D centers, and regionally concentrated supplier networks. The result will be higher productivity and quality, rising wages and more rewarding jobs for production and white-collar workers, prosperity for auto-producing regions, better products and value for North American consumers, and balanced trade with the Asian lean production system.

Contrary to the optimistic predictions of Womack *et al.* (1990), the empirical evidence referred to in this chapter points toward a less dynamic and more inegalitarian pattern of development, in which:

- New organizational methods and rapid labor productivity growth diffuse at best slowly beyond the permanent employees of major assembly company operations and some first-tier suppliers. Outside this industry core, firms compete by combining traditional mass production with low wages.
- Overall auto industry productivity growth falls as the share of total industry employment accounted for by high productivity growth assembly plants declines.
- Constrained by low productivity growth and by increasing competition with Mexico based on price and labor costs real wages in independent parts suppliers in the United States continue to fall in real terms at one per cent or more annually.
- Real hourly wages at assembly firms remain high relative to suppliers but, as from 1978 to 1993, do not rise in real terms. They could decline if newly hired workers increasingly earn lower wages.
- Within the relatively high-wage plants of assembly companies, management-dominated lean production rather than more negotiated forms of cooperation predominates.

- Union weakness, high levels of work intensity and the absence of meaningful promotion opportunities weaken worker commitment to performance improvement even in core plants.
- Shopfloor relations in supplier plants, especially below the first tier, resemble autocratic practices under mass production more than lean production or negotiated flexibility consistent with human-resource intensive business strategies.
- Autocratic relations and the lack of voice *within* suppliers limit the benefits of voice *between* assemblers and suppliers.
- Emphasis on low costs, and the geographical dispersion of low-wage branch plants impede the creation of dynamic networks of suppliers.
- Low productivity growth, transplant sourcing patterns and limited engineering and design capabilities within the North American auto and allied industries prolong the North American trade deficit in engineering-intensive parts, in high profitability specialty vehicles, and in capital equipment for auto plants.
- By the year 2000, the number of high-wage middle-class jobs in the US auto industry, already almost half a million less than in 1978, would fall by another 100 000 – to about 300 000.

In sum, in contrast to Womack *et al.*'s vision of a revitalized industry built on geographic concentrations of assembly and parts production, the restructuring of the US auto industry could produce an industry characterized by enormous labor-market segmentation and limited innovative capacity and collective learning.

For Canada and Mexico, the empirical evidence is less clear. In Canada, unions and a less polarized labor market provide stronger checks on low-wage competition. Government, industry and labor have made more attempts to institutionalize a quality and productivity-based strategy. Nonetheless, Canada's historic weakness in engineering and research and development, and low-wage pressures from the south, will be hard to overcome.

In Mexico, given anticipated industry expansion and the absence, outside the most labor-intensive segments, of lower-wage competitors, the possibilities remain more open. Even if the United States and Canada move in a segmented direction, Mexico could develop dynamic regional agglomerations of rising wage/high productivity production. Mexico's institutions, including industrial chambers and corporatist unions, are, on paper, well suited to fostering industrial districts. Some of its rhetoric about the new unionism points in the right directions.

But Mexico's practice often appears closer to the worst of US traditions – employer unilateralism, Taylorism, and low-wage strategies – than to its corporatist ideology. Under the influence of the business strategies of US and Japanese employers, sluggish macroeconomic conditions, and excess labor supply, Mexico is unlikely to follow a more dynamic path.

POLICY IMPLICATIONS

This section outlines a regulatory regime intended to reduce the social costs of auto industry restructuring and to promote a more dynamic outcome of that restructuring. Before outlining the policy proposals, three prefatory comments are appropriate.

First, the auto industry, and manufacturing generally, now account for a small and declining fraction of total employment in North America. As long as US service-sector workers are paid as little as one-quarter of auto assembly company wages, it will be virtually impossible for workers in lower-tier auto suppliers to obtain wage and contract terms similar to those of core workers. It will also be difficult to stop the shrinkage of the core itself via outsourcing and vertical disintegration. In sum, even an integrated set of auto sector trade, industrial, and labor market policies can, in the absence of complementary strategies at the level of the national and continental economy, only ameliorate the pressures toward low-wage competition in the auto sector.

Second, the state policies proposed here include a proposal for managed auto sector trade between North America and Japan, and for a measure of temporary trade management within North America. These proposals are predicated on the view that lean producers can be forced to produce locally in proportion to their market sales without sacrifices in efficiency. Thus, while some past trade management – although not the US–Canada Auto Pact – may have come at the expense of consumers, this need not be the case with trade management in the auto industry today.

Third, these proposals outline a regulatory framework for the *North American* auto sector. In practice, whether regulation will be restricted to national policies or include substantial trinational elements remains uncertain. The accelerating integration of the Mexican auto industry with those of the United States and Canada, means that an effective regulatory framework will have to have substantial continental elements.

North American Trade Relations with Japan

The trade deficit with Japan reduces auto industry employment and production in North America, especially engineering-intensive production that supports high wages and permits companies to earn sufficient profit to underwrite technology and development costs. With improvements in productivity and quality over the past decade, and the recent appreciation of the yen, it may now be cheaper to produce vehicles in North America than in Japan. Nonetheless, even if the yen remains near 100 per dollar, questions remain regarding how quickly market forces will reduce the US and North American trade deficits with Japan.

Even though US exports may now be cheaper and competitive in non-price terms, the cost of setting up distribution channels, and Japanese companies' control over existing channels, impede increases in vehicle exports – although trade negotiations or the need of Japanese companies for cash could provide US companies with access to existing Japanese distribution systems. In parts, Japanese *keiretsu* (assembler-supplier networks) limit exports from the United States.

With respect to transferring production, Japanese assemblers are unlikely to increase North American capacity more than already planned because yen appreciation has robbed them of money for new plants and led to domestic excess capacity in Japan of 15 per cent. One Nissan executive said recently, 'In order not to lower the rate of operation of domestic plants, it is impossible any more to transfer plants abroad on a large scale.'[10] Institutionally, Japanese companies keep production in Japan to maintain job security and promotion opportunities for Japanese workers and managers, and to ensure profits for Japanese suppliers. As Womack (1991a) has now acknowledged, '[lean] production, once set up in one place, has no tendency to migrate'.

It is possible that recent yen appreciation will, over time, reduce the market share of vehicles produced in Japan and thus the North American auto trade deficit. The recent dip in Japanese market share and the dramatic decline in the market share of Japanese trucks and of European producers provide precedents for exchange-rate driven effects. Japanese companies, however, are far more competitive in all segments of the car market than in the truck market, just as they are more competitive than European car makers.

For the foreseeable future, significant Japanese net auto exports to North America will deprive the United States, Canada and Mexico of market share that could help institutionalize employee and supplier commitment to performance improvement. On grounds of efficiency, reciprocity and economic self-interest, there is a case for regulating trade between Japan and North America in the global auto industry.

Past European Community and Canadian policies provide precedents for a Japan–North America Auto Pact (JNAAP) to increase the ratio of auto sector value-added to sales in either the United States or North America as a whole. The EC approach combines import limits and local-content requirements. Through 1998, the Japanese import share is restricted to roughly 16 per cent of the market. The three largest Japanese transplants are committed to achieving 80 per cent content levels within two to three years after startup.

Canada's approach under the US–Canada Auto Pact differs from the EC's in two respects. Rather than restraining finished vehicle imports, Canada required each Auto Pact producer to meet a specified ratio of the value of vehicles assembled in Canada to the net sales value of vehicles sold in Canada. Second, Canada obligates Auto Pact producers to meet a *de facto* net corporate content requirement as opposed to a content rule that applies to each vehicle.[11] Compared to import quotas or Voluntary Restraint agreements, net corporate content and assembly-to-sales ratios give corporations flexibility because they allow them to satisfy the requirement by either increasing exports or lowering imports. On either measure, the Japanese companies are currently well below the requirements Canada imposes on Auto Pact producers.[12]

A JNAAP could be made consistent with GATT via voluntary agreements that Japan agrees not to challenge in the GATT; or through tri-bloc negotiations – overseen by the new World Trade Organization – that include the Europeans and which establish a stable framework for inter-bloc auto trade that might last several decades.

Suggestions made by Mexico and Canada in the NAFTA auto talks indicate that both might be receptive to a JNAAP.[13] In the United States, the Clinton Administration has so far emphasized the notion of 'market opening' to remove barriers to US vehicle exports; and to increase purchases of parts from US-owned (and located) auto suppliers by Japanese transplants and by assemblers in Japan. Neither approach seems likely to happen on a scale sufficient to substantially reduce the trade deficit. Using an assembly-to-sales ratio or net-content or trade-balance approach to force more balanced US–Japan auto trade has not been contemplated. Nonetheless, the Administration's interest in setting targets for sectoral reductions in the trade deficit may ultimately lead in these directions. For those who see exchange rates as likely to achieve these reductions anyway, a JNAAP could be thought of as a form of insurance (and a lever to use with auto companies and Mexico in obtaining other policy changes).

The discussion above was framed in terms of a Japanese auto trade with North America, not just the United States. Given the continental integration of the North American industry, this broader approach has an underlying economic logic. It also has a political logic: Canada and Mexico will perceive any US–Japan deal that presses Japan to preferentially buy from or invest in the United States as inconsistent with the spirit of NAFTA; a continental rule from which Mexico believes it would gain production (as opposed to a US–Japan agreement from which Mexico might lose) would provide leverage for obtaining Mexican commitments on labor issues (see the discussion on industrial relations below). A continental trade approach would not obviate the need for US (and Canadian) national safeguards (that is, a lower national content or trade-balance rule); national safeguards would sustain US and Canadian supplier interest in building multi-employer associative institutions critical to dynamic industrial agglomerations. A national safeguard would also help develop more integrated and dynamic supplier agglomerations in the north and center of Mexico.

Industrial Development Policy

Established auto assemblers and suppliers would benefit substantially from implementation of a JNAAP or US–Japan Auto Pact. In exchange, the US (or US, Mexico and Canadian) government(s) could seek a general commitment to the vision of a high-wage, high-skill industry, and concrete commitments consistent with that vision. These would include commitments in the areas of industrial development and labor along the following lines.

Sectoral training and technology funds

One critical issue is the pressure toward low-wage competition. To help avoid this, and sustain movement toward integrated networks of dynamic firms, supplier companies could be required to contribute a percentage of payroll or a flat fee per worker (the latter requires relatively more contributions from low-wage, low-productivity firms) to sectoral training and technology funds. Funds could be allocated to institutes in key auto-producing regions and overseen by management–labor–community boards. If the US, Canada and Mexico simultaneously implemented mandatory contributions, this would address the collective action problem that discourages individual countries from requiring contributions for fear of losing investment.

Discipline on subsidies

The use of national and continental rules can strengthen discipline on subsidies for new investment. Over the past decade, many US states have bid for foreign auto investments via tax abatements, subsidized land and infrastructure and other subsidies. If a trade agreement guarantees that new auto investment will be made somewhere in North America (or the United States), subsidies to influence where facilities locate are irrational from the perspective of the continent (or United States) as a whole.

Social benefit funds

As emphasized by Howes (1991), new Japanese assemblers and suppliers have lower costs because they do not have old workforces, high retiree–active ratios and thus high medical and pension costs. To reduce erosion of health and pension protection by competition, industry-wide social benefit funds could be created to which companies, including foreign investors, would contribute in proportion to the size of their workforce.

Industrial Relations

Institutionalizing a less segmented auto industry pattern of development will require mitigating labor-market pressures that encourage companies to pursue core–periphery strategies which draw on the commitment and skill of only a small fraction of employees, especially in suppliers. These pressures include low-wage competition and competition from Mexican plants where workers are denied independent union representation.

To deal with this, the US could seek additional commitments from Mexico and from employers in exchange for a trade pact with Japan. From Mexico's perspective, the policies proposed below could accelerate a transition to a modernized system of labor relations, which includes more accountable unions and launches the country onto a virtuous circle of rising productivity, increasing wages and worker commitment, and further increases in productivity.

North American works councils

In Europe, the European Commission has proposed establishing 'European Works Councils' in companies that employ more than 1000 EC workers and more than 100 workers in two or more countries of the Community. Employers would provide funding for works councillors and management representatives to meet once a year (and an additional time if the need arises). European-wide works councils already operate in VW and Ford. In the North American auto industry, the creation of 'North American Works Councils' at major multinational auto companies would have two major benefits. The contact between US, Canadian and Mexican workers is likely to increase the space within Mexico for independent union leaders to operate. Second, the establishment of North American works councils might lay the groundwork for negotiation over the harmonization of Mexican, US and Canadian labor standards.

Continental wage rules

The most tangible labor-standards issue within the North American auto industry is wages. At some point over the next decade, a 'continental improvement factor' (CIF) could be negotiated which gradually raises Mexican wages towards US and Canadian levels.

There should be no illusion that a CIF would quickly equalize Mexican with US and Canadian wages: assuming a 40 per cent appreciation of the peso, a 10:1 initial wage ratio, and a CIF that sets Mexican wage growth at 4 per cent higher than US increases, it would take 36 years for Mexican wage levels to reach US levels. The length of this period is one reason that such safeguards may be necessary for the auto industry in the United States and Canada. What a CIF might do is partly remove the contentious issue of wages from annual negotiations in major assembly companies, increase shopfloor peace by giving workers confidence that they would share in the benefits of productivity growth, and assure that wage competition in Mexico does not prevent the expansion of aggregate demand. These are the kinds of benefits provided by the Annual Improvement Factor (AIF) in the United States in the aftermath of World War II.

If harmonization of US, Canadian and Mexican wages within the auto sector would exacerbate inequalities within the Mexican labor market, some fraction of scheduled wage increases could be funneled into community funds that promote development in more backward, lower-wage parts of the Mexican economy.

Limiting low-wage supplier competition

Labor policy reform to combat low-wage strategies may also be necessary at the national level. Such reforms might help give birth to vertical or horizontal-network unions. Possible policy approaches include permitting the use of economic pressure to create unions that span vertical or horizontal networks; legislative or labor-board promotion of sectoral collective bargaining; or the extension of the economic terms of pattern-setting contracts to small employers (for specific proposals, see US Congress, 1992, p. 46; and OFL, 1989). Legislation along these lines already exists in Mexico and Quebec. Article 404 of the Federal Labor Law facilitates the establishment of sectoral bargaining. Quebec has a 'Decree system' through which the economic terms of major agreements may be extended throughout designated sectors.

Shorter work time

Given that productivity increases in major assembly companies will likely exceed output growth, the total number of hours worked in such companies is likely to decline. With constant average annual work hours, lower total hours would mean lower employment and reduced promotion opportunities. It would thus make it more difficult for employers to institutionalize worker cooperation. Shorter work time, on the other hand, would create employment and promotion opportunities in all three countries of North America. Competition for investment, however, could prevent unions or legislation in the United States, Mexico and Canada from achieving the shorter work time that would benefit all three countries. Continental negotiations might solve this prisoner's dilemma and enable each country to shorten work time in the auto sector without suffering a competitive disadvantage. Shorter work time in the auto industry might set a precedent for other industries or for continental legislative standards. General reductions are likely to be an important component of any continental efforts to reduce unemployment and promote environmentally sustainable development.

CONCLUSION

The blind spots of US political debate being what they are, the restructuring of the North American auto industry may be on the verge of being labelled a success. This success, however, is a highly qualified one: a restoration of profits for North American producers, the maintenance of recent assembly plant productivity gains and of improvements in quality, reliability and value for consumers, but all within an increasingly segmented industry. This segmented structure would provide few high-wage jobs for production workers. Within it, the contribution of workers and suppliers to performance improvement would be limited by adversarial labor relations and a managerial focus on wages and costs. This would significantly erode economic performance. Replicated in the labor market as a whole, as it has been, the income inequality associated with a segmented auto industry will continue to generate social tensions and costs.

Fostering egalitarian, high-wage, high-skill development in the North American auto industry would require implementing an integrated set of trade, investment and industrial relations policies. These policies would directly and indirectly foster the development of workers' skills and of the technical capacities of auto suppliers. They would discourage the pursuit of low-wage strategies in traditional mass production operations.

Even in the best of circumstances, of course, many automobile jobs will still consist of rote tasks. Moreover, it remains unclear how much skill and technology-based strategies can insulate the US and Canada from lower-wage competition. Finally, if rapid productivity growth does diffuse throughout the industry, this will be a mixed blessing unless macroeconomic policy, shorter work time and other social policy innovations can bring back full unemployment or establish non-stigmatized sources of basic income other than private-sector employment.

Much more than in the past, the automobile industry today is not, by itself, an institutional system. Pressures from the labor market as a whole have sufficient force to undermine attempts to pursue a human-resource intensive path in the auto industry. Despite this, the auto industry still plays a powerful pattern-setting role. As we collectively search for institutional arrangements that reconcile our economic and social priorities, the automobile industry may play a central role in guiding North America toward new understandings about the role of workers, the state and employers in industrial and social development.

Notes

1. This paper contains an updated, integrated, but abbreviated version of Herzenberg, 1991b and Herzenberg, 1993. The former, in particular, provides more detail on trade and labor-market data as well as more complete references.
2. For a brief theoretical discussion of 'sectoral patterns of development' and their relationship to industrial relations system theory and to the idea of national patterns of development developed by the French Regulation School, see Herzenberg, 1991.

3. The actual requirements were to maintain the CVA at that of the base year and to achieve, for cars, a 60 per cent CVA/sales ratio for any increase in sales. Even though the base-year ratio was less than 60 per cent for some producers, the growth of sales in Canada since the base year make the requirement close to an overall 60 per cent CVA/sales ratio.

4. The US–C FTA leaves in place one inducement for the Big Three to meet the performance requirements implemented with the Auto Pact: duty remission on Canada's 9.2 per cent tariff on parts imports from third countries.

5. This paper relies primarily on official US auto trade statistics analyzed by the US International Trade Commission (ITC) (some figures have been updated to 1993 using data from the Office of Automotive Affairs of the US Department of Commerce (hereafter OAA/DOC)). For details on the ITC data series used and on disaggregated car, truck and parts imports and exports from 1984–90, see Herzenberg, 1991b. The US auto parts exports figures reported here for 1989–92 differ from the series reported in Herzenberg, 1991b by roughly 25 per cent (due to changes in the series made by the ITC). Small differences in data for car and truck imports before and after 1989 are ignored in calculations that span 1990 and the pre-1989 period.

6. This fall stemmed partly from the delayed impact of the imposition of a 25 per cent tariff of light trucks in 1981. In the years immediately after 1981, appreciation of the dollar compensated for the tariff hike.

7. Canadian figures put the 1992 US vehicle deficit at US $15.1 billion (Canadian DIST, 1993).

8. In 1988, Canadian auto assembler hourly earnings equalled only 1.19 times the manufacturing average wage. This compares with 1.58 for production workers in US SIC 3711.

9. In the late 1980s, OSHA fined each of the Big Three for under-reporting injuries, and required them to expand their ergonomics programs to reduce repetitive motion injury rates.

10. *Nippon Keizan Shimbun*, 17 August 1993, cited in Watanabe, 1993.

11. Womack (1991a) proposed a trade-balancing requirement, in essence a net-content requirement, as a means of ensuring more balanced production in the North American and Japanese auto bloc.

12. In 1992, in the United States, the ratio, in units, of Japanese-nameplate vehicles produced in North America to total Japanese-nameplate sales equalled 0.46. The same ratio equalled 0.62 for Honda, 0.47 for Nissan and 0.4 for Toyota. If one assumes that Japanese vehicles assembled in North America average 50 per cent North American content, the North American content of Japanese auto companies sales in the United States in 1992 was below 25 per cent.

13. The Mexican NAFTA auto negotiator circulated a document raising the possibility of a 10 per cent common external tariff as part of an effort by North America to achieve more balanced interbloc auto trade. Canada put forward the option of replacing the Auto Pact and Mexican Auto Decree with a common trinational regulatory framework that included national sageguards to protect the integrity of each country's industry. The Bush Administration, consistent with free-trade ideology, rejected these suggestions.

References

Canada Consulting Cresap (1991) *Report of the Automotive Parts Human Resource Study* (Toronto).

Canadian Department of Industry Science and Technology (DIST) (1993) *Statistical Review of the Automotive Industry* (Ottawa, ONT.: DIST)

CAW-Canada Research Group on CAMI (1993) *The CAMI Report: Lean Production in a Unionized Auto Plant* (Willowdale, Out: CAW-Canada Research Department).

Employment and Immigration-Canada (EIC-Canada) (1986) *Why People Count?* Report of the Automotive Industry Human Resources Task Force. Ottawa: Minister of Supply and Services Canada, Cat. No. MP43–194/1986E.

Fucini, J. and S. Fucini (1990) *Working for the Japanese: Inside Mazda's American Auto Plant* (New York: Free Press).

Herzenberg, Stephen A. and David Campbell (1993) 'Productivity Growth in US Auto Suppliers', draft Working Paper, MIT International Motor Vehicle Program, revised December.

Herzenberg, Stephen A. (1993) 'Continental Integration and the Future of the North American Auto Sector', in Maureen Appel Molot (ed.), *Driving Continentally: National Policies and the North American Auto Industry* (Ottawa, Canada: Carleton University Press).

Herzenberg, Stephen A. (1991a) *Towards A Cooperative Commonwealth? Labor and Restructuring in the US and Canadian Auto Industries*, Ph.D. dissertation, Massachusetts Institute of Technology Department of Economics.

Herzenberg, Stephen A. (1991b) 'The North American Auto Industry at the Onset of Continental Free Trade Negotiations'. Economic Discussion Paper 38, Bureau of International Labor Affairs, US Department of Labor, Washington, DC, 1 July.

Howes, Candace (1991) 'The Benefits of Youth: the Role of Japanese Fringe Benefit Policies in the Restructuring of the US Motor Vehicle Industry', *International Contributions to Labour Studies*. Are Japanese Transplants Restoring U.S. Competitiveness or Dumping their Social Problems in the U.S. Market? (Steve Babson (ed.), Lean Work:) Empowerment and Exploitation in the Global Auto Industry (Detroit, MI.: Wayne State Univ. Press, 1995).

Japanese External Trade Organization (JETRO) (1991) 'Special Issue: Survey of Japanese Manufacturers in the US: Contributions to US Economy Increase', 6(1), April.

Katz, Harry C. (1985) *Shifting Gears: Changing Labor Relations in the US Automobile Industry* (Cambridge: MIT Press).

Luria, Daniel (1993) 'A High Road Policy for US Manufacturing'. (Industrial Technology Institute), mimeo, 28 March.

Luria, Daniel (1989) 'The Case for the Base: Thinking About the Michigan Manufacturing Foundation', *Modern Michigan*, 2(1), Fall.

McAlinden, Sean P., David J. Andrea, Michael S. Flynn and Brett C. Smith (1991) *The US–Japan Automotive Bilateral Trade Deficit* (Ann Arbor: The University of Michigan Transportation Research Institute), Report No. UMTRI 91–20, May.

Middlebrook, Kevin J. (1989) 'Union Democratization in the Mexican Automobile Industry: A Reappraisal', *Latin American Research Review*, 24.

294   *Regulatory Frameworks and Development*

Ontario Federation of Labor (OFL) (1989) 'The Unequal Bargain'. Document 4, 33rd Annual OFL Convention, 20–24 November.

Parker, Mike and Jane Slaughter (1993) 'Surviving Lean Production: Two Auto Workers Locals in the United States'. Paper presented at the Lean Workplace Conference, Centre for Research and Society, York University, North York, Ontario, 30 September–3 October.

Parker, Mike and Jane Slaughter (1988) *Choosing Sides: Unions and the Team Concept* (Boston: South End Press).

Rogers, Joel and Wolfgang Streeck (1991) 'Skill Needs and Training Strategies in the Wisconsin Metalworking Sector: Executive Summary' (Madison: Center for Wisconsin Strategy), January.

Sabel, Charles F. (1990) 'Studied Trust: Building New Forms of Cooperation in a Volatile Economy'. Unpublished paper, Massachusetts Institute of Technology, 24 September.

Schippani, Mike (1990) 'Labor and Industrial Relations Strategies in the State of Michigan'. Paper presented at the Center for Labor–Management Policy Studies, the City University of New York, 29 March.

Shaiken, Harley (1992) 'The Auto and Electronics Sectors in US–Mexico Trade and Investment'. Report prepared for the US Office of Technology Assessment under Contract No. 13–1815, May.

Shaiken, Harley and Browne, Harry (1991) 'Japanese Work Organization in Mexico', in Gabriel Szekely (ed.), *Manufacturing Across Borders and Oceans: Japan, the United States, and Mexico* (La Jolla, CA: Center for US–Mexican Studies, University of California-San Diego), Monograph Series, No. 36.

Shaiken, Harley (1990) *Mexico in the Global Economy: High Technology and Work Organization in Export Industries* (La Jolla, CA: Center for US–Mexican Studies, University of California-San Diego), Monograph Series, No. 33.

Shaiken, Harley and Stephen Herzenberg (1987) *Automation and Global Production: Automobile Engine Production in Mexico, the United States and Canada* (La Jolla, CA: Center for US–Mexican Studies, University of California-San Diego), Monograph Series, No. 26.

US Congress, Office of Technology Assessment (1992) *US–Mexico Trade: Pulling Together or Pulling Apart?* (Washington, DC: US Government Printing Office), ITE–545, October.

US Department of Labor (USDOL) (1991) *Industry Wage Survey: Motor Vehicle and Parts. Part I: Motor Vehicles, June 1989. Part II: Motor Vehicle Parts, August 1989* (Washington, DC: Bureau of Labor Statistics), BLS Bulletin?.

Watanabe, Ben (1993) 'The Japanese Auto Industry: Is Lean Production on the Way Out?' Paper presented at the Lean Workplace Conference, Centre for Research on Work and Society, York University, North York, Ontario, 30 September–3 October.

Womack, James P. (1991) 'A Positive Sum Solution: Free Trade in the North American Motor Vehicle Sector', in M. Delal Baer and Guy F. Erb (eds), *Strategic Sectors in Mexican–US Free Trade*. Washington, DC: the Center for Strategic and International Studies and the US Council of the Mexico–US Business Committee, CSIS Significant Issues Series, XIII (6).

Womack, James, Daniel Jones, and Daniel Roos (1990). *The Machine that changed the World* (New York: Rawson Associates).

10 Conclusion: Competition, Politics, and the Social Construction of Flexible Labor Systems

Frederic C. Deyo

Dynamic production flexibility provides an important basis for competitive success insofar as it supports continuous change and improvement in product and process. But beyond this obvious point, important questions remain. In particular: when and under what circumstances is flexible production actually introduced? To what extent, and how, have its core features been diffused across cultures and nationalities? What forms may it take? What relationship does it bear to human resource and industrial relations practices? How does it affect labor and social welfare? What is its impact on relations with and personnel practices within supplier firms? And how is it influenced by labor politics and state policy? The following concluding comments draw on the chapters in this volume to provide provisional responses to these questions.

DYNAMIC FLEXIBILITY: LIMITATIONS AND MIXED-STRATEGIES

It has been noted that flexible production is an adaptive response to technology change, market fragmentation and volatility, and to ever higher consumer standards of quality. From this it follows that variation in these predisposing conditions is associated with corresponding variation in the degree of competitive pressure for organizations to become more flexible. As noted by Rodgers in his essay on South Korea, there remain numerous products whose markets and technology remain sufficiently stable to warrant continued adherence to standardized mass production.

It is clear as well that competitive pressures place other conflicting demands on firms which may not be compatible with dynamic flexibility, and which may thus inhibit flexibility reforms. In particular, it was noted in the introduction to this volume that immediate cost pressures may divert attention from long-term strategies and often uncertain investments in favor of shorter-term responses and static flexibilities. Finally, environmental conditions relating to government policy, labor relations, physical infrastructure and linkages with other firms, both domestic and foreign, may further constrain efforts to enhance dynamic flexibility.

Given that firms must in fact respond simultaneously to a host of competitive pressures through what may best be termed 'mixed strategies' (see Sabel, 1991), including immediate cost-reduction and cost-flexibility policies alongside longer-term organizational reforms, the question arises as to the intercompatibility of these various responses. Reliance on 'external flexibility' and temporary labor, for example, may sufficiently reduce morale, cooperation and worker stability to undercut worker participation and training programs.

In such cases of incompatibility, pursuance of a mixed strategy may require institutional segregation of these different approaches. Reliance on outsourcing to cut costs in stable-technology components alongside use of flexible in-house production of other components would be an example of such a segregated mixed-strategy, as would efforts to institutionally and socially insulate a core skilled workforce from a larger pool of temporary, lower-skilled workers within firms themselves. It should be noted in this regard that some institutional reforms (for example, use of in-house skilled contract labor and development of flexible, high-quality component suppliers) foster external and dynamic flexibility simultaneously, although these strategies too may create other morale problems within both firms and supplier chains through the inequities and labor-market dualism they create.

DYNAMIC FLEXIBLE PRODUCTION: A WORKING TYPOLOGY BASED ON DEGREE OF CENTRALIZATION

It is increasingly apparent that Japanese 'best-practice' flexible production has diffused rapidly around the world. In part, such diffusion has followed in the wake of overseas investment by Japanese firms in such countries as the US, Mexico and Thailand. In part too, however, the competitive superiority of flexible production has forced other companies to adopt at least some of its constituent elements as a condition of economic survival. While the case of Japanese transplants in the US strongly suggests that flexible work reforms may be undertaken in a wide variety of social and cultural contexts, it is also clear that such contexts, relating especially to sectoral governance institutions, may encourage adaptive hybrid *forms* of dynamic flexibility in different situations, thus challenging convergence views of global industrial restructuring (Turner and Auer, Chapter 8, this volume).

In response to increasing global competition, managers in Thailand, Mexico, the US, Japan, Canada, Germany and Sweden have introduced such core defining features of dynamic flexibility as programmable, general purpose machinery, broadly defined job classifications, flexible work rules, procedures for making quick changes in product and process, job rotation, increased multiskill training, work teams and quality circles. In all cases, these innovations have enhanced quality and product diversity.

But as striking as these commonalities is the cross-national and inter-firm variation in the forms these innovations have taken in particular historical and institutional contexts, and in the manner in which the innovations have been introduced. Associated with much of this variation are differences in the degree of centralization of organizational power underlying the introduction and functioning of flexible production: high in Thailand and Mexico, moderate in Japan and many US plants, and relatively low in Germany and Sweden.

Flexible production systems in newer Mexican auto plants and in Thailand are quite autocratic by comparison with those in Europe, Japan and the US. Workers receive substantial cross-training, participate in quality circles and other deliberative fora for improving quality and production efficiency, and in other ways meet the stringent requirements of new production systems. On the other hand, these workers and their unions remain somewhat passive players in the instituting and functioning of flexible production systems. While they are consulted in matters relating to shopfloor improvements in efficiency and defect reduction, their decisional role even in these areas is minimal. And they are not at all involved in broader decisions. Further, and in part by consequence of labor's weak bargaining position, considerations of worker welfare, safety and job enrichment rarely figure prominently in labor–management contracts, technological innovations or work reorganization (Middlebrook, Chapter 7, this volume).

Forms of flexibility in firms and countries which are global pace-setters in technology and product development are associated with more penetrating systems of human resource mobilization. Here one finds more extensive training, broader exposure to the whole production process, and greater effort to encourage shopfloor problem-solving. And the motivational base for enhanced worker contribution is in turn rooted in employment practices which encourage greater identification with enterprise performance, commitment to teamwork and group success, and willingness to go beyond (or around) formal job requirements when necessary.

But the contrasting characteristics of Toyotaism (or 'lean production') on the one hand, and German and Swedish flexible production on the other, suggest the need for a further distinction even among these more participative forms of flexibility. Under Toyotaism, individual workers, workgroups, works councils and enterprise unions participate in circumscribed decision-making confined largely to immediate production tasks and within managerially-determined parameters (Florida and Kenney, Kumar and Holmes, and Herzenberg, this volume; Parker and Slaughter, 1988). On the other hand are systems which de-emphasize such vertical, management-directed participation in favor of greater shopfloor autonomy and more worker involvement in agenda-setting and organizational strategies. These differences between what may be termed 'participatory' flexibility and 'bargained' (or negotiated) flexibility (Herzenberg, Chapter 9, this volume), are in turn associated with somewhat different strategic priorities and industrial relations systems.

Participatory flexibility, most closely associated with industry practices in Japan, in Japanese transplants in the US, and in US Big-Three plants where local unions and managers have initiated teamwork and 'jointness' programs, strongly privileges agendas and goals centered on the requirements of competitive economic success. While job security is typically a basis for union participation in participation programs, quality of worklife issues tend to be subordinated to questions of productive efficiency and product improvement. By contrast, bargained flexibility, as in many plants in Germany and Sweden and perhaps at the Saturn plant in the United States as well (Katz and MacDuffie, 1994), gives greater scope to quality of worklife issues in agenda setting, as seen in greater attention in recent work reforms to task cycle time, work pace, safety and workgroup autonomy (see also Herzenberg, this volume). Similarly, Kumar and Holmes, in Chapter 6, have reported that effective CAW involvement in Canadian work restructuring has ensured attention to such matters as time off, benefits, pacing, worker discretion on the job, and other matters affecting worker welfare.

Participatory and bargained flexibilities differ too in the nature of their associated training systems. Whereas participatory flexibility is associated with management control over training, bargained flexibility in Europe includes substantial union involvement in apprenticeship and other training programs (Dankbaar, 1994). The consequence of this difference in the nature and role of unions is that workers under participatory flexibility are more dependent on firms and managers for job security and career advancement than are their counterparts under bargained flexibility (see also Sabel, 1991).

FLEXIBILITY AND SUPPLIER RELATIONS

Do competitive strategies pursued in assembly plants and firms spill over to shape relations with and internal strategies of suppliers as well? The case studies on Japanese and Thai firms, and on US Japanese transplants suggest just such a spill-over. Florida and Kenney, in Chapter 3, have found that cooperation-based, intra-organizational flexibility in US Japanese transplants is strongly associated with cooperative, trust-based supplier relations. In addition, where assemblers have sought to adopt systems of flexible production, they have generally encouraged similar organizational and work reforms among their primary suppliers. According to Levine (Chapter 2, this volume), Japanese assemblers have successfully spread the risk of new product development by sharing the costs of product development with suppliers. This has necessitated a diffusion of participatory flexibility to suppliers in order to support on-going collaborative product and process development. Such diffusion, in turn, has necessitated the cultivation of long-term relations of trust, information-sharing, and mutual assistance in assembler–supplier relationships. In addition, in Japan and elsewhere, new quality and just-in-time standards have forced suppliers to adopt flexible production systems to meet the increasingly stringent requirements of assemblers. In the case of Japan, Levine (Chapter 2) points out that enterprise unions encompassing workers in both assembly firms and major supplier companies provide further support for these inclusionary systems of participatory flexibility.

Conversely, the cases of Japan, the US transplants and Thailand suggest that lower-tier suppliers have played quite different roles – providing low-cost production and static flexibility for assemblers and higher-tier suppliers (Herzenberg, Chapter 9, this volume; also see Cutcher-Gershenfeld and McHugh, 1994, pp. 230–1). Indeed, a strong emphasis by contractors on supplier cost-cutting, rather than on innovation and flexibility, informs relations with these lower-tier suppliers.

Such emphasis is often an explicit part of the mixed-strategies of larger firms as they have sought simultaneously to meet the demands of cost-cutting and dynamic flexibility.

DYNAMIC FLEXIBILITY AND LABOR RELATIONS

The relatively autocratic flexibility found in plants in Mexico and Thailand contradicts the notion that flexible production systems presuppose labor relations characterized by trust, worker identification with the firm, cooperation and high morale, where these characteristics are seen as encouraging skill and human-resource development, along with worker initiative and participation. The Thai and Mexican cases, in particular, suggest that participation and flexibility are at least somewhat compatible with low-trust, low-morale industrial relations, and that managerial control, rooted in part in slack labor markets and relatively high wages, can effectively sustain human-resource mobilization and development. It is also clear that autocratic flexibility is encouraged where unions are very weak, as in Thailand, or where managerial and state repression have undercut the power of labor to hinder new work reforms, as in South Korea. Rodgers (Chapter 4) has reported in this regard that South Korean companies have sought to use labor–management councils to pre-empt unions altogether. Weak unions in the newer Northern Mexican auto plants have contributed to autocratic flexibility through contractual acquiescence to uncontested management control over hiring and promotion, use of temporary workers, work rhythms and rates of production, and flexible deployment of workers on the shopfloor (Middlebrook, Chapter 7, this volume).

But this is not to argue for a more general dissociation between labor relations and flexibility. South Korea, for example, demonstrates the possible limits posed by inappropriate labor relations for the shift from autocratic to participatory flexibility. As described by Rodgers, South Korean auto companies have sought to move into innovative first-tier segments of their industry through the development of localized design and development capabilities and Japanese-style production systems. Their general lack of success in achieving these goals is attributable in part to high levels of labor turnover, confrontational labor–management relations, production sabotage and a corresponding unwillingness on the part of management to grant workers a significant role in shopfloor problem-solving. Indeed, the recent reversion to more repressive state measures to contain labor militancy further discourages the sorts of employment practices necessary for the instituting of participatory flexibility. Under such circumstances, autocratic flexibility, and with it second-tier status in the world auto industry, may define an upper limit to shopfloor reforms in these firms. At higher points in the value chain, particularly in the more industrially advanced countries, more innovation-intensive, participatory forms of flexibility have been associated with tight labor markets. In both Japan and Sweden, managers sought to retain scarce labor in the 1960s through improved pay, work conditions and job security. But the choice between participatory and bargained forms of flexibility has been most critically influenced by characteristics of national labor relations (Turner and Auer, Chapter 8, this volume; and Hollingworth and Streeck, 1994). Participatory flexibility in Japan, and increasingly in the United States, is associated with decentralized collective bargaining, tenuous political and legal guarantees for trade unionism, and relatively weak or co-opted unions. This observation is supported by the experience of loss of union leverage and the progressive decentralization of bargaining in the US (Kumar and Holmes, Chapter 6, this volume; and Katz and MacDuffie, 1994), where many of the most flexibly organized plants (transplants, NUMMI, Saturn) have collective agreements which differ substantially from national contracts adopted by UAW and Big-Three negotiators. Florida and Kenney (Chapter 3) have noted, as well, that some Japanese transplant assemblers in the US have replaced unions with employee associations for grievance handling and fostering employee participation.

Quite different is the case of bargained flexibility in Germany, Sweden and Canada, where relatively stronger national unions provide an independent political base for either opposing or negotiating new work reforms. Turner and Auer (Chapter 8) have argued that political support and a legally mandated union role in decision making have encouraged European unions to adopt pro-active cooperative strategies to shape work reorganization from the outset. Conversely, Kumar and Holmes (Chapter 6) have noted that efforts by Canadian managers to introduce managerially-dominated participatory flexibility were effectively blocked by the CAW, with the result that flexible work reforms were more limited than in the US, and, where they were successful, took more of a bargained than participatory form. The fact that the CAW enjoys less political support than its Swedish or German counterparts has encouraged a somewhat more confrontational and oppositional union stance in Canada to work reform initiatives.

FLEXIBILITY, WORK RESTRUCTURING AND THE CONSOLIDATION OF MANAGERIAL POWER

Worldwide processes of structural adjustment and economic liberalization have increased competitive pressures associated with a growing in-
terpenetration of global and national markets. These trends have been
accompanied, as well, by labor-market deregulation and the dismant-
ling of politically-secured shelters protecting workers and their unions
from managerial domination and from welfare-compromising labor-
cost competition among firms. Such labor-market deregulation, especially in developing countries, often occurs despite contrary international political pressures for enhanced labor standards as
industrialized countries seek to reduce global competitive pressures on
domestic firms by imposing their own high labor standards on low-
wage producers (Hollingsworth and Streeck, 1994). The critical source
of deregulation in the face of such political pressures is to be found in
the more compelling demands of economic competition and corresponding efforts by governments to enhance enterprise competitiveness and growth-inducing investment. Even in the highly regulated
European economies, economic recession in the early 1990s prompted
calls for labor-market deregulation (*Wall Street Journal*, 13 June
1994, p. 1).

In the past, work reforms which have empowered workers to participate in production and enterprise decision-making have flowed from
larger political processes. Japanese participatory flexibility, introduced after the defeat of radical unionism in the 1950s, re-established
managerial control over the production process. On the other hand,
many of its core elements, such as job security, participation in shopfloor decisions, and corporate welfare paternalism, are clearly rooted
in the earlier labor struggles. Similarly, worker autonomy and empowerment under Swedish and German bargained flexibility in conjunction
with legislatively mandated training were based on political victories
and party–labor alliances at national levels.

Quite different are the sources of new patterns of flexibility in the
1980s and 1990s. The driving force now is not so much political as economic, as firms seek work reforms which will help them meet intensified competitive challenges. By consequence, the agendas shaping
these reforms are less attentive to the needs of workers than to the requirements of global markets. On the one hand, competition is pushing
corporate managers toward labor-cost reduction, casualization, reliance on cheap outsourcing, and efforts to undercut or avoid unions, ef-

forts encouraged by labor-market deregulation at national levels. On the other hand, where technology, market and other considerations demand greater attention to quality, product diversification and process improvements, firms are seeking to institute forms of flexibility which seek to mobilize worker input without jeopardizing managerial control over work and production. Such efforts, along with growing competition and continued deregulation, ensure that new work reforms are tending to retain or bolster the discretionary power of managers, to subordinate worker welfare to enterprise success, and to confine worker and union participation in decision-making to narrow, shopfloor issues. The success of these reforms is reinforced, of course, by the greatly diminished power of organized labor in the face of global competition, domestic deregulation and these more aggressive corporate labor strategies themselves (Craypo and Nissen, 1993).

By consequence of these trends, there are growing indications that competitively 'soft' forms of industrial organization are vulnerable to economic assaults from leaner and tougher forms. Swedish and German variants of bargained flexibility, for example, established a compromise between the agendas of labor and capital. Growing direct competition from Japanese firms in European markets may evoke an unequal battle insofar as Japanese participatory flexibility excludes a labor agenda to a greater extent than does its European adversary. Indeed, questions are now being raised as to whether Swedish innovations in autonomous work groups and non-assembly-line work organization will for long survive new competitive pressures in the context of labor-market deregulation.

Conversely, Big-Three US auto producers, beginning with Ford and Chrysler, have achieved remarkable industrial turnarounds by the mid-1990s. This reversal of previous industrial trends, seen most dramatically in increased Big-Three market share in the US, was rooted in part in renewed growth in the US economy alongside continuing recession in Japan and an appreciated yen. But as important were the beginnings of success in introducing organizational reforms after years of fitful experimentation in the US. These reforms included the instituting of relatively top-down participatory flexibilities in the face of ambivalence and occasional though ineffectual opposition from members and locals of an increasingly beleaguered UAW (Katz and MacDuffie, 1994). It should also be noted that the highly efficient US Japanese transplants have themselves adopted somewhat less participatory forms of flexibility than their parent firms in Japan itself, in most cases excluding unions altogether (Florida and Kenney, Chapter 3, this volume). It is clear that

Conclusion

companies in the US have been far freer to impose tough, labor-shedding cost-reduction strategies alongside longer-term organizational reforms than have their European counterparts with their more highly regulated labor markets and politically protected unions. And there are even indications that Japanese auto plants in Japan itself are adopting tougher labor policies as they seek to cope with slower growth, increased competition from foreign producers, and more erratic markets, through overseas investments and outsourcing, workforce reductions and attenuated lifetime employment guarantees (*Ward's Automotive Yearbook*, 1994, p. 56).

The foregoing discussion raises an important issue regarding the role of the state in the instituting of dynamic flexibility. The historical sources of dynamic flexibility in the auto industries of Japan, Germany and Sweden are to be found in large measure in flexibility-encouraging sectoral governance institutions. In all cases, states played an important though varying role in inducing managers to adopt long-term strategies of dynamic flexibility in lieu of short-term cost cutting. Central to this role were incentives and sanctions intended to encourage effective human resource programs alongside employment and industrial relations practices conducive to trust, cooperation and participation.

Despite industrial globalization, trade liberalization and a reduced state role in directing, financing and protecting domestic industries, states continue to influence the competitive strategies of firms. In addition to providing an essential educational and training foundation for dynamic flexibility, states often seek to encourage collaboration among firms and research organizations (for example, through the establishment of industrial parks), corporate training programs, quality circles, works councils, trade and industry associations, supplier development programs, and the like.

But having said this, it nevertheless remains the case that states have played an ever more marginal governance role in national economies. While economic deregulation (for example, privatization, trade liberalization and reduced financial assistance to industry) has been pushed by international political forces, labor-market deregulation has more often resulted from economic pressures on states to remove regulatory hindrances to competitiveness. Indeed, labor-market deregulation in developing countries often occurs *despite* continuing international political pressures for improved labor standards, applied by developed countries largely to protect their own industries from foreign competition. For this reason, such deregulation has often taken unobtrusive forms, as exemplified by the non-enforcement of existing labor legislation in Thailand and elsewhere (see Deyo, Chapter 5, this volume).

Given the important role of the state in the construction of flexible production systems in Germany, Sweden and, to a lesser extent, Japan, destatization and deregulation may seem to undermine the continued development and diffusion of dynamic flexibility. Several observations help place this issue in perspective. First, in many cases, deregulation may function as much to encourage a shift to more management-dominated forms of flexibility, as suggested above, as to discourage it altogether. As important, states are but one element of larger governance systems which underpin industrial cooperation and innovation. Indeed, a growing body of literature, starting with Piore and Sabel's seminal study of 'flexible specialization' among groups of small firms in industrial districts of Italy (Piore and Sabel, 1984), suggests the ways in which private-sector institutions can foster dynamic flexibility in the absence of intrusive state policy. While this volume has focused primarily on the roles of firms, states and unions in the social construction of flexible production systems, it is clear that private-sector institutions may, as in Taiwan, Japan and elsewhere, provide an adequate basis for the organizational reforms, risk-sharing, and cooperation necessary for industrial flexibility.

Further, even where neither states nor private-sector institutions are able to play such a supportive role, dynamic flexibility is still within the reach of large firms like Toyota with sufficient resources to absorb the short-term costs and risks in undertaking major investments and reforms, to provide funding for programs and ventures with substantial economic externalities (for example, public sectoral training programs), and to institute effective interfirm collaboration (for example, supplier groups). This is particularly the case in lower-tier industry niches with their somewhat more attenuated labor relations and governance requirements.

Finally, it should be noted that, while the role of both states and unions in national economies has been substantially compromised by forces of economic globalization and neo-liberalism, the possibilities for the reconstruction of effective social governance at *international* levels has been driven ever more urgently by growing domestic political reactions to the social disruptions associated with global deregulation. In the context of international negotiations to establish regional free-trade zones, states have begun to construct new transnational systems of social governance (see Hollingworth and Streeck, 1994, p. 293) which may ultimately achieve what national systems once did: political protection against the social destruction born of unfettered market competition. Such overtures are already seen in the social and environmental agreements appended to the North American Free Trade Agreement and to the 1991 Maastricht pact uniting the economies of the European Community.

THE QUESTION OF CONVERGENCE

A growing trend toward relatively 'lean and mean' forms of autocratic and participatory flexibility in the auto industry does not preclude continued sectoral diversity within and across particular market niches. First, the growing weakness of nationally organized labor and the decline of pattern bargaining have freed local firms to adopt a variety of different labor strategies (Katz and MacDuffie, 1994). Given the somewhat loose fit between particular performance standards and competitive success, as well as the possibility that alternative organizational strategies and structures may yield equivalent performance outcomes (Hollingworth and Streeck, 1994, p. 285), the resulting diversification of labor practices and organizational reforms may not necessarily imply such marked differences in competitive success as to winnow out for survival all but a narrow range of reform experiments.

Second, continued organizational diversity is suggested by the varied competitive performance demands associated with different niches in the auto industry (Hollingsworth and Streeck, 1994, p. 280). The diversity-generating impact of differential performance demands may best be seen in the experience of developing countries. It is not at all clear, for example, that the autocratic forms of flexibility in developing countries, like bargained flexibility in more advanced countries, must be transformed into participatory forms in order to remain competitive. The automotive industries of Mexico, Thailand and South Korea are continuing to grow quite rapidly despite reliance on highly autocratic forms of flexibility rooted in authoritarian political regimes and low-trust labor–management climates. This is explained in part by the suggestion that where firms compete mainly through continuous innovation in product and process, as in the advanced industrial countries, more of the development work occurs in the process of shopfloor implementation and de-bugging, thus requiring more initiative and self-direction on the part of production workers (Sabel, 1991). Where, on the other hand, firms rely on an adoption and adaptation of new products, technologies and production systems developed and perfected elsewhere, change may most efficiently be directed and channeled through managers and production engineers (Rodgers, Chapter 4, this volume, p. 53). For this reason, countries like South Korea, Mexico and to a lesser degree Thailand, with their relatively well-developed industrial and supplier infrastructures, are likely, despite reliance on autocratic forms of flexibility, to remain competitive and even to further consolidate their position in second-tier niches of the global automobile industry over the foreseeable future. Such observations support the argument that variation in the competitive requirements facing different segments of the world automobile industry permit firms operating in different subsectors and at different levels to compete successfully through production systems with quite different types and degrees of flexibility, including mixed strategies entailing both static and dynamic flexibilities.

Third, this continuing process of organizational diversification is reinforced by labor-market deregulation on the one hand, and a growing pre-eminence of competitive/economic over social considerations in state economic policy on the other. While it is clear that both deregulation and a regulatory 'tilt' toward the needs of industry may, as noted earlier, encourage some degree of convergence on 'tough', competitive autocratic and participatory forms of flexibility, their diversity-effect is equally evident. Labor-market deregulation, by relaxing universally mandated labor standards across firms and sectors, and by undercutting both union strength and national-level collective bargaining, has encouraged diversity by increasing the freedom of firms to pursue competitive strategies appropriate to their unique economic and technological environments. Such increased diversity is further reinforced by a redirection of state economic policy toward the competitive needs of companies, and away from the social and labor agendas which have hitherto played so important a role in the social governance of market economies.

References

Amsden, Alice H. (1989) *Asian's Next Giant: South Korea and Late Industrialization* (New York: Oxford University Press).
Craypo, Charles and Bruce Nissen (1993) 'The Impact of Corporate Strategies', in Charles Craypo and Bruce Nissen (eds), *Grand Designs: The Impact of Corporate Strategies on Workers, Unions and Communities* (Ithaca: ILR Press).

Cutcher-Gershenfeld, Joel and Patrick P. McHugh (1994) 'Competition and Divergence: Collective Bargaining in the North American Auto Supply Industry', in Paula B. Voos (ed.), *Contemporary Collective Bargaining in the Private Sector* (Madison, WI: Industrial Relations Research Association).

Dankbaar, Ben (1994) 'Sectoral Governance in the Automobile Industries of Germany, Great Britain and France', in J. Rogers Hollingsworth, Philippe C. Schmitter and Wolfgang Streeck (eds), *Governing Capitalist Economies* (New York: Oxford University Press).

Hill, Richard Child (1992) 'Foundation Firms and Industrial Districts', in Akira Shigemori *et al.* (eds), *Globalization and the City* (Tokyo: Keizai Shinposha), in Japanese.

Hill, Richard Child and Yong Joo Lee 'Japanese Multinationals and East Asian Development: The Case of the Automobile Industry' (forthcoming), in Leslie Sklair (ed.), *Capitalism and Development* (London: Routledge).

Hoffman, Kurt and Raphael Kaplinski (1988) *Driving Force: The Global Restructuring of Technology, Labour and Investment in the Automobile and Components Industries* (Boulder, CO: Westview Press).

Hollingsworth, J. Rogers and Wolfgang Streeck (1994) 'Countries and Sectors: Concluding Remarks on Performance, Convergence and Competitiveness', in J. Rogers Hollingsworth, Philippe C. Schmitter and Wolfgang Streeck (eds), *Governing Capitalist Economies* (New York: Oxford University Press).

Katz, Harry and John Paul MacDuffie (1994) 'Collective Bargaining in the US Auto Assembly Sector', in Paula B. Voos (ed.), *Contemporary Collective Bargaining* (Madison, WI: Industrial Relations Research Association Series).

Lee, Naeyoung and Jeffrey Cason (1994) 'Automobile Commodity Chains in the NIC's: A Comparison of South Korea, Mexico and Brazil', in Gary Gereffi and Miguel Korzeniewicz (eds), *Commodity Chains and Global Capitalism* (Westport, CT: Praeger).

Parker, Mike and Jane Slaughter (1988) *Choosing Sides: Unions and the Team Concept* (Boston: South End Press).

Pempel, T. J. and Keiichi Tsunekawa (1979) 'Corporatism without Labor? The Japanese Anomaly', in Philippe C. Schmitter and Gerhard Lehmbruch (eds), *Trends Toward Corporatist Intermediation* (Beverly Hills: Sage).

Piore, Michael and Charles Sabel (1984) *The Second Industrial Divide: Possibilities for Prosperity* (New York: Basic Books).

Sabel, Charles (1991) 'Moebious-Strip Organizations and Open Labor Markets: Some Consequences of the Reintegration of Conception and Execution in a Volatile Economy', in Pierre Bourdieu and James S. Coleman (eds), *Social Theory for a Changing Society* (Boulder, CO: Westview Press; and New York: Russell Sage Foundation), pp. 23–61.

Ward's Automotive Yearbook (1994) (Detroit: Ward's Communications).

Womack, James P., Daniel T. Jones and Daniel Roos (1990) *The Machine that Changed the World* (New York: Rawson Associates).

Index